PAUL AND THE POWER OF SIN

Paul and the Power of Sin seeks to ground Paul's language of sin in the socio-cultural context of his original letters. T.L. Carter draws on the work of social anthropologist Mary Douglas to conduct a cross-cultural analysis of the symbolism of the power of sin in the letters, examining thoroughly Douglas' 'Grid and Group' model and defending its use as a heuristic tool for New Testament scholars. He uses this model to examine the social location of Paul and the communities to which he wrote and offers a fresh insight into key passages from 1 Corinthians, Galatians and Romans. Carter concludes that an important part of Paul's purpose was to safeguard the position of law-free Gentile believers by redrawing social boundaries along eschatological rather than ethnic lines.

T.L. CARTER is Baptist Minister at Leamington Spa Baptist Church. He has also published in the *Journal for the Study of the New Testament*.

SOCIETY FOR NEW TESTAMENT STUDIES

MONOGRAPH SERIES

General editor: Richard Bauckham

115

PAUL AND THE POWER OF SIN

Paul and the Power of Sin

Redefining 'Beyond the Pale'

T.L. CARTER

CAMBRIDGE
UNIVERSITY PRESS

PUBLISHED BY THE PRESS SYNDICATE OF THE UNIVERSITY OF CAMBRIDGE
The Pitt Building, Trumpington Street, Cambridge, United Kingdom

CAMBRIDGE UNIVERSITY PRESS
The Edinburgh Building, Cambridge CB2 2RU, UK
40 West 20th Street, New York, NY 10011-4211, USA
477 Williamstown Road, Port Melbourne, VIC 3207, Australia
Ruiz de Alarcón 13, 28014 Madrid, Spain
Dock House, The Waterfront, Cape Town 8001, South Africa

http://www.cambridge.org

First published 2002

Printed in the United Kingdom at the University Press, Cambridge

Typeface Times 10/12 pt.   *System* LaTeX 2$_\varepsilon$ [TB]

A catalogue record for this book is available from the British Library

Library of Congress cataloguing in publication data

Carter, T.L. (Timothy Leonard), 1963–
Paul and the power of sin : redefining 'beyond the pale' / by T.L. Carter.
    p.   cm. – (Society for New Testament Studies monograph series ; 115)
Includes bibliographical references and index.
ISBN 0 521 81041 8

1. Bible. N.T. Epistles of Paul – Socio-rhetorical criticism. 2. Sin – Biblical teaching.
3. Gentiles in the New Testament. I. Title. II. Monograph series (Society for New
Testament Studies) ; 115.
BS2655.S54 C37 2002
241′.3′092–dc21   2001037393

ISBN 0 521 81041 8 hardback

For my mother

*'Sin is a power in our life:
let us fairly understand that it can only be met by
another power.'*

HENRY DRUMMOND

CONTENTS

List of figures   *page* x
Preface   xi
List of abbreviations   xiii

1   Introduction   1

2   'Grid and group'   19

3   Physical and social boundaries in Corinth   45

4   Exclusive boundaries in Galatia   78

5   Small bounded groups in Rome   124

6   Inclusive boundaries in Rome   146

7   Conclusion   204

    Bibliography   210
    Index of selected subjects   227
    Index to ancient references   231

FIGURES

1 The Grid/Group matrix   *page* 20

2 Grid and Group (1970)   21

3 Customised Grid and Group   44

4 The present boundaries in Galatia   87

5 Christianity as a Jewish sect   87

6 Paul's exclusive eschatological boundary   88

7 Paul's inclusive eschatological boundaries   202

PREFACE

'Beyond the pale' is a well-known English phrase, generally applied to anything beyond the boundaries of acceptability. Christian theology in the west has often emphasised the doctrine of original sin, according to which every individual is inherently sinful and 'beyond the pale', acceptable to God only on the basis of the atoning death of his son, Jesus Christ. In his struggle against Pelagianism, Augustine sought to ground the doctrine of original sin in the writings of the apostle Paul, who portrayed sin as an active agent enslaving all humanity in its power and condemning the world to death. Accordingly the apostle is often credited with – or blamed for – a radically pessimistic assessment of the basic sinfulness of human nature.

This book endeavours to set aside Augustine's agenda and understand the apostle in the light of his own socio-cultural context. A cross-cultural model, developed by social anthropologist Mary Douglas, is employed to analyse Paul's letters and, as a result, a different picture emerges. It is argued that Paul developed the symbolism of the power of sin as a way of safeguarding the position of law-free Gentile believers within the small, bounded social groups that made up the early church. He sought to remove the ethnic boundary that separated Jew from Gentile and replace it with a new, eschatological boundary between the righteous and the sinful. In effect, Paul was seeking to redefine his readers' perception of who is and is not 'beyond the pale'. He does this by depicting sin as a power that threatens to infiltrate the boundaries surrounding the social body of the church and the physical bodies of believers. Sin becomes an active force which needs to be kept at bay, 'beyond the pale', outside those boundaries. These different meanings of the phrase 'beyond the pale' give rise to the title of this book: *Paul and the Power of Sin: Redefining 'Beyond the Pale'*.

This study is a revised version of my D.Phil. thesis, which was successfully submitted to Oxford University in 1998. The lion's share of my gratitude must go to Robert Morgan, whose rigorous supervision over many years eventually ensured that my thesis did not fall short of the required standard. I am grateful, too, to my examiners, John Ashton and Philip Esler, for their comments, as well as to John Barclay and Chris Rowland for their encouragement on the way. Members of the *Seminar on the Use of the Old Testament in the New* also helped me to sharpen my thinking on Romans 3:10–18.

Professor Mary Douglas was kind enough to spend some time discussing my use of her 'Grid and Group' model. Despite her reservations about applying the model to New Testament communities, she has been most supportive and helpful and her comments led me to make a serious reassessment of my approach. Readers of this book will see how often her work has been plundered by New Testament scholars; I am grateful to her for allowing me to add my name to the long list of those who have adapted her work to serve their own ends. If the final result of this study is deemed unsatisfactory, then the responsibility for that rests solely on my shoulders.

Thanks, too, are due to the Baptist Union of Great Britain, who drew on their Scholarship Fund to support me during my three years at Regent's Park College in Oxford. The Sir Richard Stapley Educational Trust and the Richard Newitt Fund also provided valuable financial assistance.

On leaving Oxford, I took up a pastorate at Leamington Spa Baptist Church, and I should like to record my gratitude to the members of that church for their generosity in allowing me, over a period of six years, to devote a significant proportion of my time to my studies. I suspect that there are few churches where such a thing would have been possible!

Last, but not least, I owe a debt of love to my wife, Sue, and to our children, Jackie, Sylvia and Robert. The thesis often took time which could have been spent with them, but it has been their support that made the writing of it seem worthwhile.

ABBREVIATIONS

AB   Anchor Bible
BBB   Bonner biblische Beiträge
Bib   *Biblica*
BTB   *Biblical Theology Bulletin*
CBQ   *Catholic Biblical Quarterly*
EKK   Evangelisch-Katholisch Kommentar zum Neuen Testament
EvTh   *Evangelische Theologie*
HTR   *Harvard Theological Review*
ICC   International Critical Commentary
JBL   *Journal of Biblical Literature*
JSNT   *Journal for the Study of the New Testament*
JSOT   *Journal for the Study of the Old Testament*
JTS   *Journal of Theological Studies*
LCC   Library of Christian Classics
LCL   Loeb Classical Library
NICNT   New International Commentary on the New Testament
NIGTC   New International Greek Testament Commentary
NovT   *Novum Testamentum*
NTS   *New Testament Studies*
NTSupp   Supplements to *Novum Testamentum*
PL   Patrologia Latina
RSR   *Religious Studies Review*
SBL   Society of Biblical Literature
SJT   *Scottish Journal of Theology*
SNTS   Society for New Testament Studies
ThQ   *Theologische Quartalschrift*
ThRev   *Theological Review*
TLZ   *Theologische Literaturzeitung*
TNTC   Tyndale New Testament Commentary

WBC   Word Biblical Commentary
WUNT   Wissenschaftliche Untersuchungen zum Neuen Testament
ZNW   *Zeitschrift für Neutestamentliche Wissenschaft*
ZTK   *Zeitschrift für Theologie und Kirche*

1

INTRODUCTION

The context of the power of sin

The *Oxford English Dictionary* defines sin as 'A transgression of the divine law and an offence against God, a violation (especially wilful or deliberate) of some religious or moral principle.' According to this definition, a sin is committed when someone does something wrong: human beings are the subject and sin the object. Without a perpetrator, sin would have no existence. Yet the apostle Paul portrays sin differently. In his letter to the Romans, sin comes to life. Humanity is no longer the subject, but the object. It is no longer the person who commits the sin: rather, sin is at work within the person.[1] In conjunction with death, sin rules over the entire world (Rom. 5:12–21). The law is powerless before it. It exploits the commandments of God for its own ends, using them to provoke the very things they were intended to prevent (7:7–13). Human nature, sold out to sin, is powerless to resist. Those who end up doing the evil that they deplore recognise, to their dismay, that sin has taken charge of their behaviour (7:13–25). In Romans 5–8, sin is the active agent and humanity its passive victim.

Two recent German monographs have explored what lies behind this distinctive portrait of sin. According to Röhser, sin is not some demonic being that holds sway over humankind.[2] Sin should not be referred to as a power, since this term is colourless and unbiblical. Instead, Paul conceived of sin as a personified deed. Drawing on a number of existing metaphors, the apostle personified sin in order to stress the full extent to which people are responsible for their actions. Röhser's case is strongest in Romans 5–6, where it is possible to understand the singular ἁμαρτία as

---

[1] Cf. E. Lohmeyer, 'Probleme paulinischer Theologie III: Sünde, Fleisch und Tod', *ZNW* 29 (1930), pp.1–59.
[2] G. Röhser, *Metaphorik und Personifikation der Sünde* (Tübingen: J.C.B. Mohr, 1987).

a metaphor for acts of sinning.[3] However, in Romans 7:7–25, ἁμαρτία takes on an identity of its own that is quite independent of the act of sinning and as Paul defines its relationship to the law, its character as 'power' becomes explicit.

Umbach takes issue with Röhser's depiction of sin as 'personified deed'.[4] According to Umbach, the concept of sin as deed is subordinated to the concept of sin as power in Paul's letters. For Paul, the term 'Sin' is always a power to which humankind 'in Adam' is completely subjected and from which they can only be freed by the power of the Spirit of God. According to Umbach, the concept of sin as a power is not really introduced until Romans 5:12–21, although Paul does refer to it in Galatians and 2 Corinthians 5:21. Elsewhere in his letters, Paul avoids the term when referring to deviant behaviour in the church because for him the term ἁμαρτία conveyed the deeper and more fundamental notion of sin as a power. On this basis, Umbach argues that Paul saw the church as a sin-free zone, since Christians have been freed from the power of sin and are now governed by the Spirit of God.

Although Umbach's stress on the power dimensions of Paul's sin language corrects Röhser's over-emphasis on sin as deed, he overplays his hand. It is by no means the case that ἁμαρτία always denotes sin as a power, since there are a number of occasions when it can denote the act of sinning.[5] Furthermore, he places too much emphasis on Romans 5:12–21. Although he acknowledges that it is only at this point that Paul introduces the concept of sin as a power, Umbach writes as if Paul had this passage in mind whenever he wrote in his other letters about sin. So if elsewhere Paul does not use ἁμαρτία to refer to deviant behaviour, Umbach implies that Paul avoids the term because ἁμαρτία necessarily denotes the power of Romans 5 that dominates unregenerate humanity. Where Paul does use the singular term ἁμαρτία in Galatians and 2 Corinthians 5:21, Umbach loads these references with semantic freight imported from Romans 5:12–21, even though Romans may well reflect a later development in the apostle's thought. If the error of illegitimate totality transfer is to be avoided, the meaning of each occurrence of ἁμαρτία will depend upon its own particular context.

---

[3]Cf. K. Koch, 'Sühne und Sündenvergebung um die Wende von der exilischen Zeit', *EvTh* 26 (1966), pp.217–39; B.N. Kaye, *The Thought Structure of Romans with Special Reference to Chapter 6* (Chico: Scholars, 1979).

[4]H. Umbach, *In Christus getauft – von der Sünde befreit: Die Gemeinde als sündenfreier Raum bei Paulus* (Göttingen: Vandenhoeck & Ruprecht, 1999).

[5]E.g. Rom. 3:20; 4:8; 14:23; 2 Cor. 5:21; 11:7; possibly Rom. 5:13, 20; 6:1; 7:7; cf. J.D.G. Dunn, *Romans*, 2 vols. (Waco: Word, 1988), vol.I, p.149.

As Umbach observes, references to the power of sin are not evenly distributed throughout Paul's letters. The majority are found in Romans 5:12–8:11, where Paul uses the singular noun ἁμαρτία 41 times, personifying sin and making it the subject of its own actions. Yet the question of the law is never far from Paul's mind in these chapters. After introducing the power of sin in Romans 5:12, Paul immediately clarifies its relationship with the law in 5:13. He goes on to imply that the law actually made sin abound (5:20), and by this means he introduces the discussion of dying to sin in 6:1–14, which culminates in the statement that sin will not rule over the recipients of his letter, because they are not under law, but under grace. This contrast between law and grace then introduces his exposition of enslavement to sin in 6:15–23. Those who have died to sin with Christ have also died to the law, which aroused sinful passions within their members (7:1–6). The arrival of God's law only served to reveal sin in all its sinfulness, since sin took advantage of the commandment by using it to provoke the very desire it forbade, thereby deceptively using the commandment to bring forth death instead of life (7:7–12). Those sold under sin find that any desire to do good is overruled by indwelling sin, so that they are held captive to the 'law of sin' in the body's members (7:13–25): it is only the law of the Spirit that brings release from sin's control (8:1–11), so achieving what the law was powerless to do, since it was weakened by the flesh. The requirements of the law are fulfilled in those who walk according to the Spirit.

Outside Romans, Paul uses the symbolism of the power of sin infrequently, but each reference occurs within the context of Paul's discussion of the Jewish law. In 1 Corinthians 15:56, sin is identified as the sting of death and the law as the power of sin. This verse encapsulates much of Paul's thinking in Romans on the relationship between sin and the law, but it bears little relation to the content of the rest of 1 Corinthians and can easily be isolated from its present context. For these reasons, it will be argued in chapter 3 that 1 Corinthians 15:56 should probably be regarded as a gloss.

The only other unambiguous references to the power of sin occur in Galatians. In Galatians 3:21–22 Paul declares that, instead of the law bringing righteousness and life, scripture has instead imprisoned the universe under sin, so that the promise might be given to those who have faith: the all-encompassing power of sin is introduced as part of Paul's argument that Gentiles and Jews alike are justified by faith, not works of the law. Another possible reference occurs in Galatians 2:17, where Paul defends himself against the charge that seeking justification apart from works of the law makes Christ the servant of sin. As in Romans, Paul uses the power of sin in Galatians to address the question of the status of law-free Gentile believers within the church.

This exclusive association of the power of sin with the law establishes Paul's discussion of the law as the context within which the power of sin needs to be understood, a factor which is ignored by both Röhser and Umbach in their studies. Apart from 1 Corinthians 15:56, all the above references to the power of sin and the law form part of Paul's attempt to establish the position of non-observant Gentile believers within the church. The question of Jewish–Gentile relations within the early church thus formed the social context in which Paul formulated his theology of the power of sin.[6] Yet from Augustine onwards,[7] Paul's sin language has been studied at a theological and doctrinal level, in isolation from that social context. This study will explore the role played by the power of sin in Paul's attempts to deal with the question of Jewish–Gentile relations within the early church, and will analyse how his sin language was shaped and influenced by this particular social context. In essence, the thesis of this study is that the issue of the relationship between Jewish and Gentile believers in the early church constitutes the socio-historical context in which the symbolism of the power of sin in Paul's letters needs to be understood. In placing all humanity under the power of sin, Paul was primarily concerned to establish that the Torah-observant Jew had no advantage over the law-free Gentile.

The legacy of Augustine

Since the fifth century, the writings of Augustine have exercised a decisive influence over the theology of sin in the western church. Augustine himself was clearly aware that Paul wrote his letter to the Romans in order to address the question 'whether the gospel of our Lord Jesus Christ came to the Jews alone because of their merits through works of the Law, or whether the justification which is of faith which is in Christ came to all nations, without any preceding merits for works'.[8] Yet in his controversy

[6]Cf. B. Holmberg, *Sociology and the New Testament: an Appraisal* (Minneapolis, Fortress, 1990), p.156: 'The social situation has to be included if we are to understand the reality the texts speak of, and not simply as a kind of "background" that might be useful to know about, but as a dimension of the meaning itself of this text and reality.'

[7]For a review of the pre-Augustinian perspective on sin, cf. R.A. Greer, 'Sinned we all in Adam's Fall?', in L.M. White and O.L. Yarbrough, eds., *The Social World of the First Christians* (Minneapolis, Fortress, 1995), pp.382–94.

[8]*Epistolae ad Romanos inchoata expositio*, 1; cf. P.F. Landes, *Augustine on Romans: Propositions from the Epistle to the Romans: Unfinished Commentary on the Epistle to the Romans* (Chico: Scholars, 1982).

with Pelagius at the beginning of the fifth century, Augustine used Romans primarily as a quarry of scripture references to support the doctrine of original sin. On the basis of Romans 5:12–21, Augustine argued that the entire human race sinned in Adam, and that this original sin alone suffices to damn even unbaptised infants.[9] In order to strengthen his hand against Pelagius, Augustine also revised his own interpretation of Romans 7:14–25. Initially he had thought that the 'wretched man' was under the law, bound to mortality as punishment for inherited original sin, and to sensuality as punishment for his own repeated sinning;[10] in his autobiographical *Confessiones*, he had even used the language of Romans 7 to portray his own pre-conversion struggles.[11] However, in the light of Pelagius' teaching that unaided human nature was capable of sinlessness, Augustine argued that Romans 7 must refer to Christian experience, since only the grace of God could produce the delight in the law referred to in 7:22.[12]

In *de spiritu et littera* Augustine wrote a detailed exposition of key passages from Romans in order to counter the Pelagian teaching that without God's help the mere power of the human will was able to advance towards perfect righteousness. Yet he did not do so without reference to Paul's original aim in writing the letter, which was 'to commend the grace which came through Jesus Christ to all peoples, lest the Jews exalt themselves above the rest on account of their possession of the law'.[13] At one point in the treatise Augustine may betray an awareness that his own anti-Pelagian exposition stands in tension with Paul's original meaning. In his exposition of Romans 2:11–16, Augustine is concerned to argue against Pelagius that those who have the law written on their hearts are Christian believers, who are able to keep the precepts of the law because their human nature has been restored by grace. Yet he recognises that others see a reference to unbelievers in these verses and accepts that their

[9] *De peccatorum meritis et remissione*, I 10.9; 11.10–39.70; *contra duas epistolas Pelagianorum* 4.7; *de nuptiis et concupiscentia* II 5.15; *de civitate Dei* 13.14; *enchiridion* 26.27; cf. G. Bonner, 'Augustine on Romans 5:12', in F.L. Cross, ed., *Studia Evangelica*, 7 vols. (Berlin: Akademie, 1969), vol.V, pp.242–7; A. Vanneste, 'Saint Paul et la Doctrine Augustinienne du Péché Originel', *Studiorum Paulinorum Congressus Internationalis Catholicus*, 2 vols. (Rome: Analecta Biblica, 1961), vol.II, pp.513–22; B. Delaroche, *Saint Augustin: Lecteur et Interprète de Saint Paul dans le 'De peccatorum meritis et remissione' (hiver 411–412)* (Paris, Institut d'Études Augustiniennes, 1996).
[10] *Ad Simplicianum* 1.1.10–11.
[11] *Confessiones* 8.10.
[12] *De gratia Christi* 1.39.43; *de nuptiis* 27.30–31.36; *duas epistolas* 1.8.13–11.24; *contra Julianum* II 3.5; 4.8; 5.13; III 26.61; *retractationes* 1.22–25; 2.27; cf. M. Huftier, *Le Tragique de la Condition Chrétienne chez Saint Augustin* (Paris: Desclé, 1964).
[13] *De spiritu et littera* 9.6.

interpretation of Paul's words makes a valid point: 'It may be that this is his way of proving what he had already said, that there is no respect of persons with God, and what he says later, that God is not the God of the Jews only but also of the Gentiles ...'[14] This second interpretation is fully in accord with Augustine's summary of the original purpose of the letter, and this suggests that Augustine himself may have been aware that his preference for the first interpretation was determined more by the need to counter Pelagius than by his own understanding of the letter's historical context.

Yet, while Augustine himself was aware that Romans addressed the question of Jews and Gentiles, it was his own theological interpretation of the letter as a treatise on human sin that decisively influenced subsequent understanding of the letter, particularly in the Reformation period. Unlike Augustine, Luther made the straightforward assertion that, 'The chief purpose of this epistle is ... to destroy all wisdom and righteousness of the flesh ... and to affirm and state and magnify sin, no matter how much someone insists it does not exist.'[15] After Luther's death, Protestant orthodoxy took its bearings from Calvin's *Institutes*, which defined original sin as 'a hereditary depravity and corruption of our nature, diffused into all parts of the soul, which first makes us liable to God's wrath then also brings forth in us "works of the flesh"'.[16] Paul's epistle to the Romans was used to support and undergird this doctrine without any reference to the letter's historical context.

With the Enlightenment came a readiness to read biblical authors on their own terms, rather than interpreting their writings though the grid of later doctrinal formulations. John Locke, who openly opposed the principle of hereditary depravity, pierced behind 1300 years of dogmatic interpretation when he argued that the aim of Romans was to establish that 'god is the god of the Gentiles as well as the Jews, and that now under the gospel there is noe difference between Jew and Gentile'.[17] The importance of the historical setting of the letter was also underlined over a century later by F.C. Baur, who regarded Romans as a key historical source for his reconstruction of the history of the New Testament period, since it contained the deepest and most comprehensive account of Pauline universalism against Jewish particularism. Baur interpreted the letter against the background of the supposed conflict between the

---

[14]Ibid., 49.28.

[15]*Lectures on Romans* 1.1.

[16]*Institutes of the Christian Religion*, 2.1.8a.

[17]J. Locke, *A Paraphrase and Notes on the Epistles of St. Paul*, ed. A. Wainwright, 2 vols. (Oxford: Clarendon, 1987), vol.II, p.483.

Petrine and Pauline parties of 1 Corinthians 1:12, and argued that Paul was writing to the predominantly Jewish Christian community in Rome in order to oppose their particularist understanding of the gospel.[18] However, although he set Romans within a particular social context, Baur's understanding of history as the vehicle for the self-disclosure of God's Spirit led him to define sin in terms of contemporary Hegelian philosophy, rather than seeking to understand it in the light of the historical context he reconstructed.

Baur was succeeded by Pfleiderer in undertaking the task of setting the writings of primitive Christianity in their historical connections. Unlike Baur, Pfleiderer argued that Paul wrote to effect a reconciliation between the oppressed and aggrieved Jewish minority in the church and the victorious Gentile Christian majority. Pfleiderer noted that Jewish belief in the law formed an 'insuperable barrier' separating Pharisaic Judaism from Gentiles, whether Christian or not. Yet, instead of examining Paul's theology of sin within that social context, Pfleiderer concentrated on identifying Jewish and Hellenistic elements in his thought. According to Pfleiderer, Paul's theology of sin was influenced by popular Hellenistic animism: sin was a demonic spiritual being, enthroned in the flesh of the human body.[19]

The first genuine attempt to understand Paul's sin language in its original social context was undertaken by Wernle, who emphasised that Paul related righteousness to the community, rather than to the individual. Wernle broke new ground by considering the different Pauline communities in turn: whereas in Thessalonica the problem of sin simply did not arise, Paul encountered the reality of sin in the incestuous man in Corinth. Paul saw this as an incident of sin crossing the boundary from the world into the church, but the overriding strength of his eschatological expectation enabled him to discount this as an exceptional event. Wernle argued that Paul's decision to excommunicate the offender reveals the communal dimensions of his thought, since all his instructions had the primary aim of cleansing the community and of producing a clearer separation from the world.[20]

In writing Galatians, the apostle's optimism returned, so that he saw entry into the Christian community as effecting a break with previous sins,

[18]F.C. Baur, 'Über Zweck und Veranlassung des Römerbriefs und die damit zusammenhängenden Verhältnisse der römischen Gemeinde', *Tübinger Zeitschrift für Theologie* (1836), vol.3, pp.59–178.
[19]O. Pfleiderer, *Primitive Christianity: its Writings and Teachings in their Historical Connections*, 2 vols. (Clifton: Reference Book, 1965), vol.I, pp.69, 218, 289f.
[20]P. Wernle, *Der Christ und die Sünde bei Paulus* (Leipzig, 1897), p.50.

and although he addressed the problem of the sinful individual in 6:1, he could not conceive that sin had any permanent place in the community. Indeed, the question of how Christians could find peace with God when they sinned did not even occur to him.[21]

Wernle's social analysis was not applied to Paul's letter to the Romans, since he rightly did not number this among the Pauline communities. Instead of investigating Paul's intention in writing Romans, he contrasts the apostle's theory of the relation of the Christian to sin with that of the Reformation:

> Den Reformatoren liegt alles daran, daß der Christ trotz der Sünde ein fröhliches Gotteskind sein kann; dem Paulus, daß er aus der Sünde herausgerissen sei und sein Zukunftsleben antrete.

> For the Reformers, everything hinges on the way in which a Christian can be a joyful child of God in spite of sin; for Paul, what is important is that he has been delivered from sin and is entering the life to come.[22]

The break with sin occurs conclusively on entry into the messianic community, after which it is no longer possible to sin: whoever sins is not a Christian. The possibility of a Christian sinning is faintly raised in Romans, only to receive the answer μὴ γένοιτο.[23] Thus Wernle exonerates Paul from the charge of making Christianity a 'religion of sin', and identifies Augustine as the culprit.

Wernle's insight into the communal dimensions of Paul's thought was temporarily obscured by the rise of the existentialist theology of Rudolf Bultmann. Citing Augustine's dictum that 'our heart is restless until it rests in thee', Bultmann argued that the universal existential question about the authenticity of our own existence furnishes the reader with the pre-understanding necessary to engage with the subject matter of pre-scientific biblical texts.[24] The real purpose of Paul's mythical sin language was to express people's understanding of themselves and the world in which they lived. For Bultmann, the ultimate sin is individual

[21] Ibid., p.90.

[22] Ibid., p.109.

[23] Meyer challenged Wernle on this point from a Lutheran perspective, arguing that Paul was aware of sin both in the church and in his own life: M. Meyer, *Die Sünde des Christen nach Pauli Briefen an die Korinther und Römer* (Gütersloh: Bertelsmann, 1902); *Der Apostel Paulus als armer Sünder: ein Beitrag zur paulinischen Hamartologie* (Gütersloh: Bertelsmann, 1903); cf. also H. Windisch, *Taufe und Sünde im ältesten Christentum* (Tübingen: J.C.B. Mohr, 1908).

[24] R. Bultmann, 'The New Testament and Mythology', in H.-W. Bartsch, ed., *Kerygma and Myth*, 2 vols. (London: SCM, 1972), vol.I, p.154; cf. Augustine, *Confessiones* 1.1.

self-reliance, an attitude which he saw exemplified in the supposed Jewish attempt to earn righteousness through works of the law. Bultmann argued that the very attempt to attain life by one's own efforts results in death, and this reveals the deceitfulness of sin: 'Man, called to selfhood, tries to live out of his own strength, and thus loses his self – his "life" – and rushes into death. This is the domination of sin. All man's doing is directed against his true intention – viz, to achieve life.'[25]

Bultmann's attempt to interpret Paul's thought in terms of individual self-understanding was attacked by Stendahl, who claimed that the 'introspective conscience of the west' could be traced no further back than Augustine, who was the first to interpret Paul in the light of his own personal struggles.[26] Since Paul himself had a 'robust conscience' and was untroubled by any pangs of guilt, Stendahl claimed that the apostle was not concerned with a personal quest for a gracious God, but rather with the social question of the status of Gentile believers within an originally Jewish church. Stendahl misrepresents Bultmann somewhat, in that the latter is not preoccupied with a guilty conscience, but rather with the existential question of care over one's own existence, but Stendahl's thesis that this kind of personal preoccupation cannot be traced back before Augustine still undermines Bultmann's individualistic understanding of Paul.

Bultmann was also accused by Käsemann of reducing theology to anthropology. According to Käsemann, Paul's thought should be understood from the apocalyptic perspective of the divine claim upon the cosmos, and it is not permissible to isolate the individual from the world which is marked by sin and death. Since people's behaviour is determined by the world to which they belong, sin has the character of an inescapable universal force to which everyone is subject both passively and actively. The fact that people are caught in a nexus of destiny and guilt does not absolve them of responsibility, since all confirm in their bodily conduct that they belong to a sinful world. This is particularly the case with the religious person, personified by the Jew, whose desire for life leads to the attempt to attain life by obeying the commandments. This, however, is to snatch what can only be given, and thus typifies the self-willed and rebellious nature of a world which is subject to the power of sin. Käsemann also rejected Stendahl's claim that Paul was concerned with the question of Jewish–Gentile relations, insisting that Jewish nomism represents

[25]R. Bultmann, *Theology of the New Testament*, 2 vols. (London: SCM, 1952), vol.I, p.246.
[26]K. Stendahl, *Paul Among Jews and Gentiles* (Minneapolis: Fortress, 1976).

the community of 'good' people who turn God's commandments into instruments of self-sanctification.[27]

This perspective on Judaism was exposed as a parody by Sanders' thorough analysis of Jewish writings from the Second Temple period and beyond, which showed that participation in the covenant and the salvation of the individual were matters of God's grace, not something to be attained by legalistic effort. Asking why Paul rejected Jewish covenantal nomism as a means of salvation, Sanders claimed that Paul thought backwards from solution to plight: since God had provided for the salvation of everyone in Christ, it followed that everyone, Jews and Gentiles alike, were in a plight from which only Christ could save them: 'The real plight of man, as Paul learned it not from experience, nor from observation, nor from an analysis of the result of human effort, but from the conviction that Christ came to be lord of all, was that men were under a different lordship.'[28]

According to Sanders, Paul simply placed all those not under the lordship of Christ under the lordship of sin. Paul's hamartiology is thus based entirely on his soteriology and this is why the apostle's attempts to demonstrate universal sinfulness in Romans fail to convince: 'The conclusion "all are under sin" is not accounted for by his arguments in favor of it, but by the prior conviction that all must have been under sin, since God sent his son to save all equally.'[29]

It was the conviction that God had saved both Jews and Gentiles through Christ that prompted Paul to reject Jewish covenantal nomism, but this belief inevitably led to the pressing question as to why God gave his people a law by which they could not be saved. Sanders here traces a development in Paul's thought.[30] In Galatians 3:22–24, Romans 5:20, the view is put forward that God gave the law with the express intention of increasing the trespass, so that grace might ultimately reign. God thus intended to condemn by the law, with a view to saving everyone through Christ. That, however, leads to the conclusion that the law is evil, which Paul is anxious to deny in Romans 7. Accordingly, in verses 7–13, he argues that God gave the law with a view to granting life by it, but, contrary to his will, the power of sin twisted the law to its own ends, arousing covetousness in its adherents and so condemning them to death. Paul then

---

[27] E. Käsemann, *Perspectives on Paul* (London: SCM, 1971), pp.1–31, 60–78; *Commentary on Romans* (London: SCM, 1980).

[28] E.P Sanders, *Paul and Palestinian Judaism* (London: SCM, 1977), p.500; cf. J. Denney, 'The Doctrine of Sin', *Expositor* 6.15 (1901), pp.283–95.

[29] E.P. Sanders, *Paul, the Law and the Jewish People* (London: SCM, 1983), p.151.

[30] Ibid., pp.70–81.

drops this explanation, possibly because he wished to avoid ascribing to sin the autonomy of a dualistic power, and proceeds immediately to a third theodicy, in which all connection between the law and transgression is broken. According to this scheme, God gave the law with the intention of granting life, but people are unable to obey it because of the law of sin, which resides in their fleshly human nature; it is primarily this last perspective upon the human plight that is resolved in 8:1–8, but not before Paul has uttered a cry over the theological difficulties in which he finds himself (7:24). By 8:20, Paul has reverted to the view that everything has taken place in accordance with the sovereign will of God.

Sanders' study is a watershed, in that he is the first to attempt to understand the power of sin within the historical context of the first-century debate over whether Gentile converts should keep the Jewish law. Yet in claiming that the power of sin is simply a reflex of Paul's soteriology Sanders fails either to note or to account for the way in which the power of sin is restricted in Paul's letters to his discussion of the law. When Sanders does address the relationship between sin and the law, his explanation is unconvincing, since it is scarcely credible that Paul should introduce himself to the Roman church by expressing his own inner confusion over why God gave the law. Although Paul asks what is the point of the law in Galatians 3:19, this question is not personally motivated, and it is not repeated in Romans: the issue of the role of the law seems to have troubled Sanders more than it did Paul.

Despite ongoing opposition to Sanders' thesis,[31] it is increasingly accepted both that Paul thought from solution to plight, and that his presentation of the gospel in Romans needs to be understood against the background of Jewish–Gentile relations in the first century. Attempts to integrate a Lutheran understanding of Paul with this new perspective tend to use the social setting as a framework for a traditional presentation of the gospel.[32] Even Dunn, who sees the primary function of the law as a boundary marker separating Jew from Gentile, insulates Romans 6:1–8:39 from the social context of the letter as a whole by reading this section as 'The outworking of the gospel in relation to the individual'.[33] Thus the power of sin is perceived as a feature of individual existential reality

---

[31] Cf. especially F. Thielman, *From Plight to Solution*, NT Supp. 61 (Leiden: E.J. Brill, 1989); T. Laato, *Paulus und das Judentum: Anthropologische Erwägungen* (Åbo: Akademis Förlag, 1991).

[32] E.g. S. Westerholm, *Israel's Law and the Church's Faith* (Grand Rapids: Eerdmans, 1988); P. Stuhlmacher, *Paul's Letter to the Romans: A Commentary* (Edinburgh: T&T Clark, 1994); D.J. Moo, *The Epistle to the Romans*, NICNT (Grand Rapids: Eerdmans, 1996).

[33] *Romans*, pp.viii, 243.

that has nothing to do with the different ethnic groups with which the remainder of the letter is concerned:

> The one fact which matters is that man experiences (consciously or unconsciously) a power which works in him to bind him wholly to his mortality and corruptibility, to render impotent any knowledge of God or concern to do God's will, to provoke his merely animal appetites in forgetfulness that he is a creature of God – and that power Paul calls 'sin'.[34]

Ziesler's commentary on Romans also embraces the new perspective, and Ziesler gives specific consideration to Paul's power language, suggesting that it has its roots in the ancient world's experience of subjection under an imperial power.[35] This suggestion takes due account of the first-century culture in which Paul wrote, but again pays insufficient attention to the issue of Jewish–Gentile relations, which forms the social context of the power of sin in Paul's letters.

N.T. Wright integrates Romans 5–8 with Romans 3:21–4:25 and Romans 9–11 by claiming that they address the question of God's covenant faithfulness.[36] According to Wright, the divine answer to Adam's sin was to make a covenant with Abraham that he should be the father of Israel, a new humanity. In the light of the cross and resurrection, Paul argues that that new humanity should be defined as a world-wide community of faith; in Romans 6–8, he argues that Israel's privileges of fulfilling the law and being God's children have been transferred to Christ and those in Christ. God's purpose in giving the law was always to concentrate sin in Israel (Rom. 5:20; cf. 7:7–13), and then in the messiah as Israel's representative, so that it could be dealt with on the cross (Rom. 8:3).

Wright's exposition has the strength of explaining why Paul only refers to the power of sin in the context of the law: it is the law that reveals the power of sin as the true plight of humanity, and in thus exposing it, prepares the way for it to be dealt with by Christ. Wright's case makes Romans 5:20 crucial to Paul's argument, a claim that he supports by arguing that the meaning of this verse is elucidated in Romans 7:7–13 and God's ultimate purpose is revealed in Romans 8:3. In the intervening

---

[34]Ibid., p.149, cf. J.D.G. Dunn, *The Theology of Paul the Apostle* (Edinburgh: T&T Clark, 1998). pp.111–14. The oddity of the statement that one's experience of sin may be unconscious highlights the inadequacy of defining sin in terms of individual experience.

[35]J.A. Ziesler, *Paul's Letter to the Romans* (London: SCM, 1989); cf. L. Schottroff, 'Die Schreckenherrschaft der Sünde und die Befreiung durch Christus nach dem Römerbrief des Paulus', *EvTh* 39 (1979), pp.497–510.

[36]N.T. Wright, *The Climax of the Covenant* (Edinburgh: T&T Clark, 1991), pp.18–40, 137–230.

sections, Paul warns his ex-proselyte readers that the Torah is not itself to be identified with sin (7:14–25) and release from Torah does not open the door to antinomianism (6:1–23) or anti-Judaism (9–11).

The problem with Wright's reading of the letter is that it is not clear whether Romans 5:20 will bear the weight of being the linchpin of chapters 5–8, particularly since the thread of Paul's argument in 5:20–8:3 is almost totally obscured by his intervening paraenesis and defence of the law. Furthermore, Wright's interpretation of sin in Romans sits uneasily with Galatians 3:19, 22, where he ascribes a final meaning to χάριν, and understands 3:22 as a statement that the law has been superseded. Here the power of sin plays a different role: it is not revealed through the law and concentrated in Israel and her messiah; it is simply used to explain the inability of the law to bring righteousness and life. This different understanding of the power of sin in Galatians 3:22 places a question mark over Wright's interpretation of Romans. The problem of integrating the two letters could be solved by insisting that they be read independently, and positing a development in Paul's thought from seeing the power of sin as a problem that the law could not solve (Gal. 3:22), to sin as a problem that the law was intended to expose (Rom. 5–8). Yet the question remains whether Wright's dependence on a particular interpretation of Romans 5:20 is not too fragile to be sustained alongside a very different understanding of the relationship between the law and sin in Galatians.

Stowers' rereading of Romans is a conscious attempt to understand the letter within a pre-Augustinian frame of reference.[37] Stowers claims that the letter is addressed exclusively to Gentiles who are attracted to Judaism as a means of attaining self-mastery, the coveted ancient ethic of moderation and restraint. Paul responds by claiming that Gentiles and Jews alike are caught up in the divinely appointed, apocalyptic period of sin's domination over the world before the end. God has punished the Gentiles by allowing them to be enslaved by their passions and desires (1:18–32). In 2:17–29 Paul portrays a Jewish teacher of Gentiles as one who speaks in the recognisable character of the pretentious person, and argues against him that the law is no solution to the problems of the Gentiles, since the Jews have difficulty keeping it themselves. Romans 6 demonstrates that Gentiles can only achieve self-mastery by relating in baptism to Christ's act of obedience, while Romans 7 illustrates the inner struggle of a Gentile who is unable to keep the law of God, and who can only attain self-mastery by the Spirit.

---

[37]S.K. Stowers, *A Rereading of Romans: Justice, Jews and Gentiles* (London: Yale University Press, 1994).

Stowers' reconstruction of the social context is vulnerable, in that the existence of proselytising Jewish teachers cannot be taken for granted.[38] Yet even if this is granted, Stowers still fails to locate Paul's sin language within this context, inasmuch as he claims that Paul's view of sin as a power is derived from Jewish apocalyptic, and Paul believed that the whole universe was subject to tribulation and sinfulness in the last days.[39] Not only does this have nothing to do with the social situation addressed in Romans, it actually conflicts with it, since Paul's respect for the governing authorities as God's agents for law and order in the world (13:1–7) indicates that he neither shared the pessimistic worldview of Jewish apocalyptic, nor experienced the social oppression that formed the crucible for apocalyptic thought.[40] Stowers' work in fact underlines the current lack of a convincing integration of Paul's sin language and his social context.

Conclusion

The doctrinal considerations that prompted Augustine to isolate sin from the context of Paul's letters determined the way in which sin was perceived until the time of the Enlightenment. Although Baur and Pfleiderer were both aware of the historical context of Paul's writings, they did not set sin in that context, but rather examined it from the perspective of Hegelian philosophy and the history of religions. Wernle's study stands out as an incipiently sociological approach, but his interpretation of the power of sin in Romans was driven by anti-Reformation polemic rather than by any appreciation of the historical context of Jewish–Gentile relations in the first century. In twentieth-century studies of Paul, Bultmann and Käsemann have dominated the theological interpretation of sin, and while a growing awareness of the apostle's social context has undermined their position, no study to date has specifically attempted to ground Paul's references to sin in that context. What is needed is an approach which seeks to understand Paul's language about the power of sin in the light of the apostle's own socio-cultural context, rather than in the light of subsequent theological reflection.

This study endeavours to meet that need by using the work of Mary Douglas, whose 'Grid and Group' model can be used to ground the

---

[38] Cf. J.C. Paget, 'Jewish Proselytism at the Time of Christian Origins: Chimera or Reality?', *JSNT* 62 (1996), pp.65–103.

[39] Stowers, *Rereading*, pp.176–87.

[40] Cf. C. Rowland, *The Open Heaven* (London: SPCK, 1982), pp.193–247.

meaning of symbols in social experience.[41] Working within the field of social anthropology, Douglas has used her model to explore the connection between a society's cosmology[42] and its social location. According to Douglas, symbols are influenced by social structures and can also reinforce or subvert those structures. When the model is applied to the epistles of Paul, it enables us to see not only how Paul's perception of sin is a given part of his socially determined cosmology, but also how the apostle employs the power of sin to shape the symbolic universe of the churches to whom he writes. Thus, on the one hand, Paul's language about sin is shaped by his socio-cultural location within the first-century Mediterranean church, while on the other, Paul employs the symbolism of sin as a power in order to bring his own influence to bear on the social issue of Jewish–Gentile relations within that church. 'Grid and Group' thus offers a potential means of analysing the interrelationship between the symbolism of the power of sin and the original socio-historical context of Paul's letters.

Furthermore, 'Grid and Group' was originally designed as a cross-cultural model and it specifically provides an analysis of the way in which sin is perceived and symbolised in different cultures. This makes the model a particularly useful heuristic tool, since it offers a way of understanding Paul's sin language in the light of the apostle's own first-century cultural context, thereby avoiding the prevalent error of interpreting it anachronistically through the lens of westernised individualism fashioned by Augustine. It is all too easy for modern readers to find their own experience as sinful human beings mirrored in Paul's letters and so to interpret the apostle's sin language in the light of their own self-understanding. Douglas' model highlights the way in which anthropology varies from culture to culture, and so offers the modern interpreter a way of perceiving how the original readers of Paul's letters would have understood the apostle's sin language in the light of their own, very different, culturally determined self-understanding.

After reviewing the many different permutations of Douglas' matrix and also engaging with its critics, a version of the model is developed which renders it suitable for application to Paul's letters (chapter 2). The horizontal 'group' dimension on the matrix is used to measure the extent

[41] M. Douglas, *Natural Symbols: Explorations in Cosmology* (1st edition, London: Barrie & Rockcliff, 1970; 2nd edition, London: Barrie & Jenkins, 1973; 3rd edition, USA, New York: Pantheon Books, 1982; 3rd edition, UK, London: Routledge, 1996).

[42] A society's cosmology is its 'theory of the universe as an ordered whole and of the general laws which govern it': S. Howell, 'Cosmology', in A. Bonnard and J. Spencer, eds., *Encyclopedia of Social and Cultural Anthropology* (London: Routledge, 1996), pp.129–32.

to which a given social unit is collectivist (high group) or individualist (low group), while the vertical 'grid' dimension is used to measure the extent to which an individual or group accepts (high grid) or rejects (low grid) the symbol system of the surrounding culture. By applying the model to Paul's letters, it is possible to ascertain Paul's own position on the matrix, and that of the community to which he writes, thus clarifying both Paul's concerns when he wrote the letter, and also how the letter would have been understood by its recipients.

The model is initially applied to 1 Corinthians (chapter 3), and the various applications of the model to this letter are assessed. The apostle's preoccupation with group cohesion and boundaries indicates that Paul belongs to the strong group/weak grid quadrant of the matrix, which is that of the small bounded group. Within the cosmology of this quadrant, sin is perceived as an external evil threatening the good inside of the physical and social body, and the apostle's response to the problems of sin within the Corinthian community is analysed in these terms.

Turning to Galatians (chapter 4), both Paul and his readers are found to be low grid/high group. Making use of the low grid/high group technique of witchcraft accusations, Paul redefines the boundaries surrounding the community in such a way as to exclude his judaising opponents from the eschatological community of believers, while at the same time also placing himself and his converts outside the ethnic boundary marker of the law, thereby making the law and the Spirit mutually exclusive spheres. Paul's rejection of the law as a boundary marker leads to the accusation that those who seek justification in Christ are no better than Gentile sinners (2:17). Yet Paul denies that this makes Christ the servant of sin. Galatians 2:18 should be understood as a reference, not to the rebuilding of the law, but rather to Paul's act of restoring the church which he had previously tried to destroy out of zeal for his ancestral traditions. Paul accepts that rebuilding the church makes him a transgressor of the law, but he accepts the law's sentence of death on himself, since it is by being crucified with Christ as a transgressor of the law that he now lives to God and knows Christ living within him. Paul thus identifies with his Gentile converts as outsiders to the Jewish law, and legitimates their position by asserting that it is as a transgressor of the law that he has died to the law with Christ, so that he can now live for God in the eschatological sphere.

Countering the exegesis of his opponents, Paul argues that this eschatological life is available only to those who are justified by faith, whereas all those who are of the law are under a curse (3:7–14). As part of this strategy of exclusion, Paul uses the symbolism of the power of sin to denote the cosmic wickedness outside the eschatological community of the righteous. Instead of keeping sin at bay, Paul argues that the law actually functions as a gaoler imprisoning people under the old aeon. In Galatians the power of sin thus plays its part in Paul's attempt to redefine the boundaries around the community along eschatological, rather than ethnic, lines.

In chapter 5, it is argued that Paul's letter to the Romans is the apostle's response to the social situation in Rome, where the small bounded groups of weak and strong are divided over the question of Torah observance. Romans represents Paul's low grid/high group attempt to reconcile the different groups on the basis of their common faith. As in Galatians, Paul attempts to define the boundaries surrounding the community along eschatological, rather than along ethnic lines (chapter 6). In Romans 1–4, Paul subverts the distinction between righteous Jew and sinful Gentile, making it clear that all alike are only justified through faith in Christ.

To replace the discredited boundary marker of Torah observance, Paul draws fresh boundaries along eschatological lines in Romans 5:12–21 and uses the power of sin to symbolise the evil of the old aeon. Paul portrays baptised Gentile believers as righteous insiders, who participate in the new aeon and have died to sin (6:1–23). However, Torah-observant Jews who do not have the Spirit are sinful outsiders, who are subject to the power of sin, which makes its presence felt through the common experience of the disjunction between willing and doing (7:1–25). Although the good inner mind of the Jew desires to fulfil the law, it is overpowered by the cosmic power of sin, which has taken up residence in the flesh, which again denotes both participation in the old aeon, and also the ambiguous bodily boundary between the good inside and the evil outside. It should not, however, be assumed that Paul understood the flesh to be literally sinful: his emphasis on the sinfulness of the physical body in Romans 5–8 is part of his strategy to emphasise the need of an eschatological deliverance from sin that the law could not provide. The main focus of Paul's attention throughout Romans is not on individual anthropology, but rather on those concerns which are characteristic of high group and low grid, namely the establishment of clear boundaries to protect the inner purity of the physical and social bodies against outside evil. Accordingly, Paul seeks to establish that the eschatological Spirit, rather than the law, should be seen as the sole effective boundary separating righteous insiders from sinful outsiders. On the basis of their common faith, Paul sought to legitimate the position of both Gentile believers and Torah-observant Jewish Christians within the church.

Paul's language about sin needs to be understood in this context. It is argued that the symbolism of the power of sin does not reflect a conviction on the apostle's part that all humanity is in bondage to the enslaving power of sin; instead, Paul developed this perspective on the human plight as a specific part of his strategy to establish a symbolic universe that would safeguard and legitimise the position of law-free Gentile believers within the eschatological community of the church.

In conclusion, it will be argued that the difference between our modern understandings of sin and that of the apostle is summed up in the different interpretations of the phrase 'beyond the pale'. For the modern reader, the phrase pertains to behaviour that is unacceptable, beyond the bounds of acceptability.[43] For the first-century apostle, however, 'beyond the pale' was precisely where sin belonged: beyond the boundaries of the social and physical body, and his primary concern in 1 Corinthians, Galatians and Romans was to establish effective boundaries that would keep sin at bay and affirm the identity of the church as the ethnically mixed but morally pure eschatological people of God.

---

[43] According to *Brewer's Dictionary of Phrase and Fable*, the phrase was coined in the fourteenth century. The 'English Pale' referred to the boundary surrounding the English settlement in Ireland under Henry II. The phrase 'beyond the pale' was used to denote anything beyond the bounds of civilisation or civilised behaviour.

2

'GRID AND GROUP'

Introduction

The last chapter opened with the *Oxford English Dictionary*'s definition of sin as 'A transgression of the divine law and an offence against God, a violation (especially wilful or deliberate) of some religious or moral principle.' Such a definition of sin has little relevance in a modern secular society where God no longer occupies a central position in most people's symbolic universe. Consequently the symbol of sin has lost its potency to identify and restrain deviant behaviour and the concept of sin is perceived as largely irrelevant. Yet on the margins of modern society other conceptions of sin emerge. Environmental pressure groups view the pollution of the earth as the prime sin of humankind.[1] In New Age thought, the essential divine goodness of each individual is emphasised; evil is perceived as a matter of ignorance, and is transcended by the enlightened individual.[2]

These different views of sin correspond to four types of society that Douglas identifies with her Grid and Group model,[3] which she uses to

[1] Environmental pressure groups stand here as a modern example of those who view sin in terms of pollution; cf. M. Douglas and A. Wildawsky, *Risk and Culture. An Essay on the Selection of Technical and Environmental Dangers* (London, University of California Press, 1982). In the original edition of *Natural Symbols*, Douglas used the example of the Bog Irish refusing to eat meat on Friday. This formed a natural link with Bernstein's work on the different linguistic codes employed by working- and middle-class families, which formed the basis for her own approach; cf. B. Bernstein, *Class, Codes and Control*, 2 vols. (London: Routledge & Kegan Paul, 1971).

[2] Cf. W.J. Hanegraaf, *New Age Religion and Western Culture: Esotericism in the Mirror of Secular Thought* (Leiden: E.J. Brill, 1996), pp.204–10.

[3] A model is defined as 'an abstract, simplified representation of some real world object, event or interaction, constituted for the purpose of understanding, control, or prediction', according to B.J. Malina, 'The Social Sciences and Biblical Interpretation', *Interpretation* 36 (1982), pp.229–42; cf. T.F. Carney, *The Shape of the Past: Models and Antiquity* (Kansas, Colorado Press, 1982). Although Horrell prefers the term 'typology' for this approach, Esler has pointed out that typologies lack the dynamic mechanism which enables models to explain and predict the effect of variations within the system: cf. P.F. Esler, *Community and*

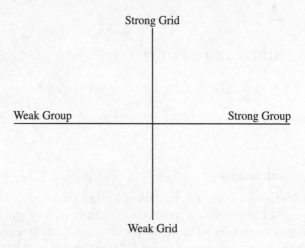

Figure 1: The Grid/Group matrix.

analyse different cultures.[4] In hierarchical societies, sin is perceived as transgression; it is regarded as irrelevant in societies which value individual competition; sin as pollution is the characteristic perspective of the sect or enclave, while sin is associated with a state of mind by those who enjoy unstructured social relations. These four different types of society Douglas plots on a matrix, the axes of which measure two variables. The horizontal axis, labelled 'group', measures the extent to which a person's lifestyle is independent or is determined by incorporation into a bounded social unit; the vertical axis, 'grid', measures the extent to which an individual's role is prescribed by the rules and classification system of any particular society (see figure 1).

The hierarchical society, which views sin as transgression, is marked by strong group and grid: high social integration and role prescription.

Gospel in Luke-Acts (Cambridge: Cambridge University Press, 1987), p.9; D.G. Horrell, *The Social Ethos of the Corinthian Correspondence: Interests and Ideology from 1 Corinthians to 1 Clement* (Edinburgh: T&T Clark, 1996), p.11. Esler's review of Horrell's book in *JTS* 49 (1998), pp.253–60 has led to a debate by both authors in *JSNT* 78 (2000), pp.83–113.

    [4]Douglas works within the field of social or cultural anthropology, the main focus of which is 'to understand cultures other than our own by means of formulating adequate models, models that are neither superficial nor inaccurate': B.J. Malina, *The New Testament World* (London: SCM, 1983), p.24. For a defence of the viability of analysing historical societies such as that of the New Testament world, cf. G. Feeley-Harnik, 'Is Historical Anthropology Possible?', in SBL Centennial Series, *Humanising America's Iconic Book* (Chico: Scholars, 1982), pp.95–126.

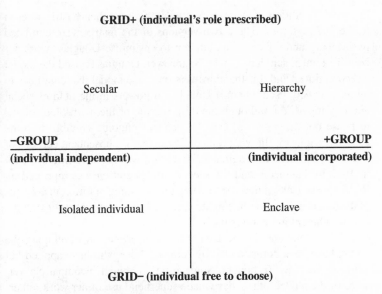

GRID+ (individual's role prescribed)

| Secular | Hierarchy |

−GROUP **(individual independent)** +GROUP **(individual incorporated)**

| Isolated individual | Enclave |

GRID− (individual free to choose)

Figure 2: Grid and Group (1970).

The enclave, with its fear of pollution, is marked by strong group and weak grid: here, there is high social integration, and group membership is defined in terms of separation from the outside world, rather than in terms of fulfilling a specific role.[5] Secular society is marked by weak group (individualism) and strong grid (high role allocation) in the first version of the model, although in subsequent versions it is spread across the matrix. The isolated individual is low group and grid in the first two versions of the matrix; however, in the final version, it is either moved up-grid or off the matrix altogether (see figure 2).

The above description gives advance warning of a serious difficulty with Douglas' matrix: it has been developed in so many incompatible ways, both by Douglas and by others, that a considerable amount of confusion has ensued. The original version of the model was published

[5]Hanson sees a biblical example of high grid/high group transgression in Leviticus 4–5, and argues for a low grid/high group perception of sin in Jeremiah 7, 26 and Acts 2; cf. K.C. Hanson, 'Sin, Purification and Group Process', in H.T.C. Sun and K.L. Eades, eds., *Problems in Biblical Theology: Essays in Honor of Rolf Knierim* (Grand Rapids: Eerdmans, 1997), pp.167–91. Cf. also the analysis of E. Sivan: 'The Enclave Culture', in M.E. Marty and R. Scott Appleby, eds., *Fundamentalisms Comprehended* (London: University of Chicago Press, 1995), pp.11–68.

in the 1970 edition of *Natural Symbols*; this was then hastily revised in the 1973 edition.[6] These two versions of the matrix were conflated by Isenberg and Owen, in an attempt to customise Douglas' work for New Testament scholars.[7] In 1978, however, Douglas revised the model a second time,[8] and it is this third version of the model that continues to be most widely used amongst Douglas' followers in the field of social anthropology.[9] Yet, although the third version of the matrix has tended to phase out the first two, Douglas has lent ongoing credibility to the earlier versions by allowing each one to appear in subsequent editions of *Natural Symbols*. The original 1970 edition was reissued in New York in 1982 by Pantheon, and the second (1973) edition was reprinted by Routledge in 1996. It must be said that this reissuing of different versions of the model only serves to heighten the confusion that is already, to some extent, inherent in the book itself.[10]

The problems caused by Douglas' inconsistency in developing the model have been compounded by some of those who have applied her work to the New Testament. Some have combined incompatible versions of the model; others have made superficial use of her work; others have developed versions of the model that scarcely bear any relation at all to Douglas' original. Consequently, the validity of Douglas' whole approach is sometimes questioned. For these reasons, it will be necessary to engage in a detailed analysis of Douglas' work. In the remainder of this chapter, each version of the model and its developments will be set out in turn, in dialogue with Douglas' critics. After analysing the different versions, a fresh adaptation will be proposed that will enable a valid application of Douglas' model to the first-century writings of the apostle Paul. Thus, while this chapter will contribute little to our understanding of the power of sin, it does provide the necessary methodological basis for what follows, and may also go some way to rehabilitating Douglas' work as a useful tool for New Testament scholars.

---

[6]This version also features in M. Douglas, *Implicit Meanings: Essays in Anthropology* (London: Routledge & Kegan Paul, 1975).

[7]S.R. Isenberg and D.E. Owen, 'Bodies, Natural and Contrived: the Work of Mary Douglas', *Religious Studies Review* 3 (1977), pp.1–17.

[8]M. Douglas, *Cultural Bias*, Royal Anthropological Institute Occasional Paper 35 (London: RAI, 1978); reprinted in *In the Active Voice* (London: Routledge & Kegan Paul, 1982), pp.183–254.

[9]E.g. M. Douglas, ed., *Essays in the Sociology of Perception* (London: Routledge & Kegan Paul, 1982).

[10]Douglas openly admits this in the introduction to the 3rd (USA) edition of *Natural Symbols*, p.xx.

Natural Symbols (1st edition, 1970, 3rd USA edition, 1982)

Douglas' preface to the groundbreaking first edition of *Natural Symbols* sets out her programme in bold terms. She claims that most symbolic behaviour must work through the human body, which is common to us all;[11] only our social condition varies, and Douglas sets out to find a way of classifying the different social experiences that are expressed through symbols based on the human body:

> All I am concerned with is a formula for classifying relations which can be applied equally to the smallest band of hunters and gatherers as to the most industrialised nations. All we need to know is the way in which these relations are structured according to two independently varying criteria which I have called grid and group. Group is obvious – the experience of a bounded social unit. Grid refers to rules which relate one person to others on an ego-centred basis.[12]

The hypothesis that underlies this matrix is that there is a concordance between symbolic and social experience, so that symbolic behaviour within a society will tend to replicate the social situation of that society. Specifically, Douglas argues that the symbolic use of the physical body corresponds to the degree of social control exercised in any society. Douglas argues that a preference for spontaneous expression and a weak degree of physical bodily control is to be explained as behaviour which is characteristic of a social body that lacks a well-articulated social structure and where a sense of group identity is weak. Correspondingly, when a social body is characterised by well-defined roles and a strong sense of group identity, one would expect to find a high value placed upon formal control of the physical body. Thus social constraints determine the way in which the physical body is perceived while, at the same time, the physical experience of the body sustains a particular view of society: physical and social experiences are mutually reinforcing.

Douglas substantiates this theory by claiming that there is a drive to achieve consonance in all levels of experience, so that formal social relations call for controlled movements and physical distance, whereas informal relations call for relaxed posture, freedom of movement and casual

---

[11] The title *Natural Symbols* is misleading, in that it could be taken to imply that the body is itself a 'natural symbol'. Douglas clarifies this in the second edition (p.xix), when she declares that there are no natural symbols; they are all social. The book would have been better entitled 'An Essay on the Limitations of the Idea of Natural Symbols'.

[12] *Natural Symbols* (1st edition), p.viii.

dress. On this basis, Douglas asserts that bodily control is an expression of social control, since bodily control cannot be imposed without the corresponding social forms and the experience of consonance in layer after layer of experience is fundamentally satisfying. Correspondingly, on the basis of an appeal to the rhetorical style of Augustine and the appearance of John Nelson Darby (founder of the Plymouth Brethren), Douglas argues that bodily expression is naturally co-ordinated with other media to facilitate communication and so to reinforce the social expressions of control or lack of control.

To test her theory of the correspondence between social control and symbolic physical behaviour, Douglas offers a comparative analysis of the religious behaviour of three neighbouring Nilotic tribes, the Dinka, the Nuer and the Mandari. She concludes that the correlation between behaviour and social structure in each case offers support for her hypothesis. The Nuer communities are concentrated in discrete villages in the wet season, and in large cattle camps in the dry season. Theirs is a rational and regulative cosmos in which moral faults are predisposed to lead to disaster, so that there is a close connection between sickness and sin; spirit possession is regarded as dangerous. Likewise amongst the Mandari, where group allegiance is important, there is a formalist attitude to sin and purification. In contrast, the Dinka have a more mobile social system and their political communities are more fluid in composition and less fixed in their spatial relations to each other; correspondingly, the Dinka are less pollution-prone and sin-conscious, and view trance as benign. On this basis, Douglas concludes that, 'The weaker the social constraints, the more bodily dissociation is approved and treated as a central ritual adjunct for channelling benign power to the community. The stronger the social pressures, the more magicality in ritual and in the definition of sin.'[13]

The Nuer and Mandari represent societies with strong grid and group, with a highly developed idea of formal transgression and its dangerous consequences. The Dinka, with their more fluid and formless social relations, represent societies marked by weak grid and group, where there is little sense of sin and the cosmos is experienced as sufficiently benign to justify faith in the inner purity and goodness of the human individual. These three tribes thus represent two of the quadrants on the matrix.

Where group is high and grid is low, small bounded groups emerge:

> Within such groups, roles are ambiguous and undefined. Leadership is precarious. The group boundary is the main definer

of roles: individuals class themselves either as members or strangers. Here the cosmos is slightly more complex. It is divided between good and bad, inside and outside. There is magical danger associated with emblems of boundary. Group members accuse deviants in their midst of allowing the outside evil to in-filtrate. The accusations lead to the fission of the group. This is a cosmos dominated by witchcraft and sorcery. It is subject to the vile, irrational behaviour of the human agents of evil. It is pre-occupied with rituals of cleansing, expulsion and re-drawing of boundaries. Its distinctive therapeutic system is based on the doc-trine of the essential goodness of that which belongs inside the body. It is an irrational cosmos since in it evil is taken to be a foreign danger, introduced by perverted or defective humans.[14]

This society is represented by the Nilotic Anuak tribe, who occupy distinct, very crowded village communities, where they are in constant and intense individual contact. Theirs is a cosmos dominated by ill will and jealousy, in which death is attributed to witches or to the vengeance of the dead. Another example of this type of group is the Exclusive Brethren, who erected a high wall between themselves and the evil outside world, and who suffered from continual schism. These groups bear the four characteristic features of a witchcraft cosmology: 'the idea of the bad outside and the good inside, the inside under attack and in need of protection, human wickedness on a cosmic scale, and these ideas used in political manipulation'.[15]

The remaining high grid/low group quadrant on Douglas' matrix is inhabited by competing individuals, who live in a manipulable cosmos where success and failure are not linked to any moral system. Here we find Lord Thomson of Fleet placed alongside the Big Men of Melanesia, who impose themselves as leaders by means of their own personal achievement and enterprise. The Big Men provide livelihood and security for everyone else, and compete with each other for followers, since their prestige and power are measured in terms of the number of their adherents. This, however, is a society in which only a few succeed, and thus it carries within it the seeds of incipient millennialism as the unsuccessful majority suffer depersonalisation and revolt against the way the social structure denies them material success. In such cases, people are forced down into the low grid/low group quadrant, where they are constrained neither by group membership, nor by society's structures. In such cases, people

[14]Ibid., pp.103–4.
[15]Ibid., p.114.

express their rejection of the system through bodily shaking, frenzy and sexual promiscuity; bodily dissociation is valued, and there is no self-consciousness about sexual or other bodily orifices and functions. In this way, unstructured social experience (low grid and group) is directly symbolised through the medium of the physical body. Similarly, people may express their alienation from strong group societies by despising and disregarding the body. Here, bodily grooming and diet are neglected in favour of experimenting with consciousness, which is approved as a form of experience which is the most personal, and which contributes the least to the wider social system. This rejection of the body symbolises their alienation from an inclusive social system.[16]

It is an important sub-theme of the book that the body symbolises social experience in most societies. In the bounded structured system of high grid and group societies, the social and physical bodies would be assimilated in such a way that the physical body would symbolise the life of the social body. Where group is strong but grid weak, anxiety about the evil world outside the boundaries of the social body would express itself in anxiety about the physical body being poisoned. Correspondingly, the emphasis on the inner good of the social body may lead to an ascetic rejection of the physical body as an empty shell. Thus the good inside and the bad outside are replicated in both the social and physical bodies. It is only in high grid/low group societies, like that of the modern middle classes, that people find themselves unable to express social identity through the physical body and have to rely instead on an elaborated language code for expression.

It is precisely for this reason that Douglas' thesis, that the physical body symbolises the social body, appears opaque to modern western eyes. Thus it is understandable that Millar and Riches demand evidence for the thesis that the body is a symbol of society and point out that a link between social

---

[16]Ibid., pp.160–2. Applying this passage to the Bog Irish, J.T. Sanders dismisses Douglas' model on the grounds of inconsistency, since although the Bog Irish are an alienated sub-group they do not reject the body, but rather cling to the dietary ritual of abstaining from meat on Fridays: J.T. Sanders, *Schismatics, Sectarians, Dissidents, Deviants: the First One Hundred Years of Jewish–Christian Relations* (London: SCM, 1993), pp.108–9. It is because Douglas misleadingly attributes rejection of the body to 'the small, interpersonal group which is alienated' (*Natural Symbols* (1st edition), p.161) that Sanders is able to accuse her of failing to account for the behaviour of the Bog Irish. However, the reason why the Bog Irish do not reject the body is that they form a close-knit social group, where individuals maintain allegiance to their common social identity by the ritual of abstention (pp.37–42). Where the individual is integrated into a close-knit social system in this way, it is possible for the body to function as a symbol of high-group social cohesion, in which case it is not simply rejected.

location and the symbolism of the physical body needs to be established.[17] Yet Douglas' thesis receives anticipatory independent substantiation from a study by Fisher and Cleveland, who conducted Rohrschach tests on different individuals to examine the relationship between bodily boundaries and personality.[18] In their analysis of psychosomatic phenomena, they found that subjects with exterior body symptoms significantly exceeded subjects with interior body symptoms in the degree to which they conceived of their bodies as surrounded by a well-differentiated boundary. Conversely, subjects with interior symptoms exceeded those with exterior symptoms in the degree to which they regarded their bodies as easily penetrated. They also found that this perception of body boundaries varied cross-culturally, with Third World Bhil, Navaho and Zuni subjects having a far higher body barrier score than those raised in the more individualistic spirit of western civilisation. Furthermore, in small group settings, those with high barrier scores were far more likely to set group goals above their own personal goals, while those with low barrier scores were more likely to withdraw. Their study would thus appear to corroborate Douglas' thesis that there is indeed a correlation between the symbolism of the physical body and the experience of the social body.[19]

Other criticisms came in an early review of *Natural Symbols*, in which Steinfels complained that Douglas had not presented an informed, fairly argued case, but instead had found a 'terribly complicated way of over-simplifying everything'.[20] Steinfels' major criticism is that Douglas' matrix can only work by flattening out the portraits of advanced societies and by ignoring the historical factors that formed them. There can be no doubt that this initial version of Douglas' matrix does struggle with modern society. The high grid/low group quadrant is vastly over-crowded and complicated, containing as it does the successful Big Men, their

---

[17] A. Millar and J.K. Riches, 'Interpretation: a Theoretical Perspective and Some Applications', *Numen* 28 (1981), pp.29–53.

[18] S. Fisher and S.E. Cleveland, *Body Image and Personality* (London: Van Nostrand, 1958). Although old, the findings of this study remain valid.

[19] The one area of tension between their findings and Douglas' theory lies in their finding that definiteness of boundaries was linked with an ability to be an independent person with definite standards, goals, and forceful striving ways of approaching tasks (p.117). According to Douglas' model, one would normally expect independence to be linked to a low boundary score. However, since western society in 1958 was a great deal less orientated towards the individual than it is now, it is not unreasonable to suppose that those with a greater sense of bodily boundaries may have been better equipped to succeed in that society. Fisher and Cleveland's study may therefore be taken as verification of Douglas' basic thesis.

[20] P. Steinfels, 'Review of *Purity and Danger, Natural Symbols*', *Commonweal* 93 (1970), pp.49–51.

unsuccessful followers and the seeds of low group/low grid millennial-ism. Furthermore, it could be argued that modern western society contains elements of all four possible societal groups. Accordingly, it is no surprise to find that the grand claim to incorporate hunters and gatherers alongside the most advanced industrial societies is quietly dropped from the second edition of *Natural Symbols*, which offers a more modest, but ultimately less satisfactory, version of the original model.

Natural Symbols (2nd edition, 1973, 3rd UK edition, 1996)

The second edition of *Natural Symbols* incorporates substantial revisions of the model, which are somewhat uneasily incorporated alongside much of the original material. This time, instead of seeking to encompass all kinds of society within a broad scope, the model adopts the more easily verifiable approach of focusing on the individual, and grid and group are accordingly redefined. Group now measures the social pressure exerted by or upon any individual: the weak group individual controls others; the strong group individual is controlled by them. Grid now measures the scope and coherent articulation of a system of classification as one social dimension in which any individual may be located. A high grid rating indicates a strong degree of conformity to the publicly accepted system of classification, while a low grid rating indicates adherence to a private system of classification.

Douglas' stated aim this time is to measure the patterns of power that underlie overt cosmologies. There is no longer a separate quadrant for each type of society; instead, Douglas thinks in terms of scatter patterns across the entire diagram to indicate the extent to which individuals are subject to different pressures and degrees of classification. Multiple group membership is accounted for, in that an individual may move across the diagram in different social contexts. The 'strong grid' Big Man society embraces both low and high group, with the faceless Big Men in charge and the rest of the population controlled by them. Should the Big Men become a law unto themselves, they spiral far down into low grid and group, controlling others according to their own private whims. The low grid/strong group quadrant is thinly populated by some small groups and infants, who inhabit a private world where they are dependent upon others. Witchcraft societies have moved out of that quadrant and are now identified as strong group/rising grid. The insane are located right at the bottom of the grid axis.

This version of the model was designed to cope with plotting social location and movement within complex modern societies, which is why

they span most of the matrix.[21] However, the model still purports to fulfil
its original purpose of analysing cultures other than our own, and the
application of the model to modern society has been more or less super-
imposed on the original cross-cultural version. The result is confusing,
since the two applications of the model are not well integrated, and the
model is not really capable of fulfilling this double function.[22]

Douglas herself uses this version of the model explicitly to explore the
effects of social dimension on behaviour and thought in modern society.
She claims that our own scientific worldview is as much influenced by
our social location as is that of the so-called primitive societies that traditionally have constituted the object of anthropological study. Inasmuch
as Durkheim was not prepared to scrutinise the social construction of his
own cognitive commitment, Douglas argues that he made scientific truth
the one sacred thing in his universe that could not be profaned.[23]

Douglas' outspoken claim that scientific beliefs about the natural world
have a social basis provoked considerable unease at her position, which
expressed itself in accusations of social determinism, functional reductionism and incoherent relativism. Of these, the charge of determinism
is the least well founded. Although it is easy to find isolated quotations that appear deterministic, Douglas explicitly denies the charge, and
clearly asserts that symbols shape society as much as they are shaped
by it.[24]

The second charge of reductionism is levelled by Sahlins, who claims
that Douglas reduces the meaningful content of symbolic utterances to
their social value: her analysis 'aims to collapse the conceptual notions of
an object into a functional message, as though cultural things were merely
substantialised versions of social solidarities'.[25] Skorupski also maintains that the social explanation of symbols can never be divorced from

[21]Douglas claims that the model can consider social change as a dynamic process
(*Natural Symbols* (2nd edition), p.84). Sanders (*Schismatics*, pp.104–8) rejects the model,
on the grounds that it can only measure social change on a very small scale, in relatively
stable situations. While this makes it unsuitable for Sanders' diachronic study of the frag-
mentation of Jewish–Christian relations, the model remains useful for a synchronic study
of the churches to which Paul wrote his letters.

[22]It is thus unfortunate that in 1996 Routledge chose to reprint the 1973 edition of *Natural
Symbols*. According to Professor Douglas, this is because the script of the original 1970
edition was no longer available.

[23]*Implicit Meanings*, pp.ix–xxi.

[24]Cf. *Natural Symbols* (1st edition), pp.xiv, 149; also 'Passive voice theories in religious
sociology', *In the Active Voice*, pp.1–15.

[25]M.D. Sahlins, *Culture and Practical Reason* (London: University of Chicago Press,
1976), p.120; Sahlins labels this 'sociability fetishism'. Cf. J.K. Riches, *Jesus and the
Transformation of Judaism* (London: DLT, 1980), pp.24–8.

the cognitive meaning ascribed to them by any actors, past or present.[26] Douglas has since acknowledged that the interpretation of a metaphor is not validated simply by its correspondence to the social structure. She has accordingly revised her approach to animal symbolism, by arguing that people impose their own understanding of human relations on the animal kingdom in such a way that animals then come to symbolise those relations. In this way, Douglas builds a cognitive bridge between the symbol and its perceived social effect.[27] In the case of the symbolism of sin, the force of the charge of reductionism is obviated by the observation that the rhetoric of sin may be developed with the precise aim of safeguarding a community from individual deviance.[28] In this respect, it would be inappropriate to isolate the symbolism of sin from its social function.[29]

The final charge of incoherent relativism is also levelled by Skorupski, who argues that Douglas' relativist claim that worldviews are socially determined fatally undermines her approach.[30] Skorupski argues that, within the relativist framework, the truth-value of a set of beliefs can be relative to the society that holds them only if reality is constructed by that mind or society. Inasmuch as Douglas analyses worldviews other than her own, her statements purport to have universal validity; yet this is impossible, since the truth about reality itself varies in each of the cultures she assesses. Skorupski concludes with a plea for recognition of his claim that modern scientific cosmologies do in fact have a relative autonomy from their social base. In her response, Douglas stands her ground, stating that his view of science has a 'strong smell of the 1950's', and maintaining that a 'world view' constitutes an overall, theoretical framework which cannot be characterised as true or false.

The debate is taken up by Spickard, who argues that Douglas is not a relativist, but an 'internal realist', whose 'active theory of knowledge'

[26]J. Skorupski, *Symbol and Theory: a Philosophical Study of Theories of Religion in Social Anthropology* (Cambridge: Cambridge University Press, 1976), pp.1–52.
[27]M. Douglas, 'Anomalous animals and animal metaphors', *Thought Styles* (London: Sage, 1996), pp.126–44.
[28]M. Douglas, *Risk and Blame: Essays in Cultural Theory* (London: Routledge, 1992), p.28.
[29]Technically, this means that it is inappropriate to refer to the *function* of Paul's sin language, since one of the tenets of functionalism is that the social effect of a certain action must be unintended by its perpetrators: cf. M. Douglas, *How Institutions Think* (London: Routledge & Kegan Paul, 1986), pp.31–43. It will be argued below that Paul developed the symbolism of the power of sin with conscious social aims in mind.
[30]J. Skorupski, 'Pangolin Power', in S.C. Brown, ed., *Philosophical Disputes in the Social Sciences* (London: Harvester Press, 1979), pp.151–76. For the debate, cf., in the same volume, M. Douglas, 'World View and the Core' (pp.177–87), and J. Skorupski, 'Our Philosopher Replies' (pp.188–94).

is committed to movement and revision in the light of the developing scientific consensus as to the nature of the world.[31] Internal realists are aware of their cognitive precariousness: they are no better founded in knowledge than anyone else, and they are aware that their own views are as socially determined as those of anyone else, but their views are regarded as true within the light of current scientific consensus.

However, having cleared Douglas of the charge of incoherent relativism, Spickard goes on to charge her with sociocentrism, inasmuch as her model is based upon the individual, which is a concept specific to western society, and certainly not common to all cultures. Spickard points to the foundational role played by the experience of the individual in Douglas' formulation of grid, and argues that this invalidates her model as an internal realist approach, since her system is biased at the very core: 'No theory which bases itself on a demonstrably particular view of the world is going to become a basis for a consensus on which science can progress.'[32]

Spickard is himself guilty of sociocentrism, however, in assuming that the scientific worldview has universal validity, whereas it is actually based on exactly the same western view of the world as is Douglas' model. The fact that Douglas' model shares a common basis with science can scarcely be used to invalidate it as a scientific approach. Spickard is right to draw attention to the problem of individualism for Douglas' model, but is wrong to dismiss it on these grounds. Since the internal realist view of knowledge is committed to constant revision, the widespread recognition that individualism is not a cross-cultural phenomenon simply means that the model needs revising in the light of this scientific consensus. Only if the model proves impossible to revise will it be necessary to dismiss it. The need for revision will be addressed on completion of the survey of developments in the model.

Isenberg and Owen, Malina, Neyrey

In 1977, Isenberg and Owen adapted Douglas' work for biblical scholars by conflating the first two versions of her model into a properly systematised matrix.[33] They set out the cosmologies of the four different

---

[31] J.V. Spickard, *Relativism and Cultural Comparison in the Anthropology of Mary Douglas: an Evaluation of the Meta-Critical Strategy of her Grid-Group Theory* (unpublished PhD dissertation, Graduate Theological Union, 1984), pp.165ff. Douglas sets out her active theory of knowledge in *Implicit Meanings*, p.xix.

[32] Spickard, *Relativism*, pp.354f.

[33] Isenberg and Owen, 'Bodies'.

possible types of social organisation under the headings of purity, ritual, magic, personal identity, body, trance, sin, cosmology and suffering and misfortune. In so doing, they incorporated a number of changes into the matrix, the first of which was an apparently unwitting alteration in Douglas' definition of group. Isenberg and Owen identify strong group as control by social pressure and weak group as the reverse. This definition simply identifies the weak group quadrant as a place where people are free from social pressure, whereas, in the second version of her model, Douglas specifies that weak group individuals actually exercise social control over others.

Their alteration to Douglas' definition of grid is deliberate,[34] and is based on the valid observation that grid and group in the second version of Douglas' model are not truly independent variables, since it is difficult to exert pressure (group) without making use of classification (grid). Accordingly, they propose that the definition of grid should be measured instead in terms of the match between the experiences of the individual, and the societal patterns of perception and evaluation that are available to bring order and intelligibility to these experiences: 'The strength or weakness of grid depends upon the "goodness of fit" between the classification system and the range of experience to be ordered.'[35] If the experience of the individual accords well with the public system of classification, the individual would have a high grid rating; on the other hand, any degree of dissonance between society's symbol system and the experiences of the individual would result in a decline in grid.

However, this definition of grid suffers from the disadvantage that it is very difficult to determine with any degree of accuracy the extent to which the *experience* of people in historical cultures either is, or fails to be, accounted for by the accepted system of classification. No indication is given as to precisely how such experiences are to be identified or quantified, and this lack of precision undermines their version of the model. In the absence of objective ways of measuring grid and group, the temptation is to abuse their matrix by making it an easy reference system, in which one identifies a certain culture by means of its known cosmological features, and fills in the gaps from the other headings.[36]

A third alteration in the model concerns their definition of sin and the body in the low grid/high group society. They rightly indicate that sin is a

---

[34] Sanders (*Schismatics*, pp.109–10) wrongly regards both this and the previous alteration as inadvertent.

[35] Isenberg and Owen, 'Bodies', p.7.

[36] Spickard reviews and criticises such 'cosmologically based studies' which neglect social analysis (*Relativism*, pp.298–308).

matter of pollution, but locate evil within the person and society. This is a direct reversal of Douglas' portrayal of the small bounded group. Douglas stresses the goodness of the inside of the social and physical bodies, and locates evil outside the boundaries of the body so that it is only the witch who is inhabited by evil, in contradistinction to the social norm. Isenberg and Owen, however, erroneously regard indwelling evil as a characteristic of low grid/high group societies. Similarly, under 'body', Isenberg and Owen claim that invaders have broken through the bodily boundaries, whereas Douglas only states that low grid/high group cosmology is marked by a fear that the physical body will be poisoned. Isenberg and Owen thus no longer perceive evil as an outside threat, but rather as an internal problem, and this represents a distortion of key aspects of this quadrant in Douglas' matrix.

Isenberg and Owen's matrix was taken up and adapted by Malina in 1978.[37] Here, group is defined as the degree of societal pressure at work in a given social unit to conform to societal norms; the significant departure from Isenberg and Owen lies in the fact that a social unit may be defined either as an individual or as a group. Malina thus breaks with Douglas' emphasis on the individual, but at the risk of incoherence: simply defining group as social pressure on a social unit means that one cannot tell whether pressure is applied to the group as a whole or to the individual within the group. In practice, Malina seems to use the group axis to measure both the incorporation of an individual into a group and pressure on a given social unit to conform, but there is no necessary connection between the two, and Malina's definition of group is unsatisfactory.

Malina also revises Isenberg and Owen's definition of grid, so that it now measures 'the degree of assent that individuals give to the symbol system of the social world'. This represents a significant advance on Isenberg and Owen, since the degree of assent to a given classification system is more easily measured than the degree to which that classification system is confirmed in personal experience.[38] Malina also refines and improves their treatment of sin, which is now described as penetrating the porous boundaries surrounding a person or a group and lodging inside. In this way, Malina correctly identifies sin as something that threatens the boundaries of the social and physical bodies from outside.

[37] B.J. Malina, 'The Social World Implied in the Letters of the Christian Bishop-Martyr (Named Ignatius of Antioch)', *SBL Seminar Papers* 2 (1978), pp.71–119.

[38] Ibid., p.101. However, Malina does not set aside Isenberg and Owen's definition, but continues to refer to grid in terms of experience in *Christian Origins and Cultural Anthropology* (Atlanta: John Knox, 1986), pp.13–20.

Malina's weakness is that he applies the model to the Hellenistic world as a whole,[39] identifying that entire culture as high group/low grid, inhabited by 'dyadic personalities', whose sense of identity was located in group membership, and who were principally concerned about group boundaries.[40] Malina's study highlights the 'others' of ancient Mediterranean culture, but it crucially fails to make any allowance for variations within that culture: apart from a small ruling elite, everyone is relegated to the same quadrant. This criticism of Malina is also levelled by Garrett, who objects to the model's high level of abstraction and lack of attention to detail.[41] She cites Marcus and Fischer, who point out that: 'Social thought has grown suspicious of the ability of encompassing paradigms to ask the right questions, let alone provide answers, about the variety of local responses to the operation of global systems.'[42] They argue that the authority of the 'grand theory' has been suspended in favour of a close consideration of contextuality: exceptions and indeterminants are more important than regularities. Malina's application of the model to entire cultures fails to make any allowance for variations within the culture. Although the use of models at such a high level of abstraction is defended by Rohrbaugh,[43] 'Grid and Group' was not originally designed to be used on this scale. According to Rayner,[44] the model can be applied on three scales. Firstly, it may be used at an individual level; secondly, it may be applied on a 'micro' scale to small populations where each individual can be assessed; thirdly, the model may be used on a 'macro' scale to assess the aggregate of grid and group pressures on a small-scale

[39] Cf. Sanders, *Schismatics*, pp.111–12.

[40] Malina, *Christian Origins*, pp.131–2. Malina's use of the term 'dyadic' does not correspond to social-scientific practice, which uses the term to refer to a '*direct*' relationship involving some form of interaction between two individuals': C.H. Landé, 'Introduction: the Dyadic Basis of Clientelism', in S.W. Schmidt, L. Guasti, C.H. Landé and J.C. Scott, eds., *Friends, Followers and Factions: a Reader in Political Clientelism* (London: University of California Press, 1977), p.xiii. 'Dyadic personalities' are better referred to as 'allocentric' (as opposed to 'idiocentric'), while cultures can be described as 'collectivist' or 'individualist': H.C. Triandis, K. Leung, M.J. Villareal and F.L. Crack, 'Allocentric versus Idiocentric Tendencies, Convergent and Discriminant Validation', *Journal of Research in Psychology* 19 (1985), pp.395–415; B.J. Malina, 'Is there a Circum-Mediterranean Person? Looking for Stereotypes', *BTB* 22 (1992), pp.66–87.

[41] S. Garrett, 'Review of *Christian Origins and Cultural Anthropology*, by B.J. Malina', *JBL* 107 (1988), pp.532–4; cf. also Sanders, *Schismatics*, pp.111–12.

[42] G.E. Marcus & M.M.J. Fischer, *Anthropology as Cultural Critique: an Experimental Moment in the Human Sciences* (Chicago: University of Chicago Press, 1986), p.9.

[43] R.L. Rohrbaugh, 'Models or Muddles: Discussion of the Social Facets Seminar', *Forum* 3 (1987), pp.23-33.

[44] S. Rayner, *The Classification and Dynamics of Sectarian Forms of Organisation: Grid/Group Perspectives on the Far Left in Britain* (unpublished PhD thesis, University of London, 1979).

social unit. The possibility of applying the model to entire cultures is, however, not even considered.

Despite its limitations, however, Malina's approach was taken up and employed by Neyrey, who initially used Malina's definitions of grid and group. He subsequently resolved the tension in Malina's definition of group by redefining group in terms of purity, namely the order and structure of the symbolic universe, while grid now measures the extent to which group members accept that ordering and find it confirmed.[45] This understanding of grid and group underlies Neyrey's later work, in which the apostle's writings are analysed through the framework of order (group) and disorder (grid) in Paul's symbolic universe.[46] At this stage, Neyrey's use of the model bears little relation to Douglas: Neyrey's 'group' is now virtually the equivalent of Douglas' 'grid', and social analysis has effectively been replaced with a psychological portrait of the apostle.

Cultural Bias (1978)

Malina and Neyrey both drew on Isenberg and Owen's conflation of the first two versions of Douglas' matrix. However, in *Cultural Bias* (1978) Douglas revised the model yet again, placing at the centre of her model the negotiating individual, who has the capacity to influence the surrounding environment, which is itself made up of all the other interacting individuals and their choices. This environment in turn moulds the individual's behaviour, since each individual needs to make sense of his or her surroundings by finding principles that will guide behaviour in sanctioned ways. As Spickard points out, 'The "drive to achieve consonance" identified in *Natural Symbols I* is no longer directly between social experience and cosmology, as in her earlier theory. It is now mediated by the arguments people use to sustain their social relations.'[47]

Group now measures the dimension of incorporation in social units sufficiently small for the individual members to know one another personally. People are allocated a zero group rating when they stand at the centre of a network of their own making that has no recognisable boundaries. Group rating increases in proportion to the extent to which each individual's life is absorbed in and sustained by group membership.

[45] E.g. J.H. Neyrey, 'Bewitched in Galatia: Paul and Cultural Anthropology', *CBQ* 55 (1988), pp.72–100.

[46] J.H. Neyrey, *Paul, in Other Words: a Cultural Reading of His Letters* (Louisville: W/JKP, 1990).

[47] J.V. Spickard, 'Guide to Grid/Group Theory', *Sociological Analysis* 50/2 (1989), pp.151–70; quotation from p.165.

Grid is now taken as the cross-hatch of rules to which individuals are subject in the course of social interaction: it measures the degree of individuation, the extent to which individuals are insulated from one another or are free to transact with each other. An individual who enjoys autonomy and is free to compete with others and to control them is classed as low grid; a high grid individual suffers from minimal autonomy, has no scope for personal transactions, and can aspire to nothing more than fulfilling an allotted role within society.

In this version of the model, the individual entrepreneur or 'Big Man' is no longer located in the upper regions of the high grid/low group quadrant; instead, the freedom of transaction enjoyed by this individual results in a low grid and group rating. To make room for this change, hermits, as the former occupants of this quadrant, are evacuated altogether, while the high grid/low group quadrant is now inhabited by peasants and domestic servants, individuals who are assigned roles in society which they are helpless to change.[48]

This is the version of the model currently used by Douglas herself, yet it has not been without its critics. Complaining that Grid and Group can easily become a parlour game for pigeon-holing social processes and cosmological patterns as fixed types, Boon argues that Douglas' method is tautologous, since the cosmological and the social are not different orders of components, but are both equally evidences of the same culture.[49] Boon's criticism is unjust at this point, since the model has been used to assess how people within the same cultural setting have different cosmologies, which reflect their social location within that setting.[50]

Boon also cites the anomalous case of the Bali, who should be located in the high group/high grid quadrant of the matrix, but who nevertheless have a (low group) proclivity for various kinds of trance. However, such an anomaly need not invalidate the model, since the study of how individual groups vary from the expected pattern on Douglas' chart may yield

[48]Malina (*Christian Origins*, pp.61–4) interprets this alteration as a relocation of the bottom rung of the high group/high grid quadrant (the peasants) in the low grid/high group area. Malina tries to integrate Douglas' third version of the model by inserting 'social catchment areas' at the bottom end of high grid spectrums, where he places such people as the untouchables in India, slaves in the Roman empire and drop-outs from modern society. Yet, in doing so, Malina notes only one aspect of the change introduced by Douglas, and fails to take into account the movement of the business entrepreneur from the high grid/low group to the low grid/low group quadrant: the different versions of the model are actually incompatible.

[49]J.A. Boon, 'America: Fringe Benefits', *Raritan* 2 (1983), p.97–121.

[50]Cf. C. Bloor and D. Bloor, 'Twenty Industrial Scientists: a Preliminary Exercise', in Douglas, ed., *Sociology of Perception*, pp.83–102; P. Bellaby, 'To Risk or not to Risk? Uses and Limitations of Mary Douglas on Risk-Acceptability for Understanding Health and Safety at Work and Road Accidents', *Sociological Review* 38 (1990), pp.465–83.

valuable insights into the makeup of a particular group or its cosmology.[51] The purpose of the model is not to categorise, but to facilitate analysis.

According to Boon, there is also built into the matrix a bias which inhibits the perception of overlapping membership and complex standards of value: pointing out that some of his best environmentalist friends still salute the flag, Boon objects to the way in which grid and group makes all membership exclusive. Yet this is not necessarily a valid criticism. Environmentalists can still be patriots if they are not deeply embedded in an anti-government organisation; patriots can have associations with environmental lobbyists if they are not high-ranking government officials. However, a high-ranking government official would find it hard to be an active member of Greenpeace: the high grid rating of the former and the strong group rating of the latter would place any individual in a situation of severe tension indeed. In such a case, the model is not guilty of making membership exclusive; it merely serves to indicate the social pressures upon a given individual.

Boon also highlights a number of cases where he feels that incompatible people or groups are summarily relegated to the same quadrant.[52] He (somewhat unfairly) queries the legitimacy of lumping Rousseau and Thoreau together as voluntary recluses, and goes on to object to the identification of Capitol Hill, the White House and Pentagon with Wall Street and Madison Avenue as the losers in a witch-hunt instigated by environmental lobbyists. In this last case, Boon's objection rests upon the incongruity of the American establishment being equated with the individual victim of a witch-hunt. However in defence of Douglas, it might be pointed out that, by means of her cross-cultural model, Douglas has merely writ large in American culture the mistrust and struggle for power which characterise 'witch-hunts' in smaller, more primitive societies.

Objections to Douglas' analysis of witch-hunts are also raised by Bergesen.[53] He points out that political witchcraft accusations, which

---

[51] Cf. Douglas' observations about the Hadza tribe, where the apparent anomaly of the menstrual taboo highlights the social hostility between the sexes: *Natural Symbols* (1st edition), pp.99–102.

[52] Similarly, Asad objects to the assimilation of the individualism of highland New Guinea societies with that of bourgeois capitalism: T. Asad, 'Anthropology and the Analysis of Ideology', *Man* 14 (1979), pp.607–27. However; according to Sahlins, 'The Melanesian Big Man seems so thoroughly bourgeois, so reminiscent of the free enterprising rugged individual of our own heritage': M.D. Sahlins, 'Poor Man, Rich Man, Big Man, Chief: Political Types in Melanesia and Polynesia', in Schmidt et al., eds., *Friends*, pp.220–31 (quotation from p.221).

[53] A. Bergesen, 'The Cultural Anthropology of Mary Douglas', in R. Wuthnow, J.D. Hunter, A. Bergesen and E. Kurzweil, eds., *Cultural Analysis: The Work of Peter L. Berger, Mary Douglas, Michel Foucault and Jürgen Habermas* (London: Routledge & Kegan Paul, 1984), pp.77–132, esp. pp.120–5.

Douglas argues are characteristic of small groups, actually take place in modern, large-scale industrial societies where there is a high level of organisation combined with well-defined roles; he cites as examples McCarthyism, the Chinese Cultural Revolution, and Stalinist purges. From this it is concluded that the key to the existence of the witch-hunt phenomenon does not lie in low levels of organisation, but probably arises in strong group situations. The hypothesis is put forward that the existence of witch-hunts in such highly structured societies may be accounted for by the supposition that strong group and strong grid are incompatible elements. Witch-hunts therefore take place in societies where highly corporate groups subvert the power and the legitimacy of institutional structures, so isolating individuals from each other to create a relationship between the atomistic individual and the all-powerful corporate group. The somewhat surprising conclusion of this analysis is that scarcely any strong group/strong grid societies actually exist.

However, the feature common to the three witch-hunts cited above is not the fact that they took place in large-scale 'strong group' industrial societies; Stalinist Russia and China in the 1960s are hardly comparable to 1950s America in this respect. What is common to all three cases is the way in which accusations of infiltration by foreign enemies were used by vulnerable leaders as a means of attacking political opponents at home. Douglas has argued that it is a combination of weak leadership and the need to maintain strong boundaries that makes witchcraft accusations endemic to the small bounded group.[54] It is the fact that each of the above societies shares these two key characteristics of the enclave which accounts for the existence of witchcraft accusations.

Douglas' third version of the matrix may thus be deemed to have withstood the criticisms directed against it, but as it stands, it cannot be applied to Paul's letters. The model was developed for the purpose of analysing extant communities, and cannot simply be applied to situations where actual fieldwork is no longer possible. This is evident from Atkins' study,[55] which seeks to respond to Garrett's criticism of Malina by employing the EXACT method of social accounting developed by Gross and Rayner,[56] in order to assemble a detailed ethnography of the Pauline churches. This technique involves questioning the text repeatedly and counting the

[54]Douglas, *How Institutions Think*, pp.31–43.

[55]R.A. Atkins, *Egalitarian Community: Ethnography and Exegesis* (University of Alabama Press, 1991).

[56]J. Gross and S. Rayner, *Measuring Culture: a Paradigm for the Analysis of Social Organisation* (New York: Columbia University Press, 1985); cf. Rayner, *Classification*, pp.62–96.

transactions that individuals have with others, in order to prepare a sheer description of the social mechanism of the Pauline church, based on the evidence of repetitive, patterned behaviour that is found in Paul's letters. This description is then used to plot the location of the Pauline communities on the version of Douglas' matrix set out in *Cultural Bias*, and developed by Ostrander.[57]

Ostrander follows *Cultural Bias* in using group to measure the extent to which a person's life depends on membership in social groups, while grid measures the extent to which social life is restricted by rules that pre-ordain social relationships. Atkins uses four criteria to measure group investment in the Pauline communities. (1) **Proximity** measures the degree of contact participants in the group have with one another. (2) **Transitivity** queries whether it is possible to infer a relationship between two people on the basis of their common relationship to a third individual in the group. (3) **Deferential involvement** assesses whether people choose to join the group or not and the commonality of their experience in group participation. (4) **Boundary** investigates the impermeability or otherwise of the boundaries surrounding the group. For grid, Atkins adopts four criteria to measure the regulation of social relationships. (1) **Role differentiation** probes whether there were recognised, permanent, authoritative, commissioned, legitimate paid offices in the Pauline churches. (2) **Authority** measures the extent to which power is institutionalised. (3) **Initiative** measures the extent to which roles in the community are ascribed to individuals, while (4) **autonomy** measures the freedom of use of time, property, clothing and association with others. The net result of this analysis is that the Pauline communities are identified as high group/low grid, leading Atkins to identify the Pauline churches as strongly bounded, egalitarian communities, which were inherently unstable due to their rejection of ascribed status and social hierarchy.

Yet Atkins' approach suffers from two weaknesses. The first relates to the difficulty in measuring individuation from written sources, where actual field observation is not possible. The four criteria he adopts for measuring grid represent only half of the predicates proposed by Gross and Rayner: the limited amount of data available from Paul's letters means that it is not possible to assess specialisation, asymmetry, entitlement or accountability. Moreover, Atkins' conclusion that the Pauline churches are egalitarian in nature is not a necessary inference from the result of the tests for grid that he is able to conduct. In his analysis, Atkins finds both

---

[57] D. Ostrander, 'One- and Two-Dimensional Models of the Distribution of Beliefs', in Douglas, ed., *Sociology of Perception*, pp. 14–30.

confusion over role differentiation, and ambiguous authority structures: given the similar nature of these two criteria, the conclusion that both are uncertain is scarcely surprising, but neither proves the egalitarian nature of the community. In examining initiative, Atkins claims that Paul subverts the pattern of ascribed patronal roles in favour of equality for all, but this assertion verges on assuming what is yet to be proven.[58] The investigation of autonomy tends to argue from silence that people enjoyed the freedom to dispose of their time and private property and to choose their company, but such freedom, again, is no firm indication of equality.

The second difficulty with Atkins' approach is that his ethnographic study still represents an inadequate response to Garrett's criticisms. Inasmuch as the EXACT method of social accounting adopted by Atkins looks for repetitive, patterned behavioural evidence, it inevitably fails to take sufficient note of the exceptions and indeterminants on which Marcus and Fischer place so much importance. Indeed, underlying Atkins' whole approach is the fallacious assumption that all Pauline congregations fit into the same mould; the possibility that different congregations might be located in different quadrants of the matrix is not even considered.[59] To be valid, Atkins' method of social accounting would need to be applied to each individual Pauline congregation. Even then, he would need to take account of the fact that the letters of Paul only reflect the social situations of the churches themselves to the extent that the apostle himself was aware of them.[60]

Atkins' study is the most thorough and detailed attempt to apply Douglas' matrix to Paul's writings, and it fails because Paul's letters do not yield enough information about the social location of the individual in each of the different churches. The question then arises as to whether it is possible to develop a version of the model that will be suitable for analysing the power of sin in Paul's letters.

Applying the matrix to Paul

The problem with applying the matrix to Paul is that Douglas designed the model for the purpose of analysing communities where social interaction

---

[58]Particularly in the light of 1 Cor. 12:28.

[59]Cf. J. Barclay, 'Thessalonica and Corinth: Social Contrasts in Pauline Christianity', *JSNT* 47 (1992), pp.49–74.

[60]Cf. B. Witherington, *Conflict and Community in Corinth: A Socio-Rhetorical Commentary on 1 and 2 Corinthians* (Exeter: Paternoster, 1995), p.151: 'The difficulty in applying modern sociological (*sic*) concepts such as group-grid analysis . . . to the Christian community in Corinth is that we have no report of what the community was like apart from Paul's assessment.'

could be observed first-hand, or where detailed ethnographic information and analysis is available. As the problems with Atkins' study show, Paul's letters do not yield such information. Malina avoids this difficulty by applying the model to first-century Mediterranean culture as a whole, but his approach gives at best a very broad brush-stroke picture of the cultural location of the apostle. Neyrey, on the other hand, analyses the apostle as an individual, ignoring the interrelation between social structure and cosmology that lies at the heart of the model.

It is the intention of this study to use the matrix to analyse the power of sin in Paul's letters. Since Paul's letters functioned as substitute for Paul's own apostolic presence with the congregation, it should not be assumed that Paul writes to the churches as an isolated individual. Rather Paul identifies himself as closely as possible with the churches as their apostle. A careful analysis of each letter will reveal the location of the apostle himself on the matrix, and this will prepare the way for interpreting the letter in the light of the cosmology of that particular quadrant, rather than in the light of later doctrinal considerations. At the same time, albeit more obliquely, Paul's letters offer a degree of insight into the specific social situations addressed by Paul in his letters. Plotting the location of the different communities on the matrix will facilitate an understanding of how the original recipients of Paul's letters would have understood and interpreted them in the light of their own social context. When Paul and his addressees are located in the same quadrant, one would expect relatively clear communication as a result of both writer and recipients sharing a common socially based agenda. However, if Paul and the church to whom he writes are located in different quadrants, there is greater potential for misunderstanding, since the church would interpret Paul's letter in the light of its own different concerns.

Seeing Paul's letters as his response to the social situation of his readers invites an analysis of the power of sin as a symbol developed by Paul precisely for the purpose of shaping their cosmology. At the same time, Paul's choice and development of that symbol is constrained by his own cultural situation as apostle to the Gentiles in the first-century Mediterranean world. Thus, even as Paul seeks to influence the churches to which he writes, he as an individual is influenced by his own culture. It is this interaction between the individual and culture which lies at the heart of Douglas' third version of the model.

In this version of the model, group is defined in terms of social incorporation, while grid measures individuation, yet it has been shown that Paul's letters yield insufficient information to allow a detailed analysis of the degree of individuation within his churches. Furthermore, Spickard's criticism of the bias towards individualism in Douglas' later work cannot be ignored. These difficulties render it necessary to adjust the model, so that grid and group are defined in such a way that they can be applied to Paul's letters in an appropriate fashion.

On the basis that individualism is not a pan-cultural phenomenon, it makes sense to use the group axis to measure the extent to which a given social unit is individualistic or collectivist. This is essentially the same as Douglas' definition of group in *Cultural Bias*. Low group would accordingly indicate an individualistic social unit, where people find themselves at the centre of a network of their own making, without any recognisable boundaries. As group increases, the individual's identity becomes defined more and more in terms of membership of clearly bounded social groups: 'The strongest effects of group are to be found where it incorporates a person with the rest by implicating them together in common residence, shared work, shared resources and recreation, and by exerting control over marriage and kinship.'[61]

Spickard's problem of a sociocentric focus on the individual can be avoided if grid is made subordinate to group. In collectivist societies, grid should be assessed with reference to the group rather than to the individual, and this will avoid imposing a modern western understanding of individual identity on cultures where it is inappropriate.

Douglas' second definition of grid as the measurement of adherence to public or private schemes of classification offers a promising starting point for defining grid, since Paul's letters yield enough information to analyse the extent to which he and his congregations accepted or rejected the surrounding culture. Furthermore, it would seem that the level of interaction with surrounding society actually has a greater degree of influence over cosmology than the existence or absence of rules which regulate the life of the individual or community. This can be illustrated from the small bounded group or enclave. Douglas herself acknowledges that hierarchical religions will tend to show sectarian anxiety when they are under stress in enclave situations: 'It is the openness of the boundary and their unsuccessful efforts to close it that put them in the same situation as an enclave, albeit preaching some hierarchical doctrines.'[62] In this case, it is the relationship with the outside world which determines the cosmology of the group. This is borne out by Bryan Wilson's analysis of sects, where he argues that the crucial factor in sectarian identity is not internal organisation, but the group's response to the

---

[61] Douglas, *Cultural Bias*, p.202.
[62] Douglas, *Natural Symbols* (3rd UK edition), p.xxiii.

world.[63] In view of the determinative influence of a group's reaction to the outside world, it is proposed that grid should be measured in terms of acceptance or rejection of the prevailing social norms.

However, as Spickard has pointed out, measuring grid in terms of acceptance or rejection of the prevailing system of classification ties grid to the cosmology of an individual or group rather than their social location. Since such a definition of grid only describes what people *think* about their experience, Spickard claims that using it results in the circular process of deriving cosmology from cosmology.[64] However, in response it may be said that, even if it is conceded that acceptance or rejection of the surrounding culture is an aspect of cosmology, it is nevertheless a clear index of the social location of an individual or group, since those who accept the prevailing classification can be expected to be integrated into society, whereas those who reject society's classifications would be expected to be socially isolated. Whereas Paul's letters do not yield enough information for a direct analysis of the extent to which individuals or groups were integrated with or isolated from society, their attitudes to society do emerge clearly, and this may be taken as a firm indication of their social location.

For the purposes of this application of Grid and Group to Paul's letters, 'Group' will therefore be defined in terms of the extent to which an individual is incorporated within a bounded social unit. 'Grid' will be measured in terms of the extent to which that individual, or the group of which he is a part, accepts or rejects the social norms of the surrounding culture. The result of defining grid and group in these terms is a matrix on which the different cosmologies are mapped out in figure 3.

The most serious disadvantage of using this version of the matrix is that it isolates this study from the third version of the matrix, which has come to be used as standard by Douglas and her associates. In fact, the version of the matrix displayed in figure 2 corresponds most closely to the first version of the model devised by Douglas in the first edition of *Natural Symbols*. However, whereas later versions of the model are increasingly developed with reference to modern western society, *Natural Symbols* contains the detailed analysis of non-western social units, on the basis of which Douglas first developed the model, and this analysis will be important in applying the model to Paul's letters. For these reasons, the

[63]B.R. Wilson, *Magic and the Millennium* (London: Heinemann, 1973), pp.18ff.; *The Social Dimensions of Sectarianism: Sects and New Religious Movements in Contemporary Society* (Oxford: Clarendon, 1990), pp.46–68.
[64]Spickard, 'Guide', pp.162–3.

+GRID
ACCEPTS PREVAILING SOCIAL MORES

Competitive individualism	Hierarchical society
Elaborated code replaces ritual	Ritual reinforces social structure and mores
Ignores body symbolism	Body symbolises social structure and boundaries
Sin irrelevant	Sin seen as transgression

−GROUP   +GROUP

INDIVIDUALIST   COLLECTIVIST

Freedom from social constraints	Sect/enclave
Emphasis on inner experience rather than ritual	Ritual focused on excluding outsiders (witchcraft accusations)
Body may be rejected	Bodily boundaries guarded to protect inner purity
Inner enlightenment the antidote to sin	Sin an outside evil threatening social and physical boundaries

−GRID
REJECTS PREVAILING SOCIAL MORES

Figure 3: Customised Grid and Group.

earlier layout of the matrix is adopted here in preference to that currently used by Douglas herself.[65]

Having developed a viable version of the model, it is now possible to begin to make use of it to analyse the communities to which Paul wrote.

[65]Cf. ibid., p.153: 'Of course the version that scholars use need not be Douglas' most recent, since there is no reason why an earlier version might not find some empirical support. Nor should scholars shy away from modifying her formulations as they see fit... But whatever variation is used, it at least should be conceptually consistent, rather than wrongly pieced together from Douglas' conflicting writings.'

3

PHYSICAL AND SOCIAL BOUNDARIES IN CORINTH

Introduction

1 Corinthians contains only one isolated reference to the power of sin, in 15:56. This verse, which may well be a gloss, speaks of the law as the power of sin. Nevertheless, the subject of sin was never far from Paul's mind as he wrote to the wayward church at Corinth and thus a chapter on 1 Corinthians earns its place in this study on Paul's hamartiology.[1] On the basis of a comparison with the sin language of 1 Corinthians, it will be possible to see whether or not Paul's use of the symbolism of the power of sin in Galatians and Romans represents a significant difference in his understanding of the human condition. This chapter will use Douglas' Grid and Group matrix to analyse 1 Corinthians, with a view to analysing the social location of Paul and the Corinthians and the influence their social location has on their different perceptions of sin. In this way, it will be possible to perceive how Paul's sin language would have been understood (or misunderstood) by the letter's original readers in the socio-cultural setting of first-century Corinth. It will also be possible to test the usefulness of the model, by seeing whether or not it can yield any fresh exegetical insights into the hamartiology of this particular letter.

A chapter on 1 Corinthians is also required because numerous scholars have applied Douglas' model to this letter and have come to substantially differing conclusions. Some have failed to appreciate the fact that Douglas has developed different, incompatible versions of the model. Others have used the model in order to support their own conclusions, little realising that the model is useless in the absence of a careful social analysis of the communities to which it is applied. The ensuing lack of consensus has undermined confidence in the validity of Douglas' approach for New Testament studies, even though the problems have often been due to an

---

[1] Space does not permit an analysis of 2 Corinthians which, in any event, does not contain any unambiguous references to the power of sin.

uncritical use of Douglas' work. It is to be hoped that this chapter will rehabilitate the model in the eyes of some of its critics by clarifying how the model should be applied to New Testament communities. It will demonstrate that an application of the model to Paul's letters can yield valid and useful insight into the social location of the recipients of the letter.

Applying 'Grid and Group' to 1 Corinthians

Early attempts to apply the matrix to Paul betray considerable confusion, caused by Douglas' own varying interpretations of the matrix. Meeks makes an early appeal to the model as he analyses the way in which Paul wants the community to have strong boundaries, and yet to maintain contact with the outside world. Arguing that Paul is thus pulled in the direction of both church and sect, Meeks claims that Paul is trying to hold together high grid and strong group, where high grid indicates increasing freedom from externally imposed classification systems.[2] Yet Douglas consistently makes this feature a characteristic of low grid. Meeks notes that the 'valence' of grid adopted in *Natural Symbols* is later reversed by Douglas and seems wrongly to deduce from this that freedom from externally imposed classification systems is now high grid. What actually happens in *Cultural Bias* is that the successful leader moves from high grid to low grid, but there is no corresponding move in the opposite direction. Meeks seems to have misunderstood the change as a reversal of the definition of grid, whereas it is in fact a reversal in the position of competitive individualism on the matrix. It may be because Meeks' fingers were burned by this early encounter with Douglas' model that he does not make explicit use of it again.

In the following year, Isenberg made a number of scattered observations on Paul and other Christian groups based on grid/group analysis.[3] Considering that he had co-operated with Owen in formulating the first coherent grid/group matrix in 1977, Isenberg's article is astonishing for its methodological carelessness. He fails to distinguish between different versions of the model when he asserts that the low grid/low group quadrant is both inhabited by pygmies and also marked by social mobility

---

[2] W. Meeks, ' "Since then you would need to go out of the world": Group Boundaries in Pauline Christianity', in T.J. Ryan, ed., *Critical History and Biblical Faith: NT Perspectives* (Villanova: College Theology Society, 1979), pp.4–29; On p.29, n.40, Meeks refers to Douglas' 'Mistletoe Lecture', which was published as *Cultural Bias*.

[3] S.R. Isenberg, 'Some Uses and Limitations of Social Scientific Methodology in the Study of Early Christianity', *SBL Seminar Papers* 18 (1980), pp.29–49.

and anxiety resulting from competition. The former description applies to *Natural Symbols* (p.34) and the latter to *Cultural Bias* (p.53), but the two are mutually incompatible.

Using diagrams from the 1973 edition of *Natural Symbols*, Isenberg charts Paul's 'conversion' as a transition from high group/high grid where he is influenced by others, to high grid/low group, where the apostle now influences others in the churches that he founds. Then, confusingly, Isenberg refers to the apostle's preference for low grid, which he claims is evident in his rejection of human hierarchies. Isenberg sees Corinth as a low grid/low group community, where individual-oriented values are satisfied at the expense of group values, and claims that Paul responds to this situation by trying to create a low grid/high group 'millennialist' social context. It is one of the features of the 1973 version of the model that the same person can appear at different times in different places on the quadrant, but the resultant fluidity results in considerable confusion in Isenberg's article. Nevertheless, Isenberg does make the important point that Paul's own position on the quadrant may be different from that of the churches to whom he writes, and it will be necessary to observe this distinction.

In an article analysing the social context of differing attitudes to the body, Gager appeals to *Natural Symbols*, but does not plot the position of Paul and the Corinthians on the matrix.[4] Nevertheless, he associates the Corinthian denial of a bodily resurrection with a belief in an immediate spiritual transformation, and argues that both their belief and Paul's are equally sectarian expressions of protest against the values of society; in other words, both Paul and the Corinthians are low grid. There can be little doubt that resurrection functions as a symbol of transformation, and Gager is probably right to claim that Paul's belief in an imminent resurrection finds its social basis in an undercurrent of protest and alienation. However, when Gager claims that the Corinthian belief in a spiritual transformation reflects a desire for individual liberation from the world, his argument is less well founded. It is true that affirmation of the spiritual and rejection of the material are characteristic of low grid, and a rejection of the body as a symbolic medium of expression may also indicate a desire for individual liberty. However, the Corinthian denial of a bodily resurrection does not necessarily imply a belief in a spiritual transformation that has already taken place, as Gager assumes, and consequently the conclusion that the Corinthians valued the spiritual over the material is insecure. On the

---

[4]J.G. Gager, 'Body Symbols and Social Reality: Resurrection, Incarnation and Asceticism in Early Christianity', *Religious Studies Review* 5 (1982), pp.345–64.

contrary, given that the resurrection is a symbol of transformation, the Corinthians' denial of bodily resurrection could well be interpreted as an affirmation of the prevailing *status quo*.

An attempt to distinguish the different positions of Paul and the Corinthians on the quadrant is made by Barton, in an article that explores the different attitudes to the boundary between church and household.[5] Barton makes limited use of the model to focus on the binary nature of boundaries, which need to be sharply defined in order to avoid dirt and keep the inside clean. Taking 1 Corinthians 14:34–35 as Pauline, Barton argues that Paul is seeking to restrict the influence of women to the household by forbidding them to speak in church. He also argues that the Lord's Supper has become an occasion for the heads of households to seek to compete at extending their influence through patronage and ostentatious consumption. Paul responds by giving prominence to metaphors of association other than the household and by emphasising the sacred nature of the meal, thereby distinguishing it from ordinary meals at home. Although Barton does not locate either Paul or the Corinthians on the matrix, attention is drawn to their differing perception of boundaries.

The same year saw the publication of Malina's adaptation of Isenberg and Owen's model for New Testament scholars in *Christian Origins and Cultural Anthropology*. He argues that group measures the degree of societal pressure on a social unit to conform, and grid measures the degree of socially constrained adherence given to the symbol system of society. In applying the model to Paul, Malina argues that Paul never lost his Jewish identity, and that since he maintained a Pharisaic concern with purity and boundaries, he should be located within the low grid/high group quadrant of the matrix.[6] Paul is distinguished from Pharisaic Judaism by the belief that Jesus is the one who saves God's people from Sin, which is the term Paul gives to 'the negative, coercive force that permeates the porous boundaries of group structures' in this quadrant.[7] However, Malina's attempt to locate Paul within the culture of the first-century Mediterranean world operates at too high a level of abstraction and his failure to analyse the specific social context within which Paul wrote his letters undermines his approach. Ultimately, Malina is more interested in developing a comprehensive model than in applying it to Paul.

[5] S. Barton, 'Paul's Sense of Place; an Anthropological Approach to Community Formation in Corinth', *NTS* 32 (1986), pp.225–46.

[6] J.T. Sanders is rightly scathing about Malina's readiness to refer to the Christian Paul as a 'Pharisaic Jew' (*Schismatics*, p.112).

[7] *Christian Origins*, p.137.

This latter task has been undertaken by Neyrey in a series of articles, which in 1990 were revised and incorporated into his book, *Paul, in Other Words: a Cultural Reading of his Letters*. In the first of these articles on 1 Corinthians,[8] Neyrey takes his matrix and his definition of grid and group from Malina. Group is thus defined as strength or weakness of pressure to conform to society's norms, while grid measures the degree of assent given to the norms, definitions and classifications of a cultural system, and the extent to which these are confirmed within an individual's experience.

As Neyrey develops his argument, however, he focuses exclusively on the group variable, setting out how strong and weak group correspond to control or a lack of control over the physical and social bodies; the question of grid is initially not discussed at all. This seems to be because Neyrey bases his argument on chapters 5 and 6 of *Natural Symbols*, which focus on the correspondence between the social and physical bodies, and how weak or strong control in the former is replicated in the latter. In these chapters, Douglas herself runs grid and group together, arguing that effervescence is characteristic of weak grid and group, while ritualism and a desire to control spirit possession are characteristic of strong grid and group.[9] Neyrey makes this sliding scale the basis for his interpretation of 1 Corinthians, identifying the effervescent Corinthian church as low grid/low group, and Paul as high grid/high group, because of the apostle's desire to impose control on the Corinthians' worship and their use of the physical body.[10] On this basis, Neyrey explains the points of conflict between Paul and the Corinthians in terms of their different attitudes towards control of the physical body.

However, in failing to pause and ascertain whether Paul and the Corinthians should be high or low grid, Neyrey invalidates his approach. Neyrey's ascription of a high grid rating to Paul is a direct result of

[8] J.H. Neyrey, 'Body language in 1 Corinthians', *Semeia* 35 (1986), pp.129–70; this article is referred to rather than the equivalent chapter in *Paul, in Other Words*, since Neyrey's later development of the model is somewhat idiosyncratic.

[9] The wrong impression that grid is tied to group when measuring ritual or effervescence is reinforced by Diagram 8 in *Natural Symbols* (1st edition: p.96; 2nd edition: p.129). Here a uniform progression is traced from low grid and group (Dinka) to high grid and group (Mandari), even though the appended explanation offers a more nuanced (albeit unclear) indication of each tribe's grid and group rating.

[10] Neyrey offers a more refined application of the model to spirit possession in *An Ideology of Revolt: John's Christology in Social-Science Perspective* (Minneapolis: Fortress, 1988), pp.173–206. Here it is recognised that in the quadrant of competitive individualism, spirit possession is not dangerous, and spirits may be found in any forms that serve individual self-realisation (pp.182–3).

his assumption that grid and group can be tied together. Yet according to the definition of grid adopted by Neyrey, this would mean that the apostle gave a high degree of assent to society's patterns of perception and evaluation. This can scarcely be said to be true of Paul as he writes 1 Corinthians. On the contrary, a preliminary reading of 1 Corinthians suggests that Paul expressly rejects the prevailing cultural norms and values in favour of the ultimate symbol of debasement, the cross of Christ (1:18–25). Furthermore, when believers air their grievances against each other in the civil court, Paul claims that this is the equivalent of appointing those who are despised in the church to sit in judgment over their disagreements (6:1–11). He is reluctant to allow his converts to participate in the idol feasts that formed part and parcel of the social life in Corinth (8–10). These are clearly not the views of a man who is in tune with the prevailing cultural system, and Neyrey's assumption that Paul is high grid is seen to be ill founded.

The same passages in the letter also call into question Neyrey's assumption that the Corinthians should be given a low grid rating. Their high opinion of rhetoric, their readiness to make use of the civil courts and to attend idol feasts can scarcely be taken as evidence of a rejection of the norms and values of the surrounding society. On the contrary, the Corinthians seem to have retained the cultural ethos of the city of Corinth all too readily. Rather than conduct a preliminary analysis of the social situation in Corinth, Neyrey seems to have assumed that Paul's difficulties with the Corinthians could be explained in terms of Douglas' contrast between ritualism and effervescence.[11]

Atkins' use of the model has already been outlined and assessed in detail; it will suffice at this point to note that he locates the Pauline communities uniformly in the low grid/high group quadrant of the matrix. Unlike Malina, who focuses on the apostle himself, Atkins concentrates on the communities, but he does not take into account the apostle's own perspective on those communities, nor does he consider the possibility of variation between the communities themselves.

Other interpreters apply the model specifically to Corinth, and follow Neyrey in making a distinction between Paul's position on the matrix

---

[11]Cf. Garrett's apposite criticism: 'The inherent tendency of the grid/group model to efface cultural differences and to reduce social discourse to what has been determined beforehand to be its "essence" or "core" would be regarded by interpretative ethnographers as culturally unacceptable. Insistence on taking account of the particularities of a people's culture is what makes cross-cultural comparison and generalisation so difficult from the interpretative viewpoint': S.R. Garrett, *The Demise of the Devil* (Minneapolis: Fortress, 1989), p.34. *Contra* Garrett, however, the problems she mentions are not inherent to the model, but rather reflect how the model is used.

and that of the church. In a critical response to Atkins, Witherington proposes that the Corinthians belong in the low group/low grid quadrant of the *Cultural Bias* version of the matrix, where ego-oriented goals were taking precedence over group unity.[12] This suggestion is also made by Wire, who sees the Corinthian church as a 'free market', where honour fell on anyone who could generate wealth and connections. This is clearly a reference to the quadrant of competitive individualism, although Wire's failure to distinguish between the different versions of the matrix used in *Cultural Bias* and in Neyrey's work results in confusion.[13]

Both Wire and Witherington agree that Paul is seeking to develop a high level of group identity in Corinth, but they disagree over where Paul himself should be located on the grid matrix. Wire argues that Paul tries to move the Corinthians towards a high grid classification since he wants to maintain a clear distinction between male and female roles within the church. Witherington, on the other hand, proposes that Paul is mid-grid, since there is a dialectic in the apostle's thought between factors that lead on the one hand to the ordering of the community and, on the other, to the levelling of its members. However, neither Wire nor Witherington makes sufficiently detailed use of the model to analyse their views in depth; both refer to the model only in order to substantiate their own views of what is taking place in the Corinthian community.

The model is also applied to 1 Corinthians by Houston, who concerns himself entirely with the question of grid and does not discuss group at all.[14] He bases his analysis on the 1973 edition of *Natural Symbols*, and so presumably accepts that work's definition of grid as the scope and coherence of the articulation of the social classification, although he does not make this explicit. The greater part of Houston's book examines the origin of the Jewish food laws, with a particular focus on the abhorrence of pork. Houston sees the priestly writers of Leviticus 11, 15 as being high grid, in view of the way they objectify the dangers to the social order in a symbolic system of external impurity. Paul's level of grid is much lower, since he sets aside the Jewish food laws (Rom. 14:14) in favour of a more subjective social order, based on the community's personal bond to the Lord and a moral appeal to its members. According to Houston,

[12]Witherington, *Conflict and Community*, pp.151–2.
[13]A.C. Wire, *The Corinthian Women Prophets* (Minneapolis: Fortress, 1990), pp.188–92. Wire refers to Neyrey's work, but is obviously using the third version of the model when she identifies the quadrant of competitive individualism as low grid/low group; in Neyrey's version of the model, it would be low group/high grid.
[14]W. Houston, *Purity and Monotheism*, JSOTSupp 140 (Sheffield: JSOT, 1993), pp.93–114.

the Corinthians are even more low grid than Paul, since the apostle has to struggle against both their natural inclinations to self-indulgence and their antinomian theology. Like Neyrey, Houston points to their informal undisciplined worship, and claims that the Corinthians have rejected structure altogether. Indeed, Houston suggests that the Corinthian church should be seen as millennialist, since they anticipated the imminent return of Christ and found their lives controlled by the remote and invisible powers of Roman domination. Douglas claims that the victims of oppressive grid react by expressing themselves by means of inarticulate, undifferentiated symbols, and Houston sees here the key to the problems in the Corinthian church.

Pickett also makes use of Neyrey's adaptation of Douglas' model in his examination of the social significance of the symbol of the cross in Corinth.[15] Pickett follows Neyrey in associating the lack of physical control with a lack of social control, and argues that this is attributable to a certain kind of spirituality which emphasised individual freedom (πάντα μοι ἔξεστιν, 6:12; 10:23). Pickett suggests that those who stressed speaking in tongues, together with the sexual libertines (1 Cor. 5–6) and ascetics (7:1–16), were emphasising the spiritual at the expense of the material in a way that reflected their lack of integration into the larger social world. Pickett distinguishes these pneumatics from those responsible for the controversies over food in chapters 8–11, to whom he ascribes a high socio-economic status. Pickett's analysis of the Corinthian situation breaks down under the strain of attributing the same slogan of individual freedom to people at opposite ends of the social spectrum (6:12; 10:23). According to Pickett, Paul responds to the situation by emphasising the purity and holiness of the community, in order to distinguish it from outside society and to preserve its unity.

Gordon analyses 1 Corinthians 7,[16] combining insights from Victor Turner's work on social drama[17] with Douglas' matrix. Basing her definitions on the first edition of *Natural Symbols*, she argues that group measures group loyalties, whereas grid refers to individual networks. Gordon's use of the model is eclectic, in that she incorporates later work by Douglas and Malina whenever it suits her argument to do so, but

[15] R. Pickett, *The Cross in Corinth: The Social Significance of the Death of Jesus*, JSNTS 143 (Sheffield: JSOT, 1997), pp.89–97.

[16] J.D. Gordon, *Sister or Wife? 1 Corinthians 7 and Cultural Anthropology*, JSNTS 149 (Sheffield: JSOT, 1997).

[17] V.W. Turner, *Dramas, Fields and Metaphors: Symbolic Action in Human Society* (New York: Cornell University Press, 1974).

she does not provide a systematic presentation of the different versions of the matrix. According to Gordon, the Corinthian church is mid- to strong-group, since the individual is under pressure to conform to community norms. Yet there is confusion as to what those norms are, since the church is split between a high grid conformity faction in favour of marriage and a low grid anti-structure group who favour celibacy, even at the cost of divorce. Paul's strong-group aim is to promote group cohesion and unity and so he attempts to undercut the absolute positions adopted by both parties by advancing arguments which advocate both marriage and singleness; this ambiguous attitude to structure makes him mid-grid. Gordon argues that Paul's attempt to find a mediate position results in a failure to address the issue directly and the apostle is ultimately prepared to sacrifice the freedom of the married women in the anti-structure group in the interests of overall group cohesion and unity.

According to Gordon, Paul uses the cross to promote a group consciousness based on his own high status leadership. However, Paul uses the symbol of the cross, not as a symbol of social cohesion, but rather as a symbol of social debasement, which in turn undermines Gordon's claim that Paul sees himself as a high status leader. Since status is more a matter of grid than group, it becomes apparent that Paul's grid rating cannot simply be determined on the basis of his mediating position between the two groups in Corinth, as Gordon seeks to do.

In analysing the Corinthians' position on the matrix, Gordon neatly splices Turner's distinction between structure and anti-structure into Douglas' matrix and seems to use this as the basis for her definition of their grid rating. Her claim that they are mid- to strong-group is based on the observation that factionalism exists and there is no clear definition of how members should relate, which is how Douglas describes the small bounded group. Given the debate over the position of the Corinthians on the matrix, Gordon would have done better to evaluate Paul and the church's positions on the matrix on the basis of 1 Corinthians as a whole, before focusing on the issues raised in chapter 7.

In reviewing the different ways in which the matrix has been applied to Paul, it becomes apparent that the apostle has been located in three of the four possible quadrants. Isenberg proposed the quadrant of the successful leader; Malina argued that Paul belongs in the quadrant of the sect or enclave, and this view is supported by Pickett's interpretation of Paul's response of distinguishing the community from 'outside' society (low grid) and promoting unity (high group). Neyrey and Wire, on the other hand, argue that Paul belongs to the stratified community of

high grid and group. Witherington differs again in proposing high group
and mid-grid, and presumably Houston and Gordon would agree with
this.

With regard to the Corinthian church, Atkins would identify it as an
egalitarian community along with all the other Pauline churches. Wire
and Witherington, on the other hand, see the church as belonging to
the quadrant of competitive individualism, while Neyrey sees the church
as made up of disorderly pneumatics who are both low grid and low
group. Houston goes one step further than Neyrey in claiming that the
Corinthian church should be seen as millennialist. Pickett argues for the
presence of both pneumatics and high status individuals in Corinth, and
Gordon sees the church as a strong-group community divided between
high grid defenders of marriage and low grid proponents of celibacy.
Clearly the issue of the location of Paul and his churches on the quadrant
is a matter for ongoing debate and will need to be resolved if the model
is to be applied to Paul with any confidence at all.

Locating Corinth on the matrix

Douglas' model offers a method of classifying societies in accordance
with two variables that, according to the definitions adopted for this study,
measure the degree of integration into a bounded social unit (group) and
the extent to which the prevailing cultural norms are either accepted or
rejected (grid). The resultant matrix sets out four different ideal types
of society, each with its own distinctive cosmology. It is tempting to cut
corners by trying to see which cosmology corresponds most closely to
the Corinthian situation, and to make this correspondence the basis for
locating the Corinthian church on the quadrant. However, the divergent
interpretations listed above indicate how easy it is to use the model this
way and to do little more than confirm one's own preconceptions. Instead,
it is necessary to conduct a cautious examination of the letter for evidence
pertaining to strength or weakness of group identity within the church,
and the church's attitude towards the surrounding culture. Once a possible
quadrant for the church has been established, it is possible to compare the
cosmology of that quadrant and the views that are held within the church.
In this way, it is possible to test the degree of correspondence between
the model and the social situation in question.

On the whole, the Corinthians' attitude to the surrounding world seems
to have been more positive than negative. Paul's repeated disparagement
of the 'wisdom of this world' is probably a reaction to the high value
placed on wisdom by the Corinthian Christians, in common with Greek

culture generally (1:18–25; 3:18–20). In the same context, Paul's defence of his preaching (1:17; 2:1–4) would appear to be a response to Corinthian criticisms of his lack of rhetorical skill, which was also highly valued in Greek culture.[18] Furthermore, the way in which Paul subverts the values of wisdom, power and noble birth (1:26) may indicate that such publicly accepted status symbols were also highly prized among the Corinthians. Confirmation that this was indeed the case is provided in 4:10, where Paul contrasts his own low social status with the Corinthians' claims to be wise, powerful and honourable.[19] In terms of their behaviour, too, at least some of the Corinthians were well integrated in society: they attended feasts in the local temples (8:7–13; 10:20–22), they continued to make use of prostitutes (6:12–20) and apparently saw no reason to avoid pursuing litigation through the local courts (6:1–11). Those who were so much at home in the surrounding society would have little reason to pin all their hopes on such a potent symbol of transformation as the eschatological resurrection of the dead (15:12).[20]

A preliminary consideration of the Corinthians' attitude towards prevailing cultural norms and the extent of their integration with the surrounding society would therefore seem to indicate that the church should be given a high grid rating.[21]

Concerning the church's group rating, it might at first appear that the existence of strife and different parties within the church (1:11–12; 3:3–4) would indicate a low group rating. Yet caution is needed here, since group fissions over leadership disputes frequently occur in the small bounded group (high group/low grid). While there is no unambiguous evidence for individualism within the fellowship, Paul's directives on spiritual gifts do emphasise the need for unity in a way that suggests an egotistic lack of concern for the fellowship as a whole (12:1–14:33). A lack of group cohesion is also apparent in 1 Corinthians 11:17–34, where Paul remarks

[18] Litfin has helped re-establish the former consensus that σοφία λόγου refers to rhetoric: D. Litfin, *St. Paul's Theology of Proclamation*, SNTS 79 (Cambridge: Cambridge University Press, 1994).

[19] According to Theissen, the terms in 4:10 are primarily sociological in meaning, as in 1:26: G. Theissen, *The Social Setting of Pauline Christianity* (Edinburgh: T&T Clark, 1982), pp.72–3. Fee contests this, claiming that Paul uses ἔνδοξοι here in place of εὐγενεῖς because the latter would not be sociologically true; according to Fee, Paul is speaking with total irony here: G. Fee, *1 Corinthians*, NICNT (Grand Rapids: Eerdmans, 1987), p.176 n.57; p.178 n.61. However, Paul's shift in vocabulary may have been determined by the need to find a suitable antonym for ἄτιμοι, and it seems likely that the Corinthians' estimation of their own position must have had at least some sociological foundation.

[20] On upper-class scepticism about the afterlife, cf. D.B. Martin, *The Corinthian Body* (Newhaven: Yale University Press, 1995), pp.108–17.

[21] This is confirmed by Horrell's careful analysis (*Social Ethos*, pp.91–123).

that each person goes ahead and eats without waiting for the others, so that some get drunk, while others go hungry (11:21). Paul indeed claims that they are not celebrating the Lord's Supper at all, since the meal which should symbolise the unity of the fellowship (10:16–17) has become the occasion when divisions within the fellowship are most apparent. They need to learn to wait for one another so that they can celebrate the meal together (11:33–34).

Thus the letter contains some clear indications of a disregard for group cohesion within the church, and there is certainly no evidence in favour of regarding the church as a close-knit social group. On balance, therefore, it would seem preferable to accept the strife in the church as a sign that the church should be given a low group rating. This would then locate the fellowship within the high grid/low group quadrant of competitive individualism, as proposed by Wire and Witherington. This hypothesis now needs to be tested by a comparison between the Corinthian church and the society dominated by impersonal rules that Douglas locates within this quadrant.

According to Douglas, the Garia tribe of the Madang District on the north coast of New Guinea exemplifies the social structure of the high grid/low group quadrant. She ascribes to them an optimistic view of the universe, in which the world exists for their benefit and they have the right to enjoy it. This culture is highly materialistic and egocentric: any sense of relationship or mutual obligation rests purely on a fiscal basis; where there is no interchange of goods or services, there is only suspicion, hostility and the risk of warfare. Religion is pragmatically regarded as a technology for overcoming risk, and there are highly magical attitudes to miracles. Spiritual values such as purity and sin are non-existent, and there is no idea of rewards or sanctions in the next world. In such a society, deviance is perceived as stupidity rather than sin, and human nature is divided between the foolish and the wise, between 'those who know' and those who do not. The successful man would be characterised by personal pre-eminence and secret ritual knowledge; the leaders are those who 'really know' and who can lure followers away from their less fortunate rivals and direct their activities to their own advantage. This is a highly egocentric, individualistic and competitive society, dominated by the 'Big Man', who imposes himself as a leader, and who derives prestige and power from the size of his following. Since the power of a leader is located in the consent of his followers, each leader seeks to lure followers away from his less successful rivals. Rival leaders compete for renown by inviting guests to a feast and presenting them with gifts, in the expectation that the recipient will not be able to reciprocate in equivalent terms; the host who is successful in discountenancing his rivals in this way attains a higher social status.[22]

This portrait offers suggestive parallels to what we can discern of the situation in Corinth from Paul's letter. In Corinth, there is no regard for any sense of purity or sin, a lack which Paul seeks to counter by his repeated use of vice lists (5:9–10, 11; 6:9–10). The slogan πάντα μοι ἔξεστιν (6:12; 10:23) comes from those who feel they have the freedom to indulge the physical and sexual appetites without any fear of judgment in the afterlife. They hold that food is for the stomach and the stomach for food, and both will simply be destroyed at death (6:13; cf. 15:12, 32–34).[23] Baptism may have been regarded as a kind of magical insurance policy, which could be taken out on behalf of those who had died (15:29). The Lord's Supper likewise was regarded as giving magical protection against any ill-effects from their behaviour (10:1–4).[24] Paul's own reluctance to accept fiscal support from these Corinthians seems to have resulted in suspicions about the validity of his apostleship (9:1–18). All these features correspond to characteristics of the 'Big Man' quadrant in Douglas' matrix.

The competition between rival leaders in 'Big Man' societies also suggests parallels with the Corinthian situation. In 1 Corinthians 1:12 we see the church split into rival parties on the basis of their allegiance to different apostles.[25] Underlying this factionalism there is an esoteric wisdom (3:18–23) that inflates the pride of those who are wise and spiritual, as opposed to being unspiritual and foolish (4:6; 2:6–16). Theissen plausibly argues that those responsible for the factionalism in Corinth were drawn from the 'not many' of 1:26 who were wise, powerful and of

[22]Douglas, *Natural Symbols* (1st edition), pp.125–39, supplemented by material from P. Lawrence, *Road Belong Cargo: a Study of the Cargo Movement in the Southern Madang District, New Guinea* (Manchester: Manchester University Press, 1964), pp.29, 225. Douglas also refers to the Siuai of Bougainville, who do not co-operate with one another on any common enterprise and where friendship is not recognised as an important social category: D.L. Oliver, *A Solomon Island Society: Kinship and Leadership among the Siuai of Bougainville* (Cambridge, MA: Harvard University Press, 1955). There is no understanding of the meaning of sin, and magic is used chiefly in order to accumulate property and wealth, albeit with an air of some scepticism. Cf. also Sahlins, 'Poor Man, Rich Man'.

[23]The qualifying negative οὐ only comes in 6:13c, which means that the whole of v.13ab should be taken as a Corinthian slogan.

[24]Cf. E. Käsemann, 'The Pauline Doctrine of the Lord's Supper', *Essays on New Testament Themes* (London: SCM, 1964), pp.108–35.

[25]Cf. M. Mitchell, *Paul and the Rhetoric of Reconciliation* (Tübingen: J.C.B. Mohr, 1991). It will be argued below that Paul should be given a high group rating, which would have led him to perceive the Corinthians' rivalry as divisive in a way that the low group Corinthians did not; cf. E.S. Fiorenza, 'Rhetorical Situation and Historical Reconstruction in 1 Corinthians', *NTS* 33 (1987), pp.386–403.

noble birth.[26] Theissen also argues that these leaders were behind the rival factions of 1:12, since it would have been people from this stratum of society who would have acted as hosts to the visiting missionaries. Such leaders may well have sought to win honour and prestige for themselves by magnifying their own adopted missionary at Paul's expense. It would also have been such socially advantaged people who would have had sufficient education to be interested in wisdom (1:18–3:23), and who would have looked down on Paul for working with his hands (4:12; 9:1–23). They would have participated in idol feasts (8–10) and would have been the ones who were excluding the poor from the Lord's Supper (11:17–34). The celebration of the Lord's Supper in Corinth may well have become a focus for competitive rivalry between leaders who used the meal as a means of seeking social advancement.[27] Tongues, too, were probably perceived as an indication of high status in Corinth,[28] and may well have been prized by rival leaders in their struggle to attain pre-eminence within the church.[29] Douglas' matrix seems to throw the role played by the local leaders in the Corinthian church into sharp relief.[30]

However, it is of course sometimes possible to read into a given text what one wants to get out of it. In the light of this knowledge it is necessary to pause and consider carefully whether it is legitimate to apply the model of the 'Big Men', based substantially on anthropological studies of tribes in New Guinea, to first-century Corinth. Is there any evidence of the existence of such people in the city at that time?

---

[26] Social Setting, pp.69–119; cf. W. Meeks, The First Urban Christians (Newhaven: Yale University Press, 1983), pp.117–25; L.L. Welborn, 'On the Discord in Corinth: 1 Corinthians 1–4 and Ancient Politics', JBL 106 (1987), pp.85–111.

[27] Cf. R.A. Campbell, 'Does Paul Acquiesce in Divisions at the Lord's Supper?' NovT 33 (1991), pp.61–70. Campbell suggests that 11:19 should be translated, 'For there actually has to be discrimination in your meetings, so that if you please, the elite may stand out from the rest'. Cf. also Barton, 'Paul's Sense of Place'; Witherington, Conflict and Community, p.244.

[28] Cf. Martin, Corinthian Body, pp.88–92.

[29] Cf. I.M. Lewis, Ecstatic Religion: a Study of Shamanism and Spirit Possession (London: Routledge, 1989), pp.114–59. Lewis analyses numerous cults, where possession is regarded as a mark of divine inspiration amongst the religious elite, who contend for leadership in the religious life of the community. Significantly, these central possession cults all occur in loosely structured societies led by big men or petty chieftains. Power tends to be won by achievement rather than prescribed by birth, and inspirational possession is the idiom in which men compete for authority. These cults firmly belong in the high grid/low group 'Big Man' quadrant of Douglas' matrix, and Lewis' work bears ample testimony to the way in which trance and possession are welcomed in such social groups, and used as a means to attaining positions of leadership within such competitive societies.

[30] As in 'Big Man' societies, the rivalry between the leaders in Corinth may well have been focused on the size of each leader's personal following; cf. T.L. Carter, ' "Big Men" in Corinth', JSNT 66 (1997), pp.45–71.

Indeed there is. A.D. Clarke has argued that the fact that the site of the city was originally chosen for its mercantile potential meant that mercantile trade was a key feature of the town's existence.[31] Furthermore, when the city was refounded in 44 BC it was populated for the most part with freedmen whose descendants would have been regarded as free-born. The relative newness of the city and the free-born nature of the population would have produced a climate that offered social mobility to those who were able to afford it, especially once the city had resumed responsibility for the Isthmian Games at the turn of the era. The possession of wealth was essential to progress, because it was only by lavish expenditure that it was possible to buy friends and win the esteem that was reserved for those who were benefactors of the community. Far from being a place where whole generations were condemned to remain in their allotted position on the social scale, Corinth was a city where social advancement was a real possibility, and where money was crucial to realising that goal. Clarke's reconstruction indicates that Corinth would have constituted suitably fertile ground for the flourishing of a materialistically based competitive individualism, akin to that of the New Guinea tribes to which Douglas refers.

The validity of this reconstruction has, however, been challenged by Meggitt.[32] Contending that reconstructions of the social makeup of the ancient world are overly dependent upon elite sources, Meggitt prefers to adopt an approach that studies 'History from Below' and analyses 'Popular Culture'. On the basis of the evidence provided by contemporary literature, legal texts, papyri, epigraphy and archaeology, Meggitt argues that there was no possibility of social advancement in the ancient Hellenistic world. With the exception of the tiny minority of the ruling elite, the entire population was trapped in absolute poverty, with no hope of any escape. On the basis of his analysis, Meggitt contends that 'Paul and the Pauline churches shared in this general experience of deprivation and subsistence. Neither the apostle nor any members of the congregations he addresses in his epistles escaped from the harsh existence that typified life in the Roman Empire for the non-élite.'[33] Meggitt's book constitutes a bold challenge to the consensus established by Judge, Theissen and Meeks that Paul's churches contained a number of relatively well-off individuals.[34]

---

[31] A.D. Clarke, *Secular and Christian Leadership in Corinth: a Socio-Historical and Exegetical Study of 1 Cor. 1–6* (Leiden: E.J. Brill, 1993), pp.9–39.

[32] J. Meggitt, *Paul, Poverty and Survival* (Edinburgh, T&T Clark, 1998).

[33] Ibid., p.75.

[34] Cf. E.A. Judge, *The Social Pattern of the Christian Groups in the First Century: Some Prolegomena to the Study of New Testament Ideas of Social Obligation* (London: Tyndale, 1960); Theissen, *Social Setting*; Meeks, *First Urban Christians*.

Yet there is sufficient contrary evidence from ancient sources to cast doubt on Meggitt's thesis. Meggitt mentions Juvenal as one ancient writer who was sensitive to the reality experienced by those beyond his clique,[35] but omits to quote those satires which reflect the resentment felt by the aristocracy to those freedmen who had recently acquired great wealth. He cites the example of one who bought a red mullet for 60 gold pieces, 'though he once went round in a loincloth of your native papyrus'.[36] He also cites a typical instance of rude words addressed by a freedman to those who are queuing to meet their patron: 'I got here first. Why shouldn't I keep my place? I don't give *that* for you. Oh, I know I'm foreign: Look here, at my pierced ears, no use denying it – born out East, on the Euphrates. But my five shops bring in four hundred thousand, see? So I qualify for the gentry.'[37]

Meggitt also is too quick to dismiss Trimalchio, the wealthy freedman in Petronius' *Satyricon*. Meggitt claims that he cannot be looked on as typifying a class of bourgeois freedmen speculators, because he inherited his initial wealth.[38] Yet while that was true of Trimalchio, it does not necessarily apply to his friends: 'That one you see lying at the bottom of the end of the sofa has eight hundred thousand. He grew from nothing. A little time ago he was carrying loads of wood on his back.'[39] Of another, Chrysanthus, it is said, 'He started with two pence, and he was always ready to pick a halfpenny out of the dung with his teeth. So whatever he touched grew like a honeycomb. Upon my word, I believe he left a clear hundred thousand, and all in hard cash.'[40] Certainly, in the case of Chrysanthus, it would appear that he accumulated his own fortune, rather than inheriting it. The way in which both Juvenal and Petronius satirise such people is evidence of their existence in some numbers. Trimalchio attained the rank of *sevir Augustalis*, and vast numbers of inscriptions bear witness to the number of freedmen who were able to purchase the title.[41] Yet Meggitt dismisses this important epigraphic evidence, on the

---

[35] *Paul, Poverty and Survival*, p.24.
[36] Juvenal, *The Sixteen Satires* (London: Penguin, 1967), 4.15.
[37] Ibid., 1.102–9.
[38] *Paul, Poverty and Survival*, pp.48–9.
[39] Petronius, *Satyricon*, LCL (London: Heinemann, 1969), 38.
[40] Ibid., 43.
[41] A.D. Nock, 'Seviri and Augustales', in *Mélanges Bidez: Annuaire de l'Institut de Philologie et d'Histoire Orientales*, 2 vols. (Brussels, 1934), vol.II, pp.627–38; S.E. Ostrow, 'The Augustales in the Augustan Scheme' in K.A. Raaflaub and M. Toher, eds., *Between Republic and Empire: Interpretations of Augustus and his Principate* (Berkeley: University of California Press, 1990), pp.364–79; N. Purcell, 'The Apparitores: A Study in Social Mobility', *Papers of the British School at Rome* 51 (1983), pp.125–73.

grounds that such arriviste groups were created by the aristocracy to replenish their ranks.

All the above counter-examples refer to freedmen becoming very wealthy, by whatever means. Within papyri from the period, there is also some evidence of people living at a standard well above subsistence level. P. Ox. 3915 indicates that a freedman was able to pay 440 drachmas (22 months' wages, according to P. Ox. 3333) for a camel; P. Ox. 3798 also records the return of a loan of 300 drachmas to the children of a veteran, the capital originally having been lent by their mother. While it is true that the evidence is not substantial, it cannot be discounted, and the conclusion is inevitable that not everyone outside the aristocracy lived in the grinding poverty that Meggitt so vividly portrays. The possibility suggested by grid/group analysis, that there were successful social climbers in the Corinthian church, must be allowed.

In summary, the application of Douglas' model to the Corinthian situation would appear to suggest that the Corinthian church should be located in the high grid/low group quadrant of competitive individualism. High grid integration with the surrounding society accounts for their appreciation of wisdom and rhetoric, and their willingness to attend the local temple and to make use of the courts; low group accounts for the lack of concern about unity within the social body of the church. A low consciousness of sin and comparative disregard for the afterlife are also features of this quadrant which contributed to a readiness to make use of prostitutes, with a disregard of bodily boundaries that characterises low group. Competition between rival leaders resulted in factionalism within the church, which may have expressed itself at the Lord's Supper and in the use of spiritual gifts. This was the plight of the church to which Paul responded in his letter.

The one aspect of the Corinthian situation that does not correspond with the church's location in the 'Big Man' quadrant of the matrix is the attitude towards marriage revealed in 1 Corinthians 7. Referring to the Corinthians' letter for the first time, Paul says that it is good for a man not to touch a woman, and the way in which this statement is contradicted in 7:2 strongly suggests that 7:1b is a quotation from the Corinthian letter.[42] It would appear that there were some in Corinth who were advocating sexual abstinence within marriage, and Paul seems to be responding to the same ascetic agenda for the remainder of the chapter. The question of divorce is raised in 7:10–11, but it is perhaps reading too much into these

---

[42]Cf. W.E. Phipps, 'Is Paul's Attitude toward Sexual Relations Contained in 1 Cor. 7:1?', *NTS* 28 (1982), pp.125–31.

verses to suggest that women in Corinth were actually divorcing their husbands.[43] Paul may be wishing to set his own advice on the question of mixed marriages in the context of the dominical prohibition of divorce (7:12–16). In advising the believer to stay in the marriage, Paul would seem to be answering fears that his or her holiness would be polluted by the unbelieving partner. Later, in his response to the question about virgins, the apostle is at pains to reassure his readers that the decision to get married is not a sin, as some apparently supposed (v.28).

Such attitudes amongst the Corinthians sit uneasily with the sexual licence and the claim that all things are lawful in 6:12–20 (cf. 10:23), and there is evidence elsewhere in the letter suggesting that there were some in the church who were unhappy with the relatively amoral behaviour of the leaders. In 8:7–13, Paul refers to the weak, whose faith is undermined by those who attend feasts in idol temples and who have qualms about any food that has been offered to idols.[44] There also seem to have been some in Corinth who wanted to ban speaking in tongues altogether (14:39). It is evident that not everyone supported the local leadership in Corinth.

Could this group be made up of those who stayed loyal to Paul (1:12)? This possibility has much to commend it. We know that there were those in Corinth who wrote to Paul, and it is unlikely that the letter would have been sent by those who had no desire to see the apostle return (4:18). It must therefore have been sent by Paul's supporters, and it follows from this that any quotations Paul may make from the letter cannot automatically be taken as representative of the position of his opponents in Corinth. Those who wrote to Paul may indeed have referred to the slogans of the strong (8:1), but they may also have put their own point of view (7:1).

If the views of this group of people are analysed in terms of Douglas' matrix, a coherent position emerges. Those who wrote to Paul expressing concern about divisions within the fellowship must be given a high group rating, and this explains their objection to the use of tongues. Combined

[43] As suggested by J. Moffatt, *The First Epistle of Paul to the Corinthians* (London: Hodder & Stoughton, 1938), p.78; Fee, *1 Corinthians*, pp.269–70; Wire, *Corinthian Women Prophets*, pp.82–90.

[44] According to Hurd, the church was united in its opposition to Paul, and so there were no weak Christians in Corinth: J.C. Hurd, *The Origin of 1 Corinthians* (London: SPCK, 1965), pp.117–25; cf. also P.D. Gooch, *Dangerous Food: 1 Corinthians 8–10 in Its Context* (Ontario: Wilfrid Laurier University Press, 1993), pp.61–72. Hurd claims that in 8:9–13 Paul puts forward a hypothetical situation to dissuade the Corinthians from eating idol meat. However, Paul seems to have actual people in view in 8:7, and this may be corroborated by Paul's use of the first class conditional in 8:13, though cf. S.E. Porter, *Idioms of the Greek New Testament* (Sheffield: Sheffield Academic Press, 1994), pp.256–7.

with this concern for group cohesion is a preoccupation with boundary-infringement, that extends even to proposing divorce between Christian and non-Christian partners. The asceticism revealed in 7:1 is indicative of low grid, and a fear of contamination from the outside world is certainly apparent in the refusal to eat any meat offered to an idol. Indeed, it is possible that this group advocated withdrawal from the world altogether on the basis of Paul's previous letter (5:9–10).[45]

It will be argued below that Paul shares the same low grid/high group quadrant with this group, and this further strengthens the proposal that they constitute his supporters in Corinth. Paul is, however, far less extreme in his views. He attributes partial credence to their reports of divisions within the fellowship (11:18) and certainly does not advocate withdrawing from the world (5:9–10). While he himself favours the single life, he affirms the rightful place of sex within a marriage relationship, and does not sanction the divorce of unbelieving partners. He does not regard idol food itself as contaminated, although he does oppose attendance at an idol's temple. Nor does he agree that the use of tongues should be banned; while he places restrictions on the use of tongues and prophecy (14:26–33), he asserts the God-given nature of inspired speech (12:4–11) and other supernatural gifts.[46]

In conclusion, the application of grid and group to Corinth suggests that the church as a whole was dominated by local 'Big Men' who were relatively amoral, but there was also a core of world-renouncing church members who maintained loyalty to the apostle Paul. This is the situation to which Paul responds in writing 1 Corinthians.

Locating Paul on the matrix

Turning to the apostle, it is now necessary to examine his view of the church in order to establish his location on the matrix. As with the church, Paul's attitudes to group cohesion and the outside world will be assessed first, and then the cosmology of the appropriate matrix checked against what Paul has to say in the letter. Having located Paul on the matrix, it will then be possible to examine Paul's sin language in 1 Corinthians in the light of the cosmology of the appropriate quadrant.

---

[45] Paul is more likely responding to an unintentional misunderstanding on the part of his supporters than a deliberate misinterpretation by his opponents (cf. Hurd, *Origin*, pp.49–51).

[46] The existence of a group within Corinth who wanted to ban tongues might explain Paul's puzzling reference to cursing Jesus in 12:3. This comment may be a response to fears within this group that someone speaking in tongues could be cursing Jesus, for all they knew.

Regarding 'group', there can be little doubt that the apostle's concern to foster unity within the fellowship is apparent throughout the letter.[47] The extent of the apostle's desire for concord is revealed in the way he immediately turns from greeting the church to address the question of quarrelling and division, urging them to come to a common mind and purpose, and charging them with dividing Christ himself (1:10–13). He goes on to attack the 'wisdom' and the boasting that he perceives to be at the root of the problem (3:18–23; 4:6–13). He responds to the rival factions by recalling the whole church to the original gospel message that he himself preached (1:17–25; 2:1–16) in an attempt to reassert his position as apostle over the church as a whole (3:10–17; 4:14–21).[48]

Faced with Corinthian abuse of the Lord's Supper, Paul claims that this is a travesty of a meal which symbolises the fellowship of Christians together in the body of Christ (10:16–17). He warns that they need to wait for one another if they are to avoid being judged by the Lord (11:27–34). Turning to the issue of spiritual gifts, Paul reminds the Corinthians that the varied gifts come from the Spirit and have the common purpose of building up the fellowship (12:1–11). Paul stresses the importance of each person's place within the fellowship by means of the symbolism of the body of Christ (12:12–31) and exalts love as the most important consideration in the use of spiritual gifts (13:1–13). Paul urges them to cultivate the gift of prophecy rather than of tongues, so that the fellowship can be strengthened (14:1–19). In short, everything is to be done for the building up of the church (14:26).[49]

Concern for group cohesion is also evident as Paul addresses the issue of food offered to idols. He accepts the Corinthians' knowledge that an idol has no existence, but points out that such knowledge puffs up the one in possession of it. Love, on the other hand, is concerned to build up one's fellow believer. Paul warns that the example of the strong could lead a weak believer to sin by eating idol food against the judgment of their conscience; to make a fellow believer stumble in this way is a sin against Christ himself (8:7–13; cf. 10:23–11:1). Paul thus makes consideration for others the primary issue in the question of whether it is right to eat food that has been offered to idols.

[47] Cf. Mitchell, *Rhetoric of Reconciliation*.

[48] Cf. N.A. Dahl, 'Paul and the Church in Corinth according to 1 Cor. 1–4', in W.R. Farmer, C.F.D. Moule and R.R. Niebuhr, eds., *Christian History and Interpretation: Studies Presented to John Knox* (Cambridge: Cambridge University Press, 1967), pp.313–37.

[49] Fee (*1 Corinthians*, pp.582–625) argues that Paul's main concern in 12:4–31 is to argue for the diversity of spiritual gifts, but he recognises that that diversity needs to be expressed within a united fellowship.

At significant points in the letter, it is therefore apparent that Paul is concerned to foster love and mutual consideration in the church. Consequently, it is clear that the apostle himself should be given a high group rating on Douglas' matrix, as one who is concerned to maintain a strong sense of group cohesion and identity.

Concerning grid, the apostle does not encourage a positive attitude towards society outside the church. His designation of the believers as 'holy' fosters a sense of being set apart from the world (1:2), and Paul expects his converts to dissociate themselves from the common practices of making use of prostitutes and of attending the local temple. Regarding the parousia as imminent, Paul advocates a detachment in all one's dealings with the world (7:29–31) and is horrified that members of the church are prosecuting each other in the civil court over everyday matters (6:1–11).

Paul also subverts the wisdom of the world by means of the ultimate symbol of debasement, the cross of Christ (1:18–25; cf. 3:18–20), and claims that God has brought to nothing the values of the world by choosing the Corinthians in their foolishness, weakness and insignificance (1:26–29). Paul associates himself with the world's dirt and refuse (4:9–13), and immediately afterwards urges the Corinthians to follow his example (4:16). This world-rejecting attitude firmly points towards a low grid rating for the apostle.[50]

This combination of a strong sense of group identity combined with a rejection of the symbol system of the surrounding culture indicates that Paul should be located within the high group/low grid quadrant of the matrix.[51] This is the home of the small bounded group, and Douglas' description of its features bears a close resemblance to Paul's view of the church in Corinth. Within this community, the group boundary is the main definer of roles, and individuals class themselves either as members or strangers. The boundaries protect the good inside of the community from the evil world outside, but these boundaries are porous, inasmuch as deviants within the group are accused of allowing the outside evil to infiltrate. This leads to a preoccupation with rituals of cleansing, expulsion and the drawing of new boundaries, and there is also an association of magical danger with boundary emblems. Within such groups, leadership is precarious, and there may well develop internal factions related to a struggle for leadership. Since the human body is a symbol of the social unit, the social idea of the good inside and the bad outside is replicated

[50]Cf. Horrell, *Social Ethos*, pp.131–57.
[51]As argued by Malina in *Christian Origins*.

in anthropology. Thus the community's distinctive therapeutic system is based upon the essential goodness of what is inside the body, while the body itself may be rejected as being the external husk or empty shell: strict ascetic controls may therefore be set on bodily enjoyment and the gateways of sensual experience.

The correspondence between this type of community and Paul's view of the Corinthian church should be obvious. As far as the apostle is concerned, the group boundary itself is the main definer of roles. While 1 Corinthians 12:28 may indicate some elementary structural ordering within the community, Paul does not develop the symbol of the body of Christ in this direction at all. The apostle does not draw on this symbol's inherent potential for developing a hierarchical structure within the community;[52] instead he employs it to stress the corporate identity and equal interdependence of all the members of the group, thereby ruling out any possibility of individualism. There is thus a strong sense of group identity, and in the absence of any strongly articulated hierarchical structure, membership is defined primarily in terms of being inside or outside of the group. It may therefore be said with some assurance that Paul wrote 1 Corinthians from the social perspective of the small, bounded group. Within the cosmology of this social unit, sin is perceived as an outside evil that threatens to penetrate the boundaries protecting the pure inside of the physical and social bodies. It is now therefore possible to examine what Paul has to say about sin in 1 Corinthians in the light of Douglas' matrix.

A preoccupation with boundaries is apparent in the case of the man who has had an incestuous relationship with his father's wife (5:1–8). The man's sin is compared to leaven, which threatens to pollute the inner purity of the community and which must be cleansed out by handing the man concerned over to Satan. Although the meaning of this command is not immediately apparent, it is elucidated in 5:11–13. Here Paul explains that he is writing now to say that members of the community are not to associate with anyone in the church who is a known sinner; such a person is to be expelled. The reference to Satan reflects the characteristically sectarian view of the world outside the community as being under the sway of evil powers.[53] This episode bears a strong

[52] The way in which the body was commonly used to symbolise hierarchical concord is well set out by Martin (*Corinthian Body*, pp.29–37), who goes on to show how Paul rather uses the symbolism of the body to establish concord and harmony (pp.38–47).

[53] This perception of the outside world renders unnecessary the claim that 5:5 refers to a curse rather than expulsion: cf. G.W.H. Lampe, 'Church Discipline and the Interpretation of the Epistles to the Corinthians', in Farmer, Moule and Niebuhr, eds., *Christian History*, pp.337–63.

resemblance to Douglas' portrait of the small bounded group, whose members accuse deviants in their midst of allowing outside evil to infiltrate. In this particular case, the accusations do not lead to the fission of the group; Paul rather uses the symbolism of cleansing (5:7) to urge the expulsion of the offender, who is placed outside the boundaries of the fellowship.

Paul's concern for the welfare of the community is evident in 5:6–7.[54] The leaven of the man's sin threatens to contaminate the entire church, and he must be expelled so that the community will then be a batch of fresh unleavened dough. Paul then adds, confusingly, that this is what in fact they are (καθώς ἐστε ἄζυμοι). The theological debate over the relation of the indicative to the imperative has now been resolved in favour of the solution that the former is the basis of the latter, so that Paul can in effect urge his converts to 'become what you are'.[55] At the social level, however, Douglas' model offers an alternative explanation based on the porosity of the boundaries that surround the sect or enclave. The purpose of such boundaries is to maintain a distinctive sense of group identity. In 6:9–11 Paul attributes such a function to baptism[56] as a rite of transfer into the community that separates believers from their sinful past in the world and identifies them as people who have been washed, sanctified and justified. In Paul's eyes, the church should be a sin-free zone, but the presence of fraud and sexual immorality within the community is evidence of the way in which the group's boundaries have failed to keep the evil of the outside world at bay. Paul's call to the church to 'become what you are' therefore expresses the tension between his expectations of the purity of the church and the reality of the presence of sin that has penetrated the porous boundaries of the community. This is why the incestuous man must be expelled from the fellowship: he is the one who has allowed the outside evil to infiltrate and threaten the purity of the entire group (5:6).

Not only does Paul say that the man's expulsion will cleanse the community (5:7); he also indicates that the intended result of this man's

---

[54]Cf. G. Forkman, *The Limits of Religious Community: Expulsion from the Religious Community within the Qumran Sect, within Rabbinic Judaism, and within Primitive Christianity* (Lund: C.W.K. Gleerup, 1972).

[55]Cf. R. Bultmann, 'The Problem of Ethics in Paul', in B.S. Rosner, ed., *Understanding Paul's Ethics: Twentieth-Century Approaches* (Grand Rapids: Eerdmans 1995), pp.195–216.

[56]ἀπελούσασθε refers to baptism here, according to G.R. Beasley-Murray, *Baptism in the New Testament* (Carlisle: Paternoster, 1997), pp.162–7. Despite Fee's doubts (*1 Corinthians*, pp.246–7), the fact that Paul puts a different emphasis on baptism in Rom. 6:1–11 does not preclude his seeing baptism as a washing away of a sinful past.

expulsion is the destruction of the flesh and the salvation of the spirit on the day of the Lord Jesus (5:5).[57] Some have argued that here, as in 5:7, Paul has the welfare of the community in mind, and that he is not concerned with the salvation of the man's spirit, but rather with the preservation of the Holy Spirit within the community.[58] However, it is hard to see in what sense the divine Spirit could be saved on the day of the Lord Jesus, and the fact that Paul always uses σώζω to denote the eschatological salvation of people tells against a reference to the Spirit of God here.[59]

Among those who accept that Paul indeed had the fate of the man in mind in 5:5, his meaning is debated. The theory that Paul refers to the physical suffering or death of the man[60] suffers from the logical difficulty that there is no convincing reason why the destruction of the flesh, so conceived, should lead to the salvation of the man's spirit.[61] The alternative view, that Paul has in mind the destruction of the man *qua* sinner and his salvation *qua* saint,[62] also suffers from a logical *non sequitur*,

---

[57]For an exposition of both aspects of Paul's intention, cf. C.J. Roetzel, *Judgement in the Community: A Study of the Relationship between Eschatology and Ecclesiology in Paul* (Leiden: E.J. Brill, 1972), pp.109–75.

[58]E.g. K.P. Donfried, 'Justification and Last Judgement in Paul', *ZNW* 67 (1976), pp.90–110; A.Y. Collins, 'The Function of "Excommunication" in Paul', *HTR* 73 (1980), pp.251–63.

[59]H.-D. Wendland, *Die Briefe an die Korinther* (Göttingen: Vandenhoeck & Ruprecht, 1962), p.39.

[60]In favour of death, cf. H. Conzelmann, *1 Corinthians*, Hermeneia (Minneapolis: Fortress, 1975), pp.97–8; W.F. Orr and J.A. Walter, *1 Corinthians*, AB (London: Chapman. 1976), pp.188–9; R.H. Gundry, *Sōma in Biblical Theology with Emphasis on Pauline Anthropology*, SNTS 29 (Cambridge: Cambridge University Press, 1976), pp.141–3. The phrase 'destruction of the flesh' would seem too strong to denote physical suffering: so L. Morris, *The First Epistle of Paul to the Corinthians*, TNTC (London: IVP, 1985), pp.88–9; Lampe, 'Church Discipline'.

[61]Cf. C.K. Barrett, *1 Corinthians* (London: A&C Black, 1971), pp.126–7, for a reference to *Sanhedrin* 6.2, where the condemned criminal is instructed to plead that his death will atone for all his sins. However, as Barrett points out, for Paul atonement is achieved through the death of Christ, not that of the sinner. Winninge suggests that Paul ascribed an atoning effect to discipline and suffering, but none of the other references quoted really support this (1 Cor. 11:29–32; 2 Cor. 2:6f.; 7:9–11). Surprisingly, he does not mention Rom. 6:7: M. Winninge, *Sinners and the Righteous: A Comparative Study of the Psalms of Solomon and Paul's Letters* (Stockholm: Almqvist & Wiksell, 1995), pp.321–32.

[62]A. Sand, *Der Begriff 'Fleisch' in den paulinischen Hauptbriefen* (Regensburg: Friedrich Pustet, 1967), pp.143–5; J. Cambier, 'La Chair et l'Esprit en 1 Cor. 5:5', *NTS* 15 (1969), pp.221–32; Fee, *1 Corinthians*, pp.212–13; Witherington, *Conflict and Community*, pp.58–9. For a cautious assessment, cf. A.C. Thiselton, 'The Meaning of ΣΑΡΞ in 1 Corinthians 5:5; a Fresh Approach in the Light of Logical and Semantic Factors', *SJT* 26 (1973), pp.204–28.

since it is far from clear why handing the man over to Satan should cause his repentance.[63]

However, Douglas' theory that the physical body is a symbol of society offers a way out of the impasse. Members of the small bounded group who draw a contrast between the good inside and the evil outside of the community will tend to regard the body as an object of anxiety or as an alien husk to be discarded. This perspective is found in 1 Corinthians 5:5, where Paul associates the salvation of the inner spirit[64] with the destruction of the outer flesh, which has been polluted by the incestuous union with the man's stepmother.[65] The rationale for the connection between the man's expulsion and his salvation is symbolic, rather than logical, and is based upon the correlation between the social and physical bodies. The inner purity of the social body is preserved by consigning the man to the destructive sphere of Satan outside the community; Paul anticipates that this same act will result in the salvation of the man's good inner spirit and the destruction of his sinful outer flesh. Salvation of the good inside and destruction of the corrupt outside is thus replicated in both the social and physical bodies.[66] Paul was probably thinking in terms of some kind of prophetic symbolism. The act of maintaining the inner purity of the community by consigning what is sinful to destruction outside is expected to have the same effect in the man himself, as evil, symbolised by the outer flesh, is destroyed, and the good inner spirit is saved.

That Paul did think in terms of some kind of anthropological duality is apparent from 1 Corinthians 5:3–4, where he talks of being absent in body, but present in spirit.[67] The presence of such an anthropological duality in Paul's thought and in Judaism has been clearly demonstrated

---

[63] Morris, *1 Corinthians*, p.88.

[64] McArthur's suggestion that πνεῦμα refers to what is left of the man after death is unlikely since Paul never uses πνεῦμα in this sense: S.D. McArthur, '"Spirit" in Pauline Usage: 1 Corinthians 5:5', in E.A. Livingstone, ed., *Studia Biblica III: Papers on Paul and Other New Testament Authors*, JSNTS 3 (Sheffield: Sheffield Academic Press, 1980), pp.249–56.

[65] Martin observes that πνεῦμα was considered to be the stuff of rationality, thought and sensation, and as such it was dangerously susceptible to pollution and corruption (*Corinthian Body*, p.24; cf. pp.168–74).

[66] The idea that society outside the community is subject to destruction is implied in 5:13.

[67] Fee argues for a dual reference to Paul's own spirit and the Holy Spirit (*1 Corinthians*, pp.203–6). Such a view is plausible for 5:3, but not 5:4: would Paul refer to the Holy Spirit as τοῦ ἐμοῦ πνεύματος? It is likely that Paul emphasises his presence 'in spirit' as a rhetorical strategy to re-establish his authority, which has been eroded in his absence (4:18). The situation demanded that Paul convey a sense of the immediacy of his presence, and this is probably what he meant by being present 'in spirit'.

by Gundry.[68] It therefore should not be assumed that Paul is here adopting a supposed Greek view of the physical flesh as being inherently sinful;[69] indeed, it is doubtful whether the majority of Greeks in Paul's day would have subscribed to such an antithetical dualism.[70] Paul simply uses the outer flesh as a symbol of the evil that must be destroyed, either through the man's repentance or through physical suffering and death.

Paul's primary concern in 5:1–8 is, however, the purity of the inside of the social body, and this concern is maintained in the command to put the wicked person outside the fellowship in 5:13. His preoccupation with the need to establish clear social boundaries separating insiders from outsiders provides the link between 5:1–13 and the subject of litigation in 6:1–11.[71] Paul is horrified that the church should go before unrighteous unbelievers when the saints will judge the world (6:1–2).[72] If disputes

[68]Gundry, *Sōma*. There has been a tendency to ignore Gundry's thesis rather than to attempt to overturn it. In a rare attempt to offset Gundry's anthropological dualism, J.A. Ziesler claims to find eight occasions in the Septuagint where σῶμα must denote the whole person: 'ΣΩΜΑ in the Septuagint', *NovT* 25 (1987), pp.133–45. Yet even these few incidents fail to persuade. In Gen. 47:12, there seems good reason to suppose that physical nourishment is in mind, and it is difficult to doubt that the job of a bodyguard is to protect the physical body of the king in 1 Chron. 28:1; 1 Esdr. 3:4. The references in Tob. 11:15 (א), 13:7 (B) are textually insecure; στόματι may have been amended to σώματι without undue regard for the sense, but even if σώματι is original, the writer may have intended nothing more than a physical expression of praise. In Prov. 11:17; Sir. 51:2; Job 33:17, Ziesler claims that σῶμα is used alongside other expressions to denote the person as a whole. However, since in each case σῶμα is used in parallel with ψυχή, there would seem to be insufficient grounds for discounting Gundry's proposal that σῶμα and ψυχή together denote the whole person. Gundry's thesis thus withstands Ziesler's attempt to dislodge it.

[69]So H. Lüdemann, *Die Anthropologie des Apostels Paulus* (Kiel, 1872); O. Pfleiderer, *Paulinism* (London: Williams & Norgate, 1877); H.J. Holtzmann, *Lehrbuch der neutestamentlichen Theologie*, 2 vols. (Tübingen: J.C.B. Mohr, 1911). W. Gutbrod is right to refer to 'a totally unstressed dichotomy': *Die paulinische Anthropologie* (Berlin: Stuttgart, 1934), p.90; cf. D. Boyarin, *A Radical Jew: Paul and the Politics of Identity* (London: University of California Press, 1994), pp.57–85.

[70]P. Brown refers to a 'benevolent dualism': *The Body and Society: Men, Women and Sexual Renunciation in Early Christianity* (Chichester: Columbia University Press, 1988), pp.26–32. Disparagement of the body in Greek literature may possibly be because the authors were an intellectual minority, who would have occupied the low group/low grid quadrant on Douglas' matrix. In any event, J.M. Dillon points out that Plato has a positive view of the body in Timaeus 90 A-D: 'Rejecting the Body, Redefining the Body: Some Remarks on the Development of Platonist Asceticism', in V.L. Wimbush and R. Valentasis, eds., *Asceticism* (Oxford: Oxford University Press, 1995), pp.80–7.

[71]According to W. Schrage, 5:1–13 and 6:1–11 are linked by the theme of the purity of the church in the world: *Der erste Brief an die Korinther*, EKK 7 (Düsseldorf: Benziger/Neukirchener Verlag, 1991–5), vol.I, p.403.

[72]The way in which Paul opposes ἀδίκων and ἁγίων in 6:1 indicates that the former term refers in general to those outside the church (cf. v.9). Paul is not referring to the injustice of the Corinthian legal system, *contra* B.W. Winter, 'Civil Litigation in Secular Corinth and the Church', *NTS* 37 (1991), pp.559–72.

arise, Paul would rather they were settled within the church (6:5), but he also makes it clear that the very existence of such disputes is a sign of failure (6:7–8). The presence of wrongdoing (ἀδικεῖτε v.8) within the fellowship undermines Paul's distinction between holy insiders and unrighteous outsiders, and as a result of this, his warning that the unrighteous will not inherit the kingdom of God (6:9) seems to threaten those within the fellowship itself. Reassurance comes in verse 11, where Paul makes it clear that the warning does not apply to his converts, who have been washed, sanctified and justified. The resultant rhetorical effect, however, is a stress on the need for the fellowship to separate itself from the sinful outside world and to maintain its own distinctive identity as a righteous and holy community.

At 1 Corinthians 6:12, the focus of attention shifts from the boundaries of the social body towards the boundaries of the physical body of the individual, as Paul returns to the subject of sexual immorality.[73] Paul points out that the body belongs to the Lord and is destined for resurrection with him (vv.12–14). Although each believer's body is spiritually united with Christ and so a member of Christ, sexual intercourse with a prostitute involves taking this member out of Christ's body, and making it a member of the prostitute's body through the act of coitus. For Paul, this is unthinkable (vv.15–17). Paul singles out sexual immorality as the only sin that one can commit against one's own body, which is the temple of the Holy Spirit and as such should be used to glorify God (vv.18–20).

Paul's claim that only sexual immorality entails sinning against one's own body has occasioned protests that drunkenness, gluttony, drug-abuse and suicide should also be seen as sins against the body.[74] Yet none of these sins breaches bodily boundaries in the same way as intercourse with a prostitute does (v.16).[75] Martin highlights the significance of the interpenetration of boundaries for Paul in this passage, claiming that

---

[73] The subject of individual sexual morality provides a natural point of transition to the Corinthians' letter to Paul. Despite the reservations of Mitchell (*Rhetoric of Reconciliation*, pp.186–91) it remains likely that Paul works his way through their letter in the remainder of 1 Corinthians: Hurd, *Origin*, pp.65–74.

[74] E.g. J. Weiss, *Der erste Korintherbrief* (Göttingen: Vandenhoeck & Ruprecht, 1910), p.135; K.E. Bailey, 'Paul's Theological Foundation for Human Sexuality: 1 Cor. 6:9–20 in the Light of Rhetorical Criticism', *ThRev* 3 (1980), pp.27–41; F. Lang, *Die Briefe an die Korinther* (Göttingen, Vandenhoeck & Ruprecht, 1986), p.84. J. Murphy-O'Connor has argued that 6:18 is a Corinthian slogan, but the transition to v.19 hardly supports this: 'Corinthian Slogans in 1 Cor. 6:12–20', *CBQ* 40 (1978), pp.391–6.

[75] 1 Cor. 6:19 should be interpreted in the light of v.16, *contra* B.N. Fisk, whose interpretation of the phrase as a reference to self-destruction takes its bearings from Sir. 19:2: 'PORNEUEIN as Body Violation: The Unique Place of Sexual Sin in 1 Cor. 6:18', *NTS* 42 (1996), pp.540–58.

72   *Paul and the Power of Sin*

the man's entry into the prostitute entails the copulation of Christ with the evil cosmos, while the man's own body is itself penetrated by sin as he penetrates the woman (v.18).[76]

Martin's case is, however, overstated. Christ is never united to the prostitute, since the man is removed from his union with Christ before his union with the woman (v.15).[77] In addition, εἰς in verse 18 cannot be pushed to mean that sin enters the man's body as he enters the prostitute: ἁμαρτάνειν εἰς occurs in too many other contexts with the clear sense of 'to sin against' to allow this aspect of Martin's thesis any validity.[78] Yet Martin's emphasis on bodily boundaries is correct. Paul sees the inside of the body as good since it is inhabited by the Holy Spirit; the evil of the world outside the body is embodied in the prostitute. The act of intercourse breaks the boundaries around the physical body that keep the two apart. It is in this sense that the man sins against his own body, and the sheer incompatibility of a simultaneous union with Christ and with a prostitute requires the breaking of the former spiritual union before the latter physical union can take place.[79] Again, Paul's perspective on sin is seen to correspond to that of Douglas' small bounded group: sin is an outside evil, which threatens to penetrate the porous boundaries of the body.

The question of boundaries again comes to the fore when Paul sets out his response to the issue of food offered to idols. In the light of their

[76] Martin, *Corinthian Body*, pp.174–9.

[77] Paul's use of ἄρας in v.15 indicates that the man's body is taken away from Christ before being united with the prostitute: J.B. Lightfoot, *Notes on the Epistles of St Paul from unpublished commentaries* (London: Macmillan, 1895), p.216.

[78] Cf. the list of references in R. Kirchhoff, *Die Sünde gegen den eigenen Leib* (Göttingen, Vandenhoeck & Ruprecht, 1994), pp.179–80, nn.302–6. The only other references to sinning against one's own body occur in Aeschines, *Against Timarchus* I 39, 195. Kirchhoff claims that these two references share with 1 Cor. 6:18 the common theme of sexual conduct that is deemed to be incompatible with membership of the community. He concludes that the sin against one's own body is bodily conduct which conflicts with one's status in the community and which leads to a loss of that status (p.181). However, Kirchhoff's thesis is undermined not only by the 400-year time lapse between Aeschines and Paul, but also by the fact that *Against Timarchus* I 39 actually refers to Timarchus' conduct as a youth, which Aeschines freely remits. Thus Aeschines does not claim at all that these sins are incompatible with Timarchus' position as a citizen; the phrase must therefore refer to sins against one's own physical body, rather than the body politic.

[79] A. Schweitzer was right to think in terms of incompatible unions, although he mistakenly referred to a literal physical union between Christ and the elect: *The Mysticism of Paul the Apostle* (London: A&C Black, 1931). E. Käsemann removed the offending elements in his thesis by proposing that σῶμα refers to the individual's capacity for relationships with the Lord and with others: *Perspectives on Paul*, pp.114–15. However, attempts to explain 1 Cor. 6:18 in terms of a disruption of communication between the individual and the Lord miss the importance of boundaries for understanding Paul's thought; cf. N. Watson, *The First Epistle to the Corinthians* (London: Epworth, 1992), pp.57–63; Schrage, *1 Korinther*, vol.II, p.31.

monotheistic knowledge that there is no such thing as an idol, the strong in Corinth were claiming that they were allowed to eat sacrificial food in an idol's temple. The weak, on the other hand, who did not share this knowledge, seem to have regarded as contaminated any meat that had been offered to an idol (8:7). Paul's own position probably falls between these two extremes: he himself sees no difficulty over the consumption of the food *per se*, provided that the consumption of idol food by the strong does not lead the weak to eat and thereby sin against their own conscience (8:9–13; 10:23–11:1). Paul is, however, deeply anxious about the practice of eating in an idol's temple.[80] This is not just because this might make a weak believer stumble (8:10–13), but also because, unlike the strong in Corinth, his knowledge of the one God does not preclude a belief in the reality of demonic powers (10:19–22).[81] Paul thus primarily responds to the Corinthian position in 8:1–13, while his own position emerges more clearly in 10:23–33. Again, Martin highlights the importance of boundaries for understanding the apostle's thought, pointing out the way in which commensality with demons disrupts the firm boundary between Christ and the cosmos, so that the body of the erring Christian becomes the site of permeation between these two incompatible worlds of meaning.[82]

By claiming that the fellowship of the Lord's table precludes eating at the table of demons, Paul attempts to establish the Lord's Supper as a firm boundary marker, separating believers from the social gatherings in idol temples:[83] infringement of that boundary brings the threat of divine retribution (10:22; cf. 10:1–13). In 11:30, Paul points to incidents of

[80]Cf. P. Borgen, ' "Yes", "No", "How Far?": the Participation of Jews and Gentiles in Pagan Cults', in T. Engsberg-Pedersen, ed., *Paul in his Hellenistic Context* (Edinburgh: T&T Clark, 1994), pp. 30–59.

[81]The existence of idols is dismissed in 8:4, which is probably a statement of the position of the strong. Paul, however, cautiously qualifies this view in 8:5–6, in that he allows the existence of so-called gods, but says that 'for us' there is only one God; cf. Barrett, *1 Corinthians*, pp.191–4. In 10:19–21, Paul states that he does not want to attribute any real existence to an idol, but neither does he want the Corinthians to have fellowship with demons. Paul does not want to contradict the strong's claim that an idol has no existence, but he himself does not appear to be convinced of its truth. Similar attitudes are found in Jubilees 11:4–6; 22:16–22; 1 Enoch 19:1; 99:6–10.

[82]Martin, *Corinthian Body*, p.182; H. Lietzmann cites Eusebius' quotation of Porphyry (*Praeparatio Evangelica* 4.3) as evidence for the way in which demons enter the body as a result of the consumption of idol food: *An die Korinther I/II* (Tübingen: J.C.B. Mohr, 1971), p.50. This reference is ignored by W.L. Willis, who argues that cultic meals were social occasions of no sacramental significance: *Idol Meat in Corinth: The Pauline Argument in 1 Corinthians 8 and 10*, SBL 68 (Chico: Scholars, 1985).

[83]Cf. Theissen, *Social Setting*, pp.130–2, for the adverse social impact of Paul's ruling for the strong.

weakness, illness and death within the fellowship as evidence of the way in which God is punishing them for their abuses at the Lord's Supper. His warning that those who fail to discern the body thereby eat and drink judgment upon themselves would appear to correspond to Douglas' claim that there is a magical danger associated with the boundary emblems of the enclave. Those who eat unworthily do so with their eye on their own social standing rather than upon Christ. Paul claims that God is punishing them so that they will not be judged along with the outside world, whose cultural values they have imported into their celebration of the Lord's Supper.

Paul can thus be seen to place a strong emphasis on the importance of the social and physical boundaries separating the good inside from the bad outside in 1 Corinthians 5–6, 8–10. This is a characteristic feature of the cosmology of the small bounded group. It has also been shown how, in 1 Corinthians, Paul portrays sin as an outside evil threatening to penetrate the boundaries surrounding the good inside of the social body of the church and the physical bodies of its members. Paul's response was to try and strengthen the boundaries and to maintain the good inner purity of the body, even by expelling a deviant member, if necessary.

It has been suggested that the problems in Corinth arose because the leaders in the church were located in the high grid/low group quadrant of competitive individualism. These 'Big Men' accepted the values of the surrounding competitive culture and had little sense of sin. Paul attempted to dissociate the Corinthians from their acceptance of the values of the surrounding culture by identifying himself and the gospel with the cross and other symbols of debasement. But this low grid technique of reinforcing boundaries backfired with the Corinthians. For those success-oriented Corinthians who belonged to the quadrant of competitive individualism, Paul's self-disparagement probably facilitated their rejection of him in favour of the super-apostles of 2 Corinthians 10–13.[84] In this case, we would appear to have an example of Paul's low grid/high group message being misinterpreted or misrepresented by his high grid/low group audience.

Given the extent to which Paul addresses the subject of sin in 1 Corinthians, it is perhaps surprising that he makes scarcely any reference to sin as a power. Were the power of sin an established feature of Paul's anthropology, one might expect Paul to refer to it in an attempt to sharpen the relatively undeveloped sense of sin among the low group/high grid members of the church. It is noteworthy that Paul does not do so. Indeed,

[84]Cf. Neyrey, *Paul*, pp.207–18.

the one reference to the power of sin comes in 1 Corinthians 15:56, where the law is identified as the power of sin, and even this reference is probably a gloss, despite the lack of supporting textual evidence.[85] The omission of 1 Corinthians 15:56 gives a far smoother reading, with Paul's offer of thanksgiving following immediately after the triumphant questioning of verses 54–55. The intrusive verse betrays a marked change in style from the doxology of the surrounding verses, and gives a rather wooden soteriological identification of the sting of death and its power. There is a clear motivation for just such an insertion, in as much as verse 57 picks up the reference to 'victory' from verses 54–5, which is snatched from death and given to believers through the Lord Jesus Christ. This, however, leaves unresolved the meaning of the 'sting' of death, and opens the door for the insertion of an explanatory gloss. However, for the Corinthian congregation, who did not have the opportunity of turning back a few pages to read Paul's letter to the Romans, the verse would have been virtually incomprehensible.[86] Paul has made no connection at all between the law and sin in this letter, and the phrase looks like an insertion made by a follower of Paul on the basis of the apostle's letter to Rome.

Even if Pauline authorship of this verse is admitted, it cannot be interpreted with reference to 1 Corinthians. If Paul wrote 1 Corinthians after Galatians,[87] it is possible that this thought strayed into 1 Corinthians from the controversy in Galatia. Here the power of sin plays a part in Paul's struggle with his opponents there over the nature of the boundaries surrounding the community. Reacting to Paul's neglect of Torah, the agitators in Galatia were insisting on circumcision as a boundary marker, whereas Paul insists that Spirit reception is sufficient. In the next chapter on Galatians, it will be argued that Paul refers to the power of sin as a way of denoting the evil beyond the boundaries of the community. The conception of sin is no different from that in 1 Corinthians, but Paul develops the symbolism of the power of sin as part of his strategy to redraw the

---

[85]Cf. Weiss, *1 Korintherbrief*; Moffatt, *Corinthians*, p.268; J. Héring, *The First Epistle of St. Paul to the Corinthians* (London: Epworth, 1962), p.182. F.W. Horn's discussion puts the burden of proof on those who wish to defend its authenticity: '1 Korinther 15.56: Ein exegetischer Stachel', *ZNW* 82 (1991), pp.88–105.

[86]This is disputed by H.W. Hollander and J. Holleman, 'The Relationship of Death, Sin and Law in 1 Cor. 15:56', *NovT* 35 (1993), pp.270–91. They argue that Paul's language would have been comprehensible to his Greek readers, who disparaged law as an ineffective means of repelling human wickedness. However, 1 Cor. 15:56 goes far beyond this in claiming that sin is actually empowered by the law.

[87]R. Jewett's chronological reconstruction is accepted here, according to which 1 Corinthians was written, after Galatians, in 55 CE: *Dating Paul's Life* (London: SCM, 1979).

boundaries around the Galatian church. It is thus possible that 1 Corinthians 15:56 is a Pauline aside which reflects this controversy. Yet whether this verse is a gloss or Paul wrote it himself, it is important to note that it links sin and the law in a way that is more characteristic of Galatians and Romans than of anything Paul writes elsewhere in 1 Corinthians.

Conclusion

Douglas' matrix has been extensively used by Pauline scholars, who have come to quite differing conclusions when they have applied the model to 1 Corinthians. Often this has been because they have used the model as a quick-reference system to substantiate their case. The most thorough application of the model to 1 Corinthians was undertaken by Neyrey, but his failure to analyse the social situation in Corinth itself leads to the false conclusion that the letter should be understood in terms of a clash between ritualism and effervescence.

The approach adopted here has distinguished between the Corinthians themselves and Paul, and has examined the letter for their different attitudes to social cohesion and to the outside world. The Corinthians were found to be low group/high grid, with a lack of concern for corporate unity and a readiness to engage with the surrounding culture. An analysis of the characteristics of the Big Man societies on which Douglas based this quadrant highlighted many parallels between the cosmology of these societies and attitudes in Corinth. The local leaders in the church at Corinth were socially advantaged individuals who competed with each other for social status and advancement. Their relatively secular and amoral cosmology resulting from this social location forms a contrast with the more conservative views of Paul's supporters in the church, who adhered to the values of the small bounded group, and who advocated a clear demarcation between the community and the world.

This application of the model to Corinth indicates that the model can be used to cast light on fairly complicated social situations. At the same time one can see that it is possible to use the definitions of grid and group adopted here to analyse a historical community through the medium of one of Paul's letters.

Regarding the apostle himself, it has been argued that Paul should be located within the high group/low grid quadrant of the enclave. The basis for this is that the apostle has a high concern for group unity and at the same time rejects the values and symbol system of Hellenistic society outside the church. Paul's concern is to maintain clear boundaries separating the good inside of the social and physical body from the evil outside. It has been shown that Paul perceives sin in this letter as an outside evil threatening the boundaries of the body, which must be dealt with by the expulsion of deviant members from the community, thereby both symbolically maintaining the inner purity of the social body of the community and saving the spirit within the physical body of the man concerned. This perception of sin resurfaces in 6:12–20, where fornication is singled out as a sin against the body because of the way it entails a breach of bodily boundaries. Such exegetical insights would appear to validate the use of the model to provide an interpretive framework for reading 1 Corinthians.

In accordance with his high group/low grid location, Paul's preoccupation in 1 Corinthians is the establishment of clear boundaries separating the community from the world. This concern is apparent in his attempt to persuade the church to reject worldly standards and values in 1 Corinthians 1–4. Correspondingly, a desire to establish clear boundaries provides a common theme in his treatment of the incestuous man (5:1–13), the practice of litigation (6:1–11), the problem of sexual immorality (6:12–20) and the Lord's Supper (11:17–34). On the issues of marriage (7:1–40) and idol feasts (8:1–13; 10:1–11:1), Paul's supporters were more conservative than the apostle himself and advocated a more rigorous separation between the church and the world than he was willing to endorse. On these issues, Paul seeks to find a middle way between the strong and the weak in the Corinthian church. However, perhaps partly as a result of their different social location, the strong rejected Paul's emphasis on low grid values and were more attracted by the overtly powerful ministry of the super-apostles to whom Paul refers in 2 Corinthians 10–13.

Since 1 Corinthians 15:56 is probably to be regarded as a gloss, it is noteworthy that Paul did not make use of the symbolism of sin as a power in 1 Corinthians, despite the problems he experienced with the Corinthians' relatively undeveloped sense of sin. As suggested in the introduction, that may well be because Paul only develops the symbolism of the power of sin in response to the issue of the relationship between Jews and Gentiles within the church. It is now time to turn to Galatians and Romans, where Paul addresses this issue, and to see whether in these letters Paul has the same concern for boundary definition as he had in 1 Corinthians, and if so, how the symbolism of the power of sin relates to this concern.

4

EXCLUSIVE BOUNDARIES IN GALATIA

Introduction

Paul's letter to the Galatians contains one clear reference to sin as a power, where Paul says that scripture has confined all things under sin (3:22). The noun ἁμαρτία also occurs in 1:4, but this time in the plural, where Paul refers to Christ giving himself for our sins, in order to rescue us from the present evil age. It also occurs in 2:17, where Paul addresses the question whether Christ is the servant of sin. In addition, the concept of sin is found elsewhere in the letter, even though Paul does not use the term ἁμαρτία: in Galatians 5:16–21; 6:8, he describes sinful behaviour in terms of 'works of the flesh'; in 2:15–21, he refers to 'Gentile sinners' and defends himself against the accusation that those who seek to be justified in Christ are found to be sinners in the process. Paul denies the charge, stating that if he is again building the things that he destroyed, he demonstrates that he is a transgressor.

Clearly these references to sin must be understood in the context of the letter as a whole. Paul wrote to the Galatians to counter what he regards as a false gospel (1:6–9), proclaimed by outsiders, who were attempting to persuade his Galatian converts to accept circumcision (5:2–3; 6:12–13). The emphasis on circumcision points decisively towards a Jewish identity for the agitators,[1] while the fact that they proclaim a different gospel

---

[1]*Contra* W. Michaelis, 'Judaistische Heidenchristen', *ZNW* 30 (1931), pp.83–9; J. Munck, *Paul and the Salvation of Mankind* (London: SCM, 1959), pp.87–9; L. Gaston, *Paul and the Torah* (British Columbia: University of British Columbia Press, 1987), p.81; all argue that the present middle or passive participle περιτεμνόμενοι in 6:13 (ℵ A C Dᵍʳ K P) identifies the agitators as Gentiles who have accepted circumcision (cf. 5:3). However, it is difficult to see how Gentile Christians who had accepted circumcision could avoid persecution by persuading others to be circumcised as well (6:12). Alternatively, according to F.F. Bruce, *The Epistle to the Galatians*, NIGNTC (Exeter: Paternoster, 1982), p.270, the participle may denote Jewish agitators, who advocate circumcision to avoid persecution and to boast in the Galatians' flesh. Such personal motivations for their policy would be highlighted by Paul's use of the middle voice for the participle; cf. Porter, *Idioms*, p.67. If the reading περιτετμημένοι is adopted, Paul's use of the perfect participle in 1 Cor. 7:18

(1:6–9) indicates that they were also Christians. Their concern to make full proselytes of Gentile believers[2] may have had its origins in a desire to avoid the church becoming a target for persecution by Jewish nationalists who attacked those who failed to maintain clear boundaries separating Jew from Gentile (6:12; cf. 2:12; 5:11).[3] The agitators could be identified with those who came from James and ended open table fellowship at Antioch, who then moved on to Galatia, taking with them a message of the need for circumcision and a full conversion to Judaism.[4] Paul himself had probably visited the Galatian churches after the incident at Antioch to warn them of just such a possibility (1:9), which would account for his amazement at the news of their rapid defection (1:6).[5]

Galatians is Paul's response to the arguments of the agitators. He defends himself against the charge that his gospel had a human origin, asserting on the contrary that he received his gospel through a revelation of Jesus Christ (1:1, 11–12). Paul insists that he did not receive his gospel 'second hand' from the apostles in Jerusalem, while at the same time he also maintains that his gospel received full recognition and approval from those same apostles (1:13–2:10).[6] His exposition of the gospel in the letter is set against the background of the alleged hypocrisy of Cephas at Antioch (2:11–21).

In the central section of the letter (3:1–5:1), Paul fights the agitators on their own ground, as he reworks their scriptural arguments[7] to demonstrate

would also indicate the Jewish identity of the agitators, *contra* R. Longenecker, *Galatians*, WBC (Dallas: Word, 1990), p.292.

[2] This is the implication of their advocacy of circumcision; full conversion to Judaism normally entailed getting circumcised: J. Nolland, 'Uncircumcised proselytes?', *Journal for the Study of Judaism* 12 (1981), pp.173–94.

[3] So R. Jewett, 'The Agitators and the Galatian Congregation', *NTS* 17 (1970), pp.198–211.

[4] J.D.G. Dunn plausibly suggests this, on the basis that Paul did not win the confrontation at Antioch; the decision taken at Antioch would have been applicable to the churches in South Galatia, since these had been founded by the Antiochene mission: *The Epistle to the Galatians* (London: A&C Black, 1993), pp.9–20.

[5] This makes sense in the light of Jewett's *Dating Paul's Life*; his hypothesis withstands Longenecker's criticisms (*Galatians*, pp.lxxv–lxxvii). According to Jewett, Gal. 2:1–10 is Paul's record of the Jerusalem Conference (Acts 15:1–29), which took place in October 51, after Paul's Corinthian ministry, when he went up and visited the church in Jerusalem, as mentioned briefly in Acts 18:22. After the conference, Paul returned to Antioch, where he confronted Cephas. According to Acts 18:23, Paul then returned to the territory of (South) Galatia and Phrygia (cf. the implied reference to a second visit in Gal. 4:13), and this is when he would have given the warning of 1:9 and mentioned the collection (1 Cor. 16:1–3). He then went to Ephesus, from where he wrote Galatians; Jewett suggests 53 CE as the date of writing (pp.162–3).

[6] J.D.G. Dunn, *Jesus, Paul and the Law* (London: SPCK, 1990), pp.108–28.

[7] C.K. Barrett, 'The Allegory of Abraham, Sarah and Hagar in the Argument of Galatians', *Essays on Paul* (London: SPCK, 1982), pp.154–70.

that the blessings of God's covenant with Abraham are inherited by those
who receive the Spirit as a result of believing the gospel; in contrast,
those who accept circumcision and Torah are cut off from Christ (5:2–6).
He continues to fight on the same front in Galatians 5:2–6:10,[8] where he
defends his gospel by arguing that the Spirit provides an adequate guide
to moral behaviour in the absence of the law. As Paul closes the letter
in his own hand, he attacks the agitators and claims that the distinction
between circumcision and uncircumcision has been abolished in God's
new creation (6:11–18). Galatians has aptly been described as a dialogical
response to Paul's opponents: 'It is a letter motivated by an intruding,
offending theology, yet it addresses the theology almost exclusively by
addressing the congregation that has been "bewitched" by the intruders.'[9]

The theme of 'bewitchment' has been explored by Neyrey in his application of Douglas' 'Grid and Group' matrix to the clash between Paul
and his opponents.[10] When Paul asks τίς ὑμᾶς ἐβάσκανεν (Gal. 3:1),
Neyrey points out that he uses a technical term in the classical Mediterranean world for the evil eye that harms and kills[11] in order to accuse his
opponents of witchcraft and so have them expelled from the community
(Gal. 4:30). According to his own particular development of the model,
Neyrey uses the horizontal 'group' axis to measure the extent to which a
particular symbolic universe is ordered and structured, while the vertical
'grid' axis measures the extent to which members of the social group accept that ordering and find it confirmed in their experience. Neyrey claims
that Paul saw the cosmos as holy and ordered under the sovereignty of
God, which was expressed in his successive covenants with Abraham
and Moses. In his death, Christ summed up the Abrahamic covenant of
faith and ended the Mosaic covenant of law. However, the appearance in
Galatia of 'Judaisers' who preached another gospel in their adherence to
the Mosaic covenant represented a chaotic threat to Paul's highly ordered
cosmology.[12]

[8]Cf. J. Barclay, *Obeying the Truth: a Study of Paul's Ethics in Galatians* (Edinburgh: T&T Clark, 1988).

[9]B.H. Brinsmead, *Galatians – Dialogical Response to Opponents*, SBL Diss. 65 (Chico: Scholars, 1982), p.187.

[10]Neyrey, 'Bewitched', cf. *Paul*, pp.181–206 (and pp.207–17 on 2 Cor. 10–13); also B.J. Malina and J.H. Neyrey, 'Jesus the Witch: Witchcraft Accusations in Matthew 12', in D.G. Horrell, ed., *Social-Scientific Approaches to New Testament Interpretation* (Edinburgh: T&T Clark, 1999), pp.29–67.

[11]Cf. J.H. Elliott, 'The Fear of the Leer: The Evil Eye from the Bible to Li'l Abner', *Forum* 4/4 (1988), pp.42–71.

[12]Neyrey identifies this cosmology as 'strong group/rising grid' ('Bewitched', p.76 n.16), but this definition bears little resemblance to Neyrey's own definitions of grid and group. Instead it is taken from Douglas' description of a typical witchcraft cosmology in *Natural Symbols* (2nd edition, 1973), although Neyrey confusingly refers the reader to

Neyrey explores the ways in which Paul uses rituals in order to create boundaries around the community and to expel invading pollutants that cross those boundaries. The most significant boundary line lies between the two covenants; it is a line which Paul himself crossed by an act of God's grace (1:13–16) and which he himself now draws in Galatians 3–5. By contrasting freedom and slavery, heaven and earth, spirit and flesh, Paul focuses on the basic distinctions between Christians and Jews in such a way as to emphasise that these are two mutually exclusive systems or ways of serving God.[13]

In contrast to this rigid ordering of the cosmos, Neyrey argues that the personal identity of both Paul and his opponents is shrouded in ambiguity. Paul is accused of preaching circumcision and pleasing people rather than God (5:11; 1:10), while his relationship to the leaders at Jerusalem is quite ambivalent (2:1–10); in turn, Paul accuses his opponents of masquerading as good, while in reality they are evil.

Neyrey then argues that the Galatian situation displays each one of six characteristics of a typical witchcraft society.[14] There are clearly marked external boundaries, but internal relations are confused (1), since there is no mechanism in place to sort out the competing claims of Paul and his opponents (2). Neyrey claims there is also close and unavoidable interaction between Paul and his churches (3), although he cannot substantiate this from Galatians.[15] The conflict in Galatia reveals underdeveloped tension-relieving techniques (4) and weakens Paul's authority over the congregation (5); the net result is intense, disorderly competition for leadership (6).

Neyrey then turns to Douglas' definition of a witch as one whose external appearance deceptively masks corrupt insides, and who attacks the pure and innocent by life-sucking or by poison. Neyrey struggles to meet these criteria. It is true, as Neyrey says, that Paul declares that the law produces a curse and that no one can be justified by the law (3:11; 2:16), but this does not mean that the agitators have corrupt insides, although

the 3rd US edition (1982), where witchcraft societies are identified as strong group/low grid.
  [13]Cf. J.L. Martyn, *Theological Issues in the Letters of Paul* (Edinburgh: T&T Clark, 1997), pp.111–23. Martyn insists that these apocalyptic distinctions only apply within the church and do not refer to Judaism (pp.77–88). However, while it is true that Paul's argument in Galatians is only directed against Jewish Christian agitators in the church, his polemical technique entails an attack on *all* those under the law.
  [14]Cf. M. Douglas, ed., *Witchcraft Accusations and Confessions* (London: Tavistock, 1979), pp.xi–xxviii; *Natural Symbols* (1st edition, 1970), pp.99–124.
  [15]Neyrey appeals to Paul's use of messengers (1 Cor. 4:17; 16:10; 2 Cor. 7:6, 13–14; 1 Thess. 3:2, 6), the oral reports and letters he receives from his churches (1 Cor. 1:11; 7:1) and his own written replies. It is debatable whether this constitutes 'close and unavoidable interaction'.

Paul does accuse them of falsehood. Surprisingly, Neyrey does not refer to Paul's charge that the agitators want to pervert the gospel (1:7), or that they desire to make a good outward show without really keeping the law (6:12–13). Paul's reference to leaven (5:9) can scarcely be compared to the ingestion of poison, as Neyrey suggests; nor may Galatians 2:2; 3:3; 4:10–11 be taken as evidence of 'life-sucking' on the part of the infiltrators. Nevertheless Neyrey goes on to cite Galatians 3:1; 1:8 as examples of 'witchcraft accusations', which identify Paul's opponents with Satan or one of his minions as part of his social strategy to discredit his rivals and persuade the Galatians to expel the 'witches' and so purify the holy group (4:30).

Notwithstanding the way in which Neyrey sometimes seems to force the evidence of the letter to fit Douglas' criteria, he is right to see the situation in Galatia as one in which witchcraft accusations would flourish, and he correctly identifies the political motive behind the accusation of 3:1. However, Neyrey only addresses the issue of sin and deviance in Galatians very briefly: he claims that Paul's strong sense of purity is reflected in the way that his list of the works of the flesh echoes the prohibitions of the Decalogue, transgression of which will result in the loss of eternal salvation. Drawing on the high group/low grid idea of sin as a pollutant, Neyrey also refers to Paul's labelling of the doctrine and practice of the Judaisers as leaven (5:9), but the references in the letter to sin and sinners are not mentioned. Thus there would seem to be scope for developing Neyrey's application of the matrix to analyse Paul's use of the concept of sin in this letter, particularly since there are aspects of Douglas' analysis of witchcraft societies that he has not applied to the letter.

Applying 'Grid and Group' to Galatians

Applying his own definitions of grid and group to Galatians, Neyrey argued that Paul is strong group/low grid at this point, since his highly structured and ordered view of the universe is under attack from the 'Judaisers'. However, since Neyrey's version of the matrix has not been adopted in this study, it is necessary to begin by examining the letter for indications of grid and group as defined above, namely acceptance or rejection of the prevailing symbolic system of classification, and the extent of integration in a bounded social unit.

In Galatians 6:14, Paul clearly reveals his own negative view of the social system: through the cross of Christ, the world has been crucified to him, as he has been crucified to the world. As in 1 Corinthians, the cross functions here as a symbol for the rejection of society's values. Paul seeks to identify the Galatians with the cross, by reminding them how, in his initial preaching, he had portrayed Christ crucified before their eyes (3:1); he also makes the point that those who belong to Christ have crucified the flesh with its passions and desires (5:24). While Paul attempts to associate the Galatians with the cross, he distances the infiltrators from it, claiming that they simply want to persuade the Galatians to be circumcised in order to avoid persecution for the cross of Christ (6:12; cf. 5:11).

Turning to the Galatians themselves, their initial readiness to embrace the message about the cross of Christ (3:1–2) could be taken as evidence of low grid, while their turning away from idol worship in response to the gospel (4:8–9)[16] indicates a readiness to set aside the prevailing religious practices of the surrounding culture. The Galatians' apparent readiness to consider accepting circumcision cannot be taken as evidence of a move up-grid, given the social dislocation that such a step entailed.[17] It would therefore seem that the Galatians were prepared to follow Paul in a low grid rejection of the values and standards of the surrounding society.

Concerning 'group', Paul stresses the unity of the church, saying that they are all one in Christ Jesus (3:28). This image of being a single person develops Paul's statement that as many as have been baptised into Christ have been clothed with Christ (3:27), a claim that clearly identifies baptism as a rite of entry into the group. Furthermore, Paul is concerned that group unity should find practical expression in a mutual care and concern (5:13–14; 6:1–2, 10), which indicates a 'high group' view of the church as a united, caring fellowship, into which baptism marks a clearly defined point of entry.

Yet the Galatians did not apparently experience the unity and harmony that Paul advocates. His appeals for mutual care seem to have been written in response to members in the church 'biting and devouring' each other (5:15),[18] and Paul has to warn them against conceit, rivalry and jealousy (5:26), since some in the congregation seem to have deluded themselves into thinking that they were something whereas in reality they were nothing (6:3). Such disunity could be taken as an expression of individualistic

---

[16]Paul's complaint that they are reverting to serve the weak and beggarly elements does not indicate that they are returning to false gods; Paul is rather associating the Torah with angels and the elemental spirits of the world (3:19; 4:1–3). His intention is also to identify the Jewish festivals they now observe (4:10) with the pagan practices they had left behind.

[17]Cf. Philo, *Spec. Leg.* 1.52; 4.178; Josephus, *Ant.* 20.38–9; Tacitus, *Hist.* 5:5.1–2. Cf. J. Barclay, *Obeying the Truth*, pp.45–60; *Jews in the Mediterranean Diaspora: From Alexander to Trajan (323 BCE – 117 CE)* (Edinburgh: T&T Clark, 1996), pp.408–10.

[18]The theory that Paul is responding to a specific Galatian situation in 5:16–26 is supported by the way in which half of the following list of 'works of the flesh' refer to community conflict: ἔχθραι, ἔρις, θυμοί, ἐριθεῖαι, διχοστασίαι, αἱρέσεις, φθόνοι; cf. Barclay, *Obeying the Truth.*

low group, or it could reflect the kind of factionalism that is a feature of the low grid/high group enclave.

A low group rating would place the Galatians in the quadrant either of competitive individualism or of relative isolation. In Corinth, rivalry was found to be a feature of the high grid/low group quadrant of competitive individualism, but since it has already been established that the Galatians were low grid, this quadrant cannot apply to them. Furthermore, rivalry and jealousy are not typical characteristics of the low group/low grid quadrant, since relationships here are too diffuse for such tensions to develop.[19] Inasmuch as the Galatians do not fit into either 'low group' quadrant of the matrix, it would seem preferable to understand the disunity as internal factionalism within the small bounded group. Such factionalism is often focused on a struggle for leadership, and Paul's warnings against conceit and rivalry serve well as responses to this kind of conflict.[20] It is therefore possible to conclude that the Galatian situation corresponded to Paul's low grid/high group view of the church as a small bounded group, distinct from the surrounding culture. One would therefore expect the Galatians to share Paul's own concerns about group cohesion and boundaries and to interpret his letter accordingly.

The combination of strong boundaries and weak leadership is characteristic of the kind of social unit that is subject to witchcraft accusations, and these are clearly present in the letter. It is possible that in 1:10–12, 16–17, Paul defends himself against the accusation that he only had an inaccurate second-hand knowledge of the gospel, and that he preached whatever would please his audience, and even sometimes advocated circumcision, if it suited the occasion (5:11). Paul vigorously denies such slanders and responds with counter-accusations of his own. He accuses the agitators of perverting the gospel (1:7) and hints that their teaching has a demonic origin (1:8; 3:1; 5:7–8). They are insincere and do not keep the law themselves: their sole aim is to avoid persecution for the cross of Christ and get the Galatians to change allegiance to their side (6:12–13), even if that means the Galatians are excluded from Christ in the process (4:17; 5:4).

Reading Galatians in the light of the cosmology of the small bounded group highlights the presence of witchcraft accusations in the letter, and

---

[19]Cf. Douglas, *Witchcraft Accusations*, p.xxx: '... among people who have very sparse, irregular social contacts, the cosmos is likely to be less dominated by the idea of dangerous human beings than in a society in which human interaction is close.'

[20]The nature of the conflict over leadership in the small bounded group is different from rivalry between leaders in the quadrant of competitive individualism: the former is marked by struggles over leadership of the group itself; the latter is marked by competition for status between different leaders.

Neyrey is right to interpret the conflict between Paul and his opponents in these terms. However, there are two important facets of Douglas' analysis of witchcraft cosmologies that Neyrey does not apply to Galatians. The first is Douglas' argument that the function of witchcraft accusations varies, depending on whether the witch is perceived as an outsider or an internal enemy.[21] Where the witch is an outsider, the function of the accusation is to reaffirm group boundaries and solidarity. Where the witch is an insider, there are a number of different possibilities. If the accused is the leader of a rival faction, the accusation serves to redefine faction boundaries and realign the hierarchy or even to split the community. If the witch is a dangerous deviant, the accusation serves as a means of exerting control in the name of community values. If the witch is an internal enemy with outside liaisons, the accusations promote factional rivalry, and may split the community or redefine the hierarchy.

In the case of Galatians, there can be no doubt that Paul perceives the agitators as outsiders who have come into the community (cf. 5:7). This means that a key part of his response to them will be a reaffirmation of group boundaries. Neyrey does focus on boundaries in his analysis, but he perceives the agitators as a threat to the existing boundaries of Paul's cosmos. It will be argued below that in Galatians, Paul in fact is engaged in the task of redefining the boundaries around the community in such a way as to exclude the intruders.

The second feature of Douglas' work ignored by Neyrey is an important summary of the four general characteristics of the witchcraft cosmology in *Natural Symbols*: '... the idea of the bad outside and the good inside, the inside under attack and in need of protection, human wickedness on a cosmic scale, and these ideas used in political manipulation'.[22] Since the power of sin symbolises universal wickedness on a cosmic scale, it will be worth investigating the role played by this symbolism in the witchcraft accusations in the letter.

It is the intention of this chapter to examine how the idea of human wickedness on a cosmic scale is combined with the idea of the good inside and the bad outside in the political manipulations of both Paul and his opponents. The issue at stake is that of where the boundaries between bad outsiders and good insiders are to be drawn. Paul's Jewish opponents essentially defined the boundaries in terms of law observance: those who adhered to the Jewish works of the law could be classed as righteous insiders, while those who did not, including Paul and his uncircumcised

---

[21] *Witchcraft Accusations*, pp.xxvi–xxvii.
[22] *Natural Symbols*, 1st edition (1970), p.114; 2nd edition (1973), p.140.

Gentile converts, belonged outside, in the class of sinners.[23] Paul responds by emphasising the boundary markers of Spirit reception and baptism. As far as the apostle is concerned, the good inside group are those who 'in Christ' share in the eschatological age of the Spirit, which is entered solely on the basis of faith in Christ. His Gentile converts are, however, under attack from infiltrators preaching a false gospel of circumcision (1:7; 4:17; 5:7; 6:12). Paul responds by redrawing the boundaries to emphasise that those who are under the law are sinful outsiders, because they still belong to the present evil age and are under the power of sin. Douglas' model suggests that Galatians should be understood in terms of a high group/low grid dispute over how to draw clear boundaries separating righteous insider from sinful outsider. Both Paul and his opponents make use of 'witchcraft accusations' in order to seek to place each other beyond the pale of the righteous.

Redrawing the boundaries

As Paul and his opponents struggle for the leadership over the Galatian congregations, both sides have a vested interest in redrawing the existing boundaries in such a way as to establish their own leadership over the insider group, while at the same time leaving their opponents on the outside. This can most easily be shown in diagrammatic form.

In figure 4, the circle on the left represents the Jewish group, whose boundaries are defined in terms of law observance, while the circle on the right represents the Christians, whose faith in Christ marks them off from the surrounding world. In the centre of the diagram, these circles overlap at the point where faith in Christ coincides with observance of the law: this central section represents the Jewish Christianity of Paul's opponents, who define themselves over against the surrounding world, both in terms of their observance of the law, and in terms of their faith in Christ. But the boundaries around this inner group also exclude the outer portions of each circle. Jewish believers are distinguished from their fellow Jews under the law, because the latter do not believe in Jesus as Messiah. While Gentile Christians share this belief, their failure to observe the law leaves them in their impure Gentile state, and thus also outside the boundaries of the community of God's people.

---

[23] P.F. Esler rightly warns against assuming that these boundaries prevented all social interaction between Jews and Gentiles: *Galatians* (London: Routledge, 1998), pp.77–81. On the contrary, boundaries prohibit interaction only at certain levels (usually connubium and commensality), in order to provide clear behavioural signals of membership and exclusion, which thus enable group members to maintain their own distinctive identity as they interact with outsiders in other non-prohibited ways; cf. F. Barth, *Ethnic Groups and Boundaries: The Social Organisation of Culture Difference* (London: Allen & Unwin, 1970), pp.9–38.

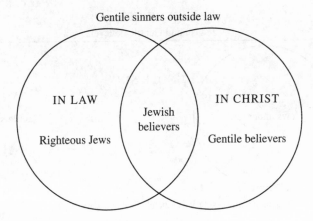

Figure 4: The present boundaries in Galatia.

It is this characteristically Jewish perception of the law as a necessary boundary marker that distinguishes righteous Jew from sinful Gentile that motivated the advocates of circumcision in Galatia. They would have perceived the admission of uncircumcised Gentile believers into the church as a corruption of the purity of God's holy people, and the attempt to persuade Paul's converts to accept circumcision was intended to draw them into the fold of Judaism, so that Christianity should maintain its former identity as a Jewish sect, safely separated from the contamination of the surrounding Gentile world by the Jewish law. The aim of Paul's opponents is thus represented in figure 5.

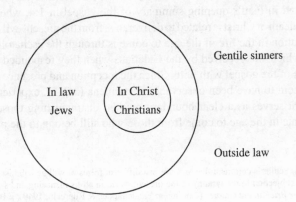

Figure 5: Christianity as a Jewish sect.

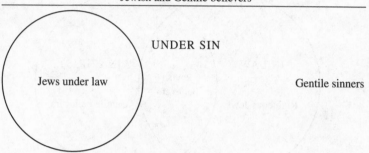

Figure 6: Paul's exclusive eschatological boundary.

Here, the circle of those who are in Christ has been drawn completely into the circle of Judaism. Thus the entire Christian community is separated from the outside world by the Jewish law, and the church is no longer subject to the threat of contamination from uncircumcised believers, who do not keep the law. Christians continue to be distinguished from unbelieving Jews by their faith in Christ. According to this model, Paul's abandonment of the law marks him out as a heretic, and places him and his followers outside the crucial boundary of the law that separates good insider from sinful outsider.

The way in which Paul himself seeks to redraw the boundaries in response to the crisis in Galatia is set out in Figure 6.

Here Paul divides humankind along eschatological lines, into those who are in Christ, and those who are not. This division is very clearly articulated in Paul's opening summary of the gospel in 1:4, where the atoning death of Christ is related to deliverance from the present evil age.[24] Participation in the life of the age to come is through the eschatological Spirit, which was received by the Galatians when they responded to the message of the gospel with faith. Since the reception and presence of the Spirit seem to have been observable phenomena (3:2–5), experience of the Spirit serves as a clear boundary marker, distinguishing those who participate in the age to come from those who still belong to the present evil age.

---

[24]Cf. H. Schlier's comment that sins are just different forms of willing submission and unwilling subjection to the tyranny of the present world in all its menacing and seductive power: *Der Brief an die Galater* (Göttingen: Vandenhoeck & Ruprecht, 1949), p.10.

To express transfer into this new aeon, Paul uses the symbolism of dying and rising with Christ, or more specifically, of co-crucifixion with Christ, in order to share in the life of the eschaton. So, in Galatians 2:19–20, Paul states that he has died to the law, so that he might live to God; he has been crucified with Christ, so that he no longer lives, but Christ lives in him. Those who belong to Christ have crucified the flesh, and live instead by the Spirit (Gal. 5:24–25). In Galatians 6:14, Paul makes his boast in the cross, which is the means by which the world is crucified to him and he to the world.[25] On the negative side, the law is associated with the flesh and the world as elements of the old aeon from which Paul has been released by dying with Christ; on the positive side, living by the Spirit and a new creation clearly denote participation in the eschatological life, something that is also implicit in the reference to 'living to God' in 2:19.[26] As a result of this transfer, neither circumcision nor uncircumcision counts for anything at all: all that counts is a new creation (6:15). In this way, ethnic boundaries have been scrubbed out and replaced with a new eschatological distinction between those who share in the life of the eschaton and those who do not.

The second boundary marker to which Paul appeals is that of baptism into Christ, which constituted a visible rite of entry into the Christian group (3:26–27).[27] For those 'in Christ', all unequal social distinctions are abolished, including the distinction between Jew and Greek that Paul's opponents are seeking to maintain, for in Christ neither circumcision nor uncircumcision count for anything: all that matters is faith working through love (5:6). This abolition of social distinctions within the social unity is typical of the small, bounded group on Douglas' matrix. Within such groups, it is the boundary, with its distinction between insider and outsider, which is the main definer of roles. Paul uses the phrase 'in Christ' to denote the righteous in-group of the eschatological community.

Since, within Douglas' small bounded group, the boundary provides the only crucial distinction between insider and outsider, it is no surprise to see that Paul uses the phrase 'in Christ' exclusively of law-free believers. Throughout the letter, the phrase 'in Christ' is used to define the position

[25]Cf. Bruce, *Galatians*, p.271: 'Because Paul has been "crucified with Christ" (2:19), the cross is a barrier by which the world is permanently "fenced off" from him and he from the world.'

[26]Cf. 4 Macc. 7:19; Luke. 20:37–38; also Rom. 6:10–11; 14:8; cf. C.H. Cosgrove, *The Cross and the Spirit: a Study of the Argument and Theology of Galatians* (Macon: Mercer, 1988), p.140.

[27]Cf. E.J. Christiansen, *The Covenant in Judaism and Paul: A Study of Ritual Boundaries as Identity Markers* (Leiden: E.J. Brill, 1995).

of believers over against those who are in, or under, the Jewish law. Being 'in Christ' and being 'in the law' are posed as mutually exclusive alternatives, so that to be in one group necessarily entails finding oneself on the outside of the other. It was the churches 'in Christ' that Paul persecuted while he was 'in Judaism' (1:13, 22). In Jerusalem, the freedom of Gentile believers in Christ is threatened by the advocates of circumcision, who are seeking to bring them into bondage (2:4). Justification in Christ is contrasted with the impossibility of justification through the law in 2:16–17, and Paul is at pains in the letter to establish that salvation belongs to the group who are 'in Christ', and not to those 'in the law'. This is made clear in 3:14, where the blessing of Abraham is said to come to the Gentiles 'in Christ', in direct contrast to those in the law, who are not justified before God and are thus under a curse (3:10–11). In 3:26, those who are in Christ are the free children of God, as opposed to those under the law, who are no better off than slaves (3:23–24; 4:1). In 4:24–26, this contrast between slavery and freedom is developed, as Paul associates the Jews with the slave girl Hagar, on the grounds that they are enslaved below with the present Jerusalem under the old covenant; the Gentile believers, on the other hand, are the free-born children, who have the heavenly Jerusalem as their mother. As Paul demonstrates by his quotation from Genesis 21:10, those who are under the law have no share in the inheritance of the free-born believers: instead, they are thrown outside (4:30). In this letter Paul admits no possibility of peaceful co-existence in Christ of Jews under the law and Gentiles outside the law.

Furthermore, in 3:7–4:7, Paul also reassigns characteristically Jewish privileges under the law to those who are in Christ. It is the Gentiles in Christ who by faith receive the blessing promised to Abraham, which Paul identifies as the eschatological Spirit. Through faith again, those who are in Christ are children of God, as is confirmed by the presence of the Spirit in their hearts crying 'Abba, Father' (3:26–4:7). In contrast, Jews are imprisoned under the law (3:23–24), and their plight is no different from enslavement to the στοιχεῖα (4:1–7). Paul leaves no room in this letter for the observance of the law, even by Jewish believers. They are justified apart from works of the law (2:16), while all those who are of works of the law are under a curse (3:10); the law is something from which Jews themselves need to be delivered (4:1–7). This uncompromising perspective (which is absent in Romans) reflects the polemical scenario of Galatians, in which Paul is struggling for the leadership and loyalty of the congregations. He employs the technique of 'witchcraft accusations' to place his opponents and those under the law firmly on the outside of the eschatological boundaries surrounding God's people. Reading Galatians in the light of Douglas' matrix underscores the comprehensive strategy of exclusion adopted by Paul in this letter.

Righteous Jew and sinful Gentile

In the course of their dispute over the drawing of boundaries, both Paul and his opponents draw on the idea of human wickedness on a cosmic scale, and use this concept to support their own position: they use the very tactics that Douglas has argued are characteristic of witchcraft societies and accusations. The language of Paul's opponents surfaces in 2:15–17, with the reference to 'Gentile sinners'. Paul responds by arguing that those who adhere to the works of the law are under a curse (3:7–14), while the law in fact imprisons people under its dominion (3:19–22). He goes on to redefine sin in eschatological terms (5:16–21). It is against this background of the political manipulation of the ideas of universal human wickedness that Paul's sin language in Galatians needs to be understood, if we are to interpret his thought correctly. Paul develops the symbolism of the power of sin as part of his strategy to oppose the contrasting ideology of his Jewish opponents in Galatia.

Jerusalem and Antioch

We begin with the distinction between righteous Jew and sinful Gentile that prompted the opposition that Paul encountered in Jerusalem and Antioch, as well as in Galatia. While there is no basis for assuming that his opponents were the same in each case, there seems to be little doubt that they shared a common concern, namely that of preserving the distinctiveness of Jewish identity over against what they perceived as the corrupting and defiling influence of the Gentile world. These attitudes suggest that they would find their place in the high group/low grid quadrant of Douglas' matrix as people who had a strong sense of group identity, but did not accept the cultural values of the prevailing symbol system by which they were surrounded.[28] In this context, the main boundary markers that set observant Jews apart from Hellenistic culture were

---

[28] As such, they would have shared common ground with the authors of Wisdom of Solomon, 3 & 4 Maccabees, *Joseph and Aseneth* and the *Sibylline Oracles*, all of which Barclay identifies as writings that reflect a high degree of antagonism towards Graeco-Roman culture, combined with a strong sense of Jewish identity (*Jews*, pp.181–228, 369–80).

abstention from participation in other cults, separation at meals, male circumcision and Sabbath observance.[29] However, not all Jews rejected Hellenistic culture: some embraced it while remaining self-consciously Jewish,[30] whereas others became assimilated to the point of losing their Jewish identity.[31] The boundaries separating the Jewish community from the Hellenistic world were thus constantly subject to erosion, and Paul's insistence that Gentile believers need not observe food laws, circumcision and Sabbath would have led to his being perceived by his fellow Jews as someone who had abandoned his Jewish identity and assimilated to Hellenism, notwithstanding his antagonism to Hellenistic culture.[32] Those who opposed Paul thus perceived him as a traitor, which is why Paul suffered persecution for the cross of Christ (5:11).

Those who opposed Paul in Jerusalem, Antioch and Galatia were therefore attempting to reinforce the boundaries between Judaism and Hellenism by insisting on circumcision, food laws and Sabbath observance.[33] We learn from Galatians 2:1–10 that the issue of circumcision was raised in Jerusalem,[34] when Paul took Titus with him on the occasion of his second visit.[35] The pressure for Titus to be circumcised will have come from those who were anxious to incorporate Gentile believers into

[29]Cf. L.H. Feldman, *Jew and Gentile in the Ancient World: Attitudes and Interactions from Alexander to Justinian* (Princeton: Princeton University Press, 1993), pp.153–70.

[30]Barclay refers to Philo, Josephus, Pseudo-Phocylides and the writer of the *Letter of Aristeas* (*Jews*, pp.138–80, 336–68). In defending Judaism's success in resisting Hellenisation, Feldman acknowledges the existence of a high level of syncretism, yet claims that it remained at the level of folklore and thus hardly diminished the people's loyalty to Judaism (*Jew and Gentile*, pp.65–9).

[31]Barclay includes the allegorists mentioned by Philo (*Mig. Abr.* 89–93) alongside Dositheos, Philo's nephew Alexander, Joseph Tobiad and Antiochus in Antioch (*Jews*, pp.104–12; 321–6).

[32]Barclay rightly describes Paul as an anomaly in this respect (ibid., pp.381–95).

[33]This is implied in Gal. 4:10, along with the other Jewish festivals.

[34]The suggestion that the false brothers raised the issue of circumcision in Antioch rather than in Jerusalem places intolerable strain on Paul's already convoluted syntax; cf. Bruce, *Galatians*, pp.115–17; R.Y.K. Fung, *Galatians*, NICNT (Grand Rapids: Eerdmans, 1988), pp.90–4.

[35]The classic question whether Gal. 2:1–10 should be identified with Acts 11:27–30 or with Acts 15:1–29 continues to be debated. *Contra* Longenecker (*Galatians*, pp.lxxvii–lxxx), the similarities between Gal. 2 and Acts 15 are sufficiently strong to indicate that the two incidents should be identified: D.R. Catchpole, 'Paul, James and the Apostolic Decree', *NTS* 23 (1977), pp.428–44. Gal. 2:10 could imply that Paul and Barnabas had brought money from Antioch to Jerusalem on the occasion of the conference if μνημονεύωμεν is understood as a continuous present, meaning that they were asked to continue to remember the poor; in this case, Luke might have made the two different reasons for going up to Jerusalem into two separate journeys. Cf. G. Lüdemann, *Paul, Apostle to the Gentiles : Studies in Chronology* (Minneapolis: Fortress, 1984), pp.149–52 for arguments that Acts 11:27ff.; 15:1ff.; 18:22 all refer to the same visit.

Judaism as proselytes, thereby maintaining a clear, unambiguous bound-ary between Jew and Gentile.[36] In the event, their arguments were not accepted by the apostles,[37] and the legitimacy of Paul's apostolic mission to the Gentiles was accepted, at least on that occasion.[38] It should be noted, however, that in retrospect Paul describes the agitators in Jerusalem as 'false brothers' (2:4). Those who threaten the freedom of his Gentile con-verts are accused by the apostle of being Christians only on the surface;[39] they are outsiders, who have been secretly introduced into the commu-nity. Paul's clear implication is that his opponents in Jerusalem have no true place in the church.

However, once the need for circumcision as the rite of entry into the Jewish community was set on one side as a result of the Jerusalem con-ference, the result was a degree of ambiguity as to where the boundary separating Jew from Gentile was to be drawn.[40] It is likely that it was this ambiguity that led to the problems at Antioch. It is safe to suppose that Titus, while he was in Jerusalem, would have fitted in with the customs of his hosts, who consequently may have assumed that it was normal practice for Gentile converts to observe Jewish food laws and Sabbath. But when the men from James came to Antioch and found Peter eating with the Gentile converts there, it became apparent that the boundaries

[36] Belief in a Jewish messiah and worship of the Jewish God clearly indicated that Gentile believers had a strong degree of sympathy to Judaism. If they were circumcised, that would have the effect of drawing them fully across the boundary separating Jew from Gentile and incorporating them within the Jewish community: cf. S.J.D. Cohen, 'Crossing the Boundary and Becoming a Jew', *HTR* 73 (1989), pp.13–33.

[37] Nor by Paul: despite T. Zahn, *Der Brief des Paulus an die Galater* (Göttingen: Vandenhoeck & Ruprecht, 1905), pp.88–91, 287–96 and B.W. Bacon, 'The Reading οἷς οὐδὲ in Gal. 2:5', *JBL* 42 (1923), pp.69–80. Gal. 2:4–5 was originally a negative anaco-luthon (𝔓[46] ℵ A B C D[1] F G Ψ). The omission of οἷς οὐδὲ (D* it[b,d] Irenaeus[lat] Tertullian) is suspect, since it gives the smoothest reading grammatically; the alteration may have been made on the strength of Acts 16:3. Marcion retains the negative but omits the relative pronoun, thereby removing the anacoluthon but retaining the sense, although the syntax is awkward. Tertullian, whose Latin text omitted both words, accused Marcion of introducing the negative (*adv. Marc.* 5.3), and it is probably on the strength of this accusation that the negative alone was omitted in D[2]. Cf. the discussion in J.B. Lightfoot, *St. Paul's Epistle to the Galatians* (London: Macmillan, 1874), pp.120–2.

[38] According to P.F. Esler, 'Making and Breaking an Agreement Mediterranean Style: a new reading of Galatians 2:1–14', *Biblical Interpretation* 3 (1995), pp.285–314, Paul emerged from the meeting at Jerusalem with honour, having inflicted a humiliating defeat on the Jewish Christian leadership.

[39] Paul's accusation that these were false brothers is polemical, and should not be taken to mean that they were non-Christian Jews, *contra* W. Schmithals, *Paul and James* (London: SCM, 1965), pp.107–8.

[40] Cf. J.D.G. Dunn, *The Theology of Paul's Letter to the Galatians* (Cambridge: Cam-bridge University Press, 1993), p.71: 'The Jerusalem agreement was probably something of a compromise which masked a variety of understandings of what had been actually agreed.'

that distinguished Jew from Gentile were also being eroded in the area of the food laws.[41]

There has been considerable debate as to the exact nature of the table fellowship being enjoyed at Antioch and about the objections that were raised by the men from James. Dunn has questioned the traditional assumption (based on Acts 10) that the table fellowship in Antioch was practised with a total disregard for Jewish food laws, and proposes instead that the degree of association between faithful Jew and God-fearing Gentile ranged across a wide spectrum from complete avoidance to regular social intercourse.[42] He argues that Gentile believers in Antioch would probably have been drawn from the ranks of the God-fearers, who thus would have been accustomed to observing the basic regulations about clean and unclean food. According to Dunn, the men from James objected to the consumption of food that was ritually impure, because it had not been tithed according to the halakhic clarifications of the law set down by the Pharisees in Palestine. Dunn therefore sees the men from James as calling for a more scrupulous observance of the rules concerning tithing and purity, so that the Gentile believers were required to submit to a stricter definition and practice of the Jewish religion than they had hitherto observed.

Dunn's position has been criticised by Esler, who argues that he has offered 'not a shred of evidence' for Jews eating with Gentiles in this period, and that the attitude of the men from James leaves no room for Dunn's proposed spectrum of degrees of table fellowship.[43] Esler argues against the existence of any commensalism between Gentiles and observant Jews in the first century. Drawing partly on Douglas' work,[44] Esler points out an intimate correlation between Jewish purity regulations, and their need to maintain separate identities from their Gentile neighbours. Seeking to support his case with evidence from a variety of Gentile and Jewish sources, Esler argues that fellowship around the Lord's table would have

[41] Paul's record of the outcome of the conference may well be tendentious, but his first-hand account is more likely to be reliable than Luke's version (Acts 15:20, 29). Acts 21:25 refers to a letter to the Gentile churches about which Paul seems to have been unaware. Possibly a decision about food was taken in the light of the incident at Antioch and Luke has retrojected this resolution of the issue on to the earlier Jerusalem conference.

[42] Dunn, *Jesus, Paul*, pp.129–82. Dunn is less specific in his commentary on Galatians, suggesting that Peter and the others accepted invitations to Gentile tables 'without asking too many questions' (*Galatians*, p.121).

[43] P.F. Esler, *Community and Gospel*, pp.71–89; *The First Christians in their Social Worlds: Social-Scientific Approaches to New Testament Interpretation* (London: Routledge, 1994), pp.52–69.

[44] M. Douglas, *Purity and Danger: An Analysis of Concepts of Pollution and Taboo* (London: Routledge & Kegan Paul, 1966); 'Deciphering a Meal', *Implicit Meanings*, pp.249–75.

been impossible for the law-abiding Jew, because of the possibility that the food eaten could be ritually defiled or the wine tainted with idolatry. He concludes by arguing that the only way in which the Gentile converts in Antioch could have been rehabilitated for the men from James was for them to become Jewish themselves by accepting circumcision.

After surveying the relevant literature, E.P. Sanders argues cogently that there was no legal barrier to social intercourse with Gentiles, so long as the Jew did not eat Gentile meat or drink Gentile wine.[45] He accepts the validity of Dunn's arguments for a broad range of social intercourse, but rejects the suggestion that the issue at Antioch concerned untithed food, because laws about tithing would not have applied outside of Palestine. He argues that Esler's blanket ban on commensalism between Jew and Gentile is inaccurate, because such exemplary stories as Aristeas clearly indicate that Jews could eat with Gentiles, so long as the Jews either brought their own food to the table, or only ate vegetables. The only real problems with associating with Gentiles were the need to obey the biblical food laws, and to avoid all contact with idolatry. Sanders concludes that a strict Jew would have wished to avoid *too much* association with Gentiles, and would not eat Gentile food or drink Gentile wine, in case it was either unclean, or had been tainted by idol worship. Thus, whether the food that Peter was eating at Antioch was clean or not, the sight of him eating Gentile food in a Gentile home would have been sufficient to produce a rebuke from the men from James.

On the basis of the evidence available, it is not possible to draw definitive conclusions as to the nature of the table fellowship at Antioch. Esler is right to argue that Jewish food laws did reinforce Jewish isolationism, but such social boundaries were constantly subject to erosion as a result of pressure to conform to the surrounding Gentile world. This is one of the characteristics of a community located in the low grid/high group quadrant of Douglas' matrix. The boundaries of first-century Judaism were subject to infiltration and erosion as a result of the willingness of some Jews to compromise with the surrounding culture. This tendency to compromise means that the possibility cannot be ruled out of the existence of a wide range of social intercourse between Jew and Gentile that may have extended even to the joint consumption of unclean food,[46] or the sharing of a eucharistic cup.

[45] E.P. Sanders, 'Jewish Association with Gentiles and Galatians 2:11–14', in R. Fortna and B.R. Gaventa, eds., *The Conversation Continues: Studies in Paul and John in Honor of J.L. Martyn* (Nashville: Abingdon, 1990), pp.170–88.

[46] 4 Maccabees was probably written to strengthen adherence to Jewish food laws, and thus provides indirect evidence for Jewish consumption of unclean food in the first century.

In such a situation of compromise, the action of the men from James is comprehensible as an exercise in strengthening the boundaries that separated Jew from Gentile. Precisely what passed between them and Peter must remain a matter for conjecture,[47] but Paul himself provides a clue in his record that Peter withdrew and separated himself, φοβούμενος τοὺς ἐκ περιτομῆς. If Paul's assessment of Peter's motivation for his behaviour is correct, then it is possible to surmise that the men from James warned Peter of the possible repercussions of his behaviour becoming known to the unbelieving Jews in Judaea.[48] As a social group belonging to the high group/low grid quadrant, preoccupied with reinforcing weak boundaries between themselves and the surrounding Gentile world, the Jews in Judaea would have had a great concern to expel deviants from the social body. Paul's own former persecution of the church is clear evidence that believers were identifiable in some way as deviant Jews, and Peter may well have withdrawn from association with the Gentiles out of a real fear of occasioning a fresh outburst of persecution against the church.

A lack of information leaves the reader in ignorance whether those who came from James were sent to Antioch with the specific aim of bringing Peter back into line, or whether Peter merely considered it prudent to withdraw from table fellowship as a result of the information that they brought him. In any event, their arrival resulted in Peter's separating himself from the Gentile believers, so sending a clear message to all concerned that he was prepared to maintain the boundary between Jew and Gentile established by the Jewish food laws, and thus leave Gentile believers on the outside.

It was this exclusion of the Gentiles that prompted Paul's single-handed attack on Peter's behaviour, demanding to know why it was that Peter, although he himself lived like a Gentile and not like a Jew, was now compelling the Gentiles to judaise (Gal. 2:14). There is no real difficulty in perceiving how Peter, by endorsing boundaries that excluded Gentiles from the people of God, was in effect compelling them to judaise; his act of withdrawal made it clear that, if they were to be accepted by their fellow Jewish believers, they themselves would have to accommodate themselves to Jewish practice by obeying Jewish food laws. That was a price that Peter may have felt was worth paying, in order to maintain his integrity as apostle to the circumcision, but it was intolerable for Paul,

---

[47]Esler (*First Christians*, pp.52–69) argues that the men from James insisted on circumcision as a condition for commensalism. His case receives some support from Luke's account of the incident at Antioch (Acts 15:1), but it is impossible to be certain whether Luke has accurately reported the Judaisers' teaching.

[48]This is the most likely referent of τοὺς ἐκ περιτομῆς: cf. Jewett, 'Agitators'.

who was not prepared to allow the Gentiles to be excluded in this fashion, and who thus mounts his attack on what he perceived to be Peter's betrayal of the truth of the gospel.

Gentile sinners justified in Christ (Gal. 2:15–16)

The outcome of Paul's confrontation with Peter at Antioch cannot be known for certain, because the apostle does not go on to record this in his letter.[49] What he does do in Galatians 2:15 is to begin to address the Galatian situation directly, under the guise of still speaking to Peter in Antioch.[50] There can be no doubt that, in Galatians 2:14, Paul summarises the words with which he took his stand against Peter at Antioch. Since there are no syntactical indications that Paul has shifted attention away from the Antioch incident in verse 15, and the flow of thought between verse 14 and verse 15 is quite smooth, it is most natural to take the ἡμεῖς of verse 15–16 as continuing to refer to Paul and Peter. Yet notwithstanding this, it is extremely unlikely that Paul has recorded *verbatim* what he had to say on that occasion; we cannot even be sure that Galatians 2:15f. is an accurate reflection of what he said. What we read at this point in Galatians is more than likely to be a response to the situation at Antioch, which Paul may only have thought out after the event. Thus Galatians 2:15f., while ostensibly addressed to Peter, is in reality written with Paul's Galatian readers in mind.[51]

For Paul, the issue at stake in Galatia when outsiders arrived advocating circumcision was basically the same as that at Antioch. The requirement that Gentile converts should adopt Jewish customs was unacceptable to the apostle, since, in his eyes, it placed outside the boundaries of God's people those Gentiles whom God had accepted on the basis of their faith. This is the point that he makes in the crucial statement of Galatians 2:15–16.[52]

Paul takes as his starting point here the distinction drawn by Jews between themselves as righteous because of their participation in God's

---

[49] Dunn plausibly suggests that Paul remained isolated at Antioch and could no longer use the church there as his base (*Jesus, Paul*, pp.159–61).

[50] G. Klein, 'Individualgeschichte und Weltgeschichte bei Paulus: Eine Interpretation ihres Verhältnisses im Galaterbrief', in *Rekonstruktion und Interpretation: Gesammelte Aufsätze zum Neuen Testament* (Munich: Chr. Kaiser, 1969), pp.180–220.

[51] Cf. A. Oepke, *Der Brief des Paulus an die Galater* (Berlin: Evangelische Verlaganstalt, 1960), p.56.

[52] Gal. 2:15–16 should be read as a single sentence: W.G. Kümmel, ' "Individualgeschichte" und "Weltgeschichte" in Galater 2:15–21', in B. Lindars and S.S. Smalley, eds., *Christ and Spirit in the New Testament* (Cambridge: Cambridge University Press, 1973), pp.157–74.

covenant, and Gentiles who are outside the covenant and therefore 'sinners'.[53] In Galatians 2:15, Paul adopts the typical Jewish perspective upon the Gentiles, but then he immediately goes on to subvert this distinction by his claim that a person is not justified by works of the law, but only by faith in Jesus Christ. δικαιοῦται is a judicial metaphor, signifying acquittal in the heavenly court; its soteriological function in Paul's letters is that of a term of transfer from a state of being unsaved to a state of being saved.[54] Paul thus asserts that it is faith in Christ,[55] not observance of works of the law, which separates the righteous from the unrighteous.

This interpretation of these verses differs considerably from that offered by Dunn, who seeks to maintain that Paul continues to operate within a Jewish framework at this point.[56] On the basis of Paul's claim to speak for his fellow Jews in verse 15, Dunn argues that they would have been wholly at one with him in seeing faith as being the key element in justification in verse 16a. Accordingly, he argues that the verb δικαιόω should not be understood here as a transfer term; instead, it should be seen as denoting the maintenance of one's position within the covenant, covering the entire period from the moment of entry until the final eschatological acquittal by God. The point at issue is the question as to what constitutes a valid expression of that faith in Israel's creator God. According to Dunn, the Jew of Paul's day would have regarded Sabbath observance, food laws and circumcision as basic expressions of

[53]This is E.P. Sanders' view of 'covenantal nomism', as expounded in *Paul and Palestinian Judaism*. That this was the basic perspective on the relative status of Jews and Gentiles has been demonstrated by Winninge (*Sinners*); cf. Ps. 9:15–17; 1 Macc. 1:34; 2:48; *Jub.* 23:23; *Ps Sol.* 1:1; 2:1–2; 17:22–25.

[54]J.A. Ziesler, *The Meaning of Righteousness in Paul* (Cambridge: Cambridge University Press, 1972).

[55]The genitive πίστις Χριστοῦ is read as objective, *contra* R.B. Hays, *The Faith of Jesus Christ: an Investigation of the Narrative Substructure of Galatians 3:1–4:11*, SBL Diss. 56 (Chico: Scholars, 1983). The noun πίστις is ambiguous, denoting either 'faith' or 'faithfulness' in English. The fact that the first meaning is common in Paul's letters, while the second is extremely rare (Rom. 1:17?; 3:9; Gal. 5:22?) suggests that πίστις Χριστοῦ denotes faith in Christ rather than the faithfulness of Christ. This is confirmed by the contexts in which Paul uses the phrase. Apart from Gal. 3:22, it is always used in contrast to 'works of the law' as a basis for justification (Rom. 3:20–26; Gal. 2:16–20; Phil. 3:9), and this is because Paul is concerned to oppose 'works', as the appropriate human response to Torah within the Sinaitic covenant, to faith, as the appropriate human response to God's act in Christ. To take πίστις Χριστοῦ as an objective genitive in Gal. 2:16 does not entail unnecessary repetition: Paul sets out successive stages of action: knowledge (v.16a); faith (v.16b); result (v.16c); scriptural warrant (v.16d).

[56]Dunn, *Jesus, Paul*, pp.183–214.

covenant loyalty.[57] These observances functioned as badges of covenant membership; insofar as they were regarded as being essential to membership of God's people, they functioned as boundary markers, separating insiders from outsiders. Paul, on the other hand, regarded faith in Jesus as messiah as the key to covenant membership, and, in verse 16a, makes the point that the requirement of faith in Christ necessarily qualifies the traditional Jewish view that justification was a matter of law observance. However, once it became apparent to Paul that his fellow Jewish believers were seeking to impose the ritual requirements of Jewish law upon Gentile converts, he reacted by pushing faith in Christ and observance of works of the law[58] into outright antithesis, to make it clear that it is faith in Christ which is the key to justification.

Dunn's reading of Galatians 2:15–16 emphasises the common ground between Jewish and Gentile Christianity, but such an eirenical reading of the passage rests uneasily with the setting of witchcraft accusations suggested by Douglas' matrix. Furthermore, Dunn's interpretation has exegetical vulnerabilities. Dunn claims that Paul continues to speak from a Jewish point of view in verse 16a, and only advances his own position from καὶ ἡμεῖς onwards. Dunn thus maintains that the phrase ἐὰν μὴ διὰ πίστεως 'Ιησοῦ Χριστοῦ qualifies, but does not exclude, justification by works of the law and it is only in verse 16b that Paul rejects the Jewish synergism of faith and works in favour of an outright antithesis. The question is, whether verse 16a is written from the Jewish point of view, in continuity with verse 15, as Dunn argues, or from Paul's own point of

---

[57]Cf. J.D.G. Dunn, 'The Theology of Galatians: the Issue of Covenantal Nomism', in J.M. Bassler, ed., *Pauline Theology I* (Minneapolis: Fortress, 1991), pp.125–46.

[58]J.D.G. Dunn argues that Paul and the authors of 4QMMT understood the 'works of the law' as a boundary marking out those of faith or faithfulness from others: '4QMMT and Galatians', *NTS* 43 (1997), pp.147–53. This is certainly how the phrase is understood in 4QMMT, where adherence to the listed halakhic rulings forms the basis for the group's secession from the others. It also corresponds to the way in which we have argued that Paul's opponents perceived the law as a boundary marker distinguishing righteous Jew from sinful Gentile. However, Dunn has argued elsewhere that in practice the phrase 'works of the law' pertained particularly to the 'covenantal badges' of circumcision, food laws and Sabbath: *Jesus, Paul,* pp.183–214; 'Yet Once More – the Works of the Law: a Response', *JSNT* 46 (1992), pp.99–117; *Galatians,* pp.135–7. In this way, Dunn is able to claim that Paul was not opposing the law *per se,* but only a wrongly placed emphasis on those aspects of the law that functioned as boundary markers. However, Dunn himself acknowledges that the phrase generally denoted 'deeds or actions which the law requires': *Galatians,* p.135; cf. J.A. Fitzmyer, *According to Paul* (New York: Paulist Press, 1993), pp.18–35. Since Paul does not explicitly redefine this publicly accepted meaning of the term, it would seem more likely that Paul's criticism of the law is actually more radical than Dunn allows (cf. also Esler, *Galatians,* pp.181–4).

view, according to which justification by faith and by works of the law are mutually exclusive alternatives, as set out in verse 16b: there can be no doubt that a shift from the first perspective to the second must take place at some point in the verse. Dunn's proposal is refuted by Räisänen's argument that Paul's use of the consecutive conjunction καί at this point renders difficult any view that perceives a major shift of focus here.[59] It is far more likely that this shift should be seen as taking place earlier, between verses 15 and 16. This shift in perspective is made explicit, if the adversative conjunction δέ is read, in accordance with the majority of manuscripts. But even if the conjunction is omitted, the participial clause still makes room for a change of one point of view to another, room that the use of καί in verse 16b does not afford. We should therefore allow the immediate context and syntax to determine the meaning of the phrase ἐὰν μή and follow the traditional understanding of this phrase as meaning 'but only'.

On exegetical grounds, it is therefore necessary to reject Dunn's reading of Galatians 2:16a: Paul does not stand on common ground with his fellow Jews in affirming that righteousness within the covenant is a matter of obeying the law and having faith in Christ. Instead, as has always been traditionally affirmed, he is stating that justification is purely a matter of faith in Christ, and has nothing to do with works of the law. The corollary to this conclusion, which Dunn is eager to avoid, is that Paul denies his fellow Jews any righteous standing under the covenant. If a person is justified only by faith in Christ and not by works of the law, then the unavoidable implication is that those who obey the law, but do not have faith in Christ, are left on the outside, as far as justification is concerned. Dunn is to be commended for emphasising the importance of boundaries for understanding what Paul has to say in these verses, but he is quite wrong in his understanding of what Paul is doing with those boundaries. Paul is not trying to widen the boundaries of the Mosaic covenant to include uncircumcised Gentile believers. Within the witchcraft cosmology that characterised the situation in Galatia, Paul's aim is to redraw the boundaries in such a way as to include all those who believe, and to exclude those under the law. His purpose at this point is not eirenical: he is trying to expel from the ranks of his community outsiders who have come in to challenge his authority, and as such, he can give them no quarter. Since the best form of defence is attack, he redraws the boundaries around the

---

[59]H. Räisänen, *Jesus, Paul and Torah: Collected Essays*, JSNTS 43 (Sheffield: Sheffield Academic Press, 1992), pp.120–1.

community in such a way as to leave his opponents firmly on the out-side. Thus, in order to safeguard the position of his Gentile converts, Paul makes faith in Christ the only means of justification and identifies law-abiding Jews as outsiders, together with the Gentile sinners. As Paul points out in 2:21, if righteousness came through the law, then Christ died in vain. Instead Paul insists that the Jewish people themselves are on the outside and, in thinking that the key to standing in a right relation to God is a matter of observing the law, they are simply trying the wrong door.

This is a radical position indeed. The law and its observance were cen-tral to the Jewish symbolic universe, fundamental to their identification of themselves as having been elected to be God's covenant people. How is it that Paul can claim Peter's support for such a radical position, bearing in mind that it is still ostensibly Peter that Paul is continuing to address at this point? Paul seems to regard Peter's act of believing in Christ as itself an indication that the law is inadequate:[60] if righteousness was in fact maintained by observing the law's requirements, it would not have been necessary to believe in Christ at all. He is thus able to point to the Jewish believers' own act of faith as an indication of their acceptance of the inadequacy of the law as a means of justification.[61]

Paul then offers scriptural warrant for his position, in his allusion to Psalm 143:2 (Gal. 2:16d). His substitution of σάρξ for ζῶν anticipates the eschatological distinction between flesh and Spirit that he will draw at the end of the letter. Sinfulness is not defined in terms of Gentiles who disregard the Jewish law; instead Paul's use of σάρξ defines sin in terms of universal participation in the present evil age (1:4). Those whose existence is determined by flesh rather than by Spirit are the wrong side of the eschatological boundary and so cannot be justified by works of Jewish Torah.[62] Galatians 2:15–16 is a clear case of boundary redefinition.

---

[60]If the participle εἰδότες is not followed by the particle δέ, it could be understood in a causal sense, in which case 2:16 indicates that the act of believing in Christ is based upon the knowledge that a person is not justified by works of the law: '... since we know that a person is not justified by works of the law but only by faith in Christ, even we have believed...'

[61]Cf. Klein, 'Individualgeschichte', p.190; H.-J. Eckstein, *Verheißung und Gesetz: Eine exegetische Untersuchung zu Galater 2,15–4,17*, WUNT 86 (Tübingen: J.C.B. Mohr, 1996), pp.35–6.

[62]Cf. J.L. Martyn, 'Events in Galatia: Modified Covenantal Nomism versus God's In-vasion of the Cosmos in the Singular Gospel: A Response to J.D.G. Dunn and B.R. Gaventa', in J.M. Bassler, ed., *Pauline Theology I*, pp.160–79: 'The teachers' fundamental issue is covenantal nomism, if you like; Paul's is evangelical, cosmic, history-creating Christology... Law observance is on the human side of the divine–human antinomy' (p.165).

A Jewish objection (Gal. 2:17)

The interpretation of Galatians 2:17 hinges on a number of questions, which can best be resolved if the verse is analysed as a three-part syllogism, consisting of two premises 'A' and 'B' and a conclusion 'C':[63]

A   εἰ δὲ ζητοῦντες δικαιωθῆναι ἐν Χριστῷ

B   εὑρέθημεν καὶ αὐτοὶ ἁμαρτωλοί,[64]

C   ἆρα[65] Χριστὸς ἁμαρτίας διάκονος;

On the basis of Paul's usage elsewhere, the concluding μὴ γένοιτο may be taken as a firm indication that the preceding clause is a question rather than a statement.[66] There is uncertainty, though, whether μὴ γένοιτο negates both clauses B and C, or just the concluding clause C. It is also unclear whether verse 17 should be understood as Paul's address to Peter, Peter's address to Paul, or Paul's rebuttal of an argument of his opponents. There are therefore a number of ways of reading the verse:

1.   Should those who seek justification in Christ sin in some way, Paul is concerned to deny that this makes Christ the servant of sin: Christ's acceptance of the sinner does not imply acceptance of whatever sins the justified believer may commit.[67]

2.   Paul himself formulates 2:17 and regards Clause B as incompatible with Clause A: should those who seek justification in Christ be found sinful, that would make Christ the servant of sin, which is unthinkable. By means of this *reductio ad absurdum* Paul claims that it cannot be sinful to seek justification in Christ instead of by works of the law.[68]

---

[63]Cf. E.D. Burton, *A Critical and Exegetical Commentary on the Epistle to the Galatians*, ICC (Edinburgh: T&T Clark, 1921), pp.127–30.

[64]M.L. Soards strains the syntax by taking εὑρέθημεν with ζητοῦντες: 'Seeking (*zetein*) and Sinning (*hamartia*) according to Galatians 2:17', in J.M. Marcus and M.L. Soards, eds., *Apocalyptic and the New Testament: Essays in Honor of J. Louis Martyn*, JSNTS 24 (Sheffield: Sheffield Academic Press, 1989), pp.237–54. According to Soards, 'seeking to be justified in Christ' declares that justification is not the work of God alone. However, this seeking is not an effort that accompanies faith, but rather is an expression of faith itself: P. Bonnard, *L'Épître de Saint Paul aux Galates* (Paris: Delacaux et Niestlé, 1972), p.54.

[65]The interrogative ἆρα occurs nowhere else in Paul's letters. The inferential ἄρα is therefore preferred, leaving open the issue of whether the clause is a statement or a question (Porter, *Idioms*, p.207).

[66]Cf. Rom. 3:4, 6, 31; 6:2, 15; 7:7, 13; 9:14; 11:1, 11; 1 Cor. 6:15; Gal. 2:20.

[67]Oepke, *Galater*, pp.60–1; Longenecker, *Galatians*, pp.88–90.

[68]R. Bultmann, 'Zur Auslegung von Galater 2:15–18', in *Exegetica*, pp.394–9; F. Mussner, *Der Galaterbrief* (Freiburg: Herder, 1974), p.176; P.C. Böttger, 'Paulus und Petrus in Antiochien', *NTS* 37 (1991), pp.77–100.

3.　　Galatians 2:17 refers to verses 11–14: Clause B refers to Peter
and Paul being identified as sinners at Antioch; Paul denies that
eating with Gentiles makes Christ the servant of sin, as is implied
by Peter's subsequent withdrawal.[69]

4.　　A Jewish objector argues that Paul's gospel makes the righteous
sinful and Christ the servant of sin; Paul denies both that those
who seek justification in Christ are sinners and that Christ is the
servant of sin (clauses B & C).[70]

5.　　A Jewish objector recognises that seeking justification in Christ
entails Jews giving up their righteous status and acknowledging
that they are no better than sinful Gentiles; Paul accepts that
those who seek justification in Christ are exposed as sinners in
this way, but denies that this makes Christ the servant of sin
(Clause C).[71]

Crucial to understanding this verse is the meaning of the word
ἁμαρτωλοί. Paul probably intends to pick up the reference to ἐξ ἐθνῶν
ἁμαρτωλοί in 2:15, since the phrase καὶ αὐτοὶ ἁμαρτωλοί would appear to suggest that those who seek justification in Christ are thereby
identified with the Gentile sinners of verse 15; any other reading evac-
uates καὶ αὐτοι of any significance. Furthermore, in Jewish writings,
ἁμαρτωλοί is consistently used to draw a distinction between in-group
and out-group.[72] The implication of the term from a Jewish perspective
is that those who seek justification in Christ are themselves 'beyond the
pale', outside the boundaries of the righteous.

[69]F. Sieffert, *Der Brief an die Galater* (Göttingen: Vandenhoeck & Ruprecht, 1899),
pp.146–51; Schmithals, *Paul and James*, pp.61–4; H. Feld, ' "Christus Diener der Sünde":
Zum Auslegung des Streites zwischen Petrus und Paulus', *ThQ* 153 (1973), pp.119–31;
Dunn, *Galatians*, p.141.

[70]H.D. Betz, *Galatians*, Hermeneia (Minneapolis: Fortress, 1979), pp.119–20; R. Kieffer,
Foi et Justification à Antioche: Interprétation d'un Conflit (Paris: Cerf, 1982), pp.53–60;
Eckstein, *Verheißung*, pp.30–41.

[71]G.S. Duncan, *The Epistle of Paul to the Galatians* (London: Hodder & Stoughton,
1934), pp.66–8; Lightfoot, p.116; Zahn, p.126; Schlier, pp.58–60; Bruce, p.141; Fung,
pp.119–20; Klein, 'Individualgeschichte', p.191; J. Lambrecht, *Pauline Studies* (Louvain:
Louvain University Press, 1991), pp.193–209; also 'Paul's Reasoning in Galatians 2:11–21,'
in J.D.G. Dunn, ed., *Paul and the Mosaic Law* (Tübingen: J.C.B. Mohr, 1996), pp.53–74.

[72]Cf. Winninge, *Sinners*, and J. Köberle's analysis of sin in terms of the distinction
between the pious and the godless: *Sünde und Gnade im religiösen Leben des Volkes
Israel bis auf Christentum: Eine Geschichte des vorchristlichen Heilbewußtseins* (Munich:
Beck'sche, 1905). The collective designation 'sinners' is not generally used by Jews of
themselves before 70 CE. It occurs in 4 Ezra 8:31: 'For we and our fathers have passed our
lives in ways that bring death, but you, because of us sinners, are called merciful.' However,
Ezra is corrected and told not to compare himself with the unrighteous in 8:47. Cf. also the
Christian *Questions of Ezra* (A) 31.

Understanding the term from a Jewish perspective rules out option 1, since Paul is not referring to sin in general terms. It also casts doubt on option 2, which fails to observe the distinction between righteous Jew and sinful Gentile underlying Paul's use of the term. Option 3 observes the distinction between righteous Jew and sinful Gentile, since it was eating with Gentiles that led to the charge of being sinners. However, Paul claims that they are found to be sinners ζητοῦντες δικαιωθῆναι ἐν Χριστῷ and there is no inherent connection between seeking justification in Christ and eating with Gentiles. Since the reference to justification refers back to verses 15–16 rather than verses 11–14, this suggests that he is concerned with the general principle that he has set down in 2:15–16, rather than the specific incident behind it.

This leaves the Jewish objections in options 4 and 5. The way in which Jews used the term ἁμαρτωλοί to denote outsiders corresponds to the re-drawing of boundaries which Douglas has identified as part of a witchcraft cosmology: Paul's Jewish accusers are placing him and other law-free Christians outside the boundaries of the righteous community. Whether Paul accepts the label ἁμαρτωλοί or not depends on where the boundaries are to be drawn. If ἁμαρτωλοί denotes being 'outside the realm of God's salvation',[73] there is no doubt that Paul would reject the label (option 4). However, for his Jewish accusers, the realm of God's salvation was defined by observance of the Torah and that is precisely the distinction between the sinful and the righteous that Paul is not prepared to accept. It is therefore more likely that Paul accepts that he and others who seek justification in Christ are sinners with respect to the law: in seeking justification apart from the law, they have abandoned the crucial boundary that separated righteous Jew from sinful Gentile.[74] As such, Paul accepts the charge of being a sinner, one outside the ethnic boundary of the law, in order to be justified in Christ.

Paul thus accepts Clause B of the syllogism, but he denies Clause C, that this makes Christ the servant of sin. It is illegitimate to import theological freight from Romans to interpret Paul's reference to ἁμαρτία here, particularly since Paul's words reflect an accusation levelled at him by his opponents.[75] The polemical nature of the question suggests that it may have been developed as a deliberate reversal of Isaiah 53:11 MT,[76]

---

[73] Betz, *Galatians*, p.120.

[74] Cf. *Aristeas* 139, 142.

[75] So Eckstein, *Verheißung*, p.36, who gives the term its full theological sense of a power at enmity with God that holds all humanity under its sway.

[76] The LXX is quite different: here it is the LORD who justifies the righteous one who serves many well: ... δικαιῶσαι δίκαιον εὖ δουλεύοντα πολλοῖς.

where the righteous servant of the Lord justifies many and bears their sins:

בְּדַעְתּוֹ יַצְדִּיק צַדִּיק עַבְדִּי לָרַבִּים וַעֲוֹנֹתָם הוּא יִסְבֹּל

To Jewish Christians, this verse would probably have been understood as a reference to Christ as the servant of the Lord who justified many by bearing their sins.[77] Galatians 2:17 is thus linked to Isaiah 53:11 by the twin concepts of Christ as the servant who justifies. In Isaiah 53:11, the righteous servant justifies many and puts them right with God. In Galatians 2:17, because those who seek justification in Christ are found to be sinners, in effect, Paul's opponents claim that Paul reverses the role ascribed to Christ in Isaiah 53:11. Their argument is that, if Christ as the servant makes people sinners instead of putting them right with God, Christ must be the servant of sin, rather than the righteous servant of the Lord.[78] It is no wonder that Paul denies the charge with an emphatic μὴ γένοιτο.

Paul's answer (Gal. 2:18f.)

The exegesis of this verse is rendered difficult by a number of points at which Paul's meaning is ambiguous. Is Paul speaking of himself personally here, or is he using the first person singular in a supra-individualistic sense? How does Paul's thought flow from verse 17 through verse 18 into verse 19? What is the referent of ταῦτα and in which sense does rebuilding 'these things' make the speaker a transgressor? Is the sentence a true-to-life, or contrary-to-fact conditional?

This verse has traditionally been understood as a warning that reconstruction of the law or the law's distinction between Jews and Gentiles is tantamount to transgression, but this interpretation suffers from the difficulty of establishing a logically viable connection between the protasis and apodosis of the conditional construction in verse 18: why should the rebuilding of the law make the one who does so a transgressor? The answer to this question hinges on the meaning of παραβάτην ἐμαυτὸν συνιστάνω.

In Romans 2:25–27 παραβάτης is used to mean transgression of the law and the cognate noun παράβασις is used by Paul to denote transgression of a commandment in Romans 2:23; 4:15; 5:14; Galatians 3:19. The

---

[77] Despite M.D. Hooker, *Jesus and the Servant* (London: SCM, 1959).
[78] The singular ἁμαρτία is used, without denoting a cosmic power, in Sir. 21:2; 27:10; T. Levi 2:3.

word group is thus never used with the sense of general wrongdoing, but always bears the specific meaning of transgressing the law. This clearly defined meaning of παραβάτης makes it unlikely that Paul uses the term here to denote a reversal of one's previous righteous status,[79] or to refer to transgression against God's revealed will in Christ.[80] Schneider retains the specific meaning of παραβάτης when he argues that placing oneself under the law will inevitably lead to concrete transgression of the law's requirements;[81] Klein argues that transgression is an inevitable part of being under the law, whether one obeys it or not,[82] while Böttger proposes that becoming subject to the law places one under the power of sin;[83] less plausible is the proposal that Paul uses the noun to indicate that returning to the law goes against the law's real intent and purpose.[84] However, these interpretations fail to do justice to the meaning of the verb συνιστάνω: Paul is not saying that building up the law again makes one a transgressor; he rather says that it demonstrates that one is a transgressor.[85] In other words, one is shown to be a transgressor in the act of rebuilding the law; one does not become a transgressor as a result of building the law. This is recognised by those who argue that the act of rebuilding the law identifies one's previous law-free behaviour as a transgression of the law.[86] Yet this interpretation is unlikely, since such a statement expresses the very position of the Judaisers that Paul wishes to refute, and furthermore, an initial reading of the verse would suggest that Paul identifies himself with this position by using the first person singular in a true-to-life conditional sentence.

---

[79] Bruce, *Galatians*, p.142; Schlier, p.60.

[80] M. Bachmann, *Sünder oder Übertreter: Studien zur Argumentation in Gal. 2:15ff.* (Tübingen: J.C.B. Mohr, 1992), pp.55–83; cf. H. Neitzel, 'Zur Interpretation von Galater 2:11–21', *ThQ* 163 (1983), pp.15–39, 131–49; Lambrecht, *Pauline Studies*, pp.211–30; Duncan, *Galatians*, pp.68–9.

[81] J. Schneider, 'παραβαίνω, παράβασις, ἀπαραβάτος, ὑπερβαίνω', in G. Kittel, ed., *Theological Dictionary of the New Testament* (Grand Rapids: Eerdmans, 1964–76), vol.v, pp.736–44; Kümmel, 'Individualgeschichte'; Fung, pp.120–1; Bonnard, p.55; Mussner, p.180; Betz, p.121.

[82] Klein, 'Individualgeschichte', p.199; cf. W. Mundle, 'Zur Auslegung von Gal. 2:17,18', *ZNW* 23 (1924), pp.152–3.

[83] Böttger, 'Paulus und Petrus'; cf. Eckstein, *Verheißung*, p.52.

[84] Burton, *Galatians*, pp.130–1; Longenecker, pp.90–1.

[85] Admittedly συνίστημι/συνιστάνω can mean 'constitute', but only when used of God's creative activity (*Enoch* 101:6; Philo, *Leg. All.* 3:10; Jos., *Ant.* 12:22; *1 Cl.* 27:4), cf. W. Bauer, *A Greek-English Lexicon of the New Testament and Other Early Christian Literature*, revised and augmented by F.W. Gingrich and F.W. Danker (London: University of Chicago Press, 1979), p.790.

[86] Sieffert, *Galater*, p.152; Zahn, p.130; Oepke, pp.61–2; Kieffer, *Foi et Justification*, pp.60–6.

Paul's use of the first person singular may of course be understood as a stylistic device to communicate a general principle, so that in verse 18 he still speaks as a representative of the Jewish Christians.[87] However, the problem with this view is that it fails to account for Paul's change from the first person plural in 2:15–17. Oepke suggested that Paul referred to himself as a tactful way of avoiding open criticism of Peter,[88] but this view founders on the fact that there is no change of subject between verse 18 and verse 19.[89] Klein proposed that the change of speaker served to carry Paul's thought forwards, indicating that in verse 18 the apostle is no longer thinking about the initial act of faith, but is now focusing on the new position of the believer.[90] Kümmel responded by reiterating the now common view that the first person singular is a stylistic device,[91] which Bachmann has sought to substantiate by arguing that in Romans 3:6–7; 7:7 Paul uses the first person singular as a stylistic device in response to the expostulation μὴ γένοιτο.[92]

Regarding the first person singular as a stylistic device has the effect of distancing Paul personally from verse 18, but it still cannot adequately account for the change from using the first person singular as negative counter-example in verse 18 to positive example in verse 19. Paul's use of the personal pronoun ἐγώ in verse 19 is not sufficient to indicate a shift from a representative to a personal understanding of the first person singular.[93] Nor is there any indication that verse 18 is to be understood as a parenthetical counter-example:[94] on the contrary, the introductory γάρ in verse 19 suggests a positive, rather than a negative correlation with verse 18. It remains fundamentally implausible that Paul would use the first person singular in one verse to describe a position he wishes to refute, and use the first person singular in the next verse to describe

---

[87] W.G. Kümmel, *Römer 7 und die Bekehrung des Paulus* (Leipzig: Hinrichs'sche, 1929), p.123.

[88] Oepke, *Galater*, p.61; cf. Longenecker, p.90; H. Merklein, ' "Nicht aus Werken des Gesetzes..." eine Auslegung von Gal. 2,15–21', in H. Merklein, K. Müller and G. Sternberger, eds., *Bibel in jüdischer und christlicher Tradition, Festschrift für Johann Maier zum 60. Geburtstag*, BBB 88 (Frankfurt: Anton Harris, 1993).

[89] Cf. Mussner, *Galaterbrief*, p.177.

[90] Klein, 'Individualgeschichte', pp.195–6.

[91] Kümmel, 'Individualgeschichte'; cf. E. Stauffer, 'ἐγώ', in Kittel, *TDNT*, vol.II, pp.343–62; Bruce, *Galatians*, p.142; Fung, p.120; Schlier, p.59.

[92] Bachmann, *Sünder*, pp.30–54. However, cf. Rom. 11:1.

[93] *Contra* V. Hasler, 'Glaube und Existenz: Hermeneutische Erwägungen zu Gal. 2,15–21', *Theologische Zeitschrift* 25 (1969), pp.241–51; E. Farahien, *Le 'Je' Paulinien – Étude pour Mieux Comprendre Gal. 2:19–21* (Rome: Editrice Pontificia Università Gregoriana, 1988); Oepke, *Galater*, p.62; Lambrecht, *Pauline Studies*, pp.193–204; Kieffer, *Foi et Justification*, pp.16–17, 62; Eckstein, *Verheißung*, pp.42–55.

[94] Bultmann, 'Auslegung', cf. Oepke, *Galater*, p.61; Schlier, p.59.

a position that he clearly applies to himself, when continuity between both verses is clearly indicated by γάϱ as the connecting conjunction. Whatever reference Paul intended by using the first person singular, his syntax indicates that there should be continuity between verse 18 and verse 19.

This difficulty is resolved, however, if verse 18 is taken as a personal reference by the apostle to his building up the church that he formerly sought to destroy.[95] Common to all the above interpretations is the un- proved assumption that the referent of ταῦτα in verse 18 is the law, or the law's distinction between Jew and Gentile. If, however, ταῦτα is taken as a reference to the church, the problems with Paul's syntax disappear. This interpretation of ταῦτα can account for Paul's shift to the first person singular in verses 18–21 and his use of the true-to-life conditional in verse 18, and can also give a coherent account of the flow of his thought.

Prima facie, it is likely that Paul's use of the first person singular in verse 18 would have been understood as a personal self-reference by his readers: Paul used the first person singular about himself as recently as 2:14, and on all other occasions in Galatians where Paul uses the first person singular, he clearly has himself in mind (1:9–2:14; 4:12–20; 5:10–12; 6:14, 17). Where Paul wishes to widen the application of his words, on the other hand, he does not hesitate to use the first person plural (1:8; 2:15–17; 3:13–14, 24–25; 4:3). Furthermore, the intensely personal nature of the letter means it is more likely that Paul would refer to his own experience in the course of defending his gospel.

In the conditional sentence of verse 18, Paul refers to building up again the things that he had destroyed. His use of the true-to-life conditional here suggests that this is something that really happened, rather than a hypothetical possibility or an option that he rejected.[96] The reference to building up (present tense) the things he destroyed (aorist)[97] points to a present reversal of past behaviour.[98] Just such a present reversal of

---

[95]Cf. P. Garnet, 'Qumran Light on Pauline Soteriology', in D.A. Hagner and M.J. Harris, eds., *Pauline Studies: Essays Presented to Professor F.F. Bruce on his 70th Birthday* (Exeter: Paternoster, 1980), p.28; Gaston, *Paul*, p.71.

[96]However, it is true that Paul is less than strict about the correctness of his conditional constructions (Gal. 2:21; 4:15; though cf. 1:10).

[97]Paul's use of the aorist tense here contrasts with the way he has previously used the imperfect tense to refer to his persecution of the church (Gal. 1:13, 23). However, this does not rule out a reference to his persecuting activity; Paul may simply have used the aorist tense here by default, since 'The perfective (aorist) aspect is the least heavily weighted of the Greek verbal aspects, and hence carries the least significant meaning attached to use of the form' (Porter, *Idioms*, p.22).

[98]πάλιν is used here with the sense of reversal, rather than repetition. It is not that Paul had previously built up the churches and was now doing so again, but rather that he was

previous behaviour has been recounted in Paul's account of his encounter with Christ in Galatians 1:13–21, which ends with the recognition by the churches in Judaea that the man who had formerly been their persecutor was now proclaiming the gospel. Furthermore, the verb καταλύω and the noun οἰκοδομή are used together of building up and destroying God's work and the church in Romans 14:19–20:

ἄρα οὖν τὰ τῆς εἰρήνης διώκωμεν καὶ τὰ τῆς οἰκοδομῆς τῆς εἰς ἀλλήλους. μὴ ἕνεκεν βρώματος κατάλυε τὸ ἔργον τοῦ θεοῦ.

This conjunction of the two terms in the context of building up and destroying the church makes it inherently likely that Paul had the church in mind in Galatians 2:18.[99] Furthermore, in Romans 14:19–20 Paul refers to building up the people and destroying the work of God, and these two different objects of building and destroying would account for Paul's indeterminate ταῦτα in Galatians 2:19.

The reason why building up the church should make Paul a transgressor of the law is the same reason why he formerly persecuted the church out of a zeal for the law: now, as one who is actively engaged in the task of building up the church, he is prepared to identify himself as a transgressor of the law.

This reading of the verse yields a coherent flow of thought from verse 17 through to verse 20. It was argued above that in verse 17, Paul accepts that those who seek justification in Christ are sinners in the eyes of the law, because they have abandoned the law as the crucial boundary marker that distinguished righteous Jew from sinful Gentile. This, however, in no way makes Christ the servant of sin. Paul's response to the μὴ γένοιτο at the end of verse 17 is only completed in verse 20. In verse 18, he accepts that his action of building up the church demonstrates that he is a transgressor of the law. In verse 19, he then goes on to state that through the law he died to the law, so that he might live for God. Paul accepts the law's sentence of death upon himself as a transgressor, and so dies through the law,[100] but in thus dying through the law, he also dies to the law in

building up churches that he had previously destroyed. Paul also uses πάλιν in this way in Rom. 11:23; Gal.4:9.

[99] Although Betz (*Galatians*, p.121) argues that καταλύω is used here in the legal sense and appeals to Bauer's *Lexicon*, the Lexicon actually proposes the figurative interpretation of 'tear down, demolish' here, as an antonym to οἰκοδομεῖν (p.414).

[100] The difficult phrase διὰ νόμου has been understood in many different ways. Duncan refers to Paul's experience of the law's ineffectiveness (*Galatians*, p.70) and Bruce to the law's role in inciting Paul to persecute the church (p.143). Lightfoot (pp.117–18) argues that the law's revelation of the sin in the life of an individual is a necessary precondition of

order to live for God. This statement is developed in the claim that he has been crucified with Christ: as Christ died under the law, so Paul has been crucified with Christ, so that he no longer lives, but Christ lives in him. It is by dying through the law as a transgressor of the law that Paul participates in the eschatological life of Christ.

As he has done in verses 15–16, Paul thus places himself firmly outside the ethnic boundary of the law, but inside the eschatological boundary between the righteous and the wicked instigated by the coming of Christ (1:4). Indeed, by saying that he died through the law so that he might live to God, Paul suggests that it is only by being placed outside the law as a transgressor that it is possible to share in the life of Christ. Within the social context of Galatians, this claim has an important double function. Firstly, Paul thereby identifies himself with his Galatian converts and signals that those who are outside the law nevertheless participate in the eschatological life of the age to come – a point he reinforces by asking on what basis they received the eschatological Spirit in 3:6. Secondly, by saying that he died to the law to live to God, Paul implies that those who are not outside the law do not share in the eschatological life, and this is a claim that he develops in 3:7–14.

Concluding this section, it is possible to see how the ideas of universal wickedness are used by Paul's opponents in their struggle over the Galatian churches. The Judaisers appeal to the universal wickedness of the Gentiles to support their case for law observance and charge Paul and the law-free believers with being 'sinners' outside the boundaries of the righteous community: they claim that Paul has effectively made Christ the servant of sin. Paul's response to this 'witchcraft accusation' is to accept the accusation that those who seek justification in Christ are 'sinners', but he denies that Christ is therefore the servant of sin. On the contrary, it is as a transgressor of the law that Paul died with Christ to his old way of life and his old identity so that he might live to God. In Galatians 3:7–5:1, Paul develops his own counter-accusation that those under the law are under a curse, and are outside the newly defined eschatological boundary of the righteous. We now turn to see how Paul himself employs

finding freedom from the law in Christ; Betz sees a reference to the law as a παιδαγωγός bringing people to Christ (p.122; cf. Longenecker, p.91). Boyarin (*Radical Jew*, pp.122–4) claims that Paul refers here to the true law of faith, through which he died to the false law of physical observances, but this distinction is not apparent in v.19. In the light of Paul's explanatory phrase Χριστῷ συνεσταύρωμαι, a more likely explanation sees a reference to the death of Christ under the law in 3:13 (Schlier, pp.60–3; Fung, p.123; Dunn, p.144). However, Paul's application of the phrase to himself makes sense within the immediate context if, as argued above, Paul is deliberately placing himself outside the pale of the law in Gal. 2:17–19.

the idea of universal human wickedness in his struggle for the control of the Galatian congregation.

The curse of the law

In Galatians 3:6, Paul introduces the figure of Abraham, and the question of establishing that law-free Gentile believers are his true descendants guides his discussion until 5:1. In what is probably a response to the exegetical arguments of his opponents,[101] Paul responds by citing Genesis 15:6; 18:18 to demonstrate that God's promised blessing through Abraham to the Gentiles is appropriated on the basis of faith, and not by the law. Indeed, Paul says that those who are ἐξ ἔργων νόμου are under a curse[102] and cites Deuteronomy 27:26 to support this claim: 'Ἐπικατάρατος πᾶς ὅς οὐκ ἐμμένει πᾶσιν τοῖς γεγραμμένοις ἐν τῷ βιβλίῳ τοῦ νόμου τοῦ ποιῆσαι αὐτά. Schoeps took this verse as evidence that Paul believed that it was impossible to keep the whole law;[103] Betz demurred, arguing instead that the establishment of the law in Paul's eyes led inevitably to the breaking of the law, so that the 'accumulation of transgressions made sin so overwhelming that "everything was confined under sin"'.[104] Both approaches take this verse as evidence of Paul's pessimistic anthropology.

Such a view has been roundly criticised by E.P. Sanders as a total misrepresentation of the Jewish understanding of the law in terms of covenantal nomism. Sanders himself proposes that Paul's argument is terminological, in that he has just linked faith and blessing (3:9), which he now sets in antithesis to law and curse by quoting Deuteronomy 27:26. According to Sanders, the content of the verse is irrelevant: he chose it simply because it is the only verse in the LXX that links law and curse.[105] Galatians 5:3 is a problem for Sanders, however, in that Paul says μαρτύρομαι δὲ πάλιν παντὶ ἀνθρώπῳ περιτεμνομένῳ ὅτι ὀφειλέτης ἐστιν ὅλον τὸν νόμον ποιῆσαι. Sanders acknowledges a

---

[101] Barrett, 'Allegory'.

[102] Bonneau's identification of the curse as 'the fear of transgressing the law' is forced, as is Stanley's argument that κατάρα denotes the *threat* of a curse: N. Bonneau, 'The Logic of Paul's Argument on the Curse of the Law in Galatians 3:10–14', *NovT* 39 (1997), pp.60–80; C.D. Stanley, 'Under a Curse: a fresh reading of Gal. 3:10–14', *NTS* 36 (1990), pp.481–511.

[103] H.-J. Schoeps, *Paul: the Theology of the Apostle in the Light of Jewish Religious History* (London: Lutterworth, 1961), pp.175–83; cf. Lightfoot, *Galatians*, p.136; Burton, pp.164–5; Mussner, pp.224–6; H. Hübner, *Law in Paul's Thought* (Edinburgh: T&T Clark, 1984), pp.15–20; Lambrecht, *Pauline Studies*, pp.231–98.

[104] Betz, *Galatians*, p.146; cf. Eckstein, *Verheißung*, p.96.

[105] Sanders, *Jewish People*, pp.17–27.

reference to 3:10 here and has to admit that 'although Paul quoted Deut. 27:26 for the connection of "curse" and νόμος, he did not forget that it said "all" '.[106] This, however, is fatal for Sanders' case, since it means that the content of the quotation was significant for Paul after all.

According to Dunn, Paul is here opposing a misunderstanding of the law, which involved restricting the scope of God's covenant people to Israel *per se,* as those people who are defined by law and marked out by its distinctive requirements.[107] Paul, however, can see that 'such an understanding of the law is *not* all that the law requires ... the law has to be understood ... as something the Gentiles can do without any reference to whether they are inside the law or outside the law'.[108] To misunderstand the law as his opponents were doing was to fall short of what the law requires and thus fall under its curse. However, if Paul were dealing with a misunderstanding of the law here as Dunn proposes, one would surely expect him to explain the nature of the misunderstanding to his readers; instead, he continues with an outright denial that the law can justify at all.

Another approach to the problem is adopted by Wright, who adapts Noth's theory that the author of Deuteronomy perceived all Israel as being under a curse for their disobedience. According to Wright, Israel's oppression by the Romans led Paul to regard the nation as still suffering the punishment of exile under the curse of the law.[109] However, even if the view of Israel's continuing exile is valid,[110] the fact remains that Paul's focus in 3:11 is on the impossibility of the individual being justified through the law, and this conclusion is not a legitimate inference from the application of the curse of Deuteronomy 27:26 to the nation as a whole.

Garlington attempts to resolve the issue by arguing that for Paul, blessing belongs to the era of Abraham and the Spirit, while the age of the Torah is epitomised as curse: the Judaisers are under a curse because they have chosen to remain in the age of law, thus opposing God's eschatological designs in Christ.[111] However, while Garlington correctly notes the eschatological dimensions of Paul's thought, the Judaisers' allegiance to

---

[106]Ibid., p.27.

[107]Dunn, *Jesus, Paul*, pp.215–41.

[108]Ibid., p.227; cf. Boyarin, *Radical Jew*, pp.136–57.

[109]Wright, *Climax*, pp.137–56; cf. Thielman, *Plight*, pp.65–72; J.M. Scott, ' "For as Many as are of Works of the Law are under a Curse" (Galatians 3:10)', in C.A. Evans and J.A. Sanders, eds., *Paul and the Scriptures of Israel*, JSNT 83 (Sheffield: Sheffield Academic Press, 1993), pp.187–221; I.-G. Hong, *The Law in Galatians*, JSNTS 81 (Sheffield: Sheffield Academic Press, 1993), pp.125–48; 'Does Paul Misrepresent the Jewish Law? Law and Covenant in Gal. 3:1–14', *NovT* 36 (1994), pp.164–82.

[110]Dunn, *Galatians*, pp.171–2.

[111]D.B. Garlington, 'Role Reversal and Paul's Use of Scripture', *JSNT* 65 (1997), pp.85–121; cf. K.A. Morland, *The Rhetoric of Curse in Galatians: Paul Confronts Another Gospel* (Atlanta: Scholars, 1995).

the wrong epoch of salvation history does not account for Paul's application of the curse of Deuteronomy 27:26 to them in Galatians 3:10. On the basis of Galatians 2:18, Garlington argues that Paul sees those who rebuild the law as transgressors in the light of the Christ event, and this is how Paul can apply Deuteronomy 27:26 to the Judaisers. Yet this is not convincing: even if one accepts Garlington's claim that Galatians 2:18 redefines transgression as allegiance to the law, this does not explain why he should use Deuteronomy 27:26 as a proof text, since this verse defines transgression in terms of non-observance of the requirements of Torah.

If however, as argued by Barrett, Deuteronomy 27:26 was quoted by Paul's opponents,[112] the reasoning behind Paul's use of the verse becomes apparent. The verse itself clearly supports their position rather than Paul's, and Paul's response is to restrict the application of the verse to those who are ἐξ ἔργων νόμου, so that the curse only applies to those who are within the law. By contrast, believing Gentiles outside the law are justified (v.11) and receive the blessing of Abraham in the form of the Spirit (v.14).

If, however, Gentiles outside the law are not under its curse, why does Paul refer to Christ redeeming us from the curse of the law? E.P. Sanders takes this to be an example of Paul's inconsistency regarding the law: the apostle makes Gentiles outside the law subject to its curse because he is working back from a universal redemption in Christ to infer a universal plight of humanity that obliterates the distinction between Jew and Gentile.[113] Howard proposes that they were suppressed under the law, but this interpretation needs to be read into the passage in direct contradiction to the import of 3:10,[114] where Paul restricts the scope of the curse to those who are ἐξ ἔργων νόμου.

If, however, the referent of ἡμᾶς is taken to be Jews who are under the law,[115] a further difficulty ensues: how does the redemption of Jews from the law's curse enable Gentiles to receive the blessing of Abraham (3:14)? Donaldson has argued that the expectation that the Gentiles will be saved after the restoration of Israel has its basis in Jewish eschatological expectation, and cites Tobit 14:5–7 and *Sib. Or.* 3:701 in support.[116] However,

---

[112]Barrett, 'Allegory'.

[113]Sanders, *Jewish People*, pp.68–9.

[114]G. Howard, *Crisis in Galatia* (Cambridge: Cambridge University Press, 1979), pp.58–61.

[115]Lightfoot, *Galatians*, p.138; Burton, p.169; Betz, p.148; Hays, *Faith*, pp.86–92, 94–112.

[116]T.L. Donaldson, 'The Curse of the Law and the Inclusion of the Gentiles', *NTS* 32 (1986), pp.94–112; Donaldson retracted this argument in *Paul and the Gentiles: Remapping the Apostle's Convictional World* (Minneapolis: Fortress, 1997), pp.191–4; cf. Hong's reference to the universal consequences of the redemption of the Jews ('Does Paul Misrepresent...').

neither text constitutes an adequate basis for his claim that the redemption of Israel is a 'necessary prelude' to the inclusion of the Gentiles.

Both the inclusive and exclusive interpretations of ἡμᾶς thus suffer from difficulties. Yet once it is recognised that Deuteronomy 27:26 is a verse used by Paul's opponents, the problem is resolved. Paul in effect uses belt and braces and employs a double argument against their charge that his Gentile converts are under a curse for not obeying the law. Firstly, he argues that, as those outside the law, they are beyond the scope of its curse (3:10a); secondly, he argues that, even if the curse did apply to them,[117] Christ has redeemed them from the curse of the law by becoming a curse himself. The fact that Paul is countering his opponents at this point explains why he includes Gentiles with Jews under the law's curse. In 3:14 the result of Christ's redeeming death is spelt out: the blessing of Abraham comes to the Gentiles (Gen. 18:18), while believing Jews and Gentiles alike receive the promised Spirit by faith (Gen. 15:6). The effect of Paul's argument again is to identify as righteous those Gentiles outside the law who have received the eschatological Spirit, while his opponents, who adhere to the ethnic boundary of the law, are placed under its curse.

The power of sin

Paul completes the process of redefining the eschatological boundary separating the righteous from the sinful in 3:19–25. Here, in keeping with the witchcraft accusations that are characteristic of the small bounded group, he redraws the boundaries in such a way as to exclude his opponents and, by using the symbolism of the power of sin, he makes explicit use of the idea of universal wickedness in his political struggle for the loyalty of the Galatian congregations.

Having established that the promise to Abraham is inherited by faith, Paul carries his argument forward by means of an objection posed by an imaginary Jewish interlocutor: Τί οὖν ὁ νόμος; Paul's reply, τῶν παραβάσεων χάριν προσετέθη, is ambiguous, and has been taken to mean that the law was given to restrict sin,[118] to provoke sin,[119] or to identify sin as transgression.[120] The proposal that the law was given to stimulate sin is undermined by the way in which this claim can only be

---

[117] Paul may have been aware of the fragile nature of his attempt to restrict the sphere of the curse of the law to those who accepted the law.

[118] E.g. Dunn, *Galatians*, pp.188–90.

[119] E.g. Lightfoot, *Galatians*, p.143; Hong, 'Does Paul Misrepresent...', p.152.

[120] E.g. Zahn, *Galater*, p.172; Burton, p.188; Oepke, p.81; Mussner, p.245.

comprehended in the light of Paul's later letter to the Romans. Paul's use of the term παραβάσεων is firm evidence for the third option, since elsewhere this word is always used of sin as transgression of the law or a commandment (cf. Rom. 2:23; 4:15; 5:14). Paul thus argues that the law had an essentially negative role of identifying and 'chalking up' sin until the coming of Christ. Nevertheless, he denies that the law is opposed to the promises of God (3:21), and responds:

> εἰ γὰρ ἐδόθη νόμος ὁ δυνάμενος ζῳοποιῆσαι,
> ὄντως ἐκ νόμου ἄν ἦν ἡ δικαιοσύνη·
> ἀλλὰ συνέκλεισεν ἡ γραφὴ τὰ πάντα ὑπὸ ἁμαρτίαν,
> ἵνα ἡ ἐπαγγελία ἐκ πίστεως Ἰησοῦ Χριστοῦ δοθῇ
>   τοῖς πιστεύουσιν.

Paul's reply in these verses takes the form of an ABBA chiasm. The first half of the chiasm considers the hypothetical possibility of righteousness and life coming by the law, and the second half sets out a contrasting picture of what has actually happened instead. Thus line 1 refers to the giving of the law, whereas line 4 mentions the giving of the promise, so that the contrast between law and promise reflects the introductory question in verse 21a. Similarly, the reference to righteousness in line 2 finds its antonym in the reference to sin in line 3, so that the two central lines of the chiasm contrast what would have been the case, had the law been able to bring life, with the reality of what actually happened. Had the law been able to make alive, there would have been no doubt that righteousness, as the precondition of eschatological life,[121] would have come through the law. The chiastic structure of the verse implies that the promise has brought the life that the law failed to deliver. It is thus not the case that the law is opposed to the promise; it is rather that the promise has achieved what the law was unable to achieve: the giving of eschatological life.

This association of the promise with life is confirmed by the identification of the promise as the Spirit in 3:14,[122] since it is the Spirit that imparts eschatological life (5:25; 6:8); the law, by contrast, brings death (2:19). Paul clearly identifies participation in the eschatological era inaugurated by the Spirit as the defining characteristic of the righteous 'in-group'; the law, by contrast, did not bring righteousness at all. Instead, under the old aeon, the scripture imprisoned everything under sin.

---

[121] Righteousness is not simply the equivalent of life here (Fung, *Galatians*, p.163).

[122] The variant reading εὐλογίαν ($\wp^{46}$ D* F G) is a secondary response to the unexpected introduction of the concept of promise.

What scripture does Paul refer to here? Does Paul use ἡ γραφή as a metonymy for God,[123] or does he refer to scripture generically without a specific verse in mind?[124] Elsewhere Paul uses ἡ γραφή with specific references in mind,[125] but there are no obvious candidates here: Psalm 143:2 (Gal. 2:16) or Deuteronomy 27:26 (Gal. 3:10) are cited as possibilities,[126] as is the catena of quotations in Romans 3:10–18.[127] Yet Galatians 3:22 is not intended to be a scriptural *citation*: whereas elsewhere Paul uses the verb λέγει with scripture,[128] here ἡ γραφή is the subject of the verb συνέκλεισεν. It is therefore misguided to embark on a fruitless search for a scriptural reference to the effect that everything is imprisoned under sin. Rather, the role of imprisoning assigned to the scripture needs to be understood within the context of Galatians 3:21–22.

Within the context of the chiasm, the false possibility of the law's bringing life and righteousness is ruled out by the scripture's imprisonment of all things under sin; instead, the promise is given to those who believe. The same constellation of ideas is found in Galatians 3:11, where the citation from Habakkuk 2:4, Ὁ δίκαιος ἐκ πίστεως ζήσεται, confirms that no one is justified before God by the law. Whether ἐκ πίστεως is taken with the preceding noun or the succeeding verb, Habakkuk 2:4 associates righteousness and life with faith. The effect of this association (which Paul would have argued was exclusive) is to rule out the possibility of righteousness and life being associated with the law, which is precisely the function attributed to the scripture in Galatians 3:22. Furthermore, Habakkuk 2:4 refers to present righteousness and future life, and this corresponds to the reference to righteousness as the precondition for life in Galatians 3:21. The association of righteousness and life with faith is also picked up in the fourth line of the chiasm, where the purpose of the scripture confining everything under sin is that 'faith in Jesus Christ should be the ground on which the promised blessing is given to those who believe' (REB). Habakkuk 2:4 thus seems a likely candidate for the scripture referred to in 3:22.

In what way, though, does this verse confine everything under sin? There is no doubt that Paul thought that believers participated in the life

---

[123]Oepke, *Galater*, p.85; Hong, 'Does Paul Misrepresent...', p.155; Eckstein, *Verheißung*, p.208.

[124]Schlier, *Galater*, p.164; Fung, p.164.

[125]Rom. 4:3; 9:17; 10:11; 11:2; Gal. 3:8; 4:30.

[126]Lightfoot, *Galatians*, p.146; Burton, pp.195–6; Longenecker, p.144.

[127]Zahn, *Galater*, pp.181–2; Dunn, p.194.

[128]In Gal. 3:8 he uses προευηγγελίσατο, which is still a verb expressing communication.

of the age to come through the Spirit, and correspondingly, righteousness, as the precondition of that life, must also be imparted by the Spirit.[129] Within the overall eschatological framework of the letter, Habakkuk 2:4 thus becomes a pledge of the eschatological realities of righteousness and life conveyed by the Spirit to believers.[130] However, if righteousness and life are identified as eschatological realities, the negative corollary of such an identification is the portrayal of the present age as sinful. Hence Habakkuk 2:4 has the negative effect of confining the present universe under sin, and ἁμαρτία here simply denotes the sinfulness of the universe under the old aeon, in accordance with the new eschatological boundaries Paul is drawing in Galatians.

The imagery of confinement is determined by the direction of Paul's argument at this point, rather than by any inherent meaning of the singular noun ἁμαρτία.[131] The idea of confinement is taken up in 3:23–25 and applied to the law as the custodian or guard of those under sin. Paul here seeks to reverse the customary perception of the law as a boundary that keeps sin at bay; instead, the law has become a gaoler that confines people under sin in the old aeon. Ebeling expresses the polemical nature of Paul's thought clearly:

> The Torah is for Israel a protective fence. It prevents contact with everything unclean, which is kept outside, and it restrains the desire to break out and overstep the salutary boundary. It would almost be possible to say that Paul takes a polemical stance towards this image of the Torah as a beneficent fence by radicalising it and thus transforming it into its opposite. It is not the law but the sin preceding the law that must first be taken into account. And it is no longer a protective fence but a prison from which there is no escape. Within this transformed metaphor the law does not have the function of partially breaking through the walls of sin, making a breach in them to open a way of escape. On the contrary, the law has the function of an additional attendant, a prison guard who makes those who live in the custody of sin

---

[129]Cf. S.K. Williams, 'The Justification of the Spirit in Galatians', *JSNT* 29 (1987), pp.91–100.

[130]Paul has already established that the Galatians received the Spirit by hearing with faith and not by obeying the law. It is because the Spirit imparts eschatological righteousness and life that Paul can safely assume the priority of Hab. 2:4, which associates righteousness and life with faith, over Lev. 18:5, which associates life with the law (Gal. 3:11–12).

[131]Paul may even have taken the use of ἁμαρτία in the singular from his opponents (Gal. 2:17).

fully aware of where they are. This φρουρεῖν is the function of
the law: it watches over those imprisoned in sin and keeps them
in custody.[132]

Douglas' model offers confirmation for Ebeling's suggestion. Paul's
language here is indeed motivated by the polemical aim of reversing the
function of the Jewish law. The characteristically Jewish perception of
cosmic wickedness perceived the law as the boundary that keeps sin at
bay. From his eschatological perspective, Paul can portray the law as a
gaoler imprisoning people under sin in the old aeon.

It is not therefore the case that the term ἁμαρτία has any inherent
connection with the symbolism of enslavement. Paul uses the term as
an antonym to δικαιοσύνη in the first line of the chiasm, and is simply
stressing the universality of sin under the old aeon.[133] His use of the
symbolism of imprisonment is here determined by his polemical aim
of subverting Jewish confidence in the law. Paul is not concerned with
developing any profound insight into the nature of the human condition
at this point: as part of his political struggle for the loyalty of the Galatian
community, his sole aim is to use the idea of human wickedness on a
cosmic scale to place those under the law beyond the eschatological pale,
firmly outside the boundaries of the righteous.

Works of the flesh

Paul further subverts the ethnic distinction between righteous Jew and
sinful Gentile by redefining sin along eschatological lines in 5:16–26,
describing sinful behaviour as 'works of the flesh' that can be overcome
only by the Spirit and so replaced with its fruit.[134]

According to Bultmann, life in the flesh is existence in the sphere of
the humanly natural and transitory: the sinfulness of the flesh arises from
an attitude of trusting that one can procure life by use of the earthly and
through one's own strength and accomplishment.[135] Bultmann therefore
characterises life according to the flesh as sinful self-reliance. Käsemann,
reacting against Bultmann's individualism, argued that existence is fundamentally conceived from the angle of the world to which one belongs:

---

[132]G. Ebeling, *The Truth of the Gospel: an Exposition of Galatians* (Philadelphia:
Fortress, 1985), p.194.

[133]Mussner, *Galaterbrief*, p.253; Bruce, p.180.

[134]R. Jewett rightly argues that it was the conflict with the Judaisers that led Paul to
connect σάρξ to the old aeon (*Paul's Anthropological Terms* (Leiden: E.J. Brill, 1971),
pp.95–116).

[135]Bultmann, *Theology*, vol.I, pp.239–46.

'Existence is "flesh" in so far as it has given itself over to the world of flesh, serves that world and allows itself to be determined by it.'[136] More recently, Barclay has rightly argued that the term σάρξ designates what is merely human, in contrast to the divine activity displayed on the cross and in the Spirit.[137] Paul thus employs the term σάρξ precisely because it sums up human existence in this age, as opposed to the life of the age to come, which is characterised by πνεῦμα. By identifying sins as 'works of the flesh', Paul brands as sinful the natural behaviour of all humanity apart from the Spirit. Esler rightly argues that Paul is seeking to forge an identity for the Galatian believers by linking community norms to the Spirit and by stereotyping the world outside the congregation as the realm of the flesh.[138]

Paul identifies walking by the Spirit as the way to overcome the desires of the flesh (5:16),[139] since the opposition between the Spirit and the flesh prevents people from doing 'whatever they want'. There is uncertainty over what the 'you' in the verse desires: are fleshly desires frustrated by the Spirit,[140] or are the promptings of conscience overridden by the flesh?[141] Alternatively, does the individual side sometimes with the flesh and sometimes with the Spirit,[142] or is this precisely the neutrality that Paul is concerned to counter?[143] The syntax of the final clause in verse 17 is curious as a result of the postponement of the main verb to the end. The clause itself (ἃ ἐὰν θέλητε ταῦτα ποιῆτε) has the possible appearance of being a slogan coined by Paul's opponents to attack what they perceived as being the libertine consequences of abandoning the moral code of the law, in which case Paul formulates the flesh/Spirit antithesis to counter the agitators' accusations that his law-free gospel places no restriction on immoral behaviour.

Paul also uses the term σάρξ against his opponents, by playing upon the ambiguity of its meaning in such a way as to associate it with the physical practice of circumcision. Thus, in 6:12–13, there can be no doubt that the references to those who want to make a good show in

---

[136]E. Käsemann, *Perspectives on Paul*, p.26.

[137]Barclay, *Obeying the Truth*, pp.178–215.

[138]P.F. Esler, 'Group Boundaries and Intergroup Conflict in Galatians: a new reading of Galatians 5:13–6:10', in M.G. Brett, ed., *Ethnicity and the Bible* (Leiden: E.J. Brill, 1996), pp.215–40.

[139]τελέσητε should be read as an indicative, and not an imperative; Paul is promising victory over the flesh rather than commanding it.

[140]Duncan, *Galatians*, pp.167–8; Barclay, *Obeying the Truth*, p.115.

[141]Lightfoot, *Galatians*, p.210; P. Althaus, 'Daß ihr nicht tut, was ihr wollt', *TLZ* 76 (1951), pp.15–18.

[142]Burton, *Galatians*, p.302; Betz, p.281; Longenecker, p.246; Dunn, p.199.

[143]Fung, *Galatians*, p.251.

the flesh and who want to boast in the Galatians' flesh are aimed at the advocates of circumcision. But since these verses follow hard upon the contrast between flesh and Spirit in 5:16–26; 6:8, it is clear that Paul wishes to associate the practice of circumcision in the physical flesh with the present evil age that is characterised by the flesh in these verses, and which is destroyed by the advent of God's new creation (6:15). Indeed, there is good reason to suppose that Paul refers to 'works of the flesh' in 5:19 in order to echo the phrase 'works of the law' in 2:16; 3:2, 5, 10. The effect is subliminally to identify circumcision, as a work of the law in the flesh, with the list of sins itemised in 5:19–21.[144]

Paul allows no place for the law in his development of the eschato-logical distinction between the righteous and the wicked. He explicitly states that those who are led by the Spirit are not under law (5:18), and suggests that the fruit of the Spirit renders the law superfluous (5:23). Paul only grants the law validity insofar as it is summed up in the love com-mandment (5:14), which is fulfilled in the mutual bearing of each other's burdens (6:2).

However, Paul's position is vulnerable to the counter-accusation that the Spirit does not make an effective boundary separating the sinful from the righteous, especially if his list of 'the works of the flesh' reflects some of the moral problems in the church in Galatia. Paul tries to tackle this problem in 6:7–8, where he warns that those who sow to the flesh will from the flesh reap destruction, while those who sow to the Spirit will reap eternal life. Paul makes the point that the whole of one's life must be oriented to the Spirit. Sin in the community of the Spirit is an anomaly, which Paul says will ultimately result in the destruction of the offender. Again, Douglas' model suggests that this often repeated exhortation to 'become what you are' is less a conscious move from the indicative to the imperative than his attempt to wrestle with the porousness of group boundaries, which means that sinful behaviour is constantly infiltrating the group from outside. This is reflected in Paul's use of the symbolism of flesh to portray this evil. Within the cosmology of the small bounded group, physical flesh is regarded with ambivalence, since it represents the porous boundary between the good inside and the evil outside. Paul uses the symbolism here, not because he regards the flesh as inherently evil, but because it accurately symbolises the ambiguous status

---

[144] A similar play on words occurs in 3:3, where Paul asks, ἐναρξάμενοι πνεύματι νῦν σαρκὶ ἐπιτελεῖσθε; here, the reference to finishing in the flesh obviously has circumcision in mind, but the effect of its being juxtaposed to the reference to the Spirit again has the effect of identifying circumcision as a practice that belongs only to the old aeon, and which is irrelevant to those who have received the eschatological Spirit.

of those who have entered into the eschatological era through receiving the Spirit, but who still have to live 'in the flesh' in the present evil age. By opposing the flesh to the eschatological Spirit, Paul adapts the tension between the good inside and evil outside symbolised by the flesh, and applies it to the eschatological tension between present and future experienced by members of the community. It is this tension which finds expression in his combination of the indicative and imperative in Galatians 5:16–6:8.

Conclusion

In this chapter, Douglas' group/grid model has been used to cast light on Paul's sin language in Galatians. It has been argued that Paul and the Galatians belong in the high group/low grid quadrant of Douglas' matrix, which means that they shared a strong sense of group identity, and rejected the prevailing symbolic system of the surrounding culture. The cosmology of this quadrant is dominated by the idea of the good inside being threatened by universal wickedness beyond the boundaries of the community. Since the small bounded group is concerned less with inward stability than with maintaining its distinctiveness over against the surrounding culture, social units in this quadrant are particularly susceptible to the kind of witchcraft accusations that Neyrey discerned within Galatians. However, Neyrey failed to note that such accusations serve the political goal of redrawing community boundaries in such a way as to exclude outsiders, who become associated with the universal human wickedness outside the community.

Douglas' witchcraft cosmology corresponds closely to the situation in Galatians, in which Paul's leadership has been challenged by Judaisers who have come into the community from outside. Both Paul and the agitators employ witchcraft accusations against each other, and redraw the boundaries around the community in such a way as to exclude their opponents and associate them with the universal wickedness outside the community. Paul's Jewish Christian opponents perceived the Gentile world as sinful, and accordingly emphasised the Torah as the only effective boundary marker between the righteous and the sinful (Gal. 2:15). They claimed that those who sought justification in Christ apart from the law were sinners, and alleged that Paul's law-free gospel made Christ the servant of sin. Only by being circumcised and keeping the law was it possible for Gentile converts to be separated from the sinfulness of the Gentile world and included within the Torah-observant community of the righteous.

Paul's response to the agitators is surprisingly bold. He accepts that all those who seek justification in Christ apart from the law are sinners, but he denies that this makes Christ the servant of sin. In a bold manoeuvre, he acknowledges that his act of rebuilding the church renders him a transgressor in the eyes of the law and subject to its sentence of death. But then he claims that with Christ he has died to the law, so that he might live for God. Although he and his converts are outside the ethnic boundary of Torah, they belong to the newly defined eschatological community of the righteous and have therefore been delivered from the present evil age (1:4).

Paul replaces the ethnic boundary of Torah observance with the eschatological boundary of Spirit reception. Characterising the Spirit as the blessing promised to Abraham, he argues that all those who are of the law are under a curse; the blessing instead is given to the Gentiles, who receive the Spirit by faith. Paul thus uncompromisingly excludes all those under Torah. Paul portrays being in Christ and being in the law as two mutually exclusive spheres. He seeks to redraw the boundaries between the righteous and the sinful along eschatological lines, in such a way as to exclude his Torah-observant opponents. The law belongs to the old aeon, which is under the dominion of sin. Far from constituting a boundary that keeps the outside evil at bay, the law functions as a prison, confining transgressors within the present evil age. Paul locates Torah firmly within the realm of sin under the old aeon, and he utilises the symbolism of the power of sin as part of his strategy of excluding his opponents. Douglas' matrix highlights the way in which both Paul and his opponents attempt to define group boundaries in such a way as to exclude each other from the community of the righteous. Paul's opponents define the boundaries along ethnic lines and identify Paul as a Gentile sinner. Paul draws the boundaries along eschatological lines and locates his opponents within the old aeon that is under the dominion of sin.

Paul's use of the symbolism of sin was determined by the specific social situation he was addressing in Galatians. It is in the context of the need to define the boundaries of the Gentile church over against Judaism that the apostle develops the symbol of sin as a power imprisoning the universe. He does not use the term ἁμαρτία in the singular because the singular noun necessarily denoted a power dominating the world; that is not how the term is used in 2:17, where it probably echoes the language of Paul's opponents. Paul's use of the term in 3:22 is determined by the social situation Paul is addressing: he develops a picture of universal human wickedness on a cosmic scale as part of his political strategy to locate law-abiding Jews firmly beyond the pale of the eschatological boundaries that he has defined around the law-free Gentile believers in Galatia. The symbolism of the power of sin is simply used to represent the evil of the world outside the boundaries of righteous, law-free believers, and is coined as part of Paul's response to this specific social situation in Galatia.

Paul also addresses the problem of deviant behaviour within the community in terms of his eschatological distinction between the righteous and the sinful. He urges members of the church to walk according to the Spirit, rather than according to the flesh. Paul uses the symbolism of flesh to identify deviance as behaviour that belongs to the present, evil age, rather than to the eschatological age of the Spirit. According to Douglas, the physical body is a symbol of the social body and within the cosmology of the small bounded group, both are threatened by sin as an outside evil that infiltrates the physical and social boundaries. Paul's use of the symbolism of flesh corresponds to this model. Since flesh marks the ambiguous boundary between the good inside and the evil outside of the physical body, it accurately symbolises the evil of the old aeon that is infiltrating the porous boundaries of the community from the world outside. In this way, Douglas' matrix illuminates Paul's choice of the term 'flesh' as a symbol for deviant behaviour.

Douglas' matrix highlights the way in which both Paul and his opponents attempt to define group boundaries in such a way as to place each other beyond the pale. Paul's opponents define the boundaries along ethnic lines and associate Paul with Gentile sinfulness. Paul redraws the boundaries along eschatological lines and locates his opponents within the old aeon that is under the dominion of sin. It was within the socio-historical context of this political struggle for the leadership of the Galatian congregations that Paul developed the symbolism of the power of sin with a view to excluding his opponents.

5

SMALL BOUNDED GROUPS IN ROME

Introduction

Paul uses the noun ἁμαρτία in the singular 45 times in Romans,[1] and 41 of these references are concentrated in chapters 5–8.[2] These chapters therefore hold the key to our understanding the symbolism of sin as a power. Traditionally, these chapters have often been read as a doctrinal exposition of the new life available to those who are saved by the gospel.[3] Such an approach insulates one's understanding of the power of sin from the socio-historical situation in which these chapters were written. If Paul wrote Romans with a view to reconciling the strong and weak factions referred to in Romans 14–16, that raises the question as to how his emphasis on the power of sin at this point in the letter relates to his overall aim in addressing this particular social situation.

Using Douglas' matrix, it will be shown how the symbolism of the power of sin in Romans is grounded in the socio-cultural context of the letter. In keeping with the cosmology of the small bounded group, Paul sees sin as an external danger that threatens the boundaries protecting the good inside of the physical and social body. His letter reflects the characteristic high group/low grid concern with boundary definition, as he responds to the question of whether Gentile believers should have to keep the Jewish law by redrawing the boundaries around the community of the righteous along eschatological, rather than ethnic, lines. Paul seeks to show that Gentile believers are released from the power of sin by dying with Christ in baptism, whereas the Torah-observant Jew is still subject to the power of sin, which holds sway within the physical body of those

[1] The plural form occurs once in 7:5, and also in scriptural citations from Ps. 32:1–2 (Rom. 4:7–8) and Isa. 27:9 (Rom. 11:26–27).
[2] The four references outside chapters 5–8 are: Rom. 3:9, 20; 4:8; 14:23.
[3] E.g., C.H. Dodd, *The Epistle of Paul to the Romans* (London: Fontana, 1959), pp.vii–viii; C.E.B. Cranfield, *The Epistle to the Romans*, ICC, 2 vols. (Edinburgh: T&T Clark, 1975–9), vol.I, pp.28–9; J. Fitzmyer, *Romans*, AB (London: Geoffrey Chapman), 1993, pp.98–9; D.J. Moo, *Romans*, pp.33–4.

who belong to the present aeon. It will be argued that Paul specifically developed such a negative anthropology in Romans 5–8 as part of his strategy to persuade other Christian groups within the capital to accept members of the law-free Gentile community as fellow believers in Christ. In this way, by means of Douglas' model, a fresh interpretation of Romans 5–8 is offered, as well as a fresh understanding of the relationship between these central chapters and Romans 1–4.

The purpose of Romans

By the time that Paul wrote Romans, in the mid- to late 50s,[4] Christianity was already well established in the capital (1:8). The origins of the church in Rome remain shrouded in obscurity, and there is insufficient evidence to determine whether Christianity was first brought to the capital as a result of direct missionary activity, or whether travelling merchants and artisans were responsible for its introduction there. The earliest evidence for the existence of Christians in Rome is Paul's letter to the Romans itself, but there can be no doubt that there had been Christians in Rome for some time before Paul wrote to them. Suetonius' account of Claudius' edict expelling the Jews for rioting *impulsore Chresto* offers secondary, indirect evidence for the existence of Christians in Rome in 49 CE.[5] If, as seems likely, Suetonius confused the title 'Christ' with the common slave name 'Chrestus', meaning 'useful', then it is possible to infer that the disturbance that occasioned the expulsion of some Jews arose out of a dispute between Jews and Jewish Christians, possibly over the question of the admission of Gentiles into the community. For how long prior to this date Jewish Christians had been peacefully associated with the local Roman synagogues it is impossible to say.

It must be deemed unlikely that Claudius expelled all Jews from the city, but it is likely that most, if not all, the Jewish Christians found themselves, like Priscilla and Aquila, banned from Rome until such time as the edict

---

[4] Jewett (*Dating Paul's Life*) dates Romans in 56–7 CE; as Cranfield points out, it is hard to be precise (*Romans*, pp.12–16). G. Lüdemann suggests the winter of 51/52 CE (*Paul*), but this is unlikely (Dunn, *Romans*, vol. I, pp.xliii–xliv).

[5] *Claudii Vita* 25.4. Orosius dates the expulsion in the ninth regnal year of Claudius, in 49 CE, but since he claims Josephus as his source and Josephus is silent on the subject, his dating must be treated with suspicion. However, according to Acts 18:2, which refers to the presence of Prisca and Aquila in Corinth following their expulsion from Rome, Paul met them there eighteen months prior to his appearance before the proconsul, Gallio (18:12–17), who held office between July 51 CE and July 52 CE (Jewett, *Dating Paul's Life*, pp.36–40). If Paul appeared before Gallio in the latter half of 51 CE his arrival at Corinth would have taken place in early 50 CE which corresponds with the expulsion of Prisca and Aquila in 49 CE. Orosius' dating of the edict thus appears to have independent confirmation, and it should therefore be accepted, despite the misgivings of Lüdemann (*Paul*, pp.164–71).

lapsed after the death of Claudius in 54 CE. On their return, they seem to have found that, during the period of their absence, Gentile Christianity had grown and that the ties with the synagogue had been severed. According to Marxsen, this scenario underlies the problem of the weak and the strong in Romans 14:1–15:13, where the strong represent Gentile, law-free Christians in Rome, while the weak are law-abiding Jews.[6] The latter returned to the capital to find that the number of Gentile Christians had increased in their absence, and that they were now in the minority. Paul then wrote to Rome to warn the Gentile majority not to despise the Jewish Christians who still observed Jewish festivals and dietary requirements, and to urge the Jewish believers not to sit in judgment on their fellow Gentile believers, who did not keep the law. Paul's aim in writing Romans was thus to reconcile these two opposing groups in the capital.

This approach to understanding Romans has, however, had its critics. Recognising the crucial role of the paraenetic section of the letter in any reconstruction of the situation in Rome, Karris analysed Romans 14:1–15:13 and concluded that this section of the letter was general paraenesis, based upon Paul's discussion of the specific problems within the Corinthian church in 1 Corinthians 8–10, which the apostle adapted for general consumption when he wrote his letter to the Romans.[7]

Karris sees Romans as a letter that sums up Paul's missionary theology and paraenesis, and thus he belongs to the camp of those who see Romans 15:14–24 as the key to understanding the letter. Here the apostle says that he has exhausted his scope for mission in the east, and that his intention after visiting Jerusalem is to visit the as yet unevangelised Spain in the west. Those who see this planned visit to Spain as the key to the letter argue that Paul was writing to the Roman congregations in order to introduce himself to them and to set before them his gospel and the basis for his missionary strategy.[8]

Another critic is Jervell, who argued that Paul's purpose in writing to the Romans was to request their support for his impending visit to Jerusalem to deliver the collection from the Gentile churches (15:25–33). According to Jervell, Paul's attention throughout the letter is focused upon the

---

[6] W. Marxsen, *Introduction to the New Testament* (Oxford: Blackwell, 1968), pp.95–103; cf. W. Wiefel, 'The Jewish Community in Ancient Rome and the Origins of Roman Christianity', in K.P. Donfried, ed., *The Romans Debate* (Peabody: Hendrickson, 1991), pp.85–101; P.S. Minear, *The Obedience of Faith* (London: SCM, 1971).

[7] R.J. Karris, 'Romans 14:1–15:13 and the Occasion of Romans', in Donfried, *Romans Debate*, pp.65–84.

[8] Cf. Dodd, *Romans*, pp.18–19; Cranfield, pp.814–26; L.A. Jervis, *The Purpose of Romans: a Comparative Letter Structure Investigation*, JSNTS 55 (Sheffield Academic Press, 1991).

objections that he anticipates encountering in Jerusalem.[9] The weakness of Jervell's position rests in the fact that he fails to give an adequate account of why Paul should write to the Roman church about issues that pertain to his forthcoming encounter with the Jewish Christian church in Jerusalem. Brown sought to correct this deficiency by suggesting that the gospel was first brought to Rome by Jewish Christian missionaries, with the result that Gentile Christians in Rome were converted to a brand of Christianity which was closely aligned with the Jerusalem church in its respect for the Jewish law. By assuring the Roman Christians of the trustworthiness of his gospel, Paul was hoping that the Roman church would recognise his gospel, and that news of this would reach Jerusalem along the excellent lines of communication between the two cities, and thus favourably influence the outcome of his own impending visit to Jerusalem.[10]

Brown also sees part of Paul's aim as being that of defending himself and his gospel against detractors in Rome itself, and here he is closely aligned with Stuhlmacher, who sees Romans as essentially a defence of Paul's gospel, written by the apostle to counter criticisms and misrepresentations of it which he has heard are circulating in Rome.[11]

There is a current tendency to try and keep as many of these different balls in the air as possible, and to explain the occasion and purpose of Romans in terms of a constellation or cluster of different circumstances, which include most or all of the different options outlined above.[12] There is nothing inherently wrong in this approach, since the options outlined above are not mutually exclusive. However, the relative importance of each of these different factors in the apostle's composition of Romans remains an outstanding issue. In particular, the crucial question that Karris posed in his response to Donfried needs an answer: '... by what criteria do we judge whether the situation behind Romans is a situation in the Roman church(es) or in the life of Paul (his missionary plans, summary of his gospel, journey to Jerusalem) or a combination of both?'[13]

---

[9] J. Jervell, 'The Letter to Jerusalem', in Donfried, *Romans Debate*, pp.53–64.

[10] R.E. Brown and J.P. Meier, *Antioch and Rome: New Testament Cradles of Catholic Christianity* (London: Chapman, 1983), pp.105–13.

[11] P. Stuhlmacher, 'The Purpose of Romans', in Donfried, *Romans Debate*, pp.231–42; 'The Theme of Romans', ibid., pp.333–45; cf. A.J.M. Wedderburn, *The Reasons for Romans* (Edinburgh: T&T Clark, 1988), pp.104, 112.

[12] J. Drane, 'Why did Paul write Romans?', in Hagner and Harris, *Pauline Studies*, pp.208–27; Wedderburn, *Reasons*, pp.5–6; F.F. Bruce, 'The Romans Debate – Continued', in Donfried, *Romans Debate*, pp.175–94; Dunn, *Romans*, pp.lv–lviii; Moo, pp.16–22; Fitzmyer, pp.68–84.

[13] R.J. Karris, 'The Occasion of Romans: a Response to Professor Donfried', in Donfried, *Romans Debate*, pp.125–7.

In response to Karris, it would seem that the paraenetic section of the letter (chs. 12–16) holds the key to the criterion he seeks. If it can be shown that the paraenesis is particular to the Roman situation, then it can be deduced that the situation in the Roman church itself was a factor in the composition of Romans. The relative importance of this factor may be assessed by the extent to which the Roman situation itself is able to account for the letter's content in its entirety: the detailed exposition of the gospel in Romans 1–8, the reflection upon the problem of Israel in 9–11, and the lengthy paraenesis in 12–16. If the whole of the letter can be interpreted in the light of the Roman situation, then we may reasonably deduce that events in Rome itself were the key factor in Paul's purpose in writing the letter. If, on the other hand, the body of the letter is not seen to have direct relevance to the Roman situation, then we may conclude that that situation played a correspondingly minor role in the composition of the letter. The way to proceed from this point onwards is therefore to analyse the paraenetic section of the letter, in order to ascertain whether or not specifically Roman difficulties lie behind the paraenesis. If this is found to be the case, then a reconstruction of that situation will be necessary, after which it will be possible to assess the extent to which the main body of the letter has direct relevance to it.

The weak and the strong

The case for regarding Romans 14:1–15:13 as general paraenesis is argued by Karris in his article, 'Rom. 14:1–15:13 and the Occasion of Romans'. Karris begins by attacking Minear's monograph, *The Obedience of Faith*, arguing that Minear's theory about five different communities in Rome simply goes beyond the evidence.[14] He refers with approval to Rauer's work of 1923, *Die 'Schwachen' in Korinth und Rom nach den Paulus-briefen*, where it is argued that the weak are individual Gentile Christians, who were abstaining from meat because of their prior religious background in Gnostic, Hellenistic mystery religions. Karris is not concerned with accepting Rauer's arguments for the religious background of the weak, but he does follow Rauer in arguing that 'the weak' and 'the strong' do not represent different communities, but refer instead to particular people, so that Paul's concern in 14:1–15:13 is simply 'to show how an established community can maintain its unity despite differences of

---

[14]Minear's five groups are: 1) the weak in faith who condemned the strong in faith; 2) the strong in faith who scorned and despised the weak in faith; 3) the doubters; 4) the weak in faith who did not condemn the strong; 5) the strong in faith who did not despise the weak.

opinion'.[15] Comparing Romans 14:1–15:13 with 1 Corinthians 8:1–11:1, Karris points out the similarity in Paul's language between these parts of each letter. He conducts a grammatical comparison between the two letters and notes that Romans 14:1–15:13 contains thirteen imperatives, but only one circumstantial 'if' clause, whereas 1 Corinthians 8 and 10 contain eight imperatives and five circumstantial 'if' clauses. On the basis of this comparison, he concludes that the combination of direct imperatives and the absence of circumstantial 'if' clauses in Romans 14:1–15:13 is an indication that this passage is a deliberate generalisation of Paul's advice to the Corinthian community, and does not address any specific situation in the Roman church at all.

It is regrettable, however, that Karris singled out Minear as his dialogue partner. Minear's thesis, with its definitive division of the Roman church into five different groups, manifestly does go beyond the bounds of plausibility, and Karris' criticism of him is just. However, simply to expose Minear's reconstruction of the Roman situation as being far-fetched will not suffice to disprove the validity of the whole approach, though this is what Karris argues. Karris' detonation of Minear's theory does nothing to disprove Wiefel's far more cautiously argued reconstruction published in Germany a year before Minear's monograph, to which Karris does not refer.[16]

Nor do Karris' grammatical observations carry any weight. As Donfried points out, neither the preponderance of imperatives, nor the absence of circumstantial 'if' clauses, constitute in themselves objective evidence that Romans 14:1–15:13 does not address a specific situation.[17] Nor do similarities of vocabulary between this passage and 1 Corinthians yield any indication as to the meaning of Romans 14:1–15:13. On the basis of this similarity, Karris argues that Paul is generalising the paraenesis of 1 Corinthians; on the same basis, others argue that Paul must be addressing the issue of idol meat in Romans, as he does in 1 Corinthians.[18] Both conclusions are unfounded: the only secure way to identify the weak and the strong is from an examination of the context of this passage within Romans itself.

[15] Karris, 'Occasion', p.79.
[16] Wiefel, 'Jewish Community', originally published as 'Die jüdische Gemeinschaft im antiken Rom und die Anfänge des römischen Christentums: Bemerkungen zu Anlass und Zweck des Römerbriefes', *Judaica* 26 (1970), pp.65–88. That Karris did not refer to it is not surprising, however: Donfried ('False Assumptions in the Study of Romans', Romans Debate, p.104, n.16) notes that Käsemann makes no reference to the article in his 1973 commentary.
[17] Donfried, 'False Assumptions', pp.108–9.
[18] F.F. Bruce, *The Epistle of Paul to the Romans* (London: Tyndale, 1963), pp.244–5; Ziesler, *Romans* , pp.322–7.

While Romans 14:1–12 could be understood as a continuation of the fairly general paraenesis of Romans 13,[19] Romans 14:13 clearly indicates that the discussion has moved on to a different level. Here Paul reiterates the plea for mutual acceptance that he has already issued in 14:3. His unwillingness to leave the theme after the natural break at the end of 14:12 is an indication of the importance he attaches to this matter. His request that the weak and the strong should no longer judge each other carries with it the clear implication that the process of judging one another is already taking place in actual fact. It follows, then, that when Paul directly addresses those who judge and despise others in 14:10, his use of the second person singular is no mere rhetorical flourish: he is addressing people whom he knows to be judging and despising others in the church.

Paul explicitly identifies himself with the position of the strong in 15:1, and he does not hesitate to address them directly with the second person plural imperative when he refers to the need to accept the weak (14:1) and to refrain from causing them to stumble (14:13, 16, 20). On the other hand, Paul's address to the weak who are judging the strong is phrased more obliquely. Here we find no direct prohibition of judging. Paul refrains from accusing the weak of judging the strong. By using the hortatory subjunctive in 14:13, Paul implies that each group is judging the other, which is not in fact the case: it is only the weak who are judging the strong; the fault of the strong is that they despise the weak. In this way, Paul treads very carefully when addressing the weak, with whom he is not personally identified.[20] Similarly, the questions of 14:4, 10 clearly imply the wrongness of judging one's fellow believer, but Paul does not stress the issue in the same way as he does when addressing the strong in 14:13–23: he prefers to allude to the wrongness of the critical attitude of the weak in the context of addressing both groups. In this way, Paul seeks to address the wrong behaviour of the weak group without antagonising them. Were this paraenesis of a purely general nature, formulated without reference to a specific situation in Rome, it is unlikely that Paul would have been so careful in the way in which he addressed the weak and strong groups. The apostle seems to be aware that he is dealing with actual factions in the Roman capital.

Further corroboration for the view that Paul was addressing a specifically Roman situation may be found in Romans 16:17–20. The abruptness with which Paul switches from greetings to this warning raises the

[19]W. Sanday and A.C. Headlam, *The Epistle to the Romans*, ICC (Edinburgh: T&T Clark, 1902), p.385.
[20]However, his use of the somewhat pejorative term 'weak' with reference to them may be deemed somewhat tactless.

suspicion of an interpolation here,[21] but it is far more likely that Paul takes the pen in his own hand at this point to conclude the letter himself, as he apparently does in 1 Corinthians 16:21–24; Galatians 6:11–18 (cf. 2 Thess. 3:17). The identity of those against whom Paul directs this invective is left unspecific: he simply warns against 'those who cause dissensions and offences' (NRSV). However, given that the problem addressed in 14:1–15:13 is one of dissension between the weak and the strong and that both passages specifically refer to σκάνδαλα (14:13; 16:17) it seems perverse to insist that Paul concludes his letter with such a strong warning against unknown schismatics, to whom he has hitherto made no reference whatsoever. It thus seems likely that Paul is warning against those who reject his conciliatory message in 14:1–15:13, and continue causing dissension and giving offence to others.

Paul's aim in addressing the weak and strong groups in 14:1–15:13 is their mutual reconciliation. To this end, he urges them to seek after peace and to try and build each other up (v.19), and prays that God will enable them to come to a common mind, so that together with one mouth they might glorify the God and Father of their Lord Jesus Christ (15:5–6). Paul writes to both parties, seeking to bring them to a mutual acceptance of one another, and to a common worship.[22]

Who, then, are the weak and the strong that Paul addresses in this section of the letter? One may infer from Romans 14:2, 21 that 'the weak' were vegetarians and abstained from wine as a matter of principle, whereas the strong in faith ate and drank freely; the weak made distinctions between different days, whereas the strong judged every day alike (14:5). In Romans 14:3, Paul urges that those who eat should not despise those who do not, while those who abstain from eating should not judge those who do. There is thus clearly friction between the two groups over the question of food.

[21]J.C. O'Neill, *Paul's Letter to the Romans* (London: Penguin, 1975), pp.252–3.

[22]This call to mutual acceptance undermines Watson's thesis that Paul's aim is to persuade the weak Torah-observant Christians to abandon the synagogue and to throw their lot in with the Pauline strong group. Watson argues that Paul 'wishes to turn a failed reform-movement into a sect': F. Watson, *Paul, Judaism and the Gentiles* (Cambridge: Cambridge University Press, 1986), p.22. Paul's call to the strong to accept the weak (14:1) does not constitute an instruction to them to welcome the weak Christian into their group; it is rather a call to accept the practices of the weak (vv.2–3). The analysis of different sects conducted by Wilson (*Magic*) highlights the dangers of Watson's attempt to deduce a standard pattern of sectarian legitimation from the Qumran and Johannine literature, which is then applied to Paul's letters. One cannot assume that a Pauline 'conversionist' sect would have the same attitude to mainline Judaism as the 'revolutionist' sect at Qumran or the 'introversionist' Johannine group: both the Qumran and Johannine communities had a far more negative attitude to the outside world than did the Pauline churches.

Furthermore, the issue of food would seem to lie behind the identification of the two groups as 'weak' and 'strong' respectively. In 14:1–2,
Paul writes: Τὸν ἀσθενοῦντα τῇ πίστει προσλαμβάνεσθε, μὴ εἰς
διακρίσεις διαλογισμῶν. ὃς μὲν πιστεύει φαγεῖν πάντα, ὁ δὲ
ἀσθενῶν λάχανα ἐσθίει. Here the reference to the weak who eats
only vegetables picks up on the preceding reference to the weak in faith,
whereas the verb πιστεύει identifies the ability to eat everything as apparently an expression of faith.[23] The terms 'weak' and 'strong' in faith
are thus directly related to differing attitudes to food, and can be satis-
factorily explained on the basis of conflicting views on diet.[24] Given the
connection Paul draws between faith and the freedom to eat anything,
the pejorative expression 'weak in faith' looks like an appellation applied
by the omnivores to those whose scruples prevented them from eating
meat.[25]

The key to establishing the identity of the groups is to be found in the
conclusion to the paraenetic section of the letter, 15:7–13. The opening
conjunction Διό establishes a close connection with the discussion that
precedes this paragraph, and the call for mutual acceptance both repeats
the charge given to the strong in 14:1, and takes up the plea for reconciliation in 15:1–6. The paragraph seems therefore to form a conclusion
to the discussion of the relationships between the weak and the strong in
14:1–15:6,[26] although any reference to weak or strong vanishes at this
point, to be replaced by a catena of quotations which follow the theme
of Jews and Gentiles worshipping together. This shift in terminology
does not presuppose a shift in Paul's focus at this point, however,[27] since
there are good grounds for broadly identifying the strong as law-free
Gentile Christians, while the weak are predominantly Torah-observant
Jews.

But at this stage an objection presents itself: if Paul is concerned in
Romans 14:1–15:13 with difficulties between Jews and Gentiles, why

---

[23]Earlier in the letter, Christian faith and believing have played a key role (1:16–17;
3:21–5:1[2]; 9:30–10:21), and 15:13 would suggest that Paul has not abandoned this
specific understanding of faith in the paraenetic section of the letter. The references to
faith and believing in 14:1–2, 22–23 should thus be understood as denoting Christian
faith rather than just 'conviction' (Käsemann, *Romans*, pp.365, 374, 379; Stuhlmacher,
p.223).

[24]Stowers' attempt to identify the weak as those whose diseases or passions of the soul
impaired their ability to attain self-mastery is weakened because he marginalises the important question of food (*Rereading*, pp.320–3).

[25]Cranfield, *Romans*, p.700; Dunn,vol.II, p.797.

[26]*Contra* Ziesler, *Romans*, pp.322–7.

[27]*Contra* Sanday and Headlam, *Romans*, pp.394–403.

does he refer to each group[28] as weak and strong? The answer probably lies in the recognition that the boundaries between the strong and the weak did not fall along strictly ethnic lines. Thus Paul himself, though a Jew, identifies himself with the strong, as presumably would Priscilla and Aquila. On the other hand, any Christians who had their origins in the ranks of the synagogue-attending God-fearers may well have continued to adhere to the dietary and Sabbath requirements of the law even as believers. It is wrong therefore to talk of any clear-cut division between Jew and Gentile: what constitutes the line of demarcation between the strong and the weak in faith is their attitude towards the Jewish law and the question of its observance. The weak maintained what might be termed a Jewish attitude towards the law, in as much as, even as believers, they continued to regard its ordinances as binding, and had a tendency to condemn those who disregarded it. The strong, on the other hand, were akin to the Gentile world in their disregard for the law, although Paul is at pains to assert that this disregard for the law should not be interpreted as a licence to sin (Rom. 6:1–23). Their faith was sufficiently strong to enable them to regard their non-observance of the Torah as being of no consequence in terms of their standing with God, since it is on the grounds of their faith in Christ alone that they are justified.[29] The degree of correspondence between the strong and the weak and Gentile and Jewish Christians is thus sufficiently strong for Paul to refer to these groups as Jews and Gentiles in 15:7–13, and quite possibly in the earlier parts of the letter as well.

An identification of the weak with Jewish-observant Christians would explain the distinction between different days that was being drawn by the weak as part of their commitment to the Lord (14:5–6).[30] From Daniel 1:8–16, we know of the Jewish practice to abstain both from pagan meat and wine for fear of idolatrous contamination; their abstinence from meat and wine and their decision to eat only vegetables corresponds to what we learn of the practices of the weak Roman Christians in Romans 14:2, 21.[31] The widespread nature of this Jewish practice can be inferred from

---

[28] Once the Jewish and Gentile identities of the weak and strong are accepted, there are no grounds left for seeing the weak and strong as individuals, rather than as groups; cf. U. Wilckens, *Der Brief an die Römer*, 3 vols. (Benziger: Neukirchener, 1978–82), vol.III, pp.109–15.

[29] Cf. Brown and Meier, *Antioch*, pp.1–26.

[30] Cf. M. Whittaker, *Jews and Christians: Graeco-Roman Views* (Cambridge: Cambridge University Press, 1984).

[31] Paul does not state in 14:2 that the weak abstained from wine as they did from meat; their refusal to drink wine can only be inferred from 14:21. This does not mean that they did not celebrate the Eucharist; no doubt the weak would have procured uncontaminated

Tobit 1:10–12; Judith 12:2, 19; Esther 14:17; Josephus, *Life*, 14. There are thus good grounds for supposing that Torah-observant Jews in the pagan environment of Rome may well have abstained from meat and wine, eating only vegetables instead.[32]

In addition, the letter itself provides further corroboration of the theory that the strong and weak can broadly be identified as Gentile and Jew respectively. In 14:3, Paul urges the strong, who eat, not to despise the weak who do not, while in turn, the weak are charged not to condemn the strong. Both of the attitudes that Paul opposes here are also mentioned earlier in the letter, specifically in the context of Jew–Gentile relations. In 2:1, Paul states that everyone who judges their fellow is thereby judged him- or herself, inasmuch as their behaviour is no better; in 2:17, the one who sits in judgment is identified by the apostle as being the Jew who relies upon the law.[33] In this way, the attack Paul launches against Jewish judgment of Gentile behaviour in Romans 2 corresponds to his request that the weak should not judge the strong in 14:3. Similarly, in Romans 11:18, Paul specifically warns Gentile believers not to despise unbelieving Israel, and this warning finds its echo in the charge that the strong should not despise the weak in 14:3. The letter itself thus offers support for the view that strong and weak are basically Gentile and Jew respectively; at the same time, the fact that references to Jews judging Gentiles and Gentiles despising Jews can be found in the earlier parts of the letter itself suggests that the letter as a whole may well have been written in order to address the tensions between Jewish and Gentile Christians in the capital.[34]

From Paul's greetings to them in Romans 16, it is apparent that these different groups of weak and strong met in small house churches, since he specifically refers to the church in the house of Prisca and Aquila (16:3–5), as well as referring to two other groups of Christians in 16:14–15; it is also possible that those of the households of Aristobulus and Narcissus (16:10–11) formed two extra groups. If, like the synagogues in Rome, these house groups lacked any central organisation, it would be natural for these different groups to develop along party lines, quite possibly in accordance with the following four different groupings suggested by

wine for this purpose. The weak objected to the practice of the strong, who probably drank any wine without discriminating as to its place of origin.

[32] Cf. Minear, *Obedience*, pp.15–22; Watson, *Paul*, pp.94–9.

[33] Arguments for the Jewish identity of the one addressed in 2:1 will be put forward in the next chapter.

[34] Cf. H. Boers, 'The Problem of Jews and Gentiles in the Macro-Structure of Romans', *Neotestamentica* 15 (1981), pp.1–11.

Brown in *Antioch and Rome*: (1) Jewish Christians and their Gentile converts who insisted on full observance of the Mosaic law, including circumcision. (2) Jewish Christians and their Gentile converts who did not insist on circumcision but did require some Jewish observances. (3) Jewish Christians and their Gentile converts who did not insist on circumcision and did not require observance of the Jewish food laws. (4) Jewish Christians and their Gentile converts who did not insist on circumcision or observance of the Jewish food laws and who saw no abiding significance in Jewish cults and feasts. In such a situation, where the different groups held differing views about the role of the Jewish law, it would be easy for a situation to develop where the more law-observant Christians ('the weak') passed judgment on the less law-observant ('the strong'), who in turn despised the weak for their adherence to practices which they deemed as being of no account. This, then, is the social context in which the Christians to whom Paul wrote were located.

It is important to note that Paul addressed his letter to *all* those loved by God in Rome, who have been called to be saints (1:7). This explains why, at different points in his letter, Paul addresses his readers either as Gentiles or as Jews:[35] the ambivalence within the letter as to the identity of the addressees reflects the disparate nature of the congregations to whom Paul is writing. It is therefore illegitimate to argue, on the basis of Paul's use of the Old Testament, that his readers must have been Jewish Christians,[36] or even Gentile God-fearers.[37] The extent to which Paul interacts with Jewish thinking in the course of the letter may possibly be an indication that Jewish Christianity exercised a degree of influence in Rome out of all proportion to its size;[38] we may suppose as well that Paul's own personal identification with the strong may well have led him to slant the argument of the letter in favour of justifying their position in the eyes of the weak, rather than the other way around. In any event, it is possible to get a reasonably coherent picture of the Christians to whom Paul wrote this particular letter: a group of disparate house churches, made up of both Jews and Gentiles, aligned on the basis of different attitudes towards the Jewish law, which had given rise to tensions and difficulties between the groups.

[35] A Gentile readership is indicated in Rom. 1:5–6, 13–15; 8:17–22; 9:3–5; 11:13–32; indications of a Jewish audience are to be found in 2:17–3:8; 4:1; 7:1; 9:24; 16:3, 7, 11.

[36] F.J. Leenhardt, *The Epistle to the Romans* (London: Lutterworth, 1961).

[37] Dunn, *Romans*, vol. I, pp.xliv–liv; P. Lampe, 'The Roman Christians of Romans 16', in K.P. Donfried, ed., *The Romans Debate* (Peabody:Hendrickson,1991), pp.216–30; Stowers, *Rereading*.

[38] P. Lampe, *Die Stadtrömischen Christen in den ersten beiden Jahrhunderten*, WUNT 18 (Tübingen: J.C.B. Mohr, 1989), p.60.

It would seem appropriate to classify these different house churches as small bounded groups, which fall into the category of high group/low grid communities on Douglas' matrix. The fact that the groups have the labels 'strong' and 'weak' suggests a strong sense of group identity, while the possibility that the believers in Rome were troubled by a sense of injustice over the level of taxation (Rom. 13:1–7)[39] suggests a degree of dislocation from the surrounding society, which is confirmed by Jeffers' argument that the Christians in Rome were largely made up of poor non-Latin non-citizens, who occupied no legal position and who were of uncertain official status.[40] Within the high group/low grid enclave, the group boundary is the main definer of roles, group members accuse deviants in the midst of allowing outside evil to infiltrate and there is a preoccupation with rituals of cleansing, expulsion and the redrawing of boundaries.

This would appear to correspond with the situation in Rome where the strong and the weak represent different groups of Christians who are separated by mutual suspicion and mistrust over their differing attitudes to the law: the weak judge the strong for their lawlessness, while the strong despise the weak for their adherence to rituals characteristic of the Jewish nation which, by and large, has rejected the gospel. It would be quite unrealistic to suppose, either that all the members of each group were uniformly of the same opinion over this question,[41] or that there was no movement of people between the different house churches. Each group will have been concerned to maintain and monitor the allegiance of its members over the issue of the law, and this would probably have led to tensions within the different house churches, in addition to the tensions between the different groups. In this context, one would expect a process of cleansing, expulsion and redrawing of boundaries to take place, as each group sought to maintain its own particular brand of purity. Paul's letter to the Romans betrays no details about these individual expulsions of course: aware of the situation from afar, Paul can only deal with the matter in the broadest terms, as he addresses the weak and the strong and their differing attitudes to one another and the law.

Yet even in Romans, it may well be that we can detect echoes of the kind of accusations that were levelled against the strong by the weak. In Romans 3:8, Paul refers to those who blaspheme against him by accusing

[39] J. Friedrich, W. Pöhlmann and P. Stuhlmacher, 'Zur historischen Situation und Intention von Röm. 13:1–7', *ZTK* 73 (1976), pp.131–66.

[40] J.S. Jeffers, *Conflict at Rome: Social Order and Hierarchy in Early Christianity* (Minneapolis: Augsburg Fortress, 1991), pp.3–35.

[41] R.E. Brown, 'Further Reflections on the Origins of the Church of Rome', in R. Fortna and B.R. Gaventa, eds., *The Conversation Continues: Studies in Paul and John in Honor of J.L. Martyn* (Nashville: Abingdon, 1987), pp.98–115.

him of encouraging people to do evil, in order that good may come. This accusation has not been levelled against Paul alone: his use of the first person plural here may perhaps indicate that there are others in the dock with him,[42] and those others could be the strong law-free Christians in Rome, who were being accused of evil behaviour – a common enough accusation in this kind of bounded group. It is also possible that Romans 6:1 represents a similar misrepresentation of the position of the strong on the part of the weak. It may be, of course, that the τινες of Romans 3:8 had no contact with Rome at all, but the fact that Paul feels it necessary to refer to this kind of accusation twice betrays his concern that this is the kind of thing that is being said about him in Rome – and if it is being said about him, then there is every likelihood that the strong Christians in Rome would have been suspected by the weak of holding such views themselves.

It has, then, been argued so far that the paraenetic section of the letter is addressed to a definite social situation in Rome of which Paul was aware, and that the disagreement between the weak and the strong was focused on the question of observance or non-observance of the Jewish law, so that the weak can broadly be identified with a Jewish attitude to the law, while the strong tended to disregard it as the Gentile world did. These strong and weak groups were based in local house churches, which should be identified as small high group/low grid communities on Douglas' matrix.

Now that this has been established, it is necessary to analyse Paul's response to the situation. To what extent did the conflict between the weak and the strong determine the theme of the letter as a whole, and what is the view of the church that Paul himself expresses as he writes in his capacity of apostle to the Gentiles to the divided house churches in the capital?

The theme of the letter

Romans 1:1–15 and 15:14–16:24 form the epistolary framework around the main body of the letter, and Paul's statement that he is not ashamed of the gospel stands at the head of the body of the letter and states the letter's theme:[43] Οὐ γὰρ ἐπαισχύνομαι τό εὐαγγέλιον, δύναμις γὰρ θεοῦ ἐστιν εἰς σωτηρίαν παντὶ τῷ πιστεύοντι, Ἰουδαίῳ τε πρῶτον καὶ Ἕλληνι.

---

[42]The referent of ἡμᾶς has changed from that of the previous first person plural personal pronoun in v.5, where ἡμῶν must refer to the Jews.

[43]Rhetorical analysis suggests that 1:16–17 should be regarded as the *propositio*, or thesis statement of the letter: so R. Jewett, 'Following the Argument of Romans', in Donfried, *Romans Debate*, pp.265–77.

The high degree of similarity between Paul's words here and Psalm 97:1–3 LXX suggests that Paul may have based his own statement on the opening verses of the psalm, which praise God for his salvation:[44]

Ἄσατε τῷ Κυρίῳ ᾆσμα καινόν, ὅτι θαυμαστὰ ἐποίησεν ὁ Κύριος· ἔσωσεν αὐτῷ ἡ δεξιὰ αὐτοῦ, καὶ ὁ βραχίων ὁ ἅγιος αὐτοῦ. Ἐγνώρισε Κύριος τό σωτήριον αὐτοῦ, ἐναντίον τῶν ἐθνῶν ἀπεκάλυψε τὴν δικαιοσύνην αὐτοῦ. Ἐμνήσθη τοῦ ἐλέους αὐτοῦ τῷ Ἰακὼβ, καὶ τῆς ἀληθείας αὐτοῦ τῷ οἴκῳ Ἰσραήλ· εἴδοσαν πάντα τὰ πέρατα τῆς γῆς τὸ σωτήριον τοῦ θεοῦ ἡμῶν.

Paul describes his gospel as the power of God for salvation (σωτηρία), while the psalm opens with the declaration that the Lord's right hand and holy arm have wrought salvation (ἔσωσεν): Paul's use of the term 'power' here merely makes explicit the psalm's metaphors of the Lord's right hand and holy arm, both of which signify God acting in power to save. The noun 'salvation' (σωτήριον) occurs twice in Psalm 97:2–3, as the psalmist records that the Lord has made known his salvation and all the ends of the earth have recognised it. It is in this context that the psalm speaks of the revelation of the Lord's righteousness , as Paul himself also does in Romans 1:17.

Within the Hebrew parallelism of Psalm 98:2 MT, the revelation of God's righteousness corresponds to the Lord making known his salvation,[45] and this fact lends strong support to the view that the phrase δικαιοσύνη θεοῦ in Romans denotes the uprightness of God, as this is manifested in the way in which God rescues his people in saving power. The parallelism of verse 3 of the psalm also links universal knowledge of God's salvation with the Lord remembering his mercy to Jacob and his truth to the house of Israel. It is surely no coincidence that in Romans 1:16 Paul asserts that the gospel is for the Jew first and also for the Gentile, and goes on to stress in the letter that the gift of salvation to the Gentiles through the gospel in no way compromises God's fidelity to his covenant with Israel (Rom. 3:1–8; 9:6–18; 11:1–12, 25–32), namely that same covenant faithfulness to which the language of 'remembering' in Psalm 98:3 MT also refers.

Significantly, faith is the only concept in Paul's summary of the gospel in Romans 1:16–17 which does not have its roots in Psalm 98:1–3, and

[44] A.J. Hultgren, *Paul's Gospel and Mission* (Minneapolis: Fortress, 1985), pp.30–4.
[45] Ps. 98:2–3 MT divides naturally in this way:

לְעֵינֵי הַגּוֹּים גִּלָּה צִדְקָתוֹ   הוֹדִיעַ יְהוָה יְשׁוּעָתוֹ

זָכַר חַסְדּוֹ|אֱמוּנָתוֹ לְבֵית יִשְׂרָאֵל   רָאוּ כָל־אַפְסֵי־אָרֶץ אֵת יְשׁוּעַת אֱלֹהֵינוּ

this is the concept which is most heavily stressed in these verses. Romans 1:16 states that the gospel is the power of God for the salvation of everyone who believes. This salvation is thus open to both the Jew and Greek, but by subordinating both nationalities to the phrase παντὶ τῷ πιστεύοντι, Paul makes it clear that both Jew and Greek can receive that salvation only by believing themselves. The offer of salvation is thus universally available to all on equal terms,[46] and it is available on those terms alone. It is the repetition of the word πίστις in verse 17 which draws attention to the importance of the phrase παντὶ τῷ πιστεύοντι in verse 16. Paul's citation of Habakkuk 2:4 makes the point that the righteous person will live by faith. Paul differs from both the MT and the LXX by leaving πίστις unqualified by a possessive adjective: the MT states that the righteous person shall live by his faithfulness, whereas in the LXX God declares that ὁ δὲ δίκαιος ἐκ πίστεως μου ζήσεται. By omitting the possessive adjective in this way, Paul leaves unspecified whose is the faith or faithfulness in question, but in all probability it is precisely this ambiguity that Paul seeks to exploit by means of the phrase ἐκ πίστεως εἰς πίστιν in the same verse: the revelation of the righteousness of God has its origin in God's faithfulness, and comes to those who themselves have faith.[47]

In Romans 1:16–17, Paul therefore makes the point that Jews and Gentiles alike receive God's salvation through their response of faith to the gospel.[48] It is no coincidence that this statement of the letter's theme has direct relevance to the concluding paraenesis, in which Paul seeks to persuade the weak and the strong, Jews and Gentiles, to recognise one another as members of a single worshipping community in Rome. Paul wrote Romans to a number of different church groups who are divided over the question of the law, and, in the course of the rest of the letter, Paul attempts to unite the different Christian factions in Rome under the common umbrella of their faith. Addressing Christians with a strong sense of group identity, Paul sets out in the letter to establish faith as the basis for that group identity.[49]

This aim is developed in 1:18–3:31, as Paul argues that Jews and Gentiles alike are all under sin (1:18–3:20), and then goes on to state that circumcised and uncircumcised alike are justified through their faith

---

[46]Cf. J.D.-S. Chae, *Paul as Apostle to the Gentiles: His Apostolic Self-awareness and Its Influence on the Soteriological Argument in Romans* (Carlisle: Paternoster, 1997).

[47]Dunn, *Romans*, vol.I, pp.43–4.

[48]Cf. Sanders, *Paul and Palestinian Judaism*, pp.488–9.

[49]Cf. W. Meeks, 'Judgement and the Brother: Romans 14:1–15:13', in G.F. Hawthorne and O. Betz, eds., *Tradition and Interpretation in the New Testament: Essays in Honor of E. Earle Ellis on his 60th Birthday* (Grand Rapids: Eerdmans, 1987), pp.290–300.

in Christ. In 4:1–25, Paul seeks to argue from Genesis 15:6 that Abraham himself was justified before God on the basis of his faith, rather than on the basis of his works. Since Abraham's faith was counted as righteousness before he was circumcised, Paul declares him to be the father of uncircumcised believers as well as the father of those circumcised Jews who have followed his example by taking the step of faith that he himself took before his circumcision (4:9–12). Paul thus claims Abraham as the father of all believers, circumcised and uncircumcised alike (4:16–17). It is therefore apparent that, in this opening part of the body of the letter, Paul's concern is to establish faith as the basis upon which both Jews and Gentiles alike are put right with God through Jesus Christ.

Paul's claim that Jews and Gentiles alike can now be put right with God only by faith raises the acute question of the problem of God's faithfulness to his people Israel, who, as a nation, did not respond to the gospel with faith. Paul addresses this issue in Romans 9–11. In Romans 9, Paul makes the point that not all Israel have been elected by God, and those whom he has called to glory include both Jews and Gentiles (v.22–24). The problem with Israel was that they persisted in seeking righteousness through works of the law rather than through faith, and thus failed to appreciate that Christ is the goal of the law,[50] bringing righteousness to all who believe (9:30–10:10). In 10:11–12 Paul cites Isaiah 28:16 in order to make the point that, since it is the one who believes who will not be put to shame, there can be no difference between Jew and Greek, for they all call on the same Lord and all are saved in the same way. The problem is that, although Israel have heard the message, they have not responded by believing and calling on the Lord in this way (10:14–21).

Nevertheless, Paul denies that God has rejected his people, and warns Gentile Christians that they are not to despise unbelieving Israel, for they are only like wild branches that have been grafted, contrary to nature, on to the olive tree of God's people which still has its Jewish roots. Even if the natural Jewish branches of the olive tree were broken off because of their unbelief, Paul holds on to the hope that the Jews will not persist in their unbelief, but that they will be grafted back on to the olive tree from which they were broken off (11:23). Indeed, Israel is still loved by God for the sake of the patriarchs, and Paul argues that this hardening has only come upon Israel temporarily, until such time as the full number of the Gentiles have come in: when this happens, all Israel will then be saved through the mercy of God (11:25–32).

[50] R. Badenas, *Christ the End of the Law*, JSNTS 10 (Sheffield: Sheffield Academic Press, 1985).

In view of God's mercies, Paul urges his readers to present their bodies as living sacrifices to God (12:1–2), and with these words he introduces the paraenetic section of the letter, which contains the practical outworking of what it means to belong to the mixed community of God's people. There is no room for superiority within the body of Christ, because all are measured by the same standard of faith (12:3),[51] and Paul goes on to spell out how the believers should behave towards one another and outsiders, including the civil authorities, in 12:9–13:10.

Whereas Paul leaves unspecified his reference to superiority in 12:3, his charge to the strong that they should not despise the weak in 14:3, 10 echoes his warning of 11:18, that Gentile believers should not despise unbelieving Israel. It seems likely that it was an attitude which dismissed the Jewish nation as having been abandoned by God that underlay the contempt of the strong for the weak, and their ongoing observance of Jewish ordinances which the strong clearly felt had been superseded. It is in order to counter such an attitude that Paul charges the strong to accept the weak in faith in 14:1.

The mutual hostility between the two groups over the issue of food is apparent in 14:3, where it is clear that those who felt free to eat anything despised those who ate only vegetables, and this second group in turn tended to judge the first. However, just as Paul has urged the strong to accept the weak, rather than despising them (v.1), so, in verse 3, he makes the point that the weak cannot judge the strong because God has accepted them. The basis for each group's acceptance is their faith, to which Paul is careful to allude in each case. Thus the strong are to receive 'the weak in faith' (v.1), but it is on the basis of their faith, albeit weak, that they are to accept them. Correspondingly, God has received the strong on the basis of their faith, since they have the faith to believe that they can eat anything (v.2). Faith is thus laid down as the basis for each group's acceptance of the other and their differing practices, and is thus established as the basis of Paul's appeal for mutual acceptance in 15:7.[52]

Paul also makes the point in 14:6 that each group's behaviour is directed to God; thus those who observe days, do so to the Lord, as do both those who eat and those who do not eat. In each case, the group's behaviour,

[51] C.E.B. Cranfield, '"ΜΕΤΡΟΝ ΠΙΣΤΕΩΣ" in Rom. XII 3', *NTS* 8 (1961), pp.345–51.
[52] According to J.M.G. Barclay, although Paul advocates mutual acceptance, he also undermines the social and cultural integrity of the law by asking the weak to make a deep social commitment to the non-observant strong: '"Do we undermine the Law?" A Study of Romans 14:1–15:6', in Dunn, *Paul and the Mosaic Law*, pp. 287–308. Barclay is quite right here, inasmuch as Paul argues for the validity of Torah observance, but robs it of its primary significance as a line of demarcation between the sinful and the righteous.

since it is directed to God, is a valid expression of its faith in God. It is important, though, that everyone be fully convinced of this in their own mind (v.5b).

Nevertheless, in 14:13–23, Paul urges the strong to moderate their behaviour out of consideration for the weak. While the strong (Paul included) may be persuaded that nothing is actually unclean at all, they nevertheless need to accept that if the weak regard something as being unclean, then it really is unclean, as far as they are concerned. It is therefore better for the strong to keep the strength of their faith to themselves and, out of love for the weak brother or sister, to refrain from doing anything that will lead them into sin. Paul explains why in verse 23: ὁ δὲ διακρινόμενος ἐὰν φάγῃ κατακέκριται, ὅτι οὐκ ἐκ πίστεως· πᾶν δὲ ὃ οὐκ ἐκ πίστεως ἁμαρτία ἐστίν.

The reference to the danger of doubting in this verse picks up what Paul had to say about the need to be fully persuaded about the rightness of one's behaviour in 14:5. In verse 23, he makes the point that if people are not so fully persuaded, but instead have doubts about what they are doing, then they have fallen under God's judgment; this is because their behaviour does not stem from faith, and everything that does not come from faith is sin.

On the basis that verse 23 has the appearance of a dogmatic statement, it has been argued that Paul is offering a definition of sin at this point,[53] or that he is establishing a basic principle for Christian paraenesis.[54] While Paul is probably able to make this assertion on the basis of his earlier exclusive association of righteousness with faith (3:21–30), this verse rather needs to be understood in its context of Paul's discussion of the weak and strong.[55] Since Paul explicitly states that the one who doubts and eats has been judged, the effect of his words would have been to reinforce the Torah-observant abstinence of the weak, because any who had been uncertain about the rightness or wrongness of eating would now be sure to stick to vegetables! Paul's words are, however, written for the benefit of the strong, whose faith expressed itself in a freedom to eat anything, and who regarded Jewish Christian scruples as evidence of weak faith. By defining sin as whatever does not proceed from faith, Paul makes the point that, for the Torah-observant Jewish Christian, eating

[53] R. Otto, *Sünde und Urschuld* (Munich: Beck'sche, 1932), pp.25–36; Dunn, *Romans*, vol.II, pp.828–9.
[54] O. Michel, *Der Brief an die Römer* (Göttingen: Vandenhoeck & Ruprecht, 1954), pp.313–15.
[55] Cf. Chrysostom, *ep. ad Romanos hom.* 26.3: 'Now all these things have been spoken by Paul of the subject in hand, not of everything.'

meat is not an expression of faith; instead it is a sin, precisely because
it does not proceed from faith. Paul's definition of sin as 'whatever does
not come from faith' is thus developed here with the specific purpose of
legitimating Jewish Christian abstention from meat.[56]

Paul then closes the paraenetic section of the letter with a plea for unity
(15:1–6) and a number of OT citations which refer to Gentiles and Jews
worshipping together (15:7–12). The wish prayer of 15:13 that Jews and
Gentiles alike might be filled with all joy and peace in believing concludes
the main body of the letter, before Paul returns to the epistolary framework
in 15:14. So it is that the body of the letter closes in the same way as it
opens, with a reference to the uniting of Jews and Gentiles together in the
gospel (1:16–17).

It has been shown, then, that the question of Jewish–Gentile relations is
crucial, not only to the paraenetic section of the letter, but also to the theme
of the letter as a whole, as this is stated in 1:16–17. If it is accepted that
Paul is addressing actual tensions within the Roman Christian community
over the question of observance or non-observance of the law in Romans
14:1–15:13, the recognition that Paul has Jew–Gentile relations in view
in these previous sections of the letter lends support to the theory that Paul
wrote the whole letter with an eye to addressing the Roman situation.

Locating Paul on the matrix

Paul's concern to unite the strong and the weak Christians on the basis of
their faith is a firm indication that once again the apostle should be given
a strong group rating as he writes to the Roman Christians. Grid is not
so easily determined. In 12:2, Paul urges his readers not to be conformed
to the present age, but to be inwardly transformed by the renewing of
their minds. Although the believers continue their bodily existence in the
present aeon, their minds are to be renewed so that they live in accordance
with the values of the new, coming age. This eschatological element in
12:2 is taken up and reinforced in the call to put off the works of darkness
and to put on the armour of light in 13:11–14. Both paragraphs indicate
that the prevailing values of the present age are passing away, and in each
case eschatology is employed to distance Paul's readers from the prevailing values of the surrounding culture in a way that is characteristic of low
grid communities. This common theme in both paragraphs also means

---

[56] *Contra* Watson, *Paul*, who argues that Paul's aim in writing to Rome was to persuade
the weak Torah-observant Christians to leave the synagogue and to throw their lot in with
the strong Pauline group; cf. Dunn's criticism (*Romans*, vol.I, p.lvii).

that together they form an *inclusio* around Romans 12–13 as a whole,[57] thereby indicating that the intervening verses address the question of what is the will of God for the eschatological people of God, as they live out their lives in the present age. Paul's exhortation here reflects the characteristic concern of the enclave to maintain clear boundaries against the outside world (low grid).

However, in 13:1–7, Paul addresses the question of obedience to rulers. As Moxnes points out, the effect of such advice would have been to strengthen an integration of the Christians in Rome into the Hellenistic symbolic universe.[58] This is a surprising response on the part of the apostle, who, in 1 Corinthians and Galatians, consistently sought to reject the symbolic system of the surrounding culture. However, while it is the case that Paul rejected the values of Hellenistic society, he had no desire to reject society itself, either by withdrawing from it or by mounting a revolution against it. Non-payment of taxes, would, however, tend to lead to one or other of these two options. But the sectarian emphasis of the apostle was neither introversionist nor revolutionary.[59] Christianity was a conversionist sect, and the need to win converts entailed keeping open boundaries between the group and the outside world. This is why Paul urges his readers to maintain their place in society by paying their taxes. It should be noted, however, that this advice comes in a passage which is framed by references to the incoming aeon, and which advises Christians how to live in the present age as people who belong to the age to come. This has the effect of relativising the position of the earthly rulers, and the perceived imminence of the end renders unnecessary any attempt to change the *status quo*. On balance, it would therefore seem appropriate to attribute to the apostle a low grid rating, in accordance with his view of the church in 1 Corinthians and Galatians.

Thus, in applying Grid and Group to both the Roman house churches and to Paul it is apparent that the high group/low grid quadrant of the enclave forms the cultural context within which it is appropriate to analyse Paul's references to the power of sin in his letter to the Romans. Both the apostle and the church would have shared the same concerns about boundaries and group unity, and the Romans would have read Paul's letter with these concerns in mind.

---

[57] Ziesler, *Romans*, p.293.

[58] H. Moxnes, 'Honour, Shame and the Outside World in Paul's Letter to the Romans', in J. Neusner, ed., *The Social World of Formative Christianity and Judaism* (Minneapolis: Fortress, 1988), pp.207–18.

[59] Cf. Wilson, *Magic*, pp.18ff.

This chapter has argued that the social situation at Rome should be taken as the starting point for interpreting Romans, and it has been suggested that the situation Paul was addressing is compatible with the scenario offered in the high group/low grid quadrant of the matrix, where group members accuse deviants in their midst of allowing outside evil to infiltrate and such accusations lead to the fission of the group. It is argued that Paul was writing to a divided community, where accusations of this kind took place (3:8; 6:1, 15), and where there may have been considerable traffic between the different house churches as members of each group came under suspicion and were forced to settle elsewhere. It was also suggested that Paul was seeking to unite these different groups on the basis of a common faith. This points to a high group rating for the apostle, whereas the eschatological perspective of the letter points to a low grid rating. Accordingly, the high group/low grid concerns about boundary definition form the appropriate socio-cultural context in which to read the letter as a whole.

6

INCLUSIVE BOUNDARIES IN ROME

Insiders and outsiders

Having ascertained the location of Paul and the Roman community on the matrix, an attempt will now be made to read Romans 1–8, understanding the power of sin within the context of the high group/low grid preoccupation with boundaries. It will be argued that Paul is concerned with demolishing the ethnic boundary of the law in Romans 1:18–4:25, and replacing it with the eschatological boundary of baptism and Spirit reception in 5:1–8:39.[1]

Paul first makes mention of the power of sin in this letter in 3:9, where he claims to have demonstrated that Jews and Gentiles alike are all under sin's power. This negative claim is the necessary precursor to his ensuing positive statement in 3:21–31, that all alike are equally justified through faith in Christ. This statement takes up Paul's summary of the theme of the letter in 1:16–17, where he proclaims that the gospel is the power of God for the salvation of all who believe, the Jew first and also the Greek. In order to show that both Jews and Greeks alike are justified on the same basis, Paul has to show that both groups alike stand in the same need of that justification. He therefore argues that the Jews have no advantage over the Gentiles by virtue of their possession of the Torah; on the contrary, Paul asserts in 3:9 that all alike are under the power of sin.

Paul's claim at this point in the letter seems, however, problematic for two reasons. Since this is the first time that the power of sin has even been mentioned, it is difficult to see how Paul can legitimately claim to have shown that all alike are under its power. Secondly, as E.P. Sanders has

[1] Limitations of space preclude a detailed consideration of Rom. 9–11. Here Paul redefines 'Israel' as the remnant who through faith have found the true goal of the law in Christ. The temporary exclusion of unbelieving Israel has served to open the door for the inclusion of believing Gentiles, who are thus 'proselyted to an "Israel" whose boundary marker is Christ rather than Torah' (Donaldson, *Remapping*, p.160). However, at the eschaton, the whole of ethnic Israel will be saved on the same basis as Gentile believers, namely that of the sovereign mercy and gracious election of God.

argued, the conclusion that all are under sin appears unwarranted, since in 1:18–2:29 he appears to entertain the possibility that some will be saved by works.[2] Such difficulties with Paul's argument arise, however, from a culturally insensitive reading of his argument. According to Douglas, the small bounded group perceives evil as a foreign danger, threatening to infiltrate the group from outside. This leads to a great deal of emphasis upon the maintenance and the redrawing of group boundaries, which have the function of preserving the distinctive purity of the group over and against the polluting evil of the outside world. It is this contrast between the good inside and the bad outside of the group which is the key to Paul's argument in Romans 1–3.

In order to fulfil his aim of establishing the equality of Jewish and Gentile believers, Paul has to overcome the typically Jewish perception of themselves as righteous within the covenant, and of the lawless Gentiles as sinful outsiders. Since the Jewish law is the foundation upon which that distinction was made, Paul sets himself the task in this part of the letter of undermining the distinction between righteous Jew and sinful Gentile, which was based on the former's observance of works of the law. By arguing that Jews under the law are in reality no better than Gentiles outside the law, Paul seeks to deny the law any effective role in establishing an effective boundary between the righteous and the sinful. It is thus because the Jew has no advantage that he can argue that all alike are under sin, the reference to the power of sin here anticipating the new, eschatological boundary between righteous insiders and sinful outsiders that the apostle will draw in 5:12ff.

Paul sets about his task of undermining the boundary constituted by the law in 1:18–32 by summarising the sinfulness of Gentile behaviour from a typically Jewish perspective. Although Paul does not specifically identify the Gentiles as those against whom the wrath of God is revealed in verse 18, it rapidly becomes apparent that these verses do in fact portray Gentile sinfulness, as this was seen through Jewish eyes.[3] Paul does not say that God has revealed himself to these people through Torah (as he surely would if he had Jews in mind), but rather through the created order; the reference to their claiming to be wise (v.22) is also probably targeted at the Hellenistic pride in and search for wisdom. Paul's linking together of idolatry, sexual immorality and other sins also reflects Jewish polemic against their Gentile neighbours.

---

[2] Sanders claims that Paul's case for universal sinfulness is 'internally inconsistent and rests on gross exaggeration' (*Jewish People*, pp.124–5).

[3] On the links with Wisdom of Solomon 11–15, cf. Sanday and Headlam, *Romans*, pp.51–2.

Although Paul does allude to Psalm 106:20/Jer. 2:11 in verse 23, this was probably not intended to bring Israel within the horizon of Paul's indictment in these verses.[4] The echo of these verses is too faint for it to be a signal that Paul is bringing Israel into the picture at this point. The psalmist and the prophet indict Israel for exchanging her glory for worthless idols: the force of the accusation lies in the contrasting values of the God they have abandoned and the idols they have accepted in his place. So, in Romans, Paul accuses the Gentiles of exchanging the glory of God for corruptible images: the allusion to glory is intended to emphasise the value of what they have abandoned, and hence their culpability in turning to idolatry.

The driving force behind this passage is the threefold declaration that God has 'given them up' (1:24, 26, 28): in each case, God gives them over to sinful behaviour as a direct result of their idolatry. This theme forges a link between this passage and Wisdom of Solomon 14–15, where this connection is also explicitly made:

> Ἀρχὴ γὰρ πορνείας ἐπίνοια εἰδώλων, εὕρεσις δὲ αὐτῶν φθορὰ
> ζωῆς   (Wisd. 14:12).

> Ἡ γὰρ τῶν ἀνωνύμων εἰδώλων θρησκεία παντὸς ἀρχὴ κακοῦ
> καὶ αἰτία καὶ πέρας ἐστιν   (Wisd. 14:27).

These parallels are significant, in that nowhere else is this causal connection between idolatry and sin made in such an explicit way. It would appear that Paul actually based Romans 1:24, 26, 28 on these verses from Wisdom 14, since Wisdom 14:8 condemns the maker of idols for naming as God something corruptible, and this is reflected in Paul's charge that people have exchanged the glory of the incorruptible God for the likeness of the image of corruptible creatures. Wisdom 14:12 identifies idolatry as the origin of sexual immorality, as does Paul in Romans 1:25–27. Wisdom 14:27 identifies the worship of idols as the beginning, cause and end of all evil at the end of a list of vices (14:25–26), and in similar fashion Paul claims that a refusal to acknowledge God gives rise to the sins listed in 1:29–31.

By picking up on Wisdom in this way, Paul adopts the stance of a Jewish insider looking out on a Gentile world that stands inexcusably under the wrath of God, and his use of the third person plural throughout this passage to denote those to whom he is referring has the effect of

---

[4] So Stowers, *Rereading*, pp.92–3.

making a distinction between 'them' and 'us'.[5] Paul thus tacitly invites his implied Jewish audience to adopt the same perspective. The tables are suddenly turned, however, when Paul turns to address his implied reader directly in 2:1: in the act of judging others the 'insider' judges himself, for he himself does the same things. Thus, like the Gentiles Paul has just described, this person, too, is 'without excuse' (2:1, cp. 1:20), and stands under the wrath of God (2:5, cp. 1:18).

Although the person Paul addresses here is not specifically identified as Jewish, until recently it was generally accepted that Paul has the Jew in mind, even though this identification is not made explicit until 2:17.[6] However, this consensus has been challenged by N. Elliott and S.K. Stowers, who argue that Paul has Gentile readers in view at this point.[7] Elliott argues that Paul must be addressing his Gentile readers in chapter 2, since for Paul to address Jewish concerns at the outset of the letter would be rhetorically ineffective, and have an alienating effect on his Gentile readership. According to Elliott, Paul puts the Jew forward as a paradigm of the one who trusts in God, but who is nevertheless held accountable, in order to show that, *a fortiori*, his Gentile readers will also be held accountable to God. Yet if, as Elliott argues, Paul's Gentile readers were disdainful of the Jews, they are scarcely likely to perceive the Jew of 2:17 as being a paradigm of trustful assent to God's will. This inconsistency fatally undermines Elliott's thesis, since the common ground, which Elliott argues is vital to Paul's rhetorical strategy, is missing at this crucial point.

According to Stowers, the original readers of 2:1–3 would instantly have recognised Paul's characterisation as that of ὁ ἀλαζῶν, the pretentious boaster or braggart who criticises others even though he does the same kind of things. However, while Stowers may be right in claiming that no one in the first century would have identified ὁ ἀλαζῶν with Judaism, the fact remains that the accusation levelled against the implied Jewish reader of 2:17–23 fits the portrait of ὁ ἀλαζῶν exactly: the Jew boasts of moral superiority by virtue of having the law, and yet actually fails to observe it. That Paul intended to identify the one who judges in 2:1–3 with the one who boasts in the law in 2:17–23 is apparent

---

[5]C.L. Porter rightly argues that Rom. 1:18–32 is a self-contained discourse similar to that used in Hellenistic Judaism in order to establish, maintain and strengthen a well-defined boundary between the Jewish community and the Gentiles: 'Romans 1:18–32: Its Role in the Developing Argument', *NTS* 40 (1994), pp.210–28.

[6]E.g. Dunn, *Romans*, vol.I, p.79; Fitzmyer, p.297; Moo, p.92.

[7]N. Elliott, *The Rhetoric of Romans*, JSNTS 45 (Sheffield: Sheffield Academic Press, 1990); Stowers, *Rereading*, pp.100–4.

from the way that the accusations of failure to keep the law in 2:17–23 impart substance to the otherwise puzzling charge that the person who judges others in 2:1–3 does the same things as those who are judged. It is the Jew who claims moral superiority and fails to keep the law who belongs to the ranks of the ὑβριστὰς ὑπερηφάνους ἀλαζόνας in 1:30.[8]

Although Paul does not explicitly identify his interlocutor as a Jew until 2:17, the way in which he has based his portrait of the Gentile world on Wisdom 12–15 would have meant that Jewish readers would readily walk into his rhetorical trap. By condemning those who endorse the behaviour of the Gentiles in 1:32, Paul ensures that his Jewish readers will distance themselves from the Gentiles by passing judgment on them. In this way they find themselves the object of his counter-accusation in 2:1–3. As the writer of Wisdom turns from focusing on the Gentiles to focus on the Jews at Wisdom 15:1, so Paul ceases to focus on the sins of the Gentiles and turns to address his Jewish interlocutor at Romans 2:1. In Romans 2:4, he takes up the references to God's grace and patience in Wisdom 15:1,[9] thus attempting to ensure that he stays on the wavelength of his Jewish Christian readers until the trap is finally sprung at 2:17 and the Jewish identity of ὁ ἀλαζῶν in 2:1–3 is established.

In this way, Paul uses the rhetorical techniques of the diatribe in order to attack that Jewish complacency, which presumes that their possession of the law secures God's mercy to them.[10] Paul argues instead that God is impartial, inasmuch as he will judge all according to their works, irrespective of whether they be Jew or Gentile, for 'God has no favourites' (2:11). Sin will be punished, whether that sin be committed inside or outside the boundaries of the law. The law itself, then, offers no protection against the wrath of God, because it is only those who do the law who will be justified – and if Gentiles, who do not have the law, nevertheless do what it requires, then that shows that they actually have the law written on their hearts.

The rhythmic structure of verse 14 and Paul's usage of φύσει elsewhere (Gal. 2:15, 4:8) suggest that φύσει should be taken with what follows it, thus indicating that Paul does not intend his readers to identify these Gentiles as Christians,[11] at least at this stage of his argument. Were Paul trying to establish the sinfulness of every individual in Romans 1–3, his

[8] Dunn plausibly proposes that Paul has emphasised sins of pride and presumption in 1:30 as a means of targeting Jewish confidence in their favoured status before God (*Romans*, vol.I, p.80).

[9] A. Nygren, *Commentary on Romans* (London: SCM, 1952), pp.113–18; Moo, pp.127–8.

[10] Dunn, *Romans*, vol.I, p.108.

[11] Leenhardt, *Romans*, p.83; Dunn, vol.I, pp.98–9.

admission of the possible existence of righteous Gentiles in 2:14 would serve to destroy his own argument. This is not, however, the point that Paul is seeking to establish. His aim is that of undermining the boundary of the law, and to this end the existence of righteous Gentiles serves to destroy the idea that righteousness is the exclusive prerogative of the Jews. Paul is not thinking here in individualistic terms at all; his attention is directed to the Jewish and Gentile people groups, and the point of his argument is that it only takes the occasional righteous Gentile to invalidate the assumption that righteousness before God is an exclusively Jewish privilege, existing only within the boundary of Torah.

In verses 17–24, Paul continues with the task of undermining the boundary marker of the law. Having outlined the Jewish sense of privilege in having the law (vv.17–20), he seeks to puncture this by means of the series of accusing questions in verses 21–24. As Dunn rightly points out, 'The detail indicates that the indictment is not intended as an accusation of wholesale Jewish profligacy, but as a pricking of the balloon of Jewish pride and presumption that being the people of God's law puts them in a uniquely privileged position in relation to the rest of humankind.'[12] It may be that Paul had isolated, albeit well-known, incidents in view,[13] but this does not invalidate his argument.[14] In asking these questions, he is not suggesting that all Jews are guilty of such crimes: that is to misread these verses through a grid of western individualism;[15] nor is he taking up Christian polemic against the synagogue.[16] Suggestions that Paul is defining sin in terms of a wrong attitude (Matt. 5:21–48) also miss the point:[17] Paul need only appeal to a few incidents of Jewish transgression of the law, to establish that the Jewish community is not free from sin: the fact that some Jews have been known to break the law by stealing and committing adultery and robbery is proof that, just because the nation has the law, that does not guarantee their righteousness.[18] The logic of Paul's argument here depends upon the culturally specific enclave view of sin as

[12]Dunn, *Romans*, vol.I, p.108.

[13]Cf. H. Strack and P. Billerbeck, *Kommentar zum Neuen Testament*, 4 vols. (Munich: Beck'sche, 1926–8), vol.III, pp.107–15.

[14]*Contra* C.K. Barrett, *Romans* (London: A&C Black, 1991), p.53.

[15]This leads H. Räisänen to charge Paul with inconsistency: *Paul and the Law* (Tübingen: J.C.B. Mohr, 1987), p.100.

[16]*Contra* Wilckens, *Römer*, vol.I, p.146.

[17]Barrett, *Romans*, p.53; Cranfield, pp.168–9.

[18]Cf. N.T. Wright, 'The Law in Romans 2', in Dunn, *Paul and the Mosaic Law*, pp.131–50. According to Wright, such sins serve to prove that Israel is still in exile. However, if there were a popular perception that Israel was still in exile as Wright argues, would Paul need to counter their boasting in their possession of the law?

an outside evil threatening the boundaries of the community.[19] Paul here argues for the existence of sin within the boundary of the law, just as, a few verses earlier, he has argued for the existence of righteous Gentiles outside its boundaries. In this way, Paul's aim in these verses is to subvert the Jewish distinction between good insiders and evil outsiders that is part of the low grid/high group outlook: the validity of regarding the law as an effective boundary marker distinguishing righteous Jew from sinful Gentile is thus further undermined.

In verses 25–29, Paul turns his attention to the primary symbol of Jewish covenant membership, namely that of circumcision. According to Douglas, there is a close connection between the social body and the individual physical body, so that a preoccupation with bodily orifices reflects a concern to guard the entrances and exits to and from the social unit.[20] In first-century Judaism, it certainly was the case that circumcision served to distinguish Jew from Gentile, inasmuch as, while God-fearers and Jewish sympathisers did adopt a number of Jewish practices, they could only be admitted to the Jewish community as proselytes by undergoing circumcision. J.J. Collins disputes this,[21] arguing, on the basis of evidence from Philo and other Jewish 'propaganda' literature, that Diaspora Judaism, in general, had sought to emphasise points of similarity to its Gentile environment. Yet, while it is true that there were Jews who sought to establish common ground with their Gentile neighbours, equally there were those Jews who reacted against this trend by seeking to reinforce the boundaries between Jew and Gentile (as Collins acknowledges).[22] Circumcision itself, however, remained a fundamentally 'low grid' symbol of Jewish 'otherness':[23] accordingly, it was downplayed by those Jews who wished to move 'up-grid' and identify themselves with Gentile society, and was emphasised by those who wished to maintain their distinctive Jewish identity over against the surrounding Gentile culture. It is this latter attitude that Paul is seeking to subvert in the opening chapters of Romans.

[19]Cf. P.W. Livermore, *The Setting and Argument of Romans 1:18–3:20: The Empirical Verification of the Power of Sin* (PhD Diss., Princeton Theological Seminary, 1979). Livermore argues that Paul here refers to idolatry, inhumanity and adultery because these are the three points at which Jews distinguished themselves most sharply from Gentiles, and he wanted to show that these sins were present in the Jewish community.

[20]Douglas, *Purity and Danger*.

[21]J.J. Collins, 'A Symbol of Otherness: Circumcision and Salvation in the First Century', in J. Neusner and E.S. Frerichs, eds., *'To See Ourselves as Others See Us': Christians, Jews, 'Others' in Late Antiquity* (Chico: Scholars, 1985), pp.163–86.

[22]Cf. S. Pattee, 'Paul's Critique of Jewish Exclusivity: A Sociological and Anthropological Perspective', *Soundings* 78 (1995), pp.589–610.

[23]Cf. Dunn, *Romans*, vol.I, pp.118–28.

In verses 25–26, Paul applies the conclusions drawn from his preceding two paragraphs to the symbolism of circumcision, and does so in reverse order. Thus verse 25 takes up the accusations of transgression levelled at the Jew in verses 17–24: circumcision is of value only to those who keep the law, but, if the law is broken, then the transgressor's circumcision has become uncircumcision. The suggestion that Gentiles do by nature what the law requires (v.14) is then taken up in verse 26: if the uncircumcised fulfil the precepts of the law, then is not their uncircumcision to be counted as circumcision? Having just sought to undermine the role of the law as an effective boundary marker between righteous Jew and sinful Gentile, Paul here seeks to turn inside out the law's distinction between insider and outsider, as this is focused in the distinctively Jewish symbol of circumcision. Now it is the Jew who has the law but who does not keep it who is the 'uncircumcised' outsider, and it is the Gentile who does not have the law but who nevertheless fulfils its requirements who is the 'circumcised' insider, and who will now judge the Jewish transgressor who formerly sat in judgment upon him (v.27; cf. v.1).[24]

Paul draws on Jewish tradition to redefine circumcision in such a way as to make it an inward matter of the heart rather than an outward mark in the flesh (vv.28–29).[25] *Contra* E.P. Sanders,[26] Paul is not referring to a circumcision of the human spirit here; he is rather referring to circumcision of the heart by the Spirit of the Lord, as he will do in 7:6 (cf. 2 Cor. 3:6). Here for the first time, he identifies the Gentiles who keep the law (cf. v.14) as those whose hearts have been circumcised by the Spirit.[27] In thus tying circumcision to the Spirit rather than the flesh, Paul seeks to negate its function as a symbol of Jewish covenant membership, and to redefine it in such a way that it applies to believers who have the Spirit. It is at this point that Paul begins to redraw the boundaries around the people of God along eschatological, rather than ethnic, lines. In the eyes of God, Jewishness is not a matter of outward circumcision of the flesh; the real Jew is one whose heart has been inwardly circumcised by the eschatological Spirit.

Paul is behaving in a manner characteristic of Douglas' small bounded group, with its preoccupation with the redrawing of boundaries.[28] In order to subvert the Torah-based judgment of law-free Gentile converts

---

[24]Cf. Chae, *Paul as Apostle*, pp.109–29.
[25]Deut. 10:16; 30:6; Jer. 4:4; 9:25–26; *Jub.* 1:23.
[26]Sanders, *Jewish People*, p.127.
[27]Käsemann, *Romans*, p.75.
[28]Cf. F. Watson, *Paul*, p.122, where he speaks of 'the sectarian claim to sole legitimate possession of the religious traditions of the community as a whole'.

by Jewish believers, Paul redraws the boundaries in such a way as to leave those Jews who put their confidence in the law on the outside of those boundaries. It is not the lawless Gentiles whom they have despised, but they themselves, who are sinners standing under the judgment of God. In this way, Paul seeks to subvert the position of those Jewish believers in Rome who were judging Gentile Christians who did not accept the Jewish law. Paul's argument in Romans 2 redefines the boundary between the righteous and the sinful: it is not those who are uncircumcised who are 'beyond the pale', but those who do not have the Spirit.

Paul sums up his position in 3:9, where he claims to have demonstrated that both Jews and Greeks are all under sin. Paul's aim in the foregoing argument has not been to demonstrate the total depravity of all humanity, but rather it has been to show that possession of the law does not set the Jews apart from the Gentiles in a class of their own. The existence of righteous Gentiles and sinful Jews means that the law does not fulfil its supposed function of demarcating the boundary between good insiders and bad outsiders. The Jew, who judges the sinfulness of the Gentile world from within the supposed security of the Torah, finds that the Torah does not protect him from the sinfulness of the outside world; instead, his claims to moral superiority serve to rank him with the ἀλαζόνας of Romans 1:30. Paul is working with the low grid/high group perception of sin as a contaminating influence which essentially belongs outside the boundaries of the righteous community. Having demolished the boundary of the law and removed the ethnic distinction between Jew and Gentile, Paul can assert that Jews and Gentiles alike are 'under sin', because the boundary between the righteous and the sinful has been redrawn along eschatological, rather than ethnic, lines.

Paul supports the claim that all are under sin by means of a catena of quotations taken from Psalms 14:1–3;[29] 5:9; 140:3; 10:7; Isaiah 59:7–8; Psalm 36:1. It is not immediately apparent what links the citations together. Only Psalm 14:3 has direct relevance to the universality of sin; while it is true that the remaining citations are joined by the theme of the sinful use of different parts of the body,[30] it is curious that Paul makes no allusion to the sinful use of the hand, despite the fact that suitable references were available (Ps. 26:10; 144:8, 11; Mic. 7:3).

---

[29]Dunn (*Romans*, vol.I, p.150) argues that the opening Οὐκ ἔστιν δίκαιος is taken from Eccles. 7:21. The wording is certainly closer there, but Paul may simply have varied his terminology in order to avoid the psalm's repetition of οὐκ ἔστιν ποιῶν χρηστότητα.

[30]J.P. Heil, *Paul's Letter to the Romans: a Reader-Response Commentary* (New York: Paulist Press, 1987), pp.36–7.

At first sight, the catena as a whole does not appear to support Paul's case for the universality of sin. However, an examination of the original literary context of each citation from the psalms reveals that they have one significant feature in common: in their original setting, the words that Paul quotes all follow references to the heart of the wicked. The first four citations all follow a reference to καρδία in the LXX, and in the MT there is a corresponding reference to לֵב in the first, third and fourth references:[31]

Romans 3:10–12

καθὼς γέγραπται ὅτι Οὐκ ἔστιν δίκαιος οὐδὲ εἷς, οὐκ ἔστιν ὁ συνίων, οὐκ ἔστιν ὁ ἐκζητῶν τὸν θεόν. πάντες ἐξέκλιναν· ἅμα ἠχρεώθησαν· οὐκ ἔστιν ὁ ποιῶν χρηστότητα, [οὐκ ἔστιν] ἕως ἑνός.

Psalm 13:1–3 LXX

Εἶπεν ἄφρων ἐν καρδίᾳ αὐτοῦ, οὐκ ἔστι Θεός· διέφθειραν καὶ ἐβδελύχθησαν ἐν ἐπιτηδεύμασιν, οὐκ ἔστι ποιῶν χρηστότητα, οὐκ ἔστιν ἕως ἑνός. Κύριος ἐκ τοῦ οὐρανοῦ διέκυψεν ἐπὶ τοὺς υἱοὺς τῶν ἀνθρώπων, τοῦ ἰδεῖν εἰ ἔστιν συνιὼν ἢ ἐκζητῶν τὸν θεόν. Πάντες ἐξέκλιναν, ἅμα ἠχρεώθησαν, οὐκ ἔστιν ποιῶν χρηστότητα, οὐκ ἔστιν ἕως ἑνός·

Psalm 14:1–4 MT

הִשְׁחִיתוּ הִתְעִיבוּ עֲלִילָה   אָמַר נָבָל בְּלִבּוֹ אֵין אֱלֹהִים
יְהוָה מִשָּׁמַיִם הִשְׁקִיף עַל־בְּנֵי־אָדָם   אֵין עֹשֵׂה־טוֹב:
דֹּרֵשׁ אֶת־אֱלֹהִים: לִרְאוֹת הֲיֵשׁ מַשְׂכִּיל
אֵין עֹשֵׂה־טוֹב   הַכֹּל סָר יַחְדָּו נֶאֱלָחוּ
אֵין גַּם־אֶחָד:

Romans 3:13a

τάφος ἀνεῳγμένος ὁ λάρυγξ αὐτῶν, ταῖς γλώσσαις αὐτῶν ἐδολιοῦσαν

---

[31] Words underlined indicate a direct quotation of the LXX.

Psalm 5:9 LXX

ὅτι οὐκ ἔστιν ἐν τῷ στόματι αὐτῶν ἀλήθεια· ἡ **καρδία** αὐτῶν ματαία· τάφος ἀνεῳγμένος ὁ λάρυγξ αὐτῶν· ταῖς γλώσσαις αὐτῶν ἐδολιοῦσαν.

Psalm 5:10 MT

כִּי אֵין בְּפִיהוּ נְכוֹנָה נְכוֹנָה קִרְבָּם הַוֹּת   קֶבֶר־פָּתוּחַ גְּרוֹנָם לְשׁוֹנָם יַחֲלִיקוּן:

Romans 3:13b

ἰὸς ἀσπίδων ὑπὸ τὰ χείλη αὐτῶν·

Psalm 139:2–3 LXX

οἵτινες ἐλογίσαντο ἀδικίας ἐν **καρδίᾳ**, ὅλην τὴν ἡμέραν παρετάσσοντο πολέμους. Ἠκόνησαν γλῶσσαν αὐτῶν ὡσεὶ ὄφεως, ἰὸς ἀσπίδων ὑπὸ τὰ χείλη αὐτῶν· **διάψαλμα**.

Psalm 140:3–4 MT

אֲשֶׁר חָשְׁבוּ רָעוֹת בְּלֵב   כָּל־יוֹם יָגוּרוּ מִלְחָמוֹת
שָׁנְנוּ לְשׁוֹנָם כְּמוֹ־נָחָשׁ   חֲמַת עַכְשׁוּב
תַּחַת שְׂפָתֵימוֹ סֶלָה:

Romans 3:14

ὧν τὸ στόμα ἀρᾶς καὶ πικρίας γέμει,

Psalm 9:27–28 LXX

Εἶπε γὰρ ἐν **καρδίᾳ** αὐτοῦ, οὐ μὴ σαλευθῶ ἀπὸ γενεᾶς εἰς γενεὰν ἄνευ **κακοῦ**. Οὗ ἀρᾶς, τὸ στόμα αὐτοῦ γέμει καὶ πικρίας καὶ δόλου, ὑπὸ τὴν γλῶσσαν αὐτοῦ κόπος καὶ πόνος.

Psalm 10:6–7 MT

לְדֹר וָדֹר אֲשֶׁר לֹא בְרָע׃ אָמַר בְּלִבּוֹ בַּל־אֶמּוֹט
תַּחַת לְשׁוֹנוֹ עָמָל וָאָוֶן׃ אָלָה פִּיהוּ מָלֵא מִרְמוֹת וָתֹךְ

The fact that a reference to 'heart' is found in all four of the original contexts of these citations from the psalms leaves the reader in no doubt at all that this was a deliberate factor in the composition of the catena. However, Romans 3:15–17 departs from the pattern, inasmuch as the verses cited neither come from the psalms, nor do they contain any reference to the heart:

Romans 3:15–17

ὀξεῖς οἱ πόδες αὐτῶν ἐκχέαι αἷμα, σύντριμμα καὶ ταλαιπωρία ἐν ταῖς ὁδοῖς αὐτῶν, καὶ ὁδὸν εἰρήνης οὐκ ἔγνωσαν.

Isaiah 59:7–8 LXX

Οἱ δὲ πόδες αὐτῶν ἐπὶ πονηρίαν τρέχουσι, ταχινοὶ ἐκχέαι αἷμα, καὶ οἱ διαλογισμοὶ αὐτῶν, διαλογισμοὶ ἀφρόνων· σύντριμμα καὶ ταλαιπωρία ἐν ταῖς ὁδοῖς αὐτῶν, καὶ ὁδὸν εἰρήνης οὐκ οἴδασι, καὶ οὐκ ἔστι κρίσις ἐν ταῖς ὁδοῖς αὐτῶν· αἱ γὰρ τρίβοι αὐτῶν διεστραμμέναι, ἃς διοδεύουσι, καὶ οὐκ οἴδασιν εἰρήνην.

Isaiah 59:7–8 MT

רַגְלֵיהֶם לָרַע יָרֻצוּ וִימַהֲרוּ לִשְׁפֹּךְ דָּם נָקִי
מַחְשְׁבוֹתֵיהֶם מַחְשְׁבוֹת אָוֶן שֹׁד וָשֶׁבֶר בִּמְסִלּוֹתָם׃
דֶּרֶךְ שָׁלוֹם לֹא יָדָעוּ וְאֵין מִשְׁפָּט בְּמַעְגְּלוֹתָם

Here, the term 'heart' has been replaced by the closely allied concept of 'thoughts' or 'intentions' which clearly have their origin in the heart.

The last citation from the catena is again from the psalms, and the term 'heart' is present, although only in the MT.

Romans 3:18

οὐκ ἔστιν φόβος θεοῦ ἀπέναντι τῶν ὀφθαλμῶν αὐτῶν.

Psalm 35:1 LXX

Φησὶν ὁ παράνομος τοῦ ἁμαρτάνειν ἐν ἑαυτῷ, οὐκ ἔστι φόβος
θεοῦ ἀπέναντι τῶν ὀφθαλμῶν αὐτοῦ.

Psalm 36:2–3 MT

נְאֻם־פֶּשַׁע לָרָשָׁע בְּקֶרֶב לִבִּי   אֵין־פַּחַד אֱלֹהִים לְנֶגֶד עֵינָיו:
כִּי־הֶחֱלִיק אֵלָיו בְּעֵינָיו   לִמְצֹא עֲוֹנוֹ לִשְׂנֹא:

Was the citation based on the LXX or the Massoretic Text of the Old
Testament? In favour of the LXX is the consideration that it is only in
the Greek that the first four citations contain the word 'heart': the word
is missing from Psalm 5:10 MT. On the other hand, it is possible that
the catena was composed on the basis of a different recension of the
Hebrew text that preceded the MT and the fact that a reference to 'heart'
is only found in the MT of the last citation could count in favour of a
Hebrew original. On balance, it is perhaps more likely that the catena
was originally based upon the Hebrew text, since this offers a rationale
for the inclusion of the citation from Isaiah 59: the way in which the
citations from the psalms are linked on the basis of the common use of the
term 'heart' employs the Jewish exegetical technique of linking different
verses on the basis of shared vocabulary, a mode of interpretation known
in rabbinic sources as *gᵉzerah shawah*.[32] The use of this technique to
link the references from the psalms would serve as an invitation to the
Jewish readers of the catena to use the principles of *gᵉzerah shawah* to
interpret the catena as a whole.[33] In the Hebrew Tanach, there is one verse
that links the key words לֵב from the psalms and מַחְשָׁבוֹת from Isaiah 59:
Genesis 6:5:[34]

[32]Cf. R. Longenecker, *Biblical Exegesis in the Apostolic Period* (Grand Rapids:
Eerdmans, 1975).
[33]Cf. U. Eco, *The Role of the Reader: Explorations in the Semiotics of Texts* (London:
Hutchinson, 1981), pp.43–51. According to Eco, an author who wishes to communicate
through a text has to foresee a model of a possible reader, one who is able to understand and
interpret the ensemble of codes used by the author in generating the text. A well-organised
text will not only presuppose a degree of competence on the part of its potential readership,
but it will work to create such a competence in its readers. Rom. 3:10–18 would appear to
be just such a text.
[34]The LXX (Gen: 6:6) lacks the term διαλογισμοί: Ἰδὼν δὲ Κύριος ὁ Θεὸς, ὅτι
ἐπληθύνθησαν αἱ κακίαι τῶν ἀνθρώπων ἐπὶ τῆς γῆς, καὶ πᾶς τις διανοεῖται
ἐν τῇ καρδίᾳ αὐτοῦ ἐπιμελῶς ἐπὶ τὰ πονηρὰ πάσας τὰς ἡμέρας.

וַיַּרְא יְהוָה כִּי רַבָּה רָעַת הָאָדָם בָּאָרֶץ
וְכָל־יֵצֶר מַחְשְׁבֹת לִבּוֹ רַק רַע כָּל־הַיּוֹם:

There is good reason to suppose that Genesis 6:5 is the hidden verse
which holds the key to the catena as a whole.[35] Genesis 6:5 was a key
verse for the Jewish doctrine of the evil *yetzer*, the principle in the heart
of humanity that lies behind the universal tendency to sin. This suggests
that the catena may originally have been composed as an exposition of the
effects of the hidden *yetzer* within the heart on human behaviour: as the
references to the heart and its intentions are hidden in the original context
of the citations, so the heart and its intentions are the hidden cause of
the sinful behaviour catalogued in the catena. Significantly, Genesis 6:5
is a verse that is of universal import: God surveys the entire world and
sees that the inclination of the thoughts of the heart was continually evil.
Accordingly, once it is seen that Genesis 6:5 lies behind the catena,[36] it
can be seen that Paul is being true to the original intention of the catena
in using it as scriptural warrant for the universality of sin.

Furthermore, there are numerous parallels between 3:10–18 and the
universal indictment of humanity in Romans 1:18–32. It has been argued
that if the citations are read in Hebrew, the link between לֵב in the psalms
and מַחְשְׁבוֹת in Isaiah 59 leads the reader to see Genesis 6:5 as the key
verse behind the catena. There is no such verbal link between the equivalent Greek words διαλογισμοί and καρδία in the Septuagint. However,
the link is frequently made in the New Testament (Matt. 15:19//Mark
7:21; Luke 2:35; 5:22; 9:47; 24:38), and Paul himself makes the connection in Romans 1:21b: ... ἀλλ᾽ ἐματαιώθησαν ἐν τοῖς διαλογισμοῖς
αὐτῶν καὶ ἐσκοτίσθη ἡ ἀσύνετος αὐτῶν καρδία.

A shared use of the words διαλογισμοί and καρδία thus links
Romans 1:21b and the original contexts of the citations in the catena.
Romans 1:21b forms part of the lengthy indictment of sinful behaviour
in 1:18–32. The two passages, 1:18–32 and 3:10–18, thus deal with the
same subject matter. Furthermore, there are broad similarities in outline
that suggest that Paul could have composed Romans 1:18–32 on the basis
of the catena.[37]

---

[35]For a similar example of 'hidden' *g*ᵉ*zerah shawah*, cf. R. Bauckham, *The Climax of
Prophecy: Studies on the Book of Revelation* (Edinburgh: T&T Clark, 1993), pp.296–307.
[36]Gen. 6:5 is also taken from the Law (cf. Rom. 3:19), unlike any of the verses actually
cited in the catena.
[37]According to L. Keck, Rom. 1:18–3:9, 19 is a sustained theological exposition of the
catena: 'The Function of Rom. 3:10–18 – Observations and Suggestions', in J. Jervell and

Romans 1:18–32 starts with the declaration that the wrath of God is revealed from heaven against the ungodliness and wickedness of those who suppress the truth. Similarly, in the subtext of the first citation, the Lord looks down from heaven to see if there is anyone who is seeking God. A heavenly perspective thus links the start of both passages. Furthermore, in the context of the first citation, Psalm 13:1 LXX starts with the fool saying in his heart that there is no God. Romans 1:21b also speaks of the foolishness of the heart of the wicked, and in the following verses (vv.22–23), that folly is displayed in the act of exchanging the glory of God for the images of people and birds and beasts and reptiles. Thus both passages associate the act of denying God with a foolish heart.

Both passages move on from denying God to the sinful use of the body. In Romans 3:13–15, the catena continues with citations from LXX Psalms 5:9, 139:3, 9:28, all of which refer to the sinful use of throat, tongue, lips and mouth. Behind each citation lies a hidden reference to the human heart. In Romans 1:21, the reference to the heart is picked up in 1:24, where God gives the wicked up to the desires of their hearts, with the result that they dishonour their bodies with each other. Both passages thus associate the heart with a sinful use of the body. The parallel is not exact: the bodily sins in Romans 1:24–27 are sexual, while in 3:13–15 the mouth is viewed as an organ of speech. However, the difference is not necessarily as great as might be supposed, given that ancient physiology may sometimes have associated the mouth and the female sexual and reproductive organs.[38]

Both passages then move on to a more generalised list of sins. The citation from Isaiah 59 takes up the theme of the body from the preceding citations, as it speaks of feet being swift to shed blood; it then continues with the statement that ruin and misery are in their paths. Behind such behaviour lie the διαλογισμοὶ ἀφρόνων referred to in the citation's original context. In Romans 1, verses 29–31 describe an assortment of different sins, which include murder and strife. These are said to arise because God has responded to people's refusal to acknowledge him, by giving them up to a debased mind (v.28). The reference to a refusal to acknowledge God in 1:28 refers the reader back to Romans 1:21–23, where such a refusal is a result of the vanity of the thoughts of the wicked and the foolishness of their hearts. In this way, there is a correlation between

W.A. Meeks, eds., *God's Christ and His People: Studies in Honor of Nils Alstrup Dahl* (Oslo: Universitetsforlaget, 1977), pp.141–57.
[38]Cf. Martin, *Corinthian Body*, pp.233–8.

Romans 1:29–31 and 3:15–17, inasmuch as both passages attribute similar sins to the foolish thinking of the wicked.

There may also be a degree of correspondence between the end of both indictment passages. Romans 1:32 closes the first passage by saying that the wicked approve of those who do such things, even though they know that God has decreed that those who behave this way should die. This disregard of the divine decree may be summarised in the concluding citation of the catena, which states that there is no fear of God in their eyes (3:18).

There are thus a number of loose parallels in subject matter and structure between Romans 1:18–32 and 3:10–18. Yet this raises another question about Paul's use of the catena. Although Romans 1:18–32 appears at first sight to be a universal indictment of humanity, it has been argued above that in fact these verses adopt the perspective of a righteous Jew who sits in judgment on the sinfulness of the Gentile world. Correspondingly, one needs to ask whether the catena is genuinely universal in its import, or does it adopt the stance of the righteous insider condemning the rest of the world as sinful? In their original contexts the individual citations of the catena adopt the perspective of the righteous, who are suffering at the hands of the wicked. If the catena itself reflects the distinction between righteous insider and sinful outsider, that threatens the legitimacy of Paul's application of the catena to those under the law (3:19). Dunn draws attention to the way in which the citations originally maintained a clear distinction between the sinful and the righteous, and suggests that Paul is arguing that these texts become universal in their import once the distinction between Jew and Gentile is undermined.[39] Davies, on the other hand, counters that Paul maintains the distinction in Romans, and that his purpose is to argue that there are no righteous among the wicked.[40] Davies' point is, however, weakened by Isaiah 59:7–8, where the reference is clearly to Israel, and not to the Gentiles. Dunn, indeed, emphasises this, claiming that Paul's point is that Jews now are like Israel was then in their presumption upon their covenant standing before God. Certainly Romans 3:19 leaves the reader in no doubt that Paul's intention is that these verses should offer scriptural warrant for abolishing any perceived distinction between righteous Israel and sinful Gentiles.

However, it is the last citation that offers a basis of Paul's application of the catena to those under the law. It is curious that this citation from

---

[39] Dunn, *Romans*, vol.I, pp.149–51.

[40] G.N. Davies, *Faith and Obedience in Romans: a Study in Romans 1–4*, JSNTS 39 (Sheffield: Sheffield Academic Press, 1990), pp.82–96.

the psalms is set apart from the others, and this may have been done in order to lend it emphasis. It should be noted that a reference to the heart is only present in the Hebrew context of the citation in Psalm 36:2–3 MT, which reads:

נְאֻם־פֶּשַׁע לָרָשָׁע בְּקֶרֶב לִבִּי   אֵין־פַּחַד אֱלֹהִים לְנֶגֶד עֵינָיו:
כִּי־הֶחֱלִיק אֵלָיו בְּעֵינָיו   לִמְצֹא עֲוֺנוֹ לִשְׂנֹא:

The significance of this particular citation lies in the awkward syntax in the Hebrew of Psalm 36:2 MT, where the noun לֵב has the first person singular pronominal suffix. Modern translations have smoothed away the difficulty by amending the sense to 'his heart'.[41] It is only the over-literal translation in the AV that accurately conveys the stilted original: 'The transgression of the wicked saith within my heart (לִבִּי), *that there is* no fear of God before his eyes.' The reader is left in some confusion as to whose heart it is in which the transgression of the wicked is heard. The natural inference to be drawn is that the voice of the wicked speaks within the psalmist's own heart, thereby effectively identifying the psalmist with the wicked. In this way, the context of the concluding citation in the catena completely subverts any supposed distinction between the righteous and the wicked. The wicked are no longer a group distinct from the righteous, to be referred to only in the third person. The use of the first person in this psalm means that the psalmist is included in the ranks of the wicked. It is thus this last verse in the catena that begins to justify the application of the catena as a whole to those who are under the law in Romans 3:19, for here the voice of the wicked speaks within the psalmist's own heart to deny the fear of God. The first person singular reference to לִבִּי, 'my heart', traps the unwary Jewish reader of the catena, who discovers an unexpected self-indictment in the context of the last citation.

In this way, the catena itself mirrors Paul's argument in Romans 1:18–3:9. Both start with a universal indictment that initially adopts the perspective of a righteous insider condemning the sinfulness of the outside world, but then moves to subvert that supposed distinction. Furthermore, the way in which Paul has referred to the heart in Romans 1:18–3:9 suggests that he may have had these quotations and Genesis 6:5 in mind. In 1:21, Paul refers to the darkening of the senseless hearts of the Gentiles, while in 2:5 he warns that the hard and impenitent heart of the Jew is

---

[41] This may well be why the LXX translators omitted a reference to 'heart' here, since their translation ἐν ἑαυτῷ also reinterprets the aberrant grammar of the Hebrew.

storing up wrath for the day of God's anger. In this way he refers to the evil heart of both Jews and Gentiles, and these first two references to the heart are balanced by Romans 2:15, 29 where Paul refers to Gentiles who have the work of the law written on their hearts, and to the one who is a Jew in secret, whose heart is circumcised by the Spirit and not by the letter. This reference to the circumcision of the heart is significant, since in the Dead Sea Scrolls, inward circumcision was the means by which the evil *yetzer* was overcome: 'No man shall walk in the stubbornness of his heart so that he strays after his heart and eyes and evil inclination, but he shall circumcise in the community the foreskin of evil inclination . . .' (1QS 5:4f.).

In Romans 1–2 therefore, Paul refers to the sinfulness of the heart of both Jew and Gentile, and claims that the true Jew is the one whose heart has been circumcised by the Spirit. This prepares the ground for 3:9–20 with its underlying motif of the evil *yetzer*. From the eschatological perspective of one whose heart has been circumcised by the Spirit, Paul looks on a world in which the hearts of Jews and Gentiles alike are subject to the evil *yetzer*, and this is another reason why Paul can apply the catena of quotations equally to Gentiles and to those under the law, without doing violence to their essential meaning. Furthermore, those who do not have the eschatological Spirit still belong to the realm of flesh, which is why Paul imports the term σάρξ into his allusion to Psalm 143:2 in Romans 3:20: no flesh shall be justified by observing the law, because those who are in the flesh belong to the old aeon and are outside the realm of the Spirit, to which believers belong.

The references to being 'under sin' (3:9) and to 'all flesh' (3:20) both indicate an eschatological distinction between the righteous and the sinners, and the way in which these references bracket the catena of quotations in 3:10–18 confirms that these verses are applied to humanity outside the eschatological community of the righteous. The boundary between Jew and Gentile that was once constituted by the law has now been completely stripped away: both groups stand alike in need of God's eschatological act of redemption in Christ. No longer does God pass over sins, as he did in the past:[42] now he displays his righteousness by justifying those who put their faith in Christ (3:21–26).

What the apostle has done at this stage in his argument (1:18–3:20) is to undermine the Jewish perception of the law as an effective boundary

---

[42] The lack of extant references to the word πάρεσις (3:25) makes it difficult to determine whether it means 'forgiveness' or 'passing over': the former is preferred by W.G. Kümmel, 'Πάρεσις and ἔνδειξις: A Contribution to the Understanding of the Pauline Doctrine of Justification', *Journal for Theology and Church* 3 (1952), pp.1–13; Wilckens, *Römer*, vol.I,

marker separating the righteous community of Israel from the surrounding Gentile sinners: it is on this basis that Paul can make his claim that all have sinned and fall short of the glory of God, and are justified by his grace as a gift, through the redemption which is in Christ Jesus (3:23–24). The equality of Jew and Gentile is thus established and, with the support of Genesis 15:6 in Romans 4, Paul is able to assert that faith is the basis for both groups' acceptance by God, and so lay the foundation for his appeal in Romans 14:1ff., that each group should accept the other on the basis of their faith. As argued in the previous chapter, Paul thus seeks to make faith a foundation upon which to base the community's strong, high group sense of identity.

Hope for a low grid community

The question of the relationship between Romans 1–4 and 5–8 was first posed by Lüdemann, who argued that there were two conceptions of flesh juxtaposed in Paul's writings, one Jewish, the other Hellenistic; the former stressed objective guilt and individual culpability (Rom. 1–4); the latter regarded material flesh as inherently sinful, and hence regarded sin as inevitable (Rom. 5–7).[43] Lüdemann also argued that there were two corresponding concepts of redemption: a 'Jewish-religious' 'juridical subjective' doctrine of redemption, which had its source in reflection on the death of Jesus, and a Hellenistic 'ethico-dualistic' system, based on the communication of the Spirit in baptism. On the basis of Lüdemann's distinction, Schweitzer argued that the doctrine of justification by faith was a subsidiary crater in Paul's gospel, and that the centre of his thought was to be found in the eschatological mysticism of Romans 5–8.[44]

On the other hand, if the relationship between Jews and Gentiles is re-garded as the letter's focus, it is difficult to avoid Romans 5–8 becoming a backwater as the flow of Paul's thought is traced directly from Romans 1–4 to Romans 9–11.[45] Minear proposes that Paul's objective in Romans

---

p.196. In favour of the latter, cf. Sanday and Headlam, *Romans*, p.90; Cranfield, vol.I, pp.211–12; Moo, pp.238–40. Paul's use of ἀνοχή at this point would certainly favour the latter alternative (cf. 2:4), as would the implicit contrast between how God dealt with sins in the past (v.25) and in the present (v.26). In addition, of the nine occurrences of ἁμάρτημα in the LXX, Wisd. 11:23 stands out as one which offers a likely background to Paul's us-age of the term here, particularly in the light of the use of the verb cognate to πάρεσις: Ἐλεεῖς δὲ πάντας, ὅτι πάντα δύνασαι, καὶ παρορᾷς ἁμαρτήματα ἀνθρώπων εἰς μετάνοιαν. The meaning 'passing over' should therefore be accepted.

[43] Lüdemann, *Anthropologie*.

[44] Schweitzer, *Mysticism*.

[45] B. Noack, 'Current and Backwater in the Epistle to the Romans', *ST* 19 (1965), pp.155–65.

5–8 is to remove the animosities between the weak and the strong and the uncertainties of the doubters, so that all could worship together: Romans 5 is addressed to all the groups in Rome; chapter 6 to the strong; 7:1–8:17 to the weak, and 8:18–39 to everyone, but especially the doubters.[46] F. Watson also claims that Romans 5–8 can be accounted for by the situation in Rome: Romans 5 expounds the hope of salvation that needs the social support afforded by the Jewish Christians leaving the synagogue and joining the Gentile fellowship. Paul then assures his Jewish Christian readers that abandoning the law does not entail abandoning all ethical restraints (Rom. 6) and claims that the effect of the law has been disastrously to intensify the dominion of sin in the Jewish community (Rom. 7:1–8:17).[47] Both approach this section by projecting the effect it would have had upon the different groups in the capital. As such, they are able to account for the presence of Romans 5–8 in the letter, but there is little sense of a coherent flow of thought within the section, nor are reasons given for its location after chapter 4.

Beker also regards the letter partly as a response to tensions between Jewish and Gentile Christians in Rome, and insists upon its occasional character. However, he excepts Romans 5–8 from the contingent situation addressed by the letter, arguing that in these chapters Paul transcends the Jewish question in order to focus on the new reality of the lordship of Christ as the proleptic manifestation of God's imminent eschatological triumph.[48] Similarly, Dunn regards the emphasis on 'Jew first but also Greek' (1:16) as the integrating motif of the letter,[49] but sets this aside when he comes to chapters 6–8. Here Dunn sees Paul pausing in his exposition of God's faithfulness to clarify how the believer should view sin, death and the law.[50] Romans 6–8 thus have nothing to do with the issue of Jews and Gentiles; instead, in these chapters Paul deals with the outworking of the gospel in relation to the individual.[51] Dunn attempts to integrate this section with the overall structure of the letter by arguing that Paul's exposition of the implications of faith for the individual and for the whole of humanity are set out in 5:1–11 and 5:12–21, and these are respectively developed in 6:1–8:39 and 9:1–11:36.[52] However,

[46]Minear, *Obedience*, pp.57–71.
[47]Watson, *Paul*, pp.143–58.
[48]J.C. Beker, *Paul the Apostle* (Edinburgh: T&T Clark, 1980), pp.83–9.
[49]Dunn, *Romans*, vol.I, pp.lx–lxiii.
[50]Ibid., p.325.
[51]J.D.G. Dunn, 'Paul's Letter to the Romans: an Analysis of Structure and Argument', in W. Haase, ed., *Aufstieg und Niedergang der römischen Welt* (Berlin: de Gruyter, 1987), vol.II, pp.3067–134 (cf. pp.2858–60).
[52]Dunn, 'Paul's Letter', pp.2855–60; *Romans*, vol.I, pp.242–4.

this interpretation of the structure of the letter seems somewhat artificial and contrived, since the universal perspective of 5:12–21 does not correspond with the focus on Israel in 9:1–11:36. Furthermore, Dunn fails to give sufficiently adequate reasons why Paul should want to expound the outworking of the gospel in relation to the individual in a letter that apparently is otherwise concerned with relations between the ethnic groups of Jew and Gentile. From this point of view, Dunn's individualistic interpretation of these chapters has the appearance of being unduly influenced by traditional Lutheran exegesis.

In Stowers' interpretation of the letter, Paul is opposing Jewish teachers who are recommending the law as a route to attaining self-mastery. According to Stowers, in Romans 5–8 Paul concludes his diatribe with the Jewish teacher and addresses his encoded Gentile readers directly, showing how the true route to self-mastery is by sharing in Christ's obedience and life. However, 5:12–21 is integrated only with difficulty: Stowers emphasises that Paul's main concern is to show how the actions of one person affect the many, but he does not explain *why* Paul should want to develop this thesis at this point in the argument of the letter.[53]

Douglas' Grid and Group model does, however, offer a rationale for Paul's thought at this point that successfully integrates Romans 5–8 into the structure of Romans as a letter that is fundamentally concerned with the issue of Jewish–Gentile relations. It has already been argued in relation to the theme of the letter that Paul is concerned to unite Jewish and Gentile Christians on the basis of their common faith in Christ. This is because Paul sees the church as a 'high group' community, with a strong sense of communal identity. However, Paul also sees the church as a low grid community which needs to be separated from the world by clearly defined boundaries. Having demolished the law as a boundary marker separating Jew from Gentile, Paul needs to put in place an effective boundary which will distinguish Christians from the surrounding culture. Accordingly, in Romans 5–8, Paul develops the theme of an eschatological distinction between the righteous and the sinful that he signalled at the end of chapter 2. In Romans 5, Paul sets up the eschatological coordinates of those boundaries; in Romans 6 he argues that law-free Gentile Christians are on the inside of the boundaries, and in Romans 7 he argues that unbelieving Jews under the law fall outside of them. The section concludes in Romans 8 with a summary of all the eschatological blessings which belong to those who possess the Spirit.

[53] Stowers, *Rereading*, pp.251–8.

In Romans 5:1–11, Paul sketches the theme of hope,[54] which he will portray again in greater detail in chapter 8.[55] After summing up the results of justification in verses 1–2a, Paul moves quickly to the theme of hope (vv.2b–4), and verses 5–8 serve to ground that hope, both subjectively in the pouring out of God's love through the Spirit, and objectively in Christ's death for sinners. In verses 9–10, Paul returns to the idea of hope, as he argues *qal wahomer* from the justifying and reconciling death of Christ to the assurance of ultimate salvation through his life. The overall thrust of the passage is thus consistently forward-looking.

That this hope is common to both Jewish and Gentile believers is apparent from the way in which Paul treats the closely associated theme of boasting in this passage. The closing claim, that 'we boast in God through our Lord Jesus Christ' (v.11), is clearly intended to pick up the Jewish claim to boast in God that Paul sought to undermine in 2:17ff. Here in 5:11 he implicitly makes the point that it is Christians, not Jews, who are able to boast in God. It is Christians who can boast in God, because they have been reconciled to God through Christ, and as such they can boast in the hope of the glory of God, of which they had formerly fallen short (5:2; cp. 3:23): Paul's use of the first person plural in this passage makes the point that both Jews and Gentiles are sinners, have been reconciled to God, and so now can boast in him and in the hope of sharing his glory.[56] Such boasting in the Christian eschatological hope replaces the Jewish boasting in the law, which Paul says has been excluded by the law of faith in 3:27.

Paul's message of hope would have had particular relevance to the Christians in Rome. For a low grid community, which rejects the symbol system of the surrounding culture and thus often finds itself to be a marginalised minority, hope plays an important part in strengthening the community's boundaries by enabling the community to resist the pressure to assimilate to the surrounding culture. The hope that the distinctive values of the group will one day be proved right gives the group the determination required to persevere through the present adversity, while the expectation of future vindication reinforces the group's separation from the world, since the future salvation of the community would almost certainly be expected to bring with it the judgment of the world outside which oppresses and afflicts them. For the Christians on the margins of society

---

[54] So Heil, *Romans*, pp.55–61; Dunn, vol.I, pp.245–6; Moo, pp.297–8.
[55] N.A. Dahl, *Studies in Paul* (Minneapolis: Augsburg, 1977), pp.70–94.
[56] Dunn, *Romans*, vol.I, p.249.

in Rome,[57] hope would have played an essential role in their ability to cope with the afflictions they were experiencing.

Principally, however, Paul introduces the theme of hope in order to prepare the ground for his depiction of Christ as second Adam, whose coming has ended the universal reign of sin and death (5:12–21). This in-breaking of the reign of God's grace gave Christians the hope that they would reign in eternal life through Jesus Christ (5:17–21). It is because the world of sin and death has yet to be transformed by the coming of the Second Adam that Paul stresses the future dimensions of the Christian hope, and he lays the foundation for this in 5:1–11, by establishing what God has already done through Christ as a basis for Christian assurance about the future. Since hope of the transformation of the world is virtually a *sine qua non* of any millennialist movement, it should come as no surprise to find that Paul spends a few verses outlining the basis for Christian hope, as a way of prefacing his introduction of Christ as Second Adam, and of Christians as the new eschatological humanity who will reign in life through him.

New boundaries for old

In Romans 5:12–21, Paul portrays Christ as the Second Adam, whose one act of obedience on the cross[58] reverses the disastrous effects of Adam's transgression (v.18). Adam is made the antitype to Christ: just as through Adam sin and death entered the world and brought all humanity under their dominion, so now Christ has inaugurated the reign of God's grace, through which people attain eternal life (v.21). Paul explicitly denies, however, any direct equivalence between Adam and Christ: the coming of God's grace through Christ completely surpasses the negative consequences of Adam's transgression, as Paul's repeated οὐχ ὡς and πολλῷ μᾶλλον in verses 16–17 are intended to convey. In addition, Paul stresses the comprehensive manner in which Christ has overturned the effects of Adam's sin. As through his trespass all people were brought under condemnation, so through Christ's act of righteousness all people are justified and receive life (v.18); just as many were made sinners through Adam, so now many will be made righteous (v.19). The superabundance of God's grace through Christ is already a present reality, as the aorists (ὑπερ)επερίσσευσεν in verses 15, 20 indicate, but the full effects of Christ's coming will not be apparent until the future, when his people are confirmed as righteous and attain eternal life (vv.17, 19, 21).

---

[57] Cf. Jeffers, *Conflict at Rome*, pp.3–35.

[58] δικαίωμα in v.18 refers to Christ's righteous act in laying down his life (so Dunn, *Romans*, vol.1, p.283; Moo, pp.354–5).

Paul's assertions about the superabundance of grace through Christ and the comprehensive overturning of the effects of Adam's transgression would have flown in the face of the *status quo* even when Paul was writing to the Romans. Then Christians were, as they are today, a minority living in a world that is all too clearly marked by the prevalence of sin and death.[59] Paul, however, seeks to assure his readers that, although they may only be a minority group at present, the future belongs to them; insignificant at present, they are the ones who will reign in righteousness and life. Paul's stress on the immeasurable superiority of the grace of God in Christ, which overturns the catastrophic results of Adam's transgression, assures members of this low grid community that they are on what will ultimately be the winning side. Paul thus seeks to reinforce the symbol system of the Christian community in Rome over against that of the surrounding culture.

Romans 5:12–21 also has the effect of establishing and strengthening the boundaries around the group. Paul portrays the world as subject to the powers of sin and death as a result of Adam's transgression, but the Christians he is addressing have received the abundant gift of God's grace and righteousness, and so will reign in life through Christ. The effect of Paul's contrast between Adam and Christ is to divide humanity into two groups: those who are still subject to the reign of sin and death under the old Adamic aeon, and those who have entered the new aeon of righteousness and life, which has Christ at its head. When this passage is read in the light of its own social context, it becomes apparent that this distinction between sinful and righteous humanity dovetails neatly with the low grid/high group tendency to divide humanity into the two distinct groups of righteous insiders and sinful outsiders. In Romans 5:12–21, Paul draws the dividing line between these two groups along eschatological lines. In this way, he can portray the church as the righteous eschatological community of Christ as second Adam, while the rest of humanity remains identified with the first Adam, under the dominion of sin and death within the old aeon.

Paul starts by referring to the entry of sin and death into the world through the transgression of Adam:

> Διὰ τοῦτο ὥσπερ δι' ἑνὸς ἀνθρώπου ἡ ἁμαρτία εἰς τὸν κόσμον εἰσῆλθεν
> καὶ διὰ τῆς ἁμαρτίας ὁ θάνατος,
> καὶ οὕτως εἰς πάντας ἀνθρώπους ὁ θάνατος διῆλθεν,
> ἐφ' ᾧ πάντες ἥμαρτον ... (5:12)

---

[59] Cf. J.C. Beker, 'The Relationship between Sin and Death in Romans', in Fortna and Gaventa, eds., *The Conversation Continues*, pp.55–61.

Romans 5:12 is an anacoluthon, in that Paul leaves unfinished the intended contrast between Adam, as the one through whom sin and death entered the world, and Christ, the one who inaugurated the aeon of righteousness and peace.[60] Since in verses 15–17 Paul is concerned to show the ways in which Christ is superior to Adam,[61] the intended contrast of 5:12 is not resumed until the οὕτως καί in 5:18.[62] Since Paul depicts Christ as Second Adam, standing at the head of a new aeon of righteousness and life inaugurated by his resurrection, the introductory Διὰ τοῦτο probably picks up the reference to salvation through Christ's life in 5:10, with the intervening verse (5:11) serving to summarise the preceding theme of reconciliation and boasting.

The four lines of the verse form a chiasm, in which the entry of death through sin (v.12b) corresponds to death coming to all people (v.12c), and the entry of sin into the world (v.12a) corresponds to all people sinning (v.12d).[63] Thus the first half of the chiasm focuses on the entry of sin and death into the world; the second half upon their universality.

The phrase ἐφ' ᾧ can either be understood in a conjunctival sense, or it may introduce a relative clause. In the latter case, however, it is difficult to find a suitable antecedent for ᾧ. Augustine took *in quo* in a locative sense with reference to Adam,[64] and Cambier has argued for a causative reference back to Adam ('à cause duquel'),[65] but notwithstanding the chiasm, ἑνὸς ἀνθρώπου is too far removed to be the antecedent of ᾧ. ὁ θάνατος is a more obvious candidate grammatically, but death is not the ground of sin, and to give ἐφ' ᾧ the meaning 'towards which' is awkward.[66] Danker's suggestion that νόμος is the missing antecedent is unlikely.[67] More plausible is Zahn's suggestion that the phrase refers to the situation outlined in v.12a–c and suggests the meaning 'on the basis of which'.[68]

Alternatively, the phrase could be understood as a conjunction, and the majority of commentators ascribe to it the meaning 'because'.[69] Similar

[60]Cranfield, *Romans*, vol.I, pp.272–3; Fitzmyer, p.411.

[61]Cf. K. Kertelge, 'The Sin of Adam in the Light of Christ's Redemptive Act According to Romans 5:12–21', *Communio* 18 (1991), pp.502–13.

[62]Cf. R. Bultmann, 'Adam and Christ according to Romans 5', in W. Klassen and G.F. Snyder, eds., *Current Issues in New Testament Interpretation* (London: SCM, 1962), pp.143–65.

[63]J. Cambier,'Péchés des Hommes et Péché d'Adam en Rom.V12', *NTS* 11(1964–5), pp.217–55 (esp. pp.250–1); Wilckens, *Römer*, vol.II, pp.314ff.; Moo, p.321.

[64]*Contra duas epistolas Pelagianorum*, 4.4.7.

[65]Cambier,'Péchés'.

[66]Cf. Cranfield, *Romans*, vol.I, pp.275–6; Fitzmyer, pp.414–15.

[67]F.W. Danker,'Romans V12: Sin under Law', *NTS* 14 (1967–8), pp.424–39.

[68]T. Zahn, *Der Brief des Paulus an die Römer* (Leipzig: Deichert, 1910), pp.263–7.

[69]Fitzmyer lists those who adopt this view: *Romans*, p.415.

in meaning is Lyonnet's suggestion that the phrase means 'étant remplie la condition que',[70] whereas Moule proposes the meaning 'inasmuch as'[71] and Fitzmyer has argued for 'with the result that'.[72]

To decide between these alternatives, it is helpful to examine Paul's use of the phrase elsewhere in Philippians 4:10; 3:12; 2 Corinthians 5:3–4. Certainly the translation 'because' would be inappropriate in Philippians 4:10, where Paul corrects his foregoing statement that the Philippians have revived their concern for him, by pointing out that they had always been concerned, but they had only lacked opportunity to show it. In this way, Paul seems to use ἐφ' ᾧ to redefine what he had meant by the preceding φρονεῖν. The same usage is apparent in Philippians 3:12, where Paul puts a different slant on the verb καταλαμβάνω, grounding his efforts to attain the resurrection of the dead (εἰ καὶ καταλάβω) in the fact that Christ has taken hold of him (ἐφ' ᾧ καὶ κατελήφθην ὑπὸ Χριστοῦ). In both cases, the phrase 'inasmuch as' would seem to be the appropriate translation, but two cases alone are insufficient to establish a regular pattern of usage, and textual doubts overshadow the other occurrence of the phrase in 2 Corinthians 5:3–4. Yet if ἐκδυσάμενοι is read in verse 3,[73] the ἐφ' ᾧ clause in verse 4 makes good sense as a clarificatory expression that Paul is not groaning and burdened because he wants to be unclothed of his body (οὐ θέλομεν ἐκδύσασθαι), but rather because he wants to be clothed with life (v.4). If this is the case, then we have here a third example of Paul using ἐφ' ᾧ to introduce a clause which in some sense explains and redefines a preceding verb. Here, as in Philippians 4:10; 3:12, the translation 'inasmuch as' captures the sense.

This translation of ἐφ' ᾧ also makes good sense in Romans 5:12, in which the final line of the chiasm repeats and reinterprets the first line: sin came into the world, *inasmuch as* all sinned.[74] But the question of how ἥμαρτον is to be understood in this context is also a matter of debate. Does

[70]S.J. Lyonnet, 'Le sens de ἐφ' ᾧ en Rom. 5:12 et l'Exégèse des Pères Grecs', *Bib* 36 (1955), pp.325–55.

[71]C.F.D. Moule, *An Idiom Book of New Testament Greek* (Cambridge: Cambridge University Press, 1959), p.153.

[72]J.A.Fitzmyer,'The Consecutive Meaning of ΕΦ 'Ω in Romans 5:12', *NTS* 39 (1993), pp.321–39.

[73]D*c it^ar,d,f,v,r,g,o geo¹ Marcion; Macrius/Symeon; Tertullian Ambrosiaster (½); Ambrose, Pelagius, Speculum, Augustine (⅐). ἐνδυσάμενοι is read by 𝔓46 ℵ B C D² 075 0150 0243 6 33 81 104 256 263 365 424 436 459 1175 1241 1319 1573 1739 1852 1881 1912 1962 2127 2200 2464; *Byz* [K L P] *Lect* it^b,fᶻt,r vg syr^p,h,pal cop^sa,bo arm eth geo² slav Clement Didymus Chrysostom Cyril; Ambrosiaster (½); Augustine (⁶⁄₇). Despite the strong attestation, the reading ἐνδυσάμενοι is probably secondary, since it follows on more smoothly from the idea of being clothed in v.2, and removes the apparent contradiction of being unclothed but not naked if ἐκδυσάμενοι is read in v.3.

[74]Cf. D. Zeller, *Der Brief an die Römer* (Regensburg: Pustet, 1985), pp.116–17.

it refer to people sinning in solidarity with Adam,[75] or to people sinning in their own capacity as individuals?[76] Paul's use of the verb elsewhere certainly supports the latter interpretation,[77] but a final decision cannot be taken until the meaning of verse 13 has been established.

In 5:13 Paul breaks his flow of thought to refer to the presence of sin in the world which is not counted by law,[78] and it is therefore appropriate to regard this interruption as being occasioned by the need to explain 5:12d. As Cranfield points out, 5:13 may be understood as offering support for either the individual or the corporate sense of ἥμαρτον, according to whether the stress is placed on the first or second clauses.[79] If the first clause is emphasised and the second clause read concessively, the apostle is to be understood as breaking off to make the point that, although the sins of individuals are not counted apart from law (4:15), nevertheless the reign of death in the period between Adam and Moses is evidence of universal sinfulness, even though this sinful behaviour was not clearly defined as transgression of a commandment.[80] If, on the other hand, the first clause is understood concessively and the emphasis is placed upon the second clause, the statement that sinful deeds are measured only from the time of the arrival of the law is the key to the whole argument. The reign of death over those between Adam and Moses, who did not disobey a specific command, points to the presence of sin apart from transgression of the law; in that sinful acts are only quantifiable under the law, ἥμαρτον must then refer to sinning in solidarity with Adam.[81]

Of the two alternatives, the scales tip in favour of the first. It has the advantage of retaining the normal sense of ἁμαρτάνω, and the need to resolve the apparent contradiction between 4:15 and 5:12 may be deemed sufficient grounds for Paul to interrupt the flow of his argument here. The second alternative suffers from a number of difficulties. Firstly, it requires an unnatural reading of ἥμαρτον. Secondly, it is curious that Paul should specifically distinguish the sin of those over whom death reigned from the sin of Adam (v.14), if in fact the former took place in the latter, as is suggested by the idea of sinning in solidarity with Adam. Thirdly, such

---

[75]E.g. Bruce, *Romans*, pp.129f.; Moo, pp.323–8.

[76]E.g. Cranfield, *Romans*, vol.I, pp.274–81.

[77]Rom. 2:12; 3:23; 5:14, 16; 6:15;1 Cor. 6:18; 7:28, 36; 8:12; 15:34.

[78]The purpose of the law was to put sin on record: G. Friedrich, "'Αμαρτία οὐκ ἐλλογεῖται: Röm: 5:13', *TLZ* 77 (1952), pp.523–8.

[79]Cranfield, *Romans*, vol.I. pp.281–3.

[80]E. Brandenburger, *Adam und Christus: Exegetisch-Religionsgeschichtliche Untersuchung in Röm. 5:12–21 (1 Kor. 15)* (Neukirchener: Neukirchener Verlag, 1962), pp.180–205.

[81]Moo, *Romans*, pp.322–9.

an interpretation has an unrealistic view of the law. Despite his comment of 4:15, Paul did not regard sin as being reckoned only under the law; it must be remembered that Jews regarded Gentiles apart from the law as sinful. In Romans 4:15, Paul posits a period free of transgression before the law only to demonstrate that God's promises to Abraham could not be invalidated by transgressions. His statement of 5:12, that sin was in the world before the law was given, conflicts with 4:15, and so Paul breaks off at 5:13 to cover his flank on this point.

For these reasons, 5:13 should be understood concessively, and ἥμαρτον accorded its normal meaning of sinning voluntarily and individually. The phrase ἐφ᾽ ᾧ πάντες ἥμαρτον thus explains the entry of sin into the world in terms of the universally sinful behaviour of all humanity, just as the entry of death into the world (5:12b) is interpreted by the universal experience of dying (5:12c). Thus, although in 5:12ab, Paul writes of sin and death as though they were mythological powers, in 5:12cd he clarifies his meaning by tying the nominative singular of both noun to the universal human experience of sinning and dying.

At this stage in the letter Paul uses the symbolism of the power of sin to express the universal fact that everyone sins.[82] Käsemann's interpretation of Paul's sin language expresses the apostle's thought well. Paul looks out on a world caught up in a nexus of sin and death, in which every individual is caught up in such a way that they cannot but manifest their belongingness to the world in their behaviour: 'In our lives we confirm the fact that a world in revolt surrounds us. The cycle of sin and destiny cannot be rationalised in terms of individual existence. All is fruit and all is seed.'[83]

The connection between the sin of Adam and the sinfulness of the rest of humanity indicated in verse 19a is probably to be perceived in these terms, since any notion of an inherited sinful nature needs to be read into Paul's argument.[84] The most likely explanation of Paul's thought at this point is that offered by Barrett, who notes that the terms 'sinners' and 'righteous' are words of relationship and not of character.[85] When Adam sinned, his own harmonious relationship with God was severed, as was that of the whole created order. It is this estrangement from God that therefore renders people sinners, and which is worked out and expressed in the sinful deeds and acts which they perform. In Romans 5:12–21, Paul declares that as a result of Adam's transgression, the world has

---

[82]Cf. Kaye, *Thought Structure*; Wilckens, *Römer*, pp.310–28.
[83]Käsemann, *Romans*, p.154.
[84]*Contra* Sanday & Headlam, *Romans*, p.134; Cranfield, vol.I, pp.290–1.
[85]Barrett, *Romans*, p.109.

been out of touch with God and enmeshed in sin. It is Christ as Second Adam who has set people free from sin, and restored God's reign of grace and righteousness and life.[86] The overall thrust of Paul's argument is polemical: it is in Christ as Second Adam, and not in Jewish law, that this freedom from sin is to be found.

As verse 20 makes clear, Paul's aim in doing this is to replace the discredited ethnic boundary of Torah observance with the new eschatological boundary of the new aeon. Far from dealing with the problem of sin, the arrival of the law served only to increase the trespass by making it 'bookable', by turning undefined trespass into the definite transgression of a commandment.[87] The effect of the law's coming was thus to make matters worse by causing sin to abound. As he redraws the boundaries around the righteous in-group, Paul thus explicitly assigns the Jewish law its place under the old aeon, alongside sin and death. In this way he is continuing to seek to legitimate the position of law-free Gentile believers within the church.

Paul's personification of sin plays an integral part in this redrawing of the boundaries. As Paul disallows the Torah any role in distinguishing the righteous from the sinful, so too he moves away from the characteristically Jewish perception of sin as polluting uncleanness. Instead, in accordance with his eschatological redefinition of the people of God, he portrays sin as a ruling power which entered the world by means of Adam's transgression, and which now holds sway over all humanity under the old aeon, including Jews under the law.

Believing Gentiles as righteous insiders

Throughout Romans 6–7, Paul uses rhetorical questions to indicate fresh stages in his argument, which occur at 6:1, 6:15, 7:1, 7:7, 7:13; with the exception of 7:1, all these questions take the form of (Jewish) objections to Paul's position, which he uses to advance his discussion.[88] The opening section of Paul's argument in these chapters thus runs from 6:1 through to 6:14. The major shift in gear occurs at 6:15, where Paul specifically addresses the question as to whether freedom from the law is a licence to sin. Whereas in 6:1–14 Paul focuses on dying to sin with Christ in

---

[86] If sin did indeed enter the world as a result of humankind's alienation from God, this explains Paul's use of the symbol of reconciliation in Rom. 5:10–11. It is because we have been reconciled to God in Christ that the reign of sin and death has been broken.

[87] Cranfield, *Romans*, vol.I, pp.292–3; Käsemann, p.158; Beker, *Paul the Apostle*, pp.243–5.

[88] The Jewish interjection in each case except 7:13 is Τί οὖν ἐροῦμεν;

baptism, in 6:15–23, his focus is more specifically on freedom from sin outside the law as he develops the extraordinary claim of 6:14 that it is precisely because his readers are not under the law that sin will have no dominion over them. The boldness of this statement means that Paul has to defend it to his Jewish Christian readers in two ways. Firstly, he seeks to establish his thesis that it is indeed those who are under grace and not the law who are righteous (6:15–23). He then continues in 7:1–23 to give evidence in support of the unspoken corollary to the claim of 6:14, namely that those who are under the law are in fact under the dominion of the power of sin. In this way, having drawn eschatological boundaries, Paul locates the strong on the inside, but places Jews under the law on the outside, thus legitimating the position of the strong in Rome.

In 6:1 Paul asks, 'Should we continue in sin, in order that grace may abound?' The clear parallel with 3:8 is an indication that this question again reflects the kind of accusations that were being levelled against Paul on account of his law-free gospel: there were clearly Jewish Christians who felt that Paul's emphasis on grace rather than law amounted to a condoning of sinful behaviour. The wording of Paul's question in 6:1 is, however, very carefully chosen. He does not ask, 'Shall we go on sinning, so that grace may increase?' (NIV); such a question would simply be a reformulation of the interlocutor's question in 3:8. Instead, Paul asks 'Shall we continue *in sin* . . . ?' This rephrasing of the question picks up the contrast that Paul has drawn in Romans 5 between the dominions of sin and grace, and asks whether it is right to remain in the sphere of sin, so that grace might abound.[89] In answering 'No', Jewish Christian objectors will find themselves hoist by their own petard, for Paul has just argued that it is precisely under the law that sin abounded, but grace increased all the more (5:20): the theme of grace abounding establishes a link between 6:1 and 5:20. Paul's reformulation of the Jewish Christian objection in 6:1 thus carries within it the germ that will destroy their position, for if it is not right to remain in sin so that grace may abound, it cannot be right either to remain under the law, since within the old aeon the law only serves to increase the trespass. A different means of deliverance from the power of sin is needed, and in 6:1–14 Paul sets out how Jews and Gentiles alike die to sin with Christ in baptism, which marks the point of entry into the community, and the separation of believers from the outside world. As Christ has died to sin and now lives to God, they are to count themselves dead to sin but alive to God in him (v.11). Through the rite of

---

[89]Cf. Dunn, *Romans*, vol.I, p.306.

baptism, Paul declares that believers are transferred out of the realm of sin and death and into God's realm of righteousness and life.[90]

Paul thus retains the eschatological distinction between insider and outsider that he has made in 5:12–21, and makes baptism the point of transition between the two groups. The absence of any such eschatological interpretation of baptism in Paul's earlier letters raises the possibility that Paul develops this interpretation of the rite here for the first time.[91] What we may see here is a reformulation of the significance of baptism, a reinterpretation of the rite deliberately intended to distinguish it from the Jewish rite of proselyte baptism from which the practice of Christian baptism was probably originally derived.[92] Whereas the Jewish practice of baptising proselytes symbolised a cleansing from the defiling nature of Gentile sin,[93] Paul avoids any reference to the cleansing effect of baptism in Romans, which is surprising, in view of the obvious nature of the symbolism (cf. 1 Cor. 6:11). It seems likely that Paul is avoiding the symbolism of cleansing because it was inextricably tied up with the Jewish view of Gentile sin as something polluting, and it is precisely this ethnic distinction between righteous and sinner that the apostle is seeking to subvert. It is therefore with a view to redrawing eschatological boundaries around the elect that Paul interprets baptism as a rite of transition from the old Adamic aeon of sin to God's new aeon of righteousness.

Paul combines this interpretation of baptism with a radical view of the sinfulness of the body as he redefines sin in eschatological terms. In Romans 6–8, Paul repeatedly portrays the body as being completely dominated by the powers of sin and death. This is apparent first of all in Paul's use of the phrase τὸ σῶμα τῆς ἁμαρτίας in Romans 6:6. That Paul views the body itself as sinful in this section of Romans is confirmed by Romans 6:12, where believers are urged to stop letting sin reign in their mortal bodies, so that they no longer obey the body's own evil

---

[90]This is completely missed by Cranfield in his otherwise detailed discussion of the possibilities (*Romans*, vol.I, pp.298–300).

[91]Although Paul's question in 6:3 might be understood as implying that his readers should be aware of this significance of baptism, there is no guarantee that this was in fact the case (Dunn, *Romans*, vol.I, p.312).

[92]Despite the lack of direct evidence for Jewish proselyte baptism at this time, it seems more than likely that it was practised then; cf. E. Schürer, *The History of the Jewish People in the Age of Jesus Christ*, 4 vols. (Edinburgh: T&T Clark, 1973–87), vol.III.1, pp.173ff. Given the contemporary existence of this practice, its influence on Christian baptism via the ministry of John the Baptist seems incontrovertible.

[93]On the Jewish view of sin as defilement, cf. A. Büchler, *Studies in Sin and Atonement in the Rabbinic Literature of the First Century* (London: Oxford University Press, 1928).

desires. Romans 7:5, 23 make it clear that those who are in the flesh are subject to the law of sin and the sinful passions at work in their bodily members.[94] In Romans 7:24, Paul pleads for deliverance from 'the body of this death', while in 8:10, he refers to the body being dead because of sin; the indwelling Spirit will bring life to their mortal bodies (8:11), but only as by the Spirit they mortify the deeds of the body (8:13). Prior to its redemption (8:23), Paul seems to portray the body as being evil in his letter to the Romans.[95]

Only in Romans 12:1 do we find a more positive view of the body, since believers are here urged to present their bodies as living sacrifices, which are holy and acceptable to God. Yet this view of the believer's body as being set apart for the Lord is what we find elsewhere in the paraenetic sections of Paul's letters. In 1 Corinthians 7:34, the unmarried woman and the virgin are said to be holy in body and spirit, while in 1 Thessalonians 5:23, Paul refers to the spirit, soul and body being kept blameless until the parousia. The body may be frail and weak and lowly, but it is God's purpose to raise it up and transform it (1 Cor. 15:42–44; 2 Cor. 4:7–5:5; Phil. 3:21). In 1 Corinthians 6:12–20, the prospect of the future redemption of the body is used to make the point that the body belongs to the Lord, and thus should not be used for sinful purposes: the body is for the Lord (v.13), who will raise it up (v.14); it is a member of Christ (6:15) and the temple of the Holy Spirit (6:19), and believers are thus exhorted to glorify God in their bodies (6:20). Only 1 Corinthians 9:27 echoes the negative view of the body set out in Romans 6–8: here, Paul talks about pummelling his body and subduing it, which may be taken as a reference to bringing the sinful desires of the body under control; yet, on the other hand, Paul may well simply be continuing the athletic metaphor from verses 24–26 in order to make the point that his training for God's service is every bit as rigorous as that of an athlete entering a competition.

According to Douglas, the high group/low grid cosmology regards the inside of the social and physical body as good, whereas the outside is evil. The body itself forms the boundary between the inside and the outside, which is precisely why high group/low grid communities are so concerned to guard the body's points of entry. The body is thus an object

---

[94] On the possible Jewish background for this idea, cf. E. Schweizer, 'Die Sünde in den Gliedern', in O. Betz, M. Hengel and P. Schmidt, eds., *Abraham unser Vater: Juden und Christen im Gespräch über die Bibel* (Leiden: E.J. Brill, 1963), pp.437–9.

[95] Jewett (*Paul's Anthropological Terms*, pp.290–8) minimises Paul's emphasis on the sinfulness of the body, to the point of ignoring it altogether.

of anxiety, with a dominant fear of poisoning and debilitation, and may be rejected as an empty shell.[96]

There is thus a degree of ambiguity about the body in high group/low grid social units, and this is reflected in Paul's varying attitudes to the body in his writings.[97] In Romans 6–8, however, he clearly portrays the body as if it has been taken over by the power of sin which reigns in the world, and thereby he identifies sin as being an inescapable part of bodily human existence under the old aeon. This is why he can use the metaphor of the destruction of the body through crucifixion to express release from the grip of the power of sin. By locating sin in the body in this way, Paul is able to portray the problem of sin as being too deep-rooted for it to be dealt with by acceptance of the Jewish law, since acceptance of the commandments of God still leaves one in the grip of sin in the present aeon. Only by undergoing the eschatological process of dying and being raised to a new life is it possible to be released from the power which dominates physical existence in the world. It is only by dying with Christ that the sinful body is destroyed, so that people are no longer enslaved to sin (6:6); it is only those who have been raised from death in Christ who have been liberated from sin, so that they can then dedicate the members of their bodies to God's service instead (6:11–13). The anguished plea for deliverance of Romans 7:24 is the cry of the law-abiding Jew longing for the deliverance from sin that only Christ can bring (v.25). It is those who have the Spirit who are able to put to death the misdeeds of the body, because they are not in the flesh, but in the Spirit (8:9–13): their reception of the Spirit has transferred them out of the dominion of the present age into the life of the age to come. Paul therefore emphasises the sinfulness of the body in Romans 6–8 in order to make the point that release from sin can only come about through the radical step of dying with Christ and being raised to new life, of exchanging the fleshly life of the old aeon for the eschatological life of the Spirit in the new. As part of his polemic against Jewish confidence in Torah, Paul develops a new plight and a new solution. Just as Christ in his death left the realm of sin and now lives for God, believers are to count themselves dead to sin and alive to God. They have died with Christ, and so have been set free from sin; as such, Paul can adapt and apply the rabbinic principle that 'All who die obtain

[96] Douglas, *Natural Symbols* (1970), pp.143, 160.

[97] This ambiguity reflects the eschatological tension out of which Paul lives: the body both belongs to this world and is also the sole medium through which eschatological realities can be expressed in this world: cf. R. Scroggs, 'Paul and the Eschatological Body', in E.H. Lovering Jr and J.L. Sumney, eds., *Theology and Ethics in Paul and His Interpreters: Essays in Honor of Victor Paul Furnish* (Nashville: Abingdon, 1996), pp.14–29.

expiation through death' and apply it to his readers: as those who have died (with Christ) they are now justified from sin (6:7).[98]

The symbolism of dying to sin, being buried, and being raised to walk in newness of life emphasises the completeness, and indeed the apparent finality, of the separation from sin. The contrast between the complete break with sin that Paul appears to refer to here and the ongoing struggle with sin experienced by the Christian and referred to in 6:11–23 has caused Pauline scholars some difficulty. Holtzmann put all the emphasis upon the imperative and regarded the indicative as an example of 'heaven-storming idealism'.[99] Sanday and Headlam argued that, according to Paul, the Christian has done once for all with sin, but then go on to qualify this claim by the parenthetic statement that 'This at least is the ideal, whatever may be the reality.'[100] The 1920s saw the debate between Bultmann and Windisch over the question of whether or not Paul expected the believer to lead a sinless life.[101] In his *Theology*, Bultmann argued that the imperative results from the indicative, in the sense that 'the life conferred by baptism must prove itself in the present by its freedom from the power of sin'.[102] Kirchgässner argues for a synergism, in which the indicative refers to the objective event of redemption, while the imperative denotes a subjective appropriation of this in terms of one's conduct.[103] Beker argues that Paul now sees sin as an impossible possibility: instead of being unable not to sin, the believer is now for the first time put in the position of being able not to sin.[104] Dunn, on the other hand, argues that Paul is here deliberately setting up an eschatological tension, in which the already of the indicative is qualified by the not yet of the imperative.[105]

Yet Douglas' matrix once more offers a rationale for the move that Paul makes from the indicative to the imperative in Romans 6. Social boundaries in the low grid/high group quadrant of the matrix suffer from a degree of porousness, inasmuch as they fail to keep out altogether the polluting influence of the outside world. It is precisely this porousness of boundary that characterises what Paul has to say about baptism in these

---

[98] The quotation comes from *Sifre Num.* 112; cf. K.G. Kuhn, 'Rm 6,7', *ZNW* 30 (1931), pp.305–10.

[99] Holtzmann, *Lehrbuch*, vol.II, p.164.

[100] Sanday and Headlam, *Romans*, p.153.

[101] H. Windisch, 'Das Problem des paulinischen Imperativs', *ZNW* 23 (1924), pp.265–81; Bultmann, 'Problem of Ethics'.

[102] Bultmann, *Theology*, vol.I, p.333.

[103] A. Kirchgässner, *Erlösung und Sünde im Neuen Testament* (Freiburg: Herder, 1950), pp.1–157.

[104] Beker, *Paul the Apostle*, p.217.

[105] Dunn, *Romans*, vol.I, pp.302–3.

verses. The social function of the rite of baptism is that of separating the believer from the outside world; it symbolises the believer's death to sin. Yet, as Paul's move from the indicative to the imperative indicates, the break with sin is not complete: the boundaries of the community are under attack from the outside world. Since the physical body symbolises the social body, Paul can portray the social problem of porous boundaries in terms of the danger of allowing sin to regain control over the physical body. His focus is not upon the individual here; rather he is rallying the members of the community to take their stand under the banner of righteousness, and resist the attempts made by the power of sin to gain control over their lives.

As Paul moves from the indicative to the imperative in 6:11, he also switches from the inclusive first person plural to address his readers in the second person, and he continues to use this mode of address for the rest of chapter 6, with the exception of the rhetorical question in 6:15. There are a number of indications that Paul specifically has Gentile believers in mind when he uses the second person plural in Romans 6. Firstly, in 6:14 he states that sin will no longer rule over them, since they are not under law, but under grace; such words would not be applicable to weak believers in Rome who wished to remain under the law. Furthermore, in verses 17–23, Paul refers to a history of voluntary enslavement to sin, which would be an inappropriate description of either a Jew or a Torah-observant God-fearer. Finally, Paul's description of sin as uncleanness and lawlessness in 6:19 reflects a characteristically Jewish perception of Gentile behaviour, as does his reference to the things of which his readers are now ashamed.[106] It is unthinkable that Paul could write such words with Jewish readers in mind, but his words are those of a Jew who can assume that Gentiles are *de facto* sinful in their behaviour.

Yet these typically Jewish images of sin as unclean, lawless and shameful behaviour are subsumed under the overarching description of sin as bondage to a power. Paul describes the past sinful behaviour of Gentile converts as an enslavement to sin, from which they have now been set free (17–18). In verse 19, he states that, whereas they used to be enslaved to uncleanness and lawlessness, they are now to present themselves as slaves to righteousness, because they are no longer subject to the power of sin, but to God (19–23). The message that Paul is seeking to convey is that the problems of Gentile uncleanness and lawlessness are dealt with by the transfer from the deadly rule of sin into the service of divine

---

[106]Cf. Michel, *Römer*, p.137; Dunn, vol.I, pp.346–8.

righteousness.[107] There is no need for Gentile converts to separate themselves still further from the pollution of their sinful past by coming inside
the boundaries of Torah: they have already been released, and the result of
their present service in the household of righteousness is that they are holy
(v.19): the Jewish symbol of holiness is here applied to Gentile believers.
In this way, Paul here transforms the Jewish perception of themselves
as the righteous and holy insiders and the Gentile as sinful and polluted
outsiders. The boundaries are once again redrawn in such a way as to
place Gentile believers on the inside.

Paul is concerned to emphasise that, although sin may have held sway
over these converts in the past, it does so now no longer. He encourages
Gentile Christians to view their past as sinful, as something from which
they have been released in order to serve God: sin belongs in the past;
it has no place in the present. Whereas the result of the former service
was simply more lawlessness and eventually death, the result of serving
righteousness is holiness, which leads to life. Paul stresses that there are
only two options open to people: either enslavement under the power
of sin which leads to death, or the service of obedience which leads
to righteousness (v.16). Paul encourages them to dedicate themselves to
God's service by comparing the deathly wages of sin with God's gracious
gift of eternal life (6:19–23).

In this second part of Romans 6, the power of sin fulfils two important social functions in the context of Paul's argument. Firstly it fulfils
a paraenetic function: by portraying sin as a power which formerly held
sway over their lives, Paul is seeking to persuade his converts to break
completely with their former way of life and to conform to the moral
standard expected of the people of God. To reinforce this process of reso-
cialisation, Paul draws a stark contrast between the two masters contained
within the image of release from an oppressive taskmaster whose only
wage is death, into the gracious service of God whose gift is eternal life.

At the same time, the Gentiles' past way of life is portrayed as an
enslavement to this power, an enslavement from which they have now
been set free as Gentiles outside the Jewish law: Paul grants them the
characteristically Jewish privileges of righteousness, holiness and life.
As those who experience eschatological freedom from the power of sin

---

[107]From the parallelism of v.16, one would expect Paul to balance the reference to sin
leading to death with one about righteousness leading to life. The effect of referring to
slavery to obedience which leads to righteousness is to stress the ethical dimension of
God's gift of righteousness. Contrary to Jewish fears, the righteousness of law-free Gentile
believers was not a licence for antinomianism, but expressed itself in practical obedience
to God.

under the old aeon, Gentile believers have no need of the Jewish law to regulate their behaviour. The symbol of the power of sin is thus also used by Paul again to redefine the boundaries of the righteous in-group along eschatological lines. The concluding words in 6:23 echo the contrast between the two aeons that Paul has drawn in 5:12–21: the contrast between the aeon of grace, righteousness and life, and the aeon of sin and death. In Romans 6 Paul seeks to portray Gentile Christians outside the law as those who belong to the new aeon of righteousness: they belong inside the boundaries surrounding the people of God that Paul is seeking to draw in this letter. They are the community of the righteous, and have no need of the boundary of the Jewish law to keep sin at bay.

Release from the law

In Romans 7:1 Paul specifically identifies those he is addressing as 'those who know (the) law',[108] and it seems likely that it is the Jewish law that Paul has in mind here.[109] At this point, then, Paul probably ceases to address Gentile readers who have been converted from a pagan background (6:17–18) and turns his attention to his fellow Jews who know the law.[110] They, he will claim, have been put to death as far as the law is concerned through the body of Christ, because the law is only binding on a person for as long as they are alive (7:1). The marriage illustration of 7:2–3 focuses upon the woman who, upon the death of her husband, is released from the law of marriage to marry again in this life. However, in his application of the metaphor Paul focuses not on the woman, but on the man who has died. In 7:4, Paul invites believers to identify with the husband who has died: inasmuch as they have died with Christ[111] they are released from the law (cf. 7:2), so that they now belong to Christ, who has himself passed through death and who has been raised to life. Thus, while the metaphor itself focuses on this life and the woman's release from the law of marriage on the death of a partner, the application of the

---

[108] Although the article is missing here, Paul regularly uses anarthrous νόμος to denote the Torah.

[109] As Dunn (*Romans*, vol.I, pp.359–60) points out, the marriage illustration reflects the principles of Jewish, not Roman, law; it is therefore most likely that it is the Torah that Paul has in view here.

[110] The phrase γινώσκουσιν γὰρ νόμον λαλῶ may be taken as indicating a change in addressee: M.-J. Lagrange, *Saint Paul: Epître aux Romains* (Paris: Gabalda, 1931), p.163; Minear, *Obedience*, p.62; N.T. Wright, *The Messiah and the People of God* (unpublished D.Phil dissertation, Oxford: 1980), p.147.

[111] This is surely what Paul meant by being killed to the law through the body of Christ (7:4); there is no reference to the church here, *contra* Dodd, *Romans*, p.120.

metaphor looks at the one who has died, who is released from the law through death, and now belongs to Christ in the new aeon of the Spirit.

Paul claims that for those who are in the flesh and who have not died with Christ in this way, the law is the instrument through which sinful passions are aroused in their members and which go on to bear fruit for death (7:5). Within the old aeon, the law is thus caught up in the destructive alliance between the flesh, the power of sin and death that Paul has hinted at in 6:14,[112] and it is for this reason that a dying to the law is necessary.[113] However, those who have been separated from the law through death are now able to serve in the newness of the Spirit rather than the old way of the letter (7:6). Paul here clearly intends a contrast between the old and the new covenants (2 Cor. 3:1–18): the old covenant given at Sinai on tablets of stone has now been replaced by God's new covenant, which is written by the Spirit upon the heart (Rom. 2:29). Romans 8:1–30 picks up on and expounds what Paul means by serving in the Spirit in 7:6, just as 7:7–25 expound the relationship between the law and sin that Paul has mentioned in 7:5.

A Torah-observant Jew as a sinful outsider

The thought structure of Romans 7:7–25 is determined by the rhetorical questions of 7:7, 13, which are used by Paul to further his argument.[114] Each question draws false conclusions from Paul's position on the law, and these conclusions Paul vigorously denies: he is not saying that the law is sin, nor that God's good law is responsible for anyone's death. To some extent, Paul's answers to these questions constitute an apology for the law to his Jewish readers, as he maintains that the law is holy and spiritual (vv.12, 14).[115] Nevertheless it is also the case that Paul here

---

[112] On this triad, cf. Lohmeyer, 'Probleme paulinischer Theologie'.

[113] Cranfield minimises the force of Paul's words by arguing that he refers to a release from the condemnation of the law (*Romans*, vol.I, p.338); Käsemann, on the other hand, claims that Paul refers to a dying to the law itself (*Romans*, pp.189–91). While Paul's language here is unambiguous (ἐθανατώθητε τῷ νόμῳ... κατηργήθημεν ἀπὸ τοῦ νόμου...), Paul does nevertheless allow the weak to observe the law's dietary requirements in 14:1–15:13. The conundrum is resolved if Paul is understood to refer to the need to die to the law in its alliance with sin and death under the old aeon; this death marks the decisive break from sin, and Paul can then rehabilitate the law in the new aeon as the work of the Spirit (8:2–4), interpreting it as the love command (13:8–10) and safeguarding the right of the weak to observe the food laws (14:1–15:13). Cf. K.R. Snodgrass, 'Spheres of Influence: a Possible Solution to the Problem of Paul and the Law', *JSNT* 32 (1988), pp.93–113.

[114] The change of tense in v.14 does not determine the structure of the argument, although there is a sense in which v.13 both concludes vv.7–12 and introduces vv.14–25.

[115] Stendahl, *Paul*, p.92.

depicts life under the law as being completely dominated by the power of sin. It is sin which hijacked the commandment and used it to bring about death rather than life (7:7–12), and it is sin in the flesh which prevents fulfilment of the law, no matter how much the individual of 7:13–25 may desire it. While Paul thus defends the law against the charge that it is an active collaborator with the power of sin, he also makes it clear that the law is unable to deliver anyone from its power: life under the law is a life lived under the oppressive regime of sin.[116] It is only God's new law of the Spirit of life in Christ Jesus which can release people from the law of sin and death (8:2).

When set in its socio-cultural context, Romans 7:7–25 forms part of Paul's attempt to redraw the boundaries around the community of God's people. In Romans 1–3, Paul argues that the law did not constitute an effective boundary marker distinguishing righteous Jew from sinful Gentile; on the contrary, both groups alike need to be justified by faith, and it is faith which unites them together into a single community with Abraham as their father (Rom. 4). In Romans 5:1–11, Paul reinforces the low grid outlook of the Christians in Rome by reminding them of the Christian eschatological hope, and in 5:12–21 he replaces the Torah-based ethnic distinction between righteous insider and sinful outsider with an eschatological distinction, based on Christ as second Adam, and with baptism as the means of entry into the newly defined righteous in-group (6:1–14). In 6:15–23, Paul seeks to establish that participation in the new aeon does separate Gentile believers from their sinful past, because they have changed allegiance from sin to God. In 7:1–8:17, Paul argues that Jews under the law still need release from the power of sin through God's eschatological Spirit. Romans 7:7–25 consists of an exposition of the ineffective struggle of the Jew under the law against the power of sin, and is an exposition and justification of Paul's claim in 5:20 that the law multiplies transgression instead of dealing with sin, with the result that deliverance from the power of sin can only happen through being delivered from the law under the old aeon (6:14), by dying with Christ to the law (7:4, 6).

Paul's answers to both questions in Romans 7:7–25 are phrased in the first person singular, and establishing the identity of the ἐγώ in Romans 7 is crucial to understanding Paul's argument. The ἐγώ of verses 7–12 was once alive apart from the law, knowing neither sin nor covetousness (vv.7, 9a). But when the commandment prohibiting covetousness came,

---

[116]M.A. Seifrid, *Justification by Faith: the Origin and Development of a Central Pauline Theme* (Leiden: E.J. Brill, 1992), p.224.

sin came to life, took advantage of the commandment and used it to arouse all kinds of covetousness in the ἐγώ, so deceiving and killing the ἐγώ (vv.8–11). In verses 14–25, the tense shifts from past to present, as the ἐγώ acknowledges that it is fleshly and sold under sin (v.14). The ἐγώ does not know what it is doing for it does not do what it wants, but what it hates (v.15). Acting in this way against its own will, the ἐγώ acknowledges that the law is good, and finds that indwelling sin is responsible for its behaviour (vv.16–17). Within the ἐγώ nothing good dwells, and this is demonstrated by the way the ἐγώ can will what is right, but cannot do it; instead it finds itself doing evil against its own will, and indwelling sin is again identified as responsible for this behaviour (vv.18–20). When the ἐγώ desires to do good, then it finds that evil is close at hand, and despite delighting in the law in its innermost being, the ἐγώ finds another law at work in its members, fighting against the law of the mind and imprisoning it under the law of sin in its members (vv.21–23). The wretched person cries out for deliverance from the body of this death (v.24) and, after an expression of thanksgiving to God through Jesus Christ, the situation is summed up in 7:25: ἄρα οὖν αὐτὸς ἐγὼ τῷ μὲν νοΐ δουλεύω νόμῳ θεοῦ, τῇ δὲ σαρκὶ νόμῳ ἁμαρτίας. While Paul speaks in the person of the ἐγώ throughout Romans 7:7–25, it will nevertheless be necessary to consider 7:7–12 and 7:13–25 separately.

Forbidden desire (7:7–12)

In his monograph, Kümmel argued that the search for a particular identity of the ἐγώ was misdirected: it was better to think of oneself as the subject.[117] Others have argued, however, for a more specific identity of the ἐγώ, whether that be Paul himself,[118] the people of Israel,[119] or Adam.[120] According to Stowers, Paul has in view the Gentile who tries to base his life upon the law.[121]

---

[117]Kümmel, *Römer 7*, p.132; cf. G. Bornkamm, 'Sin, Law and Death (Romans 7)', *Early Christian Experience* (London: SCM, 1969), pp.87–104.

[118]E.g. Augustine, *Contra duas epistolas Pelagianorum* 8:14; Zahn, Römer, pp.341–4; Dodd, pp.122–33; Bruce, pp.147–9; R.H. Gundry, 'The Moral Frustration of Paul before his Conversion: Sexual Lust in Rom. 7:7–25', in Hagner and Harris, *Pauline Studies*, pp.238–45.

[119]Moo, *Romans*, pp.423–31.

[120]Michel, *Römen*, p.148; Leenhardt, pp.180–6; Käsemann, pp.195–7; Dunn, pp.378–85; Ziesler, pp.180–5; Stuhlmacher, pp.106–7; G. Theissen, *Psychological Aspects of Pauline Christianity* (Edinburgh: T&T Clark, 1987), pp.202–8.

[121]Stowers, *Rereading*, pp.273–84.

Of these options, it is most likely that Romans 7:7–12 is a retelling of the story of the Fall, with the ἐγώ cast in the role of Adam and sin fulfilling the role of the serpent.[122] When read in this way, the parallels between this passage and Genesis 2–3 are striking: just as the serpent takes advantage of the commandment of God to deceive and kill in the paradise story, sin does the same thing here. It was the striking nature of these parallels that led Käsemann to claim that 'There is nothing in the passage that does not fit Adam, and everything fits Adam alone'.[123] Amongst recent advocates of this view, Theissen stands out as one who has taken the trouble to defend it in detail against its critics: he argues that Adam should be seen as the model of the conflict in Romans 7:7ff., rather than as the actual subject, and states that 'the I assumes the role of Adam and structures it in the light of personal experience of conflict'.[124]

Knowledge of such a conflict between prohibition and desire is attested in ancient literature long before Augustine wrote of his desire for forbidden fruit.[125] As examples, Theissen cites Euripides, 'Love reproved more urgent grows' (Plutarch, *Moralia* 71A) and Ovid: 'We ever strive for what is forbid, and ever covet what is denied'; 'What one may not do pricks more keenly on' (*Amores* 3.4.17; 2.19.3).[126]

Jews under the law were also well acquainted with forbidden desires: 'When we are attracted to forbidden foods, how do we come to reject the pleasures to be gained from them? Is it not because reason has power to control the appetites? I believe it is. Accordingly, when we crave seafood or fowl or the meat of four-legged beasts or any sort of food that is forbidden to us under the Law, it is through the mastery of reason that we abstain.'[127] Similarly, R. Eliezer stated that one should not say he has no desire to eat pig, or to engage in illicit intercourse: '. . . but he must say, "Yes, I would like to do these acts, but what can I do? My Father who is in heaven has forbidden them." '[128]

While neither of these references explicitly refers to an arousal of the desire for forbidden things by reason of their prohibition, the inherent desirability of what is forbidden is implied in both cases, and is made explicit in the following example: 'R. Mena (on the Day of Atonement) went to visit R. Haggai who was ill. R. Haggai said, "I am thirsty." R. Mena

[122] Cf. S.J. Lyonnet, 'L'Histoire du Salut selon la Chapitre VII de l'Epître aux Romains', *Biblica* 43 (1962), pp.117–51.

[123] Käsemann, *Romans*, p.196.

[124] Theissen, *Psychological Aspects*, p.203.

[125] Augustine, *Confessiones* 2.6.

[126] Theissen, *Psychological Aspects*, p.224.

[127] 4 Maccabees 1:33–34.

[128] *Sifra* 93d.

said, "Drink." Then he left him. After he came again and said, "How about your thirst?" He said, "No sooner had you permitted me to drink than the thirst left me." '[129]

In the light of these rabbinic references, it would appear that Jews under the law would have been able to identify with the ἐγώ in its struggle with coveting what is forbidden by the law in Romans 7:7–12.

What Paul does here is to take the common human experience of contra-suggestibility and interpret it as the result of the activity of the power of sin in the life of the Jew under the law. The apostle thus attributes the desire for what is forbidden to the power of sin. In this way, the apostle is able to portray the power of sin as living and active within the life of the Jew under the law, and so set out a plight from which the Torah-observant Jew needs delivering.

Paul casts the ἐγώ in the role of Adam here in order to make the point that, far from effectively serving as a boundary keeping sin at bay, the law in fact proved to be the loophole through which sin entered the system; the boundary of Torah is not just under attack, as one would expect in a high group/low grid community; it has been completely overwhelmed. Like the French Maginot Line in 1940, the commandment offered life, but the ἐγώ sheltering under its protection was defenceless against sin's surprise assault from the rear. Paul wishes to make it clear to his Jewish readers that life lived under the law in the old aeon is a life lived in the grip of the power of sin, from which they need deliverance.

In the light of this, Paul's conclusion that the commandment is holy and just and good may well seem surprising, for there seems little after the emphatic μὴ γένοιτο in verse 7 to substantiate this conclusion. He has just argued that, instead of providing a secure bulwark against sin, the prohibitions and commandments of the law actually serve to provoke and stimulate sin within the heart. Yet Paul exonerates the law and pins the blame entirely on the power of sin, which has become exceedingly sinful through the commandment (v.13). Paul probably does this with an eye on the social situation in Rome, since he cannot afford to alienate the 'weak' Christians or to jeopardise their position by writing off the law altogether. Paul therefore exculpates the law by highlighting the sinfulness of sin, and in so doing he emphasises the plight of those under the law. If the commandment serves to stimulate sinful desire and the law is holy and just and good, the problem must reside in the hold that sin has over the lives of those under the law. That, of course, is precisely the point that Paul wishes to make: even though the law is

[129]T.J. Yana vi 4.43d line 21.

holy and just and good, it nevertheless does not deal with the problem of the power of sin under the old aeon, which Paul here identifies as the feelings of contra-suggestibility aroused by the commandment. The power of sin thus serves Paul's aim of subverting Jewish confidence in the Torah as a means of keeping sin at bay. Paul maintains this dual aim of exonerating the law and emphasising the plight of those under the law in 7:13–25.

The conflict between willing and doing

The rhetorical question with which Paul opens the next stage of his argument (v.13) queries whether the good law is responsible for the death of the ἐγώ. This Paul vehemently denies, emphasising that sin is responsible for the death of the ἐγώ, and is thereby revealed in all its sinfulness. He affirms that the law is spiritual; the problem is that the ἐγώ is fleshly, sold under sin (7:14). This verse points clearly towards the non-Christian identity of the ἐγώ in 7:14–25, since the believer has been delivered from sin (6:2, 14, 17–18, 22) and the law (7:4, 6) and is said to be in the Spirit and not in the flesh (8:9).

The change of tense in verse 14 therefore does not signal a change from non-Christian to Christian experience.[130] Yet Dunn attempts to minimise the difficulty of the description of the ἐγώ in 7:14 in two ways.[131] Firstly, he points out that in Romans 6–8, Paul contrasts sin and grace, death and life, flesh and Spirit. He suggests that the absence of any antithesis to the law in Romans 7 means that the law cannot be set unequivocally among the negative factors. Yet this line of argument would seem to collapse in the light of the contrast between law and grace in 6:14–15, and between the letter and the Spirit in 7:6. Secondly, Dunn refers to a pattern of an eschatological tension between the already and the not yet that is repeated with respect to sin (6:1–11 vs. 6:12–23) and the flesh (8:1–9 vs. 8:10–30) and claims that this is repeated with respect to the law, so that the claim to be released from the law in 7:1–6 is modified in 7:7–25. However, 7:7–25 is not comparable with 6:12–23 and 8:10–30, since these other passages are clearly paraenetic, exhorting people to leave sinful and fleshly behaviour behind; Romans 7:7–25, by contrast, leaves the ἐγώ a helpless victim of sin, and has no paraenetic value whatsoever.

The partisan claim that Romans 7:14–25 must refer to Christian experience since only a Christian who has the Spirit can experience the kind

[130]Nygren, *Romans*, p.283; Cranfield, vol.I, pp.344–7.
[131]Dunn, *Romans*, pp.302–3; 376–8.

of struggle against sin described here[132] is weakened by the fact that this passage makes no reference to the Spirit,[133] and demolished by the fact that the Dead Sea Scrolls display both a knowledge of an internal struggle against sin (IQS 3:14–4:26) and also a deep-seated sense of personal sinfulness (IQS 11:9–15; cf. IQH 3:19–36; 4:30–38; 12:24–34; 18:22–29). Nor can the position of the expression of thanksgiving be used to support the Christian experience position,[134] since 7:25b is a summary restatement of the position of the ἐγώ of 7:13–25 before the nature of God's deliverance in Christ is expounded in Romans 8.[135] The interpretation of Romans 7:14–25 in terms of Christian experience must be rejected as exegetically unsound.

Kümmel argues cogently that the ἐγώ of verses 7–12 must represent the same person as the ἐγώ of verses 13–25, since there is no indication that the identity of the speaker has changed.[136] Looking at what is said of the ἐγώ in Romans 7:7–25, it should be noted that verses 7–12 describe the effect of an initial encounter with the commandment: prior to that encounter the ἐγώ was alive, but after the commandment came, sin sprang to life and the ἐγώ died. Following on from this, the use of the present tense in verses 13–25 then refers most naturally to the ongoing experience of the ἐγώ under the law (vv.14, 21–23), and the change in tense indicates a shift from the narration of the event of the coming of the commandment to the description of the condition of the ἐγώ under the law.[137] There is thus an ongoing continuity in the identity of the ἐγώ, although Paul ceases to use Adam as the model for experience of the law after verse 12.

In 7:15–20, the ἐγώ describes the experience of having good intentions, but being unable to put them into practice; instead of achieving the desired course of action, the ἐγώ does what it hates. This is attributed to the ἐγώ's loss of control to the indwelling power of

[132]Nygren, *Romans*, pp.284–303. This consideration played no small part in influencing Augustine's shift to understanding the passage in terms of Christian experience: the suggestion that the unregenerate person could delight in God's law opened the door to Pelagianism.

[133]Although ὁ ἔσω ἄνθρωπος is renewed by the Spirit in 2 Cor. 4:16 (cf. Eph. 3:16), it is illegitimate to infer from this that Paul must therefore be referring to Christian experience in Rom. 7:22, despite Cranfield, *Romans*, vol.I, p.363.

[134]Ziesler (*Romans*, pp.193–4) regards this as perhaps the best piece of evidence for the Christian interpretation.

[135]Cf. Rom. 5:11; Gal. 3:29 for a similar technique.

[136]Kümmel, *Römer 7*, p.89.

[137]Wilckens, *Römer*, vol.II, p.85. In his psychological analysis of Rom. 7, Theissen argues that Paul's unconscious conflict with the law is raised to consciousness in these verses (*Psychological Aspects*, pp.228–50), but in the absence of the subject, such a theory is difficult to verify.

sin: εἰ δὲ ὃ οὐ θέλω τοῦτο ποιῶ, σύμφημι τῷ νόμῳ ὅτι καλός. νυνὶ δὲ οὐκέτι ἐγὼ κατεργάζομαι αὐτὸ ἀλλὰ ἡ οἰκοῦσα ἐν ἐμοὶ ἁμαρτία (7:16–7). Here the lack of assent to the ἐγώ's behaviour entails the recognition that the law is good, while the behaviour itself is attributed to the indwelling power of sin.

This recognition that the law is good rules out Bultmann's trans-subjective interpretation of this passage, according to which the intention of verse 16 is the unconscious aim of achieving life, which results in death under the law because, in the very act of serving the law, the law's aim is perverted.[138] If θέλω in verse 16a refers to the aim of achieving life as Bultmann claims, the sentence lacks any logical basis for the apodosis of verse 16b, which concludes on the basis of this unfulfilled intention that the law is good. *Contra* Bultmann, the recognition that the law is good indicates that θέλω refers to a conscious moral aim.

This throws us back on the view rejected by Bultmann, that Paul here is expressing the kind of inner conflict attributed to Medea in Ovid, *Met.* 7.17–21: 'meliora proboque, deteriora sequor.'[139] Huggins outlines three different classical solutions to the problem of the tension between reason and passion, and concludes that none of them forms a true parallel to Romans 7.[140] Firstly, according to Socrates, evil conduct stems from ignorance, and right knowledge will inevitably lead to right conduct.[141] Huggins rightly argues that Paul does not attribute the problems of the ἐγώ to ignorance. The second, Aristotelian solution was to attribute one's failure to do what one knows to be right to the problem of incontinence (ἀκρασία).[142] Huggins argues Aristotle's solution cannot be applied to the ἐγώ, on the grounds that Aristotle defines ἀκρασία as a departure from the general standard of behaviour adopted by the majority of people; whereas Paul includes the mass of humanity under sin, even those whom Aristotle would have considered continent. Thirdly, Huggins also refers to the tragic motif of the fatal error, according to which a character makes a

---

[138] R. Bultmann, 'Romans 7 and the Anthropology of Paul', *Existence and Faith* (London: Fontana, 1964), pp.173–85; cf. Käsemann, *Romans*, pp.201–6.

[139] Around the first century CE, Euripides' portrayal of the plight of *Medea* (1077–80) was much debated: Ovid, *Metamorphoses* 7.17–21; Plutarch, *Moralia* 446A; Epictetus, *Diss.* 1.28.6–8; 2.26.1–4; Galen, *Hippoc. et Plat.* 4.244.2–9; 4.274.15–22. Cf. Theissen, *Psychological Aspects*, pp.212–19; Thielman, *From Plight to Solution*, pp.104–6; Stowers, *Rereading*, pp.260–4.

[140] R.V. Huggins, 'Alleged Classical Parallels to Paul's "What I want to do I do not do, but what I hate, that I do" (Rom. 7:15)', *Westminster Theological Journal* 54 (1992), pp.153–61.

[141] Plato, *Protagoras* 352b–56c.

[142] Aristotle, *Ethica Nicomachea* 7; cf. A. van den Beld, 'Romans 7:14–25 and the problem of *Akrasia*', *Interpretation* 21 (1985), pp.495–515; Stowers, *Rereading*, pp.269–72.

single disastrous response to a particularly trying set of circumstances.[143] Since Romans 7 is concerned with the general condition of life, rather than a single tragic fatal error, Huggins again denies any parallel and concludes that none of the classical discussions of the question is conceptually parallel to Paul's thought.

However, Huggins underestimates the parallel between Romans 7:13–25 and the problem of ἀκρασία. The acknowledgement by the ἐγώ that the law is good corresponds to the condition of the ἀκρατής, who is 'mastered by passion sufficiently for him not to act in accordance with right principle, but not so completely as to be of such a character as to believe that the reckless pursuit of pleasure is right'.[144] Aristotle compares such a person to a city which votes in excellent laws without enforcing them. This is the position of the fleshly ἐγώ who recognises the law as spiritual, but does not keep it. Huggins' attempt to dismiss the parallel on the grounds that Aristotle perceived the majority of people as continent is invalid: Paul is writing here of Jewish experience under the law, and it is clear from both Qumran and rabbinic writings that Torah-observant Jews, who perceived themselves as righteous and morally continent, were no strangers to such internal moral conflict. 1 QS 4:23–35 reads, 'Until now the spirits of truth and injustice struggle in the hearts of men and they walk in both wisdom and folly. According to his portion of truth so does a man hate injustice, and according to his inheritance in the realm of injustice so he is wicked and hates the truth.' The rabbis interpreted this conflict in terms of the presence of the evil *yetzer*:[145]

> Raba said, 'Though God created the evil *Yetzer ha-Ra*, He created the Law, as an antidote against it.'[146]

> The evil *yetzer* has no power against the Law, and he who has the Law in his heart, over him the *yetzer* has no power.[147]

> The words of the Law are likened to a medicine of life. Like a king who inflicted a big wound on his son, and he put a plaster on his wound. He said, 'My son, so long as this plaster is on your wound, eat and drink what you like, and wash in cold or warm water, and you will suffer no harm. But if you remove it, you will get a bad boil.' So God says to the Israelites, 'I created within

[143]Here Huggins cites Ovid, *Metamorphoses* 7:21; Euripides, *Medea* 1078–80; *Hippolytus* 379–83; 433–4; 525–8; 540–5; 595–668; 774.

[144]Aristotle, *Eth. Nic.* 7.8.5.

[145]Cf. also 1QS 5:4–5.

[146]*Bab.B.* 16a.

[147]*Midr. Ps.* on CXIX, 10 (246b, 7).

you the evil *yetzer*, but I created the Law as a drug. As long as you occupy yourselves with the Law, the *yetzer* will not rule over you. But if you do not occupy yourselves with the Torah, then you will be delivered into the power of the *yetzer*, and all its activity will be against you.'[148]

Thus, it is evident that Jews under the law were no strangers to the kind of moral conflict that Paul depicts in 7:13–25. But while the rabbis explained this disjunction between willing and doing in terms of the evil *yetzer*, Paul attributes it to the power of sin. It is sin that is responsible for the common experience of knowing what is right and doing what is wrong, and Paul repeats this conclusion twice to emphasise the point (7:17, 20). Paul's point is that sin is present and active in the flesh of the Torah-observant Jew. Whereas the rabbis saw the solution to the problem of the *yetzer* in adherence to Torah, Paul portrays the Torah as overwhelmed by the law of sin in the members of the ἐγώ. In this way, Paul indicates that the ethnic boundary of the law does not hold the eschatological power of sin at bay, since the struggles of the Torah-observant Jew against the problem of ἀκρασία reveal that sin is actually resident within the fleshly members.

Crucial to the interpretation of 7:21–23 is the question of the referent of νόμος: does Paul use this term uniformly to denote the Torah, which bifurcates in verse 21 into the law of the mind and the law of sin,[149] or does νόμος in verse 21 mean 'principle'?[150] Despite the growing popularity of the first view that νόμος denotes the Torah throughout this passage, there are two indications in verse 23 that this was not Paul's intended meaning. Firstly, there is the problem of the location of this law: Paul declares twice that this other law, the law of sin, is 'in my members', and this is scarcely true of the Torah. Secondly, as Räisänen has shown, νόμος can quite possibly refer to 'the regularity which naturally pertains in life or in one of its subordinate parts; the ruling order; the normal situation'.[151] If it is granted that 'the law of sin' manifests itself in the experience of the conflict between willing and doing that Paul has spelt out in verses 15, 19, then the widespread discussion of this theme in the ancient world would warrant identifying this conflict as being a νόμος or principle of

---

[148] *Kiddushim* 30b.

[149] Wilckens, *Römer*, vol.II, pp.89–92; E.P. Sanders, *Jewish People*, pp. 74–5; Heil, *Romans*, p. 78; Theissen, *Psychological Aspects*, p.189; Dunn, *Romans*, vol.I, pp.392–3; Snodgrass, 'Spheres of Influence', pp.105–6.

[150] Cranfield, *Romans*, vol.I, pp.361–2; Käsemann, p.205; Moo, pp.462–4; Fitzmyer, pp.475–6.

[151] Räisänen, *Jesus, Paul and Torah*, p.82; cf. pp.69–94.

human existence. For these reasons it is better to understand verses 21–25 in terms of the ἐγώ being caught between wanting to obey the Torah in its mind and finding itself unable to do so because of the principle of sin in its members. Read this way, Paul's claim that the law is spiritual (v.14) stands: it is not Torah but the ἐγώ which has become entrammelled in sin, with the result that evil always accompanies the desire to do good (v.21). It is this result which constitutes the principle of verse 21, and which provokes the cry of anguish in verse 24.

When read in the light of Douglas' matrix, it is apparent that Paul retains here the high group/low grid anthropology of the good inside and the evil outside: the innermost being of the ἐγώ delights in the law of God, but the mind is rendered helpless by the power of sin which has taken up residence in the flesh (7:22–3).[152] In this way, the good inside has been overwhelmed by the evil outside, so that sin is no longer an outside evil that needs to be kept at bay: it is now the controlling principle in the life of the ἐγώ, having taken up residence in the body's members. This is not to say that Paul regarded the physical flesh as inherently sinful: it is rather the case that Paul uses the contrast between the good inner person and the evil outer flesh to symbolise the eschatological distinction that he wishes to draw: he associates sin with the flesh under the old aeon, so that he can attribute effective deliverance from this plight to the eschatological Spirit.

The similarity between Paul's language here and passages from Qumran such as 1QS 11:9–12; 1QM 4:3; 1QH 1:21–27 cannot be denied. On the basis of these similarities, Kuhn argued that Paul and the Qumran community both understood the human plight in terms of sinful flesh: 'Man is flesh because and inasmuch as he sins and stands under ungodly power.'[153] E.P. Sanders, however, countered by arguing that the

---

[152]Schmithals attempts to salvage the Lutheran doctrine of *totus peccator* by arguing Paul succumbed at this point to the influence of Hellenistic dualism. Behind this inadequate dualistic anthropology, Schmithals claims that Paul saw the real truth that the *whole* person who strives for life actually achieves evil, because this person's expectation of life is based upon achievement: W. Schmithals, *Die theologische Anthropologie des Paulus* (Stuttgart: Kohlhammer, 1980), p.64. Douglas' matrix points to a more natural reading of 7:22–3, and warns against the doctrinally based assumption that the unregenerate are incapable of genuinely delighting in God's law.

[153]K.G. Kuhn, 'New Light on Temptation, Sin and Flesh in the New Testament', in K. Stendahl, ed., *The Scrolls and the New Testament* (London: SCM, 1958), pp.94–113 (p.102); cf. H. Braun, 'Römer 7,7–25 und das Selbstverständnis des Qumran-Frommen', *ZTK* 56/1 (1959), pp.1–18. According to J. Becker, *Das Heil Gottes* (Göttingen: Vandenhoeck & Ruprecht, 1964) and H. Thyen, *Studien zur Sündenvergebung* (Göttingen: Vandenhoeck & Ruprecht, 1970), pp.77–97, the Qumran community shared Paul's view of sin as a power. The inadequacy of this thesis is exposed in E.P. Sanders, *Paul and Palestinian Judaism*, pp.274–9.

Scrolls differ from Paul in that the Qumran sectarians did not perceive the human plight in term of the fleshly nature, since the flesh *does not damn*: it is those who are in the community of the saved who confess their human inadequacy and nothingness before God.[154] Sanders insists that the human plight must be defined in terms of those sins which exclude one from the sect, namely, avoidable transgressions.

Yet the fact that the Qumran sectarians are not damned on account of their fleshly nature does not preclude the sinfulness of the flesh from being part of the human plight. It is rather the case that, were the author of 1 QS 11 not a member of the community, then his sinful fleshly condition would be enough to damn him. It is not that the physical flesh itself is evil;[155] it is rather that the writer is conscious that his own flesh is something he has in common with sinful humanity outside the community, and he is contaminated by this sense of shared identity:

> As for me,
> I belong to wicked mankind,
> to the company of unjust flesh.
> My iniquities, rebellions, and sins,
> together with the perversity of my heart,
> belong to the company of worms
> and to those who walk in darkness.[156]

Thus, while Sanders is right to argue that the sinfulness of the flesh is not sufficient to place the author outside the community of the righteous, it would be true to say that the writer is only saved because he has been separated from the rest of sinful humanity by his participation in the community of those who will be saved.[157]

Seifrid is therefore more accurate than Sanders when he describes the penitential prayers and confessions of early Judaism as expressions of personal guilt, which are made in the consciousness of a surrounding framework of divine mercy.[158] The psalmist expresses his own intrinsic

---

[154] *Paul and Palestinian Judaism*, pp.279–82.

[155] Cf. H. Hübner, 'Anthropologischer Dualismus in den Hodayot?', *NTS* 18 (1971–2), pp.268–84.

[156] 1QS 11:9–10; cf. 'flesh' meaning common humanity in 1QS 9:12; 1QH 7:17; 9:16; 13:16; 18:14, 23. The same idea may underlie 1 QH 1:21–23.

[157] In accordance with the low grid/high group cosmology of Douglas' matrix, the covenanters at Qumran were conscious of the need to be separate from the rest of sinful humanity, but they could not escape the fleshly identity they shared in common with those outside, and this was one of the ways in which they perceived sin infiltrating the community.

[158] M.A. Seifrid, 'The Subject of Rom. 7:14–25', *NovT* 34 (1992), pp.313–33.

lack of soteriological resources, but is confident of salvation through participation in God's covenant (1QS 11:11–12).

According to Seifrid, Paul bases Romans 7:14–25 upon 'the confessing ἐγώ of early Judaism'. Since Paul believes that Christ is the sole agent of God's saving grace, and that the Torah is therefore excluded from God's saving purposes, he seeks to demonstrate the inadequacy of the law to overcome transgression by locating evil in the ἐγώ, who acknowledges that it is the prisoner of sin and under divine condemnation. In this passage, Paul portrays the inadequacy of the intrinsic soteriological resources available to a fallen human being confronted with the law. By using the first person singular, Paul invites his readers to participate in the same theological self-judgment about the necessity of excluding the law from God's saving purposes and of putting one's faith in God's saving act in Christ (7:25a; 8:1–4). This salvation is, according to Seifrid, extrinsically accomplished; intrinsically, believers remain as much sinful people in the new order as they did under the old (8:10–13). Although the condemnation worked by the law is still applicable to them intrinsically, it has now been overcome extrinsically by God's act of salvation in Christ. All believers are therefore *simul iustus et peccator*.[159]

Seifrid's proposal that Paul is consciously using Jewish penitential psalms and confessions as a model at this point has a high degree of plausibility about it, as does his claim that Paul is intending to persuade his readers of the validity and necessity of excluding the law from God's saving purpose. However, Seifrid's attempt to conform Paul to the Lutheran doctrine of *simul iustus et peccator* undermines his argument, since the new extrinsic soteriological resources supplied in Christ change nothing intrinsically at all: 'the ἐγώ is not what Paul once was: it is what he still is, intrinsically considered ... Sin remains a continuing reality, inherent to the life of the fallen human being.'[160] Thus all that Paul achieves in Romans 7–8 is a shifting of the tune of the Jewish lament into a different key, in which the individual now laments subjection to the power of sin, but relies on God's extrinsic provision for salvation in Christ rather than in the law. If, however, the transfer from the law to Christ produces no tangible difference in the situation of the individual, why make the transfer at all? This difficulty is greatly increased because in Seifrid's reconstruction of Paul's argument, the apostle does not explicitly remove the safety-net of God's mercy and covenant faithfulness from the Jewish Christian reader: he gives no reason why the Jewish Christian reader should not be able

---

[159] Cf. Seifrid, *Justification by Faith.*
[160] Seifrid, 'Subject', p.326

simply to rely on God's mercy. Seifrid's proposal therefore requires some emendation.

It is appropriate to begin by examining afresh the parallels between Romans 7:14–25 and Qumran. It should be noted that the reason behind the lament in Qumran is fundamentally different from that in Romans 7. The ἐγώ in Romans 7 agonises over an inability to fulfil the law; the Qumran laments over personal sinfulness, on the other hand, are an expression of human inadequacy in the face of the mystery of God. Thus, in 1QS 11:9; 1QH 4:29, the introductory phrase 'As for me' heralds a shift in focus away from a wondering acknowledgment of the marvellous mysteries of God in the preceding lines to a recognition of the sinful unworthiness of the psalmist. The same contrasting shift is heralded by the phrase 'And yet I' in 1QH 1:21, where the psalmist turns from considering the marvellous mysteries of God's providence in order to reflect on his identity as 'a shape of clay kneaded in water, a ground of shame and a source of pollution, a melting pot of wickedness and an edifice of sin...' A similar self-portrait follows the 'And yet I' in 3:19, where the psalmist turns from thanking God for his redemption to reflect on his own unworthiness. These confessions of sinfulness are not made with a view to seeking forgiveness, as is the case with the confessions in canonical Psalms 38; 40; 51, or with the pseudepigraphical confessions in *Jos. & As.* 12:1–13:15; 21:10–21; *Pr. Man.* 9–15. In the Qumran hymns, awareness of personal sin is more than matched by an awareness of the sufficiency of God's mercy: 'As for me, if I stumble, the mercies of God shall be my eternal salvation. If I stagger because of the sin of flesh, my justification shall be by the righteousness of God which endures for ever' (1QS 11:11; cf. 1QH 1:31–33; 4:33). The confessions of the Qumran hymns are thus firmly located within the context of the psalmist's ultimate security in his membership of the covenant, as Seifrid correctly observes.

However, in Romans 7:14–25, the lament of the ἐγώ is prompted, not by the wonderful mysteries of God's mercy and providence, but rather by the spiritual nature of the law, which places its fulfilment beyond the grasp of one who is fleshly. Thus, although the language of this lament is very similar to that found at Qumran, the setting of Romans 7:14–25 is more akin to the petitions of Psalms 19:7–13; 40:6–12; 119:169–176, where the psalmist's recognition of the essential goodness of the law leads him to an awareness of his own sinfulness and his need of God's help. What links the Qumran hymns with the canonical psalms is a deep awareness of sin on the part of the covenant member, and this is what Paul plays upon in Romans 7:14–25. Here the presence of sin is expressed in terms of an inability to keep the law as one would wish, and there can be no doubt that this experience lies behind the confessional literature, even if it is not formulated in this way. Paul, however, reinterprets the experience of sin in terms of an inability to keep the law because it is Jewish confidence in the law as boundary marker against sin that he is seeking to undermine. By setting the lament in the context of one's own sinfulness before the law, Paul has thus removed the laments from the immediate context of God's covenant faithfulness.

Furthermore, by relating the common human experience of the disjunction between willing and doing to the power of sin, Paul directs his Jewish readers to understand that their experience is a direct result of the power of sin which rules the Adamic aeon, and which has taken up residence in the flesh. Here 'flesh' is used, not to describe their solidarity with the rest of sinful humanity as in Qumran, but to express their participation in the old aeon which is dominated by sin and death. Sin has invaded the flesh and assumed control of the members, overpowering the mind. Even the person who delights in Torah is subject to the power of sin; the tragedy is, it is precisely through the law that sin was able to enter and gain control in the first place (7:9). No wonder the ἐγώ cries out in despair, ταλαίπωρος ἐγὼ ἄνθρωπος. Paul has identified the Jew under the law as a sinful outsider, one who is excluded from the righteous eschatological in-group. As Paul goes on to argue in Romans 8, it is possession of the Spirit of God that demarcates the difference between the righteous from the sinful, which is all-important for the small bounded group which rejects the world beyond its boundaries as evil. In Romans 7, Paul makes it clear that the Jew within the law but without the Spirit of God is lost: it is only the Spirit of God which can set people free from the power of sin and the flesh.

The eschatological Spirit

Paul begins Romans 8 by identifying the Spirit of Christ as the antidote to the human problem of sin in the flesh which he has depicted in Romans 7. There is no condemnation for those in Christ Jesus, for the law of the Spirit of life in Christ Jesus has set them free from the law of sin and death (8:1–2).[161] The real culprit of 7:7–25, namely sin, has been condemned by God's act of sending his Son to the cross in the likeness of sinful flesh (8:3). In this way, God achieved what the law was powerless to do,

---

[161] There can be no doubt that σε (א B F G) is the correct reading in 8:1, as opposed to με (A D) or ἡμᾶς (ψ). Paul probably uses the second person singular to indicate that he is no longer speaking in the person of a Torah-observant Jew, as he has done in Rom. 7.

since it was weakened by the flesh (8:3). Consequently, the righteous requirements of the law are now fulfilled in those who no longer walk according to the flesh, but who walk according to the Spirit (8:4). The plight caused by sin in the flesh, against which the law was powerless, has been effectively answered by the eschatological solution of the Spirit of life.

Paul emphasises the eschatological dimensions of the human plight and of God's solution in Christ by using the contrast between flesh and Spirit to stress the total sinfulness of fleshly human existence within the present aeon. The association of flesh and sin began in 7:5 with Paul's statement that the sinful passions aroused by the law were at work in the members of those who were in the flesh. This link was strengthened in 7:14, where Paul correlated being fleshly and being sold under sin. On account of the indwelling power of sin, Paul said that nothing good dwells in the flesh of the ἐγώ (7:17–18). It is with the flesh that the ἐγώ serves the law of sin (7:25) and the law could not bring life because it was weakened by the flesh (8:3). Paul even refers to the incarnation as Christ coming in the likeness of 'sinful flesh' (8:3). He then continues by saying that those who live according to the flesh set their minds on the things of the flesh (8:5): the outlook[162] of the flesh is death and those who think according to the flesh are God's enemies; they cannot please God or keep his law (8:6–8). By contrast, those who are in the Spirit set their minds on the things of the Spirit, and the mindset of the Spirit is life and peace (8:6b). In this way, Paul portrays the whole of fleshly human existence in the present aeon as sinful, suffering a plight to which the eschatological Spirit is the sole effective solution.

This contrast between life according to the flesh and life according to the Spirit is not paraenetic: Paul is not exhorting his readers to live according to the Spirit rather than according to the flesh. On the contrary, Paul makes it clear that he considers his readers to be in the Spirit and not in the flesh, since the Spirit of God dwells in them: were that not the case, they would not belong to Christ (8:9). However, since they have the Spirit, the mortal consequences of sin are overcome, inasmuch as those who are indwelt by the Spirit of God will share in the resurrection of Christ (8:10–11).

In 8:5–9 Paul has separated those who live according to the Spirit and those who live according to the flesh into two mutually exclusive groups,

---

[162]The REB wisely uses the English word 'outlook' instead of 'mind' to translate φρόνημα in 8:6–7, so avoiding confusing what is said here of the φρόνημα of the fleshly person with what is said of the νοῦς in 7:23.

as he attempts to redraw the boundaries that separate the righteous in-group from the sinful out-group along eschatological lines. In Romans 8:1–11, Paul uses πνεῦμα as a label to identify those who belong to the in-group of the eschatological community, and σάρξ as a label for the sinful out-group, those who participate in the present aeon of sin and death, irrespective of whether or not they observe Jewish Torah.

In Romans 7, Paul portrays the Jewish Torah as compromised by its association with sin and the flesh. In 7:5, Paul refers to sinful passions being aroused by the law. In 7:7–12, he describes how sin came to life through the commandment and resulted in the death of the ἐγώ. In 7:13–25, the ἐγώ delights in the law of God, but is hindered from fulfilling it by the indwelling power of sin. In 8:1–11, Paul indicates that the law has been weakened by the flesh and states that the mindset of the flesh cannot submit to the law of God; the righteous requirement of the law is fulfilled only in those who walk according to the Spirit. The law is thus a constantly recurring feature in Paul's exposition of the plight of being in the flesh. This in turn suggests that, in his contrast between flesh and Spirit in Romans 8, Paul is still seeking to redraw the boundaries between the righteous and the sinful along eschatological lines, so as to subvert Jewish Christian confidence in the Torah as an effective moral boundary marker.

However, the validity of Paul's argument appears threatened as he confronts his readers in 8:12–13 with the alternatives of living either according to the Spirit or according to the flesh: Paul tells them that if they live according to the flesh, they will die, but if by the Spirit they put to death the deeds of the body, they will live.[163] Perhaps under the influence of Galatians 5:16–26, these verses are generally understood as paraenetic: Paul's comment that those who have the Spirit ought to put to death the deeds of the body implies that those who have the Spirit still have to wrestle with the lingering presence of the power of sin, the ongoing presence of which is attested by the mortality of the physical body (8:10). Yet if correct, this interpretation of 8:12–13 has serious repercussions for the validity of Paul's claim that the eschatological Spirit alone constitutes an effective antidote to the indwelling power of sin.

However, the phrase κατὰ σάρκα ζῆν in 8:12–13 must be understood in the light of the literary context of Romans 7–8, rather than in the light

---

[163]Cf. O. Kuss, *Der Römerbrief*, 3 vols. (Regensburg: Pustet, 1957–78), vol.II, pp.596–7: 'The boundaries between the realm of the Spirit and the realm of the flesh ... do not run simply and clearly between the believers on the one side and the nonbelievers, but go right through the believers, through each individual believer' (ET cited in Dunn, *Romans*, vol.I, p.448).

of Galatians 5. Paul's discussion of the contrast between life in the flesh
and life in the Spirit in Rom. 7–8 is introduced in 7:5–6:

> ὅτε γὰρ ἦμεν ἐν τῇ σαρκά, τὰ παθήματα τῶν ἁμαρτιῶν
> τὰ διὰ τοῦ νόμου ἐνηργεῖτο ἐν τοῖς μέλεσιν ἡμῶν εἰς
> καρποφορῆσαι τῷ θανάτῳ· νυνὶ δὲ κατηργήθημεν ἀπὸ τοῦ
> νόμου, ἀποθανόντες ἐν ᾧ κατειχόμεθα, ὥστε δουλεύειν
> ἡμας ἐν καινότητι πνεύματος καὶ οὐ παλαιότητι
> γράμματος.

It is generally accepted that in Romans 7:7–25 Paul expounds the
mortal plight of those who are in the flesh, and in 8:1 begins to consider
what it means to serve in newness of the Spirit: Romans 7–8 is thus
a development of the contrast that Paul has drawn in Romans 7:5–6.
In 7:5, however, Paul describes life in the flesh as life lived under the
law, and his subsequent exposition of fleshly existence describes how
the desire of a Torah-observant Jew to fulfil the law's requirements is
frustrated by sin in the flesh and is in fact made possible only by means
of the eschatological Spirit. However, the fact that Paul uses the Torah-
observant Jew as an example of one who lives life in the flesh should
caution us against assuming that those who live according to the flesh in
8:12–13 are those who choose an immoral lifestyle. Up to this point in
Romans, Paul has not used σάρξ to denote a sinful lifestyle: the symbol
σάρξ rather denotes life lived in the present aeon.[164] When Paul stresses
the sinfulness of σάρξ in 8:5–8, he does not do so in order to establish
σάρξ as a symbol for sin;[165] his intention is rather to persuade his readers
that human life lived within the present aeon is *de facto* sinful. If life κατὰ
σάρκα in 8:12–13 refers to life lived in the present aeon, that means that
Paul is not exhorting his readers to adopt a moral rather than an immoral
lifestyle: he is rather stating that eschatological life is only available to
those who, by the Spirit, put to death the deeds of the body; those who
live according to the present aeon (i.e. κατὰ σάρκα) will die – and the
preceding context indicates that that includes those who rely on Torah,[166]
which Paul has argued is an ineffective antidote to the misdeeds of the
body.

This reading of 8:12–13 makes these verses consistent with Paul's
preceding attempt to redraw the boundaries between the sinful and the
righteous along eschatological, rather than along ethnic, lines. Paul is

[164]This is true also of Rom. 13:14, where the desires and sins with which σάρξ is
associated all belong to the present evil age which is already passing away (13:12).

[165]*Contra* Bultmann, *Theology*, vol.I, p.237.

[166]Paul uses κατὰ σάρκα with reference to ethnic Israel in Rom. 4:1; 9:3, 5.

continuing to write with a view to addressing his Jewish Christian readers in Rome at this point. This interpretation also accounts for the potentially awkward transition to 8:14–17:[167] having assured his readers that it is only those who have the Spirit who will live, Paul simply continues by referring to the hitherto characteristically Jewish privileges of being children and heirs of God, and ascribes them exclusively to the ethnically mixed, eschatological community of the Spirit,[168] who will come to share in the glory of God (8:18–30).

In the rest of Romans 8, Paul reiterates the themes of Romans 5:1–11, as he focuses on eschatological hope and the love God has for his people in the midst of tribulation.[169] These themes of hope and love with which Romans 5–8 begins and ends are essential to the maintenance of the low grid small group, which regards itself as right and the rest of the world as wrong. The Roman believers' experience of marginalisation needed to be counteracted by Paul's affirmation of God's love for them in the midst of tribulation, and the apostle's stress on the hope of ultimate glory serves to assure them of future vindication.

Yet it is not just the beginning and end of this section of the letter that are concerned with the establishment of low grid values. The burden of this chapter has been that use of Douglas' matrix invites us to read the whole of Romans 5–8 as an attempt to define the kind of clear distinction between righteous insider and sinful outsider which is essential to the symbol system of a low grid/high group community. This distinction Paul seeks to draw in Romans 5:12–21 on the basis of whether or not one belongs to the first Adam and the aeon of sin and death, or the second Adam and the aeon of righteousness and life. He asserts that Gentile believers are indeed set apart from the uncleanness of their past by the rite of baptism, which symbolises their dying with Christ to sin and their corresponding transfer of allegiance to the service of righteousness (Rom. 6:1–23). In Romans 7:1–25, Paul argues that Jews under the law need to die to the law as written code and have the law rewritten on their hearts by the Spirit of God, for fleshly existence under the law is completely dominated by the power of sin. It is thus only the Spirit of God and not the law which can serve to distinguish the righteous from the sinful. Paul's aim in Romans 5–8 can therefore be seen to be the establishment of a clear eschatologically based distinction between righteous insider and sinful outsider.

Paul's aim in Romans can be portrayed diagrammatically as in Figure 7.

---

[167]Cf. Dodd, *Romans*, pp.142–3.

[168]It is thus probably at 8:14 that Paul ceases specifically to address Torah-observant Jewish Christians in his letter.

[169]Cf. N.A. Dahl, 'Two Notes on Romans 5', *Studia Theologica* 5 (1951), pp.37–48.

THE AEON OF RIGHTEOUSNESS AND LIFE

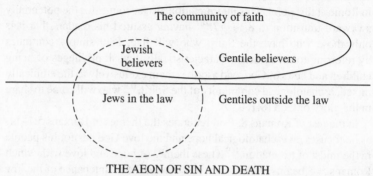

THE AEON OF SIN AND DEATH

Figure 7: Paul's inclusive eschatological boundaries.

Here the division between the two aeons is represented by the horizontal dividing line. The ellipse with a broken line represents the Jewish law, which does not form a boundary between Jew and Gentile in Paul's redefined symbolic universe. Both Jews within the law and Gentiles outside the law are located within the aeon of sin and death, where they are subject to the power of sin. Above the line, in the new aeon of righteousness and life, Gentile and Jewish believers are united in a single community of faith, in which Jewish believers are still at liberty to observe the dietary requirements of Torah.

Conclusion

This chapter has offered a reading of Romans 1–8 in the light of Douglas' matrix, in which it has been argued that chapters 5–8 reflect the characteristically high group/low grid concern about the redrawing of clear boundaries around the group. When Romans 5–8 is read in the light of Douglas' matrix, one can see that in these chapters Paul is reinforcing the 'low grid' identity of members of the community. He does this by combating their sense of marginalisation through emphasising the importance of Christian hope, and also by seeking to establish participation in the eschatological aeon of the Second Adam as the factor which serves to distinguish believers from the sinful mass of the rest of humanity. Those who have the Spirit are the righteous insiders, whereas sinful outsiders are those who are in the flesh, and in this way Paul draws the boundaries in such a way as to include baptised law-free Gentile believers, but to exclude unbelieving Jews under the law.

Paul uses the power of sin in Romans 5–8 as part of this process of boundary definition, by associating the power of sin with bodily existence within the old aeon. In this way, Paul can argue that baptised believers have died with Christ to sin, whereas the power of sin living within the members of the body is responsible for the inner moral conflict experienced by Jews under the law. It is only the eschatological Spirit which brings release from this conflict, and which enables the law to be fulfilled in terms of the love commandment.

In this way the apostle seeks to demolish Jewish confidence in the function of the law as a boundary marker, and to legitimate the position of law-free Gentile believers within the church. Within Romans, the symbolic language of the power of sin is employed as a means to achieve this end, and indeed the way in which Paul's use of the symbolism can be accounted for in terms of its function within the overall purpose of the letter makes it likely that Paul developed this understanding of the human plight and its solution precisely with this aim in mind. Paul's use of the symbolism of the power of sin does not indicate that the apostle had a singularly negative view of human nature: he rather developed and used the symbolism of the power of sin with the specific social aim of legitimating the position of 'strong' law-free believers in Rome. In this way, reading Romans 5–8 in the light of Douglas' matrix enables these chapters to be integrated with the rest of the letter which was written to address the tensions between the strong and the weak in Rome.

7

CONCLUSION

This study opened with the observation that references to sin as a power in Paul's letters are to be found within the context of his discussion about the social question of the relationship between Jewish and Gentile believers in the church. While Augustine recognised this, the theological need to counter Pelagianism resulted in a reading of Paul's letters that neglected the socio-historical setting of Paul's sin language in favour of developing an anthropology that stressed the radical sinfulness of the individual. With the Enlightenment came a fresh recognition of the importance of the Jew–Gentile question, but this insight did not lead to an analysis of Paul's sin language within that context. Instead, the recognition that Paul was not concerned with formulating a doctrine of original sin opened the door to a more optimistic view of human nature, and responsibility for the traditional emphasis on human sinfulness was placed at Augustine's door.

In the twentieth century, Bultmann's attempt to recover a Lutheran theology of sin that was relevant to individuals in a secular society was effectively challenged in the 1970s. Bultmann had interpreted Paul's letters using the existential question about the authenticity of our existence as a hermeneutical bridge, but Stendahl argued that this approach was anachronistic, on the grounds that such personal introspection could be traced no further back than Augustine: Paul was concerned with the social question of Jewish–Gentile relations, not with the individual's search for a gracious God. Stendahl's claim received vigorous support from Sanders, who argued that Paul's perception of the human plight was simply the inverse of his soteriology: those who were not under the lordship of Christ were simply under the lordship of sin. Yet, although Stendahl and his successors effectively argued for the importance of the Jew–Gentile question for understanding Romans and Galatians, there has to date been no real attempt to ground Paul's sin language in that context. This study has attempted to meet that need.

For this purpose, it was decided to make use of Douglas' 'Grid and Group' model, which was originally developed to assist social anthropologists in the task of studying cultures other than their own. Douglas' matrix is well suited to the task of interpreting Paul's sin language within its original socio-historical context, since it sets out the way in which a society's cosmology (and in particular its sense of sin) is related to its social location. This model was therefore chosen in the hope that it would demonstrate how Paul's use of the symbolism of the power of sin relates to the context of the social question of Jewish–Gentile relations in the first century. Another advantage of the model is that one is made aware of one's own inherent cultural bias in the process of using it. As such, it offers a way of reading Paul's sin language that is not unduly influenced by Augustine's legacy of westernised individualism.

However, electing to use Douglas' model posed a number of problems. Douglas herself has revised the model a number of times, with the result that there are three incompatible versions of the matrix. Douglas herself did not design the model with a view to analysing ancient societies, and those who adapted her work for this purpose did so with such varying degrees of success that the validity of the model has been placed in some jeopardy. For this reason, some time was spent analysing the model and seeking to establish a firm methodological base for its application to the communities addressed in 1 Corinthians, Galatians and Romans. In this revised version of the model, 'group' is used to measure the extent to which a given social unit is collectivist or individualistic, while 'grid' is used to measure the extent to which that social unit accepts or rejects the symbol system of the surrounding culture. The decision to use Douglas' matrix may be deemed worthwhile, if it can be shown that her model has yielded fresh insights into the symbolism of sin as a power in Paul's letters.

The model was first applied to 1 Corinthians, since this letter has been the subject of several analyses using Douglas' model. Having reviewed the different approaches, it was argued that the church in Corinth should be regarded as a high grid/low group community dominated by competitive individualism, although not everyone in Corinth fits into this mould. When 'Grid and Group' is used to analyse varying attitudes to group cohesion and the outside world, a coherent picture emerges of a group in Corinth who shared Paul's perception of the church as a high group/low grid bounded community. They objected to the divisive use of tongues in the church, and their concern for physical and social purity undergirded their opposition to sexual intercourse (even within marriage) and to any participation in idol feasts. While he shares their concerns, Paul attempts to adopt a mediating position between the two groups over these divisive issues.

In a manner characteristic of the quadrant of competitive individualism, the local leaders in Corinth had a low consciousness of sin, and Paul
responded by emphasising the low grid/high group distinction between
the good inside and the evil outside of the social and physical bodies.
Since the physical body symbolises the social body, Paul can claim that
the expulsion of the incestuous man will have the dual effect of both maintaining the purity of the community from outside contamination, and of
the salvation of the man's good inner spirit and the destruction of the flesh.
Douglas' matrix also enables us to see why Paul singles out fornication as
a sin against the body, since this alone entails a breach of the all-important
boundaries around the physical and social body. In both these cases, use
of 'Grid and Group' enables us to see more clearly the logic of Paul's argument, as he attempts to shape the symbolic universe of the competitive
individuals in accordance with his own strong group/low grid cosmology. However, Paul's attempt to rectify the Corinthians' accommodation
to the social mores of the surrounding society by emphasising symbols
of abasement backfired, in that his strategy was misinterpreted by the
success-oriented high grid Corinthians, who consequently were inclined
to look down on Paul and honour the super-apostles of 2 Corinthians
10–13.

The 'Grid and Group' matrix also makes a significant contribution towards establishing an appropriate context for reading Galatians. Douglas
draws attention to the way in which witchcraft accusations are used by
members of high group/low grid communities to redraw boundaries in
such a way as to exclude their political opponents. In Galatians, both Paul
and his judaising opponents employ the idea of human wickedness on a
cosmic scale as part of their political struggle for the leadership of the
congregation. The matrix invites a reading of Galatians which emphasises the clash over whether the boundary between the righteous and the
sinful should be drawn along ethnic or eschatological lines. The agitators
seek to place Paul beyond the pale with their accusation that he has made
Christ the servant of sin by abolishing the distinction between righteous
Jew and sinful Gentile. Paul counters that he is indeed condemned by the
law as a transgressor; however, he has been crucified with Christ to the
law, in order that he might live for God (2:15–21). Paul accepts that he
and his Gentile converts are outside the boundaries of the Jewish law, but
he redefines the distinction between the righteous and the sinful along
eschatological lines. Paul and his converts belong within the new eschatological boundary established by Spirit baptism. Paul makes 'in Christ'
and 'under law' mutually exclusive spheres and so seeks to exclude the
Judaisers and those who support them. He argues that all those under the

law are under its curse (3:1–14) and, substantiating his case with an appeal to Habakkuk 2:4, he claims that the law's failure to bring eschatological life means that it did not bring righteousness either. On the contrary, all the law can do is imprison people under the power of sin, which dominates the present aeon (3:19–25). In his struggle against the Judaisers for the loyalty of the Galatian Christians, Paul employs the power of sin to symbolise the evil which lies outside the eschatological boundaries surrounding the righteous community of Gentile believers, and unequivocally places Jews under the law outside those boundaries as a means of legitimating his own apostolic position. Douglas' matrix highlights the clash between the different boundaries drawn between righteous insider and sinful outsider that is at the centre of this reading of Galatians.

At the end of the letter, the continuing presence of sin within the church is identified as 'works of the flesh', vestiges of the old aeon which have no place within the eschatological community (5:22–6:8). When this passage is read in the light of Douglas' model, our understanding of the symbolism of σάρξ is enriched, since, according to Douglas, the flesh represents the ambiguous boundary between the good inside and evil outside of the body. Accordingly, it not only symbolises the tension between the present and the future; it also functions as an ideal symbol of evil's infiltration of the porous boundaries that separate the righteous eschatological community from the world outside.

In Romans, Paul is addressing the tensions between law-free strong and Torah-observant weak groups within the capital, and his overall purpose is to reconcile these different bounded groups on the basis of their common faith in Christ. Douglas' model invites a reading of Romans 1–8 as a high group/low grid attempt to redefine the boundaries surrounding the community of the righteous. The matrix clarifies the structure of the first part of the letter: in chapters 1–4, Paul seeks to remove the ethnic boundary of Torah observance, while in 5–8, he then seeks to redefine the low grid distinction between good inside and bad outside in terms of a distinction between the old and new aeons, represented by Adam and Christ respectively (5:12–21). Making baptism the rite of transition from the old aeon to the new, Paul redraws the boundaries in such a way that law-free believers are on the inside (6:1–23), while non-Christian Torah-observant Jews are on the outside (7:1–25). Paul draws on the common human experience of contra-suggestibility and identifies this as evidence of the presence of the power of sin, which prevents the Torah-observant Jew from carrying out the good intentions of the inner mind. Against such a power, Paul argues that Torah is valueless: it is only the eschatological Spirit that can deliver believers from sin and death.

In his concern to establish eschatological boundaries around the community, Paul found a congenial symbol in the physical body. Paul repeatedly associates the power of sin with the physical body and its members (Rom. 6:6, 12; 7:5, 23; 8:10, 13). Were Paul concerned with individual anthropology, it would be hard to avoid the conclusion that Paul perceived the material body as evil. However, Douglas' theory of a correlation between the social and physical bodies can explain this feature of Paul's thought. Entry into the eschatological in-group is through baptism, which symbolises the death of the body and emphasises a radical separation from the outside world. The body represents the community's contact with the evil of the outside world which is under the dominion of sin. Whereas the outer body is already dead because of sin, the inner Spirit is the source of life. In Romans 8, Paul does not use 'flesh' as a symbol for a sinful way of life, as he does in Galatians. Rather, 'flesh' refers to life under the old aeon, and specifically includes Jewish Torah observance. Paul makes it clear that membership of the righteous in-group is defined by possession of the Spirit: to continue in the flesh will result in death. Douglas' theory explains Paul's anthropology, inasmuch as it shows that Paul's portrayal of the body as sinful in Romans is motivated by his need to subvert the ethnic boundary of Torah observance and to establish in its place clear eschatological boundaries around the community of the church.

This reading of the letter integrates Romans 5–8 with the overall theme of the letter, rather than reading it as a digression which applies the gospel to the individual. Having argued in Romans 1–4 that faith is the basis for (high group) church unity, in Romans 5–8 Paul goes on to argue that Gentile believers are separated from their sinful past and the outside world by dying with Christ in baptism, whereas the Jewish law acts as the Trojan horse that allows sin to take control of people's lives through the commandment. The argument of Romans is a sustained attempt to establish the identity of the church as an eschatological community of faith.

When read in the socio-cultural context of the letter as a whole, it is thus apparent that the symbolism of sin does not reflect a conviction on Paul's part that the whole of humanity was in bondage to sin as an enslaving power. Instead, in Romans 5–8 Paul develops a fresh understanding of the human plight and its solution in order to legitimate the position of law-free Gentile believers.

In the thesis, the model is used to guide exegesis, not control it. Thus, for example, the examination of Romans 3:9–20 did not focus on the contrast between insiders and outsiders, or on aspects of the body. Instead, independent exegesis led to the conclusion that Paul had adapted an existing Jewish collection of verses on the sinful effects of the inclination of the heart. Such independent exegesis has exerted a degree of control on the results of the study, in that the texts have not been pressed into serving the model. Rather, the model has been used to suggest a way of understanding the symbolism of the power of sin by seeking to ground it in Paul's own socio-cultural context.

Douglas' matrix invites a fresh reading of Paul's hamartiology, which grounds the apostle's perception of sin in the socio-cultural context of a need to establish non-permeable boundaries around the social and physical body of believers. There is a close fit between Douglas' theory and Paul's view of sin, and the exegetical insights yielded justify the use of her model, despite the difficulties encountered in using it. Douglas' work offers a coherent way of understanding Paul's thought which avoids the individualistic bias that has been a usual consequence of the western mind-set. Since the time of Augustine, Romans has been read as an exposition of divine grace overcoming individual depravity. However, Douglas' matrix invites us to understand the symbolism of the power of sin as part of a specific attempt on Paul's part to redefine the boundaries around the community of the righteous along eschatological, rather than ethnic, lines. The focus of Paul's concern throughout is not on the individual, but rather on the community.

The fact that Paul's language about sin in both Romans and Galatians can be explained in terms of the apostle's response to these specific social situations leads to the conclusion that it was Paul's concern to legitimate the position of law-free Gentile believers within the church which determined the development of the symbolism of the power of sin, rather than any insight into the depravity of human nature. Paul did not see human beings as being 'beyond the pale', in terms of the complete sinfulness of each and every individual. Rather, for Paul, sin was 'beyond the pale' in the sense that it represented the evil beyond the boundaries protecting the good inside of the physical and social bodies of the righteous. In his view of human nature, Paul was less of a pessimist than is commonly supposed: his real concern was to redefine 'beyond the pale' in such a way as to establish a clear boundary to safeguard the place of Gentile converts within the righteous, eschatological community of the church.

BIBLIOGRAPHY

Althaus, P., 'Daß ihr nicht tut, was ihr wollt', *TLZ* 76 (1951), pp.15–18.

Asad, T., 'Anthropology and the Analysis of Ideology', *Man* 14 (1979), pp.607–27.

Atkins, R.A., *Egalitarian Community: Ethnography and Exegesis* (Alabama: University of Alabama Press, 1991).

Augustine, Bishop of Hippo, *Sancti Aurelii Augustini Hipponensis Episcopi Opera Omnia post Lovanensium theologicarum recensionem*, PL 32–47.

Ed. M. Dods, *The Works of Aurelius Augustine* (Edinburgh: T&T Clark, 1872).

Ed. J.H.S. Burleigh, *Earlier Writings*, LCC 6 (London: SCM, 1953).

Ed. A.C. Outler, *Confessions and Enchiridion*, LCC 7 (London: SCM, 1955).

Ed. J. Burnaby, *Later Works*, LCC 8 (London: SCM, 1955).

Bachmann, M., *Sünder oder Übertreter: Studien zur Argumentation in Gal. 2:15ff.* (Tübingen: J.C.B. Mohr, 1992).

Bacon, B.W., 'The Reading οἷς οὐδὲ in Gal. 2:5', *JBL* 42 (1923), pp.69–80.

Badenas, R., *Christ the End of the Law*, JSNTS 10 (Sheffield: Sheffield Academic Press, 1985).

Bailey, K.E., 'Paul's Theological Foundation for Human Sexuality: 1 Cor. 6:9–20 in the Light of Rhetorical Criticism', *ThRev* 3 (1980), pp.27–41.

Barclay, J., *Obeying the Truth: a Study of Paul's Ethics in Galatians* (Edinburgh: T&T Clark, 1988).

'Thessalonica and Corinth: Social Contrasts in Pauline Christianity', *JSNT* 47 (1992), pp.49–74.

'"Do we undermine the Law?" A Study of Romans 14:1–15:6', in J.D.G. Dunn, ed., *Paul and the Mosaic Law* (Tübingen: J.C.B. Mohr, 1996), pp.287–308.

Jews in the Mediterranean Diaspora: From Alexander to Trajan (323 BCE – 117 CE) (Edinburgh: T&T Clark, 1996).

Barrett, C.K., *1 Corinthians* (London: A&C Black, 1971).

Essays on Paul (London: SPCK, 1982).

Romans (London: A&C Black, 1991).

Barth, F., *Ethnic Groups and Boundaries: The Social Organisation of Culture Difference* (London: Allen & Unwin, 1970).

Barton, S.,'Paul's Sense of Place; an Anthropological Approach to Community Formation in Corinth', *NTS* 32 (1986), pp.225–46.

Bassler, J.M., ed., *Pauline Theology I* (Minneapolis: Fortress, 1991).

Bauckham, R., *The Climax of Prophecy: Studies on the Book of Revelation* (Edinburgh: T&T Clark, 1993).

Bauer, W., *A Greek-English Lexicon of the New Testament and Other Early Christian Literature*, revised and augmented by F.W. Gingrich and F.W. Danker (London: University of Chicago Press, 1979).

Baur, F.C., 'Über Zweck und Veranlassung des Römerbriefs und die damit zusammenhängenden Verhältnisse der römischen Gemeinde', *Tübinger Zeitschrift für Theologie* (1836), vol.3, pp.59–178.

Beasley-Murray, G.R., *Baptism in the New Testament* (Carlisle: Paternoster, 1997).

Becker, J., *Das Heil Gottes* (Göttingen: Vandenhoeck & Ruprecht, 1964).

Beker, J.C., *Paul the Apostle* (Edinburgh: T&T Clark, 1980).

'The Relationship between Sin and Death in Romans', in R. Fortna and B.R. Gaventa, eds., *The Conversation Continues: Studies in Paul and John in Honor of J.L. Martyn* (Nashville: Abingdon, 1987), pp.55–61.

Bellaby, P., 'To Risk or not to Risk? Uses and Limitations of Mary Douglas on Risk-Acceptability for Understanding Health and Safety at Work and Road Accidents', *Sociological Review* 38 (1990), pp.465–83.

Bergesen, A., 'The Cultural Anthropology of Mary Douglas', in R. Wuthnow, J.D. Hunter, A. Bergesen and E. Kurzweil, eds., *Cultural Analysis: The Work of Peter L. Berger, Mary Douglas, Michel Foucault and Jürgen Habermas* (London: Routledge & Kegan Paul, 1984), pp.77–132.

Bernstein, B., *Class, Codes and Control*, 2 vols. (London: Routledge & Kegan Paul, 1971).

Betz, H.D., *Galatians*, Hermeneia (Minneapolis: Fortress, 1979).

Bloor, C., and Bloor, D., 'Twenty Industrial Scientists: a Preliminary Exercise', in M. Douglas, ed., *Essays in the Sociology of Perception* (London: Routledge & Kegan Paul, 1982), pp.83–102.

Boers, H., 'The Problem of Jews and Gentiles in the Macro-Structure of Romans', *Neotestamentica* 15 (1981), pp.1–11.

Bonnard, A., and Spencer, J., eds., *Encyclopedia of Social and Cultural Anthropology* (London: Routledge, 1996), pp.129–32.

Bonnard, P., *L'Epître de Saint Paul aux Galates* (Paris: Delacaux et Niestlé, 1972).

Bonneau, N., 'The Logic of Paul's Argument on the Curse of the Law in Galatians 3:10–14', *NovT* 39 (1997), pp.60–80.

Bonner, G., 'Augustine on Romans 5:12', in F.L. Cross, ed., *Studia Evangelica*, 7 vols. (Berlin: Akademie, 1969), vol.v, pp.242–7.

Boon, J.A., 'America: Fringe Benefits', *Raritan* 2 (1983), pp.97–121.

Borgen, P., ' "Yes", "No", "How Far?": the Participation of Jews and Gentiles in Pagan Cults', in T. Engsberg-Pedersen, ed., *Paul in his Hellenistic Context* (Edinburgh: T&T Clark, 1994), pp.30–59.

Bornkamm, G., 'Sin, Law and Death (Romans 7)', *Early Christian Experience* (London: SCM, 1969), pp.87–104.

Böttger, P.C., 'Paulus und Petrus in Antiochien', *NTS* 37 (1991), pp.77–100.

Boyarin, D., *A Radical Jew: Paul and the Politics of Identity* (London: University of California Press, 1994).

Brandenburger, E., *Adam und Christus: Exegetisch-Religionsgeschichtliche Untersuchung in Röm. 5:12–21 (1 Kor. 15)* (Neukirchen: Neukirchener Verlag, 1962).

Braun, H., 'Römer 7,7–25 und das Selbstverständnis des Qumran-Frommen', *ZTK* 56/1 (1959), pp.1–18.

Brett, M.G., ed., *Ethnicity and the Bible, I* (Leiden: E.J. Brill, 1996).

Brinsmead, B.H., *Galatians – Dialogical Response to Opponents*, SBL Diss. 65 (Chico: Scholars, 1982).

Brown, P., *The Body and Society: Men, Women and Sexual Renunciation in Early Christianity* (Chichester: Columbia University Press, 1988).

Brown, R.E., 'Further Reflections on the Origins of the Church of Rome', in R. Fortna and B.R. Gaventa, eds., *The Conversation Continues: Studies in Paul and John in Honor of J.L. Martyn* (Nashville: Abingdon, 1987), pp.98–115.

Brown, R.E., and Meier, J.P., *Antioch and Rome: New Testament Cradles of Catholic Christianity* (London: Chapman, 1983).

Brown, S.C., ed., *Philosophical Disputes in the Social Sciences* (London: Harvester Press, 1979).

Bruce, F.F., *The Epistle of Paul to the Romans* (London: Tyndale, 1963).

The Epistle to the Galatians, NIGNTC (Exeter: Paternoster, 1982).

'The Romans Debate – Continued', in K.P Donfried, ed., *The Romans Debate* (Peabody: Hendrickson, 1991), pp.175–94.

Büchler, A., *Studies in Sin and Atonement in the Rabbinic Literature of the First Century* (London: Oxford University Press, 1928).

Bultmann, R., 'Romans 7 and the Anthropology of Paul', *Existence and Faith* (London: Fontana, 1964), pp.173–85.

Theology of the New Testament, 2 vols. (London: SCM, 1952).

'Adam and Christ according to Romans 5', in W. Klassen and G.F. Snyder, eds., *Current Issues in New Testament Interpretation* (London: SCM, 1962), pp.143–65.

Ed. E. Dinkler, *Exegetica: Aufsätze zur Erforschung des Neuen Testaments* (Tübingen; J.C.B. Mohr, 1967).

'The New Testament and Mythology', in H.-W. Bartsch, ed., *Kerygma and Myth*, 2 vols. (London: SCM, 1972).

'The Problem of Ethics in Paul', in B.S. Rosner, ed., *Understanding Paul's Ethics: Twentieth-Century Approaches* (Grand Rapids: Eerdmans, 1995), pp.195–216.

Burton, E.D., *A Critical and Exegetical Commentary on the Epistle to the Galatians,* ICC (Edinburgh: T&T Clark, 1921).

Calvin, J., *Institutes of the Christian Religion*, LCC 20–1 (London: SCM, 1960).

Cambier, J., 'Péchés des Hommes et Péché d'Adam en Rom. V 12', *NTS* 11 (1964–5), pp.217–55.

'La Chair et l'Esprit en 1 Cor. 5:5', *NTS* 15 (1969), pp.221–32.

Campbell, R.A., 'Does Paul Acquiesce in Divisions at the Lord's Supper?', *NovT* 33 (1991), pp.61–70.

Carney, T.F., *The Shape of the Past: Models and Antiquity* (Kansas, Colorado Press, 1982).

Carter, T.L., ' "Big Men" in Corinth', *JSNT* 66 (1997), pp.45–71.

Catchpole, D.R., 'Paul, James and the Apostolic Decree', *NTS* 23 (1997), pp.428–44.

Chae, J.D.-S., *Paul as Apostle to the Gentiles: His Apostolic Self-awareness and Its Influence on the Soteriological Argument in Romans* (Carlisle: Paternoster, 1997).

Christiansen, E.J., *The Covenant in Judaism and Paul: A Study of Ritual Bound-
    aries as Identity Markers* (Leiden: E.J. Brill, 1995).
Clarke, A.D., *Secular and Christian Leadership in Corinth: a Socio-Historical
    and Exegetical Study of 1 Cor. 1–6* (Leiden: E.J. Brill, 1993).
Cohen, S.J.D.,'Crossing the Boundary and Becoming a Jew', *HTR* 82 (1989),
    pp.13–33.
Collins, A.Y.,'The Function of "Excommunication" in Paul', *HTR* 73 (1980),
    pp.251–63.
Collins, J.J., 'A Symbol of Otherness: Circumcision and Salvation in the First
    Century', in J. Neusner and E.S. Frerichs, ed., *'To See Ourselves as Others
    See Us': Christians, Jews, 'Others' in Late Antiquity* (Chico: Scholars,
    1985), pp.163–86.
Conzelmann, H., *1 Corinthians*, Hermeneia (Minneapolis: Fortress, 1975).
Cosgrove, C.H., *The Cross and the Spirit: a Study of the Argument and Theology
    of Galatians* (Macon: Mercer, 1988).
Cranfield, C.E.B., ' "ΜΕΤΡΟΝ ΠΙΣΤΕΩΣ" in Rom. XII 3', *NTS* 8 (1961),
    pp.345–51.
    The Epistle to the Romans, ICC, 2 vols. (Edinburgh: T&T Clark, 1975–9).
Cross, F.L., ed., *Studia Evangelica,* 7 vols. (Berlin: Akademie, 1969).
Dahl, N.A., 'Two Notes on Romans 5', *Studia Theologica* 5 (1951), pp.37–48.
    'Paul and the Church in Corinth according to 1 Cor. 1–4', in W.R. Farmer,
    C.F.D. Moule and R.R. Niebuhr, eds., *Christian History and Interpretation:
    Studies Presented to John Knox* (Cambridge: Cambridge University Press,
    1967), pp.313–37.
    Studies in Paul (Minneapolis: Augsburg, 1977).
Danker, F.W., 'Romans V 12: Sin under Law', *NTS* 14 (1967–8), pp.424–39.
Davies, G.N., *Faith and Obedience in Romans: a Study in Romans 1–4*, JSNTS
    39 (Sheffield: Sheffield Academic Press, 1990).
Delaroche, B., *Saint Augustin: Lecteur et Interprète de Saint Paul dans le 'De
    peccatorum meritis et remissione' (hiver 411–412)* (Paris: Institut d'Études
    Augustiniennes, 1996).
Denney, J., 'The Doctrine of Sin', *Expositor* 6/15 (1901), pp.283–95.
Dillon, J.M., 'Rejecting the Body, Redefining the Body: Some Remarks on the
    Development of Platonist Asceticism', in V.L. Wimbush and R. Valentasis,
    eds., *Asceticism* (Oxford: Oxford University Press, 1995), pp.80–7.
Dodd, C.H., *The Epistle of Paul to the Romans* (London: Fontana, 1959).
Donaldson, T.L., 'The Curse of the Law and the Inclusion of the Gentiles', *NTS*
    32 (1986), pp.94–112.
    Paul and the Gentiles: Remapping the Apostle's Convictional World
    (Minneapolis: Fortress, 1997).
Donfried, K.P., 'Justification and Last Judgement in Paul', *ZNW* 67 (1976),
    pp.90–110.
    (ed.) *The Romans Debate* (Peabody: Hendrickson, 1991).
Douglas, M., *Purity and Danger: An Analysis of Concepts of Pollution and Taboo*
    (London: Routledge & Kegan Paul, 1966).
    Natural Symbols: Explorations in Cosmology (1st edition, London: Barrie &
    Rockcliff, 1970; 2nd edition, London: Barrie & Jenkins, 1973; 3rd edi-
    tion, USA, New York: Pantheon Books, 1982; 3rd edition, UK, London:
    Routledge, 1996).

Implicit Meanings: Essays in Anthropology (London: Routledge & Kegan Paul, 1975).

'World View and the Core', in S.C. Brown, ed., *Philosophical Disputes in the Social Sciences* (London: Harvester Press, 1979), pp.177–87.

Cultural Bias, Royal Anthropological Institute Occasional Paper 35 (London: RAI, 1978); reprinted in *In the Active Voice* (London: Routledge & Kegan Paul, 1982), pp.183–254.

In the Active Voice (London: Routledge & Kegan Paul, 1982).

How Institutions Think (London: Routledge & Kegan Paul, 1986).

Risk and Blame: Essays in Cultural Theory (London: Routledge, 1992).

'Anomalous animals and animal metaphors', *Thought Styles* (London: Sage, 1996), pp.126–44.

Thought Styles (London: Sage, 1996).

(ed.) *Witchcraft Accusations and Confessions* (London: Tavistock, 1979).

(ed.) *Essays in the Sociology of Perception* (London: Routledge & Kegan Paul, 1982).

Douglas, M., and Wildawsky, A., *Risk and Culture. An Essay on the Selection of Technical and Environmental Dangers* (London, University of California Press, 1982).

Drane, J., 'Why did Paul write Romans?', in D.A. Hagner and M.J. Harris, eds., *Pauline Studies: Essays Presented to Professor F.F. Bruce on his 70th Birthday* (Exeter: Paternoster, 1980), pp.208–27.

Duncan, G.S., *The Epistle of Paul to the Galatians* (London: Hodder & Stoughton, 1934).

Dunn, J.D.G., 'Paul's Letter to the Romans: an Analysis of Structure and Argument', in W. Haase, ed., *Aufstieg und Niedergang der römischen Welt* (Berlin: de Gruyter, 1987), vol.II, pp.3067–134.

Romans, 2 vols. (Waco: Word, 1988).

Jesus, Paul and the Law (London: SPCK, 1990).

'The Theology of Galatians: the Issue of Covenantal Nomism', in J.M. Bassler, ed., *Pauline Theology I* (Minneapolis: Fortress, 1991), pp.125–46.

'Yet Once More – the Works of the Law: a Response', *JSNT* 46 (1992), pp.99–117.

The Epistle to the Galatians (London: A&C Black, 1993).

The Theology of Paul's Letter to the Galatians (Cambridge: Cambridge University Press, 1993).

'4QMMT and Galatians', *NTS* 43 (1997), pp.147–53.

The Theology of Paul the Apostle (Edinburgh: T&T Clark, 1998).

(ed.) *Paul and the Mosaic Law* (Tübingen: J.C.B. Mohr, 1996).

Ebeling, G., *The Truth of the Gospel: an Exposition of Galatians* (Philadelphia: Fortress, 1985).

Eckstein, H.-J., *Verheißung und Gesetz: Eine exegetische Untersuchung zu Galater 2,15–4,17*, WUNT 86 (Tübingen: J.C.B. Mohr, 1996).

Eco, U., *The Role of the Reader: Explorations in the Semiotics of Texts* (London: Hutchinson, 1981).

Elliott, J.H., 'The Fear of the Leer: The Evil Eye from the Bible to Li'l Abner', *Forum* 4/4 (1988), pp.42–71.

Elliott, N., *The Rhetoric of Romans*, JSNTS 45 (Sheffield: Sheffield Academic Press, 1990).

Engsberg-Pedersen, T., ed., *Paul in his Hellenistic Context* (Edinburgh: T&T Clark, 1994).

Esler, P.F., *Community and Gospel in Luke-Acts* (Cambridge: Cambridge University Press, 1987).

'Making and Breaking an Agreement Mediterranean Style: a new reading of Galatians 2:1–14', *Biblical Interpretation* 3 (1995), pp.285–314.

'Group Boundaries and Intergroup Conflict in Galatians: a new reading of Galatians 5:13–6:10', in M.G. Brett, ed., *Ethnicity and the Bible* (Leiden: E.J. Brill, 1996), pp.215–40.

Galatians (London: Routledge, 1998).

'Review of D.G. Horrell, *The Social Ethos of the Corinthian Correspondence*', *JTS* 49 (1998), pp.253–60.

'Models in New Testament Interpretation: a Reply to David Horrell', *JSNT* 78 (2000), pp.107–13.

(ed.) *The First Christians in their Social Worlds: Social-Scientific Approaches to New Testament Interpretation* (London: Routledge, 1994).

Evans, C.A., and Sanders, J.A., eds., *Paul and the Scriptures of Israel*, JSNTS 83 (Sheffield Academic Press, 1993).

Farahien, E., *Le 'Je' Paulinien – Étude pour Mieux Comprendre Gal. 2:19–21* (Rome: Editrice Pontificia Università Gregoriana, 1988).

Farmer, W.R., Moule, C.F.D., and Niebuhr, R.R., eds., *Christian History and Interpretation: Studies Presented to John Knox* (Cambridge: Cambridge University Press, 1967).

Fee, G., *1 Corinthians*, NICNT (Grand Rapids: Eerdmans, 1987).

Feeley-Harnik, G., 'Is Historical Anthropology Possible?', in SBL Centennial Series, *Humanising America's Iconic Book* (Chico: Scholars, 1982).

Feld, H., ' "Christus Diener der Sünde": Zum Auslegung des Streites zwischen Petrus und Paulus', *ThQ* 153 (1973), pp.119–31.

Feldman, L.H., *Jew and Gentile in the Ancient World: Attitudes and Interactions from Alexander to Justinian* (Princeton: Princeton University Press, 1993).

Fiorenza, E.S., 'Rhetorical Situation and Historical Reconstruction in 1 Corinthians', *NTS* 33 (1987), pp.386–403.

Fisher, S., and Cleveland, S.E., *Body Image and Personality* (London: Van Nostrand, 1958).

Fisk, B.N., 'PORNEUEIN as Body Violation: The Unique Place of Sexual Sin in 1 Cor. 6:18', *NTS* 42 (1996), pp.540–58.

Fitzmyer, J.A., *According to Paul* (New York: Paulist Press, 1993).

Romans, AB (London: Geoffrey Chapman, 1993).

'The Consecutive Meaning of 'ΕΦ 'Ω̣ in Romans 5:12', *NTS* 39 (1993), pp.321–39.

Forkman, G., *The Limits of Religious Community: Expulsion from the Religious Community within the Qumran Sect, within Rabbinic Judaism, and within Primitive Christianity* (Lund: C.W.K. Gleerup, 1972).

Fortna, R., and Gaventa, B.R., eds., *The Conversation Continues: Studies in Paul and John in Honor of J.L. Martyn* (Nashville: Abingdon, 1987).

Friedrich, G., ' Ἁμαρτία οὐκ ἐλλογεῖται: Röm. 5:13', *TLZ* 77 (1952), pp.523–8.

Friedrich, J., Pöhlmann, W., and Stuhlmacher, P., 'Zur historischen Situation und Intention von Röm. 13:1–7', *ZTK* 73 (1976), pp.131–66.

Fung, R.Y.K., *Galatians*, NICNT (Grand Rapids: Eerdmans, 1988), pp.90–4.

Gager, J.G., 'Body Symbols and Social Reality: Resurrection, Incarnation and Asceticism in Early Christianity', *Religious Studies Review* 5 (1982), pp.345–64.

Garlington, D.B., 'Role Reversal and Paul's Use of Scripture', *JSNT* 65 (1997), pp.85–121.

Garnet, P., 'Qumran Light on Pauline Soteriology', in D.A. Hagner and M.J. Harris, eds., *Pauline Studies: Essays Presented to Professor F.F. Bruce on his 70th Birthday* (Exeter: Paternoster, 1980), pp.19–32.

Garrett, S., 'Review of *Christian Origins and Cultural Anthropology*, by B.J. Malina', *JBL* 107 (1988), pp.532–4.

The Demise of the Devil (Minneapolis: Fortress, 1989).

Gaston, L., *Paul and the Torah* (British Columbia: University of British Columbia Press, 1987).

Gooch, P.D., *Dangerous Food: 1 Corinthians 8–10 in Its Context* (Ontario: Wilfrid Laurier University Press, 1993).

Gordon, J.D., *Sister or Wife? 1 Corinthians 7 and Cultural Anthropology*, JSNTS 149 (Sheffield: JSOT, 1997).

Greer, R.A., 'Sinned we all in Adam's Fall?', in L.M. White and O.L. Yarbrough, eds., *The Social World of the First Christians* (Minneapolis, Fortress, 1995), pp.382–94.

Gross, J., and Rayner, S., *Measuring Culture: a Paradigm for the Analysis of Social Organisation* (New York: Columbia University Press, 1985).

Gundry, R.H., *Sōma in Biblical Theology with Emphasis on Pauline Anthropology*, SNTS 29 (Cambridge: Cambridge University Press, 1976).

'The Moral Frustration of Paul before his Conversion: Sexual Lust in Rom. 7:7–25', in D.A. Hagner and M.J. Harris, eds., *Pauline Studies: Essays Presented to Professor F.F. Bruce on his 70th Birthday* (Exeter: Paternoster, 1980), pp.238–45.

Gutbrod, W., *Die paulinische Anthropologie* (Berlin: Stuttgart, 1934).

Hagner, D.A., and Harris, M.J., eds., *Pauline Studies: Essays Presented to Professor F.F. Bruce on his 70th Birthday* (Exeter: Paternoster, 1980).

Hanegraaf, W.J., *New Age Religion and Western Culture: Esotericism in the Mirror of Secular Thought* (Leiden: E.J. Brill, 1996).

Hanson, K.C., 'Sin, Purification and Group Process', in H.T.C. Sun and K.L. Eades, eds., *Problems in Biblical Theology: Essays in Honor of Rolf Knierim* (Grand Rapids: Eerdmans, 1997), pp.167–91.

Hasler, V., 'Glaube und Existenz: Hermeneutische Erwägungen zu Gal. 2,15–21', *Theologische Zeitschrift* 25 (1969), pp.241–51.

Hays, R.B., *The Faith of Jesus Christ: an Investigation of the Narrative Substructure of Galatians 3:1–4:11*, SBL Diss. 56 (Chico: Scholars, 1983).

Heil, J.P., *Paul's Letter to the Romans: a Reader-Response Commentary* (New York: Paulist Press, 1987).

Héring, J., *The First Epistle of St. Paul to the Corinthians* (London: Epworth, 1962).

Hollander, H.W., and Holleman, J., 'The Relationship of Death, Sin and Law in 1 Cor. 15:56', *NovT* 35 (1993), pp.270–91.

Holmberg, B., *Sociology and the New Testament: an Appraisal* (Minneapolis, Fortress, 1990).

Holtzmann, H.J., *Lehrbuch der neutestamentlichen Theologie*, 2 vols. (Tübingen: J.C.B. Mohr, 1911).

Hong, I.-G., *The Law in Galatians*, JSNTS 81 (Sheffield: Sheffield Academic Press, 1993).

'Does Paul Misrepresent the Jewish Law? Law and Covenant in Gal. 3:1–14', *NovT* 36 (1994), pp.164–82.

Hooker, M.D., *Jesus and the Servant* (London: SCM, 1959).

Horn, F.W., '1 Korinther 15.56: Ein exegetischer Stachel', *ZNW* 82 (1991), pp.88–105.

Horrell, D.G., *The Social Ethos of the Corinthian Correspondence: Interests and Ideology from 1 Corinthians to 1 Clement* (Edinburgh: T&T Clark, 1996).

'Models and Methods in Social-Scientific Interpretation: A Response to Philip Esler', *JSNT* 78 (2000), pp.83–105.

(ed.) *Social-Scientific Approaches to New Testament Interpretation* (Edinburgh: T&T Clark, 1999).

Houston, W., *Purity and Monotheism*, JSOTSupp 140 (Sheffield: JSOT, 1993).

Howard, G., *Crisis in Galatia* (Cambridge: Cambridge University Press, 1979).

Howell, S., 'Cosmology', in A. Bonnard and J. Spencer, eds., *Encyclopedia of Social and Cultural Anthropology* (London: Routledge, 1996), pp.129–32.

Hübner, H., 'Anthropologischer Dualismus in den Hodayot?', *NTS* 18 (1971–2), pp.268–84.

Law in Paul's Thought (Edinburgh: T&T Clark, 1984).

Huftier, M., *Le Tragique de la Condition Chrétienne chez Saint Augustin* (Paris: Desclé, 1964).

Huggins, R.V., 'Alleged Classical Parallels to Paul's "What I want to do I do not do, but what I hate, that I do" (Rom. 7:15)', *Westminster Theological Journal* 54 (1992), pp.153–61.

Hultgren, A.J., *Paul's Gospel and Mission* (Minneapolis: Fortress, 1985).

Hurd, J.C., *The Origin of 1 Corinthians* (London: SPCK, 1965).

Isenberg, S.R., 'Some Uses and Limitations of Social Scientific Methodology in the Study of Early Christianity', *SBL Seminar Papers* 18 (1980), pp.29–49.

Isenberg, S.R., and Owen, D.E., 'Bodies, Natural and Contrived: the Work of Mary Douglas', *Religious Studies Review* 3 (1977), pp.1–17.

Jeffers, J.S., *Conflict at Rome: Social Order and Hierarchy in Early Christianity* (Minneapolis: Augsburg Fortress, 1991).

Jervell, J., 'The Letter to Jerusalem', in K.P. Donfried, ed., *The Romans Debate* (Peabody: Hendrickson, 1991), pp.53–64.

Jervis, L.A., *The Purpose of Romans: a Comparative Letter Structure Investigation*, JSNTS 55 (Sheffield: Sheffield Academic Press, 1991).

Jewett, R., 'The Agitators and the Galatian Congregation', *NTS* 17 (1970), pp.198–211.

Paul's Anthropological Terms (Leiden: E.J. Brill, 1971).

Dating Paul's Life (London: SCM, 1979).

'Following the Argument of Romans', in K.P. Donfried, ed., *The Romans Debate* (Peabody: Hendrickson, 1991), pp.265–77.

Judge, E.A., *The Social Pattern of the Christian Groups in the First Century: Some Prolegomena to the Study of New Testament Ideas of Social Obligation* (London: Tyndale, 1960).

Juvenal, *The Sixteen Satires* (London: Penguin, 1967).

Karris, R.J., 'Romans 14:1–15:13 and the Occasion of Romans', in K.P. Donfried, ed., *The Romans Debate* (Peabody: Hendrickson, 1991), pp.65–84.

'The Occasion of Romans: a Response to Professor Donfried', in K.P. Donfried, ed., *The Romans Debate* (Peabody: Hendrickson, 1991), pp.125–7.

Käsemann, E., *Essays on New Testament Themes* (London: SCM, 1964).

Perspectives on Paul (London: SCM, 1971).

Commentary on Romans (London: SCM, 1980).

Kaye, B.N., *The Thought Structure of Romans with Special Reference to Chapter 6* (Chico: Scholars, 1979).

Keck, L., 'The Function of Rom. 3:10–18 – Observations and Suggestions', in J. Jervell and W.A. Meeks, eds., *God's Christ and His People: Studies in Honor of Nils Alstrup Dahl* (Oslo: Universitetsforlaget, 1977), pp.141–57.

Kertelge, K., 'The Sin of Adam in the Light of Christ's Redemptive Act According to Romans 5:12–21', *Communio* 18 (1991), pp.502–13.

Kieffer, R., *Foi et Justification à Antioche: Interprétation d'un Conflit* (Paris: Cerf, 1982).

Kirchgässner, A., *Erlösung und Sünde im Neuen Testament* (Freiburg: Herder, 1950).

Kirchhoff, R., *Die Sünde gegen den eigenen Leib* (Göttingen, Vandenhoeck & Ruprecht, 1994).

Kittel, G., ed., *Theological Dictionary of the New Testament*, 10 vols. (Grand Rapids: Eerdmans, 1964–76).

Klein, G., 'Individualgeschichte und Weltgeschichte bei Paulus: Eine Interpretation ihres Verhältnisses im Galaterbrief', in *Rekonstruktion und Interpretation: Gesammelte Aufsätze zum Neuen Testament* (Munich: Chr. Kaiser, 1969), pp.180–220.

Köberle, J., *Sünde und Gnade im religiösen Leben des Volkes Israel bis auf Christentum: Eine Geschichte des vorchristlichen Heilbewußtseins* (Munich: Beck'sche, 1905).

Koch, K., 'Sühne und Sündenvergebung um die Wende von der exilischen Zeit', *EvTh* 26 (1966), pp.217–39.

Kuhn, K.G., 'Rm 6,7', *ZNW* 30 (1931), pp.305–10.

'New Light on Temptation, Sin and Flesh in the New Testament', in K. Stendahl, ed., *The Scrolls and the New Testament* (London: SCM, 1958), pp.94–113.

Kümmel, W.G., *Römer 7 und die Bekehrung des Paulus* (Leipzig: Hinrichs'sche, 1929).

'Πάρεσις and ἔνδειξις: A Contribution to the Understanding of the Pauline Doctrine of Justification', *Journal for Theology and Church* 3 (1952), pp.1–13.

' "Individualgeschichte" und "Weltgeschichte" in Galater 2:15–21', in B. Lindars and S.S. Smalley, eds., *Christ and Spirit in the New Testament* (Cambridge: Cambridge University Press, 1973), pp.157–74.

Kuss, O., *Der Römerbrief*, 3 vols. (Regensburg: Pustet, 1957–78).

Laato, T., *Paulus und das Judentum: Anthropologische Erwägungen* (Åbo: Akademis Förlag, 1991).

Lagrange, M.-J., *Saint Paul: Epître aux Romains* (Paris: Gabalda, 1931).

Bibliography 219

Lambrecht, J., *Pauline Studies* (Louvain: Louvain University Press, 1991).
'Paul's Reasoning in Galatians 2:11–21', in J.D.G. Dunn, ed., *Paul and the Mosaic Law* (Tübingen: J.C.B. Mohr, 1996), pp.53–74.
Lampe, G.W.H., 'Church Discipline and the Interpretation of the Epistles to the Corinthians', in W.R. Farmer, C.F.D. Moule and R.R. Niebuhr, eds., *Christian History and Interpretation: Studies Presented to John Knox* (Cambridge: Cambridge University Press, 1967), pp.337–63.
Lampe, P., *Die Stadtrömischen Christen in den ersten beiden Jahrhunderten*, WUNT 18 (Tübingen: J.C.B. Mohr, 1989).
'The Roman Christians of Romans 16', in K.P. Donfried, ed., *The Romans Debate* (Peabody: Hendrickson, 1991), pp.216–30.
Landé, C.H., 'Introduction: the Dyadic Basis of Clientelism', in S.W. Schmidt, L. Guasti, C.H. Landé and J.C. Scott, eds., *Friends, Followers and Factions: a Reader in Political Clientelism* (London: University of California Press, 1977), pp.xiii–xxxvii.
Landes, P.F., *Augustine on Romans: Propositions from the Epistle to the Romans: Unfinished Commentary on the Epistle to the Romans* (Chico: Scholars, 1982).
Lang, F., *Die Briefe an die Korinther* (Göttingen, Vandenhoeck & Ruprecht, 1986).
Lawrence, P., *Road Belong Cargo: a Study of the Cargo Movement in the Southern Madang District, New Guinea* (Manchester: Manchester University Press, 1964).
Leenhardt, F.J., *The Epistle to the Romans* (London: Lutterworth, 1961).
Lewis, I.M., *Ecstatic Religion: a Study of Shamanism and Spirit Possession* (London: Routledge, 1989).
Lietzmann, H., *An die Korinther I/II* (Tübingen: J.C.B. Mohr, 1971).
Lightfoot, J.B., *St. Paul's Epistle to the Galatians* (London: Macmillan, 1874).
Notes on the Epistles of St Paul from unpublished commentaries (London: Macmillan, 1895).
Lindars, B., and Smalley, S.S., eds., *Christ and Spirit in the New Testament* (Cambridge: Cambridge University Press, 1973).
Litfin, D., *St. Paul's Theology of Proclamation*, SNTS 79 (Cambridge: Cambridge University Press, 1994).
Livermore, P.W., *The Setting and Argument of Romans 1:18–3:20: The Empirical Verification of the Power of Sin* (PhD Diss., Princeton Theological Seminary, 1979).
Livingstone, E.A., ed., *Studia Biblica: Papers on Paul and Other New Testament Authors*, 3 vols. (Sheffield: Sheffield Academic Press, 1980).
Locke, J., *A Paraphrase and Notes on the Epistles of St. Paul*, ed. A. Wainwright, 2 vols. (Oxford: Clarendon, 1987).
Lohmeyer, E., 'Probleme paulinischer Theologie III: Sünde, Fleisch und Tod', *ZNW* 29 (1930), pp.1–59.
Longenecker, R., *Biblical Exegesis in the Apostolic Period* (Grand Rapids: Eerdmans, 1975).
Galatians, WBC (Dallas: Word, 1990).
Lüdemann, G., *Paul, Apostle to the Gentiles: Studies in Chronology* (Minneapolis: Fortress, 1984).
Lüdemann, H., *Die Anthropologie des Apostels Paulus* (Kiel, 1872).

Luther, M., *Luther's Works* (St. Louis: Concordia, 1972).
Lyonnet, S.J., 'Le sens de ἐφ'ᾧ en Rom. 5:12 et l'Exégèse des Pères Grecs', *Bib* 36 (1955), pp.325–55.
    'L'Histoire du Salut selon la Chapitre VII de l'Epître aux Romains', *Biblica* 43 (1962), pp.117–51.
Malina, B.J., 'The Social World Implied in the Letters of the Christian Bishop-Martyr (Named Ignatius of Antioch)', *SBL Seminar Papers* 2 (1978), pp.71–119.
    'The Social Sciences and Biblical Interpretation', *Interpretation* 36 (1982), pp.229–42.
    The New Testament World (London: SCM, 1983).
    Christian Origins and Cultural Anthropology (Atlanta: John Knox, 1986).
    'Is there a Circum-Mediterranean Person? Looking for Stereotypes', *BTB* 22 (1992), pp.66–87.
Malina, B.J., and Neyrey, J.H., 'Jesus the Witch: Witchcraft Accusations in Matthew 12', in D.G. Horrell, ed., *Social-Scientific Approaches to New Testament Interpretation* (Edinburgh: T&T Clark, 1999), pp.29–67.
Marcus, G.E., and Fischer, M.M.J., *Anthropology as Cultural Critique: an Experimental Moment in the Human Sciences* (Chicago: University of Chicago Press, 1986).
Marcus, J.M., and Soards, M.L., eds., *Apocalyptic and the New Testament: Essays in Honor of J. Louis Martyn*, JSNTS 24 (Sheffield: Sheffield Academic Press, 1989).
Martin, D.B., *The Corinthian Body* (Newhaven: Yale University Press, 1995).
Marty, M.E., and Appleby, R. Scott, eds., *Fundamentalisms Comprehended* (London: University of Chicago Press, 1995).
Martyn, J.L., 'Events in Galatia: Modified Covenantal Nomism versus God's Invasion of the Cosmos in the Singular Gospel: A Response to J.D.G. Dunn and B.R. Gaventa', in J.M. Bassler, ed., *Pauline Theology I* (Minneapolis: Fortress, 1991), pp.160–79.
    Theological Issues in the Letters of Paul (Edinburgh: T&T Clark, 1997).
Marxsen, W., *Introduction to the New Testament* (Oxford: Blackwell, 1968).
McArthur, S.D., ' "Spirit" in Pauline Usage: 1 Corinthians 5:5', in E.A. Livingstone, ed., *Studia Biblica III: Papers on Paul and Other New Testament Authors*, JSNTS 3 (Sheffield: Sheffield Academic Press, 1980), pp.249–56.
Meeks, W., ' "Since then you would need to go out of the world": Group Boundaries in Pauline Christianity', in T.J. Ryan, ed., *Critical History and Biblical Faith: NT Perspectives* (Villanova, PA: College Theology Society, 1979), pp.4–29.
    The First Urban Christians (Newhaven: Yale University Press, 1983).
    'Judgement and the Brother: Romans 14:1–15:13', in G.F. Hawthorne and O. Betz, eds., *Tradition and Interpretation in the New Testament: Essays in Honor of E. Earle Ellis on his 60th Birthday* (Grand Rapids: Eerdmans, 1987), pp.290–300.
Meggitt, J., *Paul, Poverty and Survival* (Edinburgh, T&T Clark, 1998).
Merklein, H., ' "Nicht aus Werken des Gesetzes..." eine Auslegung von Gal. 2,15–21', in H. Merklein, K. Müller and G. Sternberger, eds., *Bibel in jüdischer und christlicher Tradition, Festschrift für Johann Maier zum 60. Geburtstag*, BBB 88 (Frankfurt: Anton Harris, 1993).

Meyer, M., *Die Sünde des Christen nach Pauli Briefen an die Korinther und Römer* (Gütersloh: Bertelsmann, 1902).

Der Apostel Paulus als armer Sünder: ein Beitrag zur paulinischen Hamartologie (Gütersloh: Bertelsmann, 1903).

Michaelis, W., 'Judaistische Heidenchristen', *ZNW* 30 (1931), pp.83–9.

Michel, O., *Der Brief an die Römer* (Göttingen: Vandenhoeck & Ruprecht, 1954).

Millar, A., and Riches, J.K., 'Interpretation: a Theoretical Perspective and Some Applications', *Numen* 28 (1981), pp.29–53.

Minear, P.S., *The Obedience of Faith* (London: SCM, 1971).

Mitchell, M., *Paul and the Rhetoric of Reconciliation* (Tübingen: J.C.B. Mohr, 1991).

Moffatt, J., *The First Epistle of Paul to the Corinthians* (London: Hodder & Stoughton, 1938).

Moo, D.J., *The Epistle to the Romans*, NICNT (Grand Rapids: Eerdmans, 1996).

Morland, K.A., *The Rhetoric of Curse in Galatians: Paul Confronts Another Gospel* (Atlanta: Scholars, 1995).

Morris, L., *The First Epistle of Paul to the Corinthians*, TNTC (London: IVP, 1985).

Moule, C.F.D., *An Idiom Book of New Testament Greek* (Cambridge: Cambridge University Press, 1959).

Moxnes, H., 'Honour, Shame and the Outside World in Paul's Letter to the Romans', in J. Neusner, ed., *The Social World of Formative Christianity and Judaism* (Minneapolis: Fortress, 1988), pp.207–18.

Munck, J., *Paul and the Salvation of Mankind* (London: SCM, 1959).

Mundle, W., 'Zur Auslegung von Gal. 2:17,18', *ZNW* 23 (1924), pp.152–3.

Murphy-O'Connor, J., 'Corinthian Slogans in 1 Cor. 6:12–20', *CBQ* 40 (1978), pp.391–6.

Mussner, F., *Der Galaterbrief* (Freiburg: Herder, 1974).

Neitzel, H., 'Zur Interpretation von Galater 2:11–21', *ThQ* 163 (1983), pp.15–39, 131–49.

Neyrey, J.H., 'Body language in 1 Corinthians', *Semeia* 35 (1986), pp.129–70.

An Ideology of Revolt: John's Christology in Social-Science Perspective (Minneapolis: Fortress, 1988).

'Bewitched in Galatia: Paul and Cultural Anthropology', *CBQ* 55 (1988), pp.72–100.

Paul, in Other Words: a Cultural Reading of His Letters (Louisville: W/JKP, 1990).

Noack, B., 'Current and Backwater in the Epistle to the Romans', *ST* 19 (1965), pp.155–65.

Nock, A.D., 'Seviri and Augustales', in *Mélanges Bidez: Annuaire de l'Institut de Philologie et d'Histoire Orientales*, 2 vols. (Brussels, 1934), vol.II, pp.627–38.

Nolland, J., 'Uncircumcised proselytes?', *Journal for the Study of Judaism* 12 (1981), pp.173–94.

Nygren, A., *Commentary on Romans* (London: SCM, 1952).

Oepke, A., *Der Brief des Paulus an die Galater* (Berlin: Evangelische Verlaganstalt, 1960).

Oliver, D.L., *A Solomon Island Society: Kinship and Leadership among the Siuai of Bougainville* (Cambridge, MA: Harvard University Press, 1955).

222   *Bibliography*

O'Neill, J.C., *Paul's Letter to the Romans* (London: Penguin, 1975).

Orr, W.F., and Walter, J.A., *1 Corinthians*, AB (London: Chapman. 1976).

Ostrander, B., 'One- and Two-Dimensional Models of the Distribution of Beliefs', in M. Douglas, ed., *Essays in the Sociology of Perception* (London: Routledge & Kegan Paul, 1982), pp.14–30.

Ostrow, S.E., 'The Augustales in the Augustan Scheme', in K.A. Raaflaub and M. Toher, eds., *Between Republic and Empire: Interpretations of Augustus and his Principate* (Berkeley: University of California Press, 1990), pp.364–79.

Otto, R., *Sünde und Urschuld* (Munich: Beck'sche, 1932).

Paget, J.C., 'Jewish Proselytism at the Time of Christian Origins: Chimera or Reality?', *JSNT* 62 (1996), pp.65–103.

Pattee, S., 'Paul's Critique of Jewish Exclusivity: A Sociological and Anthropological Perspective', *Soundings* 78 (1995), pp.589–610.

Petronius, *Satyricon*, LCL (London: Heinemann, 1969).

Pfleiderer, O., *Paulinism* (London: Williams & Norgate, 1877).

Primitive Christianity: its Writings and Teachings in their Historical Connections, 2 vols. (Clifton: Reference Book, 1965).

Phipps, W.E., 'Is Paul's Attitude toward Sexual Relations Contained in 1 Cor. 7:1?', *NTS* 28 (1982), pp.125–31.

Pickett, R., *The Cross in Corinth: The Social Significance of the Death of Jesus*, JSNTS 143 (Sheffield: JSOT, 1997).

Porter, C.L., 'Romans 1:18-32: Its Role in the Developing Argument', *NTS* 40 (1994), pp.210–28.

Porter, S.E., *Idioms of the Greek New Testament* (Sheffield: Sheffield Academic Press, 1994).

Purcell, N., 'The Apparitores: A Study in Social Mobility', *Papers of the British School at Rome* 51 (1983), pp.125–73.

Raaflaub, K.A., and Toher, M., eds., *Between Republic and Empire: Interpretations of Augustus and his Principate* (Berkeley: University of California Press, 1990).

Räisänen, H., *Paul and the Law* (Tübingen: J.C.B. Mohr, 1987).

Jesus, Paul and Torah: Collected Essays, JSNTS 43 (Sheffield: Sheffield Academic Press, 1992).

Rayner, S., *The Classification and Dynamics of Sectarian Forms of Organisation: Grid/Group Perspectives on the Far Left in Britain* (unpublished PhD thesis, University of London, 1979).

Riches, J.K., *Jesus and the Transformation of Judaism* (London: DLT, 1980).

Roetzel, C.J., *Judgement in the Community: A Study of the Relationship between Eschatology and Ecclesiology in Paul* (Leiden: E.J. Brill, 1972).

Rohrbaugh, R.L., 'Models or Muddles: Discussion of the Social Facets Seminar', *Forum* 3 (1987), pp.23–33.

Röhser, G., *Metaphorik und Personifikation der Sünde* (Tübingen: J.C.B. Mohr, 1987).

Rosner, B.S., ed., *Understanding Paul's Ethics: Twentieth-Century Approaches* (Grand Rapids: Eerdmans, 1995), 353.

Rowland, C., *The Open Heaven* (London: SPCK, 1982).

Ryan, T.J., ed., *Critical History and Biblical Faith: NT Perspectives* (Villanova, PA: College Theology Society, 1979).

Bibliography 223

Sahlins, M.D., *Culture and Practical Reason* (London: University of Chicago Press, 1976).
'Poor Man, Rich Man, Big Man, Chief: Political Types in Melanesia and Polynesia', in S.W. Schmidt, L. Guasti, C.H. Landé and J.C. Scott, eds., *Friends, Followers and Factions: a Reader in Political Clientelism* (London: University of California Press, 1977).
Sand, A., *Der Begriff 'Fleisch' in den paulinischen Hauptbriefen* (Regensburg: Friedrich Pustet, 1967).
Sanday, W., and Headlam, A.C., *The Epistle to the Romans*, ICC (Edinburgh: T&T Clark, 1902).
Sanders, E.P., *Paul and Palestinian Judaism* (London: SCM, 1977).
Paul, the Law and the Jewish People (London: SCM, 1983).
'Jewish Association with Gentiles and Galatians 2:11–14', in R. Fortna and B.R. Gaventa, eds., *The Conversation Continues: Studies in Paul and John in Honor of J. L. Martyn* (Nashville: Abingdon, 1990), pp.170–88.
Sanders, J.T., *Schismatics, Sectarians, Dissidents, Deviants: the First One Hundred Years of Jewish–Christian Relations* (London: SCM, 1993).
Schlier, H., *Der Brief an die Galater* (Göttingen: Vandenhoeck and Ruprecht, 1949).
Schmidt, S.W., Guasti, L., Landé, C.H. and Scott, J.C. eds., *Friends, Followers and Factions: a Reader in Political Clientelism* (London: University of California Press, 1977).
Schmithals, W., *Paul and James* (London: SCM, 1965), pp.107–8.
Die theologische Anthropologie des Paulus (Stuttgart: Kohlhammer, 1980).
Schneider, J., 'παραβαίνω, παράβασις, ἀπαραβάτος, ὑπερβαίνω', in G. Kittel, ed., *Theological Dictionary of the New Testament* (Grand Rapids: Eerdmans, 1964–76), vol.v, pp.736–44.
Schoeps, H.-J., *Paul: the Theology of the Apostle in the Light of Jewish Religious History* (London: Lutterworth, 1961).
Schottroff, L., 'Die Schreckenherrschaft der Sünde und die Befreiung durch Christus nach dem Römerbrief des Paulus', *EvTh* 39 (1979), pp.497–510.
Schrage,W., *Der erste Brief an die Korinther*, 2 vols., EKK 7 (Düsseldorf: Benziger/Neukirchener Verlag, 1991–5).
Schürer, E., *The History of the Jewish People in the Age of Jesus Christ*, 4 vols. (Edinburgh: T&T Clark, 1973–87).
Schweitzer, A., *The Mysticism of Paul the Apostle* (London: A&C Black, 1931).
Schweizer, E., 'Die Sünde in den Gliedern', in O. Betz, M. Hengel and P. Schmidt, eds., *Abraham unser Vater: Juden und Christen im Gespräch über die Bibel* (Leiden: E.J. Brill, 1963), pp.437–9.
Scott, J.M., ' "For as Many as are of Works of the Law are under a Curse" (Galatians 3:10)', in C.A. Evans and J.A. Sanders, eds., *Paul and the Scriptures of Israel*, JSNT 83 (Sheffield: Sheffield Academic Press, 1993), pp.187–221.
Scroggs, R., 'Paul and the Eschatological Body', in E.H. Lovering Jr and J.L. Sumney, eds., *Theology and Ethics in Paul and His Interpreters: Essays in Honor of Victor Paul Furnish* (Nashville: Abingdon, 1996), pp.14–29.
Seifrid, M.A., *Justification by Faith: the Origin and Development of a Central Pauline Theme* (Leiden: E.J. Brill, 1992).
'The Subject of Rom. 7:14–25', *NovT* 34 (1992), pp.313–33.

Sieffert, F., *Der Brief an die Galater* (Göttingen: Vandenhoeck & Ruprecht, 1899).

Sivan, E., 'The Enclave Culture', in M.E. Marty and R. Scott Appleby, eds., *Fundamentalisms Comprehended* (London: University of Chicago Press, 1995), pp.11–68.

Skorupski, J., *Symbol and Theory: a Philosophical Study of Theories of Religion in Social Anthropology* (Cambridge: Cambridge University Press, 1976).

'Pangolin Power', in S.C. Brown, ed., *Philosophical Disputes in the Social Sciences* (London: Harvester Press, 1979), pp.151–76.

'Our Philosopher Replies', in S.C. Brown, ed., *Philosophical Disputes in the Social Sciences* (London: Harvester Press, 1979), pp.188–94.

Snodgrass, K.R., 'Spheres of Influence: a Possible Solution to the Problem of Paul and the Law', *JSNT* 32 (1988), pp.93–113.

Soards, M.L., 'Seeking (*zētein*) and Sinning (*hamartia*) according to Galatians 2:17', in J.M. Marcus and M.L. Soards, eds., *Apocalyptic and the New Testament: Essays in Honor of J. Louis Martyn*, JSNTS 24 (Sheffield: Sheffield Academic Press, 1989), pp.237–54.

Spickard, J.V., *Relativism and Cultural Comparison in the Anthropology of Mary Douglas: an Evaluation of the Meta-Critical Strategy of her Grid-Group Theory* (unpublished PhD dissertation, Graduate Theological Union, 1984).

'Guide to Grid/Group Theory', *Sociological Analysis* 50/2 (1989), pp.151–70.

Stanley, C.D., 'Under a Curse: a fresh reading of Gal. 3:10–14', *NTS* 36 (1990), pp.481–511.

Stauffer, E., 'ἐγώ', in G. Kittel, ed., *Theological Dictionary of the New Testament*, 10 vols. (Grand Rapids: Eerdmans, 1964–76), vol.II, pp.343–62.

Steinfels, P., 'Review of *Purity and Danger, Natural Symbols*', *Commonweal* 93 (1970), pp.49–51.

Stendahl, K., *Paul Among Jews and Gentiles* (Minneapolis: Fortress, 1976).

Stowers, S.K., *A Rereading of Romans: Justice, Jews and Gentiles* (London: Yale University Press, 1994).

Strack, H., and Billerbeck, P., *Kommentar zum Neuen Testament*, 4 vols. (Munich: Beck'sche, 1926–8).

Stuhlmacher, P., 'The Purpose of Romans', in K.P Donfried, ed., *The Romans Debate* (Hendrickson: Peabody, 1991), pp.231–42.

'The Theme of Romans', in K.P Donfried, ed., *The Romans Debate* (Hendrickson: Peabody, 1991), pp.333–45.

Paul's Letter to the Romans: A Commentary (Edinburgh: T&T Clark, 1994).

Sun, H.T.C., and Eades, K.L., eds., *Problems in Biblical Theology: Essays in Honor of Rolf Knierim* (Grand Rapids: Eerdmans, 1997).

Theissen, G., *The Social Setting of Pauline Christianity* (Edinburgh: T&T Clark, 1982).

Psychological Aspects of Pauline Christianity (Edinburgh: T&T Clark, 1987).

Thielman, F., *From Plight to Solution*, NT Supp. 61 (Leiden: E.J. Brill, 1989).

Thiselton, A.C., 'The Meaning of ΣΑΡΞ in 1 Corinthians 5:5; a Fresh Approach in the Light of Logical and Semantic Factors', *SJT* 26 (1973), pp.204–28.

Thyen, H., *Studien zur Sündenvergebung* (Göttingen: Vandenhoeck & Ruprecht, 1970).

Triandis, H.C., Leung, K., Villareal, M.J., and Crack, F.L., 'Allocentric versus Idiocentric Tendencies, Convergent and Discriminant Validation', *Journal of Research in Psychology* 19 (1985), pp.395–415.

Turner, V.W., *Dramas, Fields and Metaphors: Symbolic Action in Human Society* (New York: Cornell University Press, 1974).

Umbach, H., *In Christus getauft – von der Sünde befreit: Die Gemeinde als sündenfreier Raum bei Paulus* (Göttingen: Vandenhoeck & Ruprecht, 1999).

van den Beld, A., 'Romans 7:14–25 and the problem of *Akrasia*', *Interpretation* 21 (1985), pp.495–515.

Vanneste, A., 'Saint Paul et la Doctrine Augustinienne du Péché Originel', *Studiorum Paulinorum Congressus Internationalis Catholicus*, 2 vols. (Rome: Analecta Biblica, 1961).

Watson, F., *Paul, Judaism and the Gentiles* (Cambridge: Cambridge University Press, 1986).

Watson, N., *The First Epistle to the Corinthians* (London: Epworth, 1992).

Wedderburn, A.J.M., *The Reasons for Romans* (Edinburgh: T&T Clark, 1988).

Weiss, J., *Der erste Korintherbrief* (Göttingen: Vandenhoeck & Ruprecht, 1910).

Welborn, L.L., 'On the Discord in Corinth: 1 Corinthians 1–4 and Ancient Politics', *JBL* 106 (1987), pp.85–111.

Wendland, H.-D., *Die Briefe an die Korinther* (Göttingen: Vandenhoeck & Ruprecht, 1962).

Wernle, P., *Der Christ und die Sünde bei Paulus* (Leipzig, 1897).

Westerholm, S., *Israel's Law and the Church's Faith* (Grand Rapids: Eerdmans, 1988).

White, L.M., and Yarbrough, O.L., eds., *The Social World of the First Christians* (Minneapolis, Fortress, 1995).

Whittaker, M., *Jews and Christians: Graeco-Roman Views* (Cambridge: Cambridge University Press, 1984).

Wiefel, W., 'The Jewish Community in Ancient Rome and the Origins of Romans Christianity', in K.P. Donfried, ed., *The Romans Debate* (Peabody: Hendrickson, 1991), pp.85–101.

Wilckens, U., *Der Brief an die Römer*, 3 vols. (Benziger: Neukirchener, 1978–82).

Williams, S.K., 'The Justification of the Spirit in Galatians', *JSNT* 29 (1987), pp.91–100.

Willis, W.L., *Idol Meat in Corinth: The Pauline Argument in 1 Corinthians 8 and 10*, SBL 68 (Chico: Scholars, 1985).

Wilson, B.R., *Magic and the Millennium* (London: Heinemann, 1973).

—— *The Social Dimensions of Sectarianism: Sects and New Religious Movements in Contemporary Society* (Oxford: Clarendon, 1990).

Wimbush, V.L., and Valentasis, R., eds., *Asceticism* (Oxford: Oxford University Press, 1995).

Windisch, H., *Taufe und Sünde im ältesten Christentum* (Tübingen: J.C.B. Mohr, 1908).

—— 'Das Problem des paulinischen Imperativs', *ZNW* 23 (1924), pp.265–81.

Winninge, M., *Sinners and the Righteous: A Comparative Study of the Psalms of Solomon and Paul's Letters* (Stockholm: Almqvist & Wiksell, 1995).

Winter, B.W., 'Civil Litigation in Secular Corinth and the Church', *NTS* 37 (1991), pp.559–72.

Wire, A.C., *The Corinthian Women Prophets* (Minneapolis: Fortress, 1990).

Witherington, B., *Conflict and Community in Corinth: A Socio-Rhetorical Commentary on 1 and 2 Corinthians* (Exeter: Paternoster, 1995).

Wright, N.T., *The Messiah and the People of God* (unpublished D.Phil dissertation, Oxford: 1980).

The Climax of the Covenant (Edinburgh: T&T Clark, 1991).

'The Law in Romans 2', in J.D.G. Dunn, ed., *Paul and the Mosaic Law* (Tübingen: J.C.B. Mohr, 1996), pp.131–50.

Wuthnow, R., Hunter, J.D., Bergesen, A., and Kurzweil, E., eds., *Cultural Analysis: The Work of Peter L. Berger, Mary Douglas, Michel Foucault and Jürgen Habermas* (London: Routledge & Kegan Paul, 1984).

Zahn, T., *Der Brief des Paulus an die Galater* (Göttingen: Vandenhoeck & Ruprecht, 1905).

Der Brief des Paulus an die Römer (Leipzig: Deichert, 1910).

Zeller, D., *Der Brief an die Römer* (Regensburg: Pustet, 1985).

Ziesler, J.A., *The Meaning of Righteousness in Paul* (Cambridge: Cambridge University Press, 1972).

'ΣΩΜΑ in the Septuagint', *NovT* 25 (1987), pp.133–45.

Paul's Letter to the Romans (London: SCM, 1989).

INDEX OF SELECTED SUBJECTS

Adam, 2, 4, 5, 12, 168–70, 172–4, 184–7, 189, 201, 202, 207

aeon, 17, 89, 115, 117, 118, 120, 122, 123, 125, 143, 144, 163, 169, 170, 174–8, 182–4, 187, 188, 193, 197–203, 207, 208

anthropology, 9, 15, 17, 20, 22, 66, 74, 111, 125, 193, 204, 208

believers, 4, 5, 9, 16–18, 50, 65, 67, 73, 75, 79, 86–90, 92–4, 96, 99–101, 110, 111, 116, 119, 123, 124, 126, 133, 134, 136, 140, 141, 143, 146, 147, 153, 154, 163, 167, 174–8, 180–2, 184, 195, 199, 201–4, 207–9

Big Man, 28, 36, 37, 56–8, 61, 76

body, 3, 7, 16–18, 23, 25, 26, 32, 47, 49, 61, 64–6, 69–74, 76, 96, 123, 124, 128, 137, 140, 141, 143, 152, 154, 160, 171, 176–8, 180, 182, 185, 193, 199, 200, 203, 206, 207, 208, 209

boundaries, 16–18, 25–7, 33–5, 38, 39, 42, 46, 48, 61, 65–7, 70–2, 74–7, 79, 81, 84–6, 88, 89, 91–3, 95–7, 100, 103, 104, 110, 114, 117, 118, 120–4, 133, 136, 144, 146, 147, 150, 152–4, 166, 167, 169, 174–6, 179, 181, 182, 184, 197, 199, 200, 202, 206–9

boundary, 7, 11, 16, 17, 18, 24, 27, 42, 48, 63, 65, 66, 73, 75, 77, 81, 86, 87–9, 91, 93, 96, 99, 101, 104, 109, 110, 114, 117, 118, 120–4, 136, 145–7, 149, 151, 153, 154, 163, 166, 174, 177, 179, 182, 184, 187, 192, 197, 199, 202, 203, 206–9

circumcision, 75, 78–81, 83, 84, 86, 87, 89, 90, 92, 93, 95–9, 119, 120, 135, 140, 152, 153, 163

commandment, 3, 105, 115, 120, 172, 174, 184, 186, 187, 189, 199, 203, 208

cosmology, 15, 16, 25, 32, 33, 35, 37, 41–3, 54, 63, 66, 74, 76, 80, 84, 85, 100, 104, 120, 121, 123, 124, 177, 194, 205, 206

covetousness, 10, 184

curse, 16, 66, 81, 90, 91, 110–14, 122, 207

death, 1, 3, 6, 9, 10, 16, 25, 57, 68–70, 74, 75, 80, 88, 103, 109, 114, 115, 122, 126, 164, 165, 167–70, 172–4, 176, 178, 180–3, 185, 188, 190, 197–202, 207, 208

evil, 1, 10, 16, 17, 19, 25, 26, 33, 65–7, 69, 70, 72, 74–6, 78, 80, 81, 86, 88, 101, 120, 122, 123, 136, 137, 145, 147, 148, 152, 159, 163, 176, 177, 185, 190, 191, 192–5, 197, 200, 206–9

faith, 3, 4, 12, 16, 17, 24, 62, 80, 86, 88–90, 97–102, 107, 109, 111, 114, 116, 117, 122, 128, 131–3, 138–43, 145, 146, 163–7, 184, 195, 202, 207, 208

flesh, 3, 6, 7, 17, 68–70, 78, 81–3, 89, 101, 118–20, 123, 153, 163, 164, 177, 178, 183, 184, 188, 192–4, 196–200, 202, 206–8

Gentiles, 3, 6, 7, 9, 10, 13, 41, 73, 77, 78, 86, 90, 92–8, 101, 103–5, 110–14, 122, 125, 131, 132, 134, 135, 137–40, 143, 146–50, 152–4, 161–5, 167, 173–5, 180, 181, 202

grace, 3, 5, 10, 81, 150, 164, 168, 169, 174, 175, 180, 182, 188, 195, 209

grid, 6, 16, 17, 20, 21, 23–8, 31–43, 46–56, 58, 61, 63, 65, 70, 74, 76, 77, 80–4, 86, 91, 95, 96, 121, 124, 136, 137, 143–6,

151, 152, 154, 166, 167, 169, 177–9, 184, 187, 193, 194, 201, 202, 205–7

group, 15–17, 20, 21, 23–8, 32–43, 46–58, 61–7, 69, 70, 72, 74, 76, 77, 80–6, 89, 91, 95, 96, 99, 103, 106, 114, 115, 120–4, 130, 131, 133, 135–7, 139, 141, 143–7, 152–4, 162, 164, 166, 167, 169, 174, 177–9, 182, 184, 187, 193, 194, 197, 201, 202, 205–8

heart, 8, 41, 153, 155, 157–60, 162, 163, 183, 187, 191, 194, 209

individual, 7–12, 16, 17, 19, 20, 21, 24–8, 30–43, 47, 49, 52, 71, 72, 109, 112, 119, 128, 136, 150, 152, 161, 164, 165, 172, 173, 180, 184, 195, 199, 204, 208, 209

individualism, 15, 21, 31, 37, 42, 46, 49, 51, 54–6, 59, 61, 66, 74, 84, 118, 151, 205, 206

Israel, 11–13, 98, 103, 112, 113, 117, 128, 134, 138, 140, 141, 146, 148, 151, 161, 164, 166, 185, 200

Jews, 3–6, 9, 10, 13, 17, 73, 77, 81, 83, 86, 88, 90–100, 103–5, 113, 114, 122, 125, 132–5, 137, 139, 140, 143, 146, 147, 149–52, 154, 161, 163–7, 173–5, 182, 184, 186, 187, 191, 192, 201–3, 207

Judaism, 7, 10, 13, 29, 48, 67, 69, 79, 81, 87–90, 92, 93, 95, 98, 122, 131, 139, 143, 144, 149, 152, 153, 165, 193–5

justification, 3, 4, 16, 90, 98–105, 109, 110, 121, 122, 146, 164, 167, 184, 196

law,
  affirmation of, 5, 13, 166, 183–5, 187, 188, 190, 191, 193, 196, 199
  boundary of, 16, 17, 87, 88, 104, 109, 110, 114, 117, 118, 146, 147, 150–4, 163, 166, 192, 197, 203
  curse of, 16, 81, 111–14, 122, 207
  death to, 3, 16, 89, 109, 110, 122, 183, 184, 201, 206
  food laws, 51, 92–6, 98, 133, 135
  free from, 4, 18, 89, 104, 106, 110, 111, 119, 121, 123, 125, 126, 132, 137, 153, 165, 166, 174, 175, 182–4, 188, 202, 203, 207–9

  fulfilment of, 12, 17, 82, 88, 111, 150, 153, 184, 196–8, 203
  in heart, 5, 150, 163, 191, 201
  inadequacy of, 1, 3, 10, 13, 81, 89–91, 101, 112, 115, 192, 195, 197–9, 207
  Jewish, 3, 7, 11, 16, 80, 87, 88, 90, 99, 101, 112, 118, 124, 127, 133–7, 139, 147, 149–51, 154, 167, 174, 178, 182, 202, 206
  and justification, 90, 101, 104, 109, 112, 116, 121, 122, 150
  observance of, 85, 86, 90, 91, 98–101, 110, 121, 122, 126, 135, 136, 143, 163, 178
  outside, 90, 110, 112–14, 147, 154, 175, 181, 182, 202
  Paul's view of, 3, 4, 11, 16, 17, 88, 90, 105, 108, 109, 111–13, 115, 119, 120, 122, 133, 147, 172, 183, 184, 188–90, 199, 200
  possession of, 5, 150, 151, 153, 154
  purpose of, 10–13, 106, 114, 115, 118, 122, 154, 191, 192, 195
  requirements of, 5, 112, 153, 187, 198–200
  and righteousness, 101, 115, 116, 175
  and sin, 2–4, 10–13, 17, 45, 75, 76, 106, 117, 118, 122, 165, 172–5, 177, 183–5, 187, 192, 197–9, 208
  and Spirit, 3, 16, 120, 184, 197, 201
  transgression of, 1, 11, 16, 19, 105, 106, 109–11, 113, 115, 122, 151, 153, 172, 173, 206
  under, 3, 5, 86, 90, 100, 106, 110, 113, 118, 120, 147, 161–3, 166, 172, 174, 175, 180, 184, 186–9, 191, 192, 197, 201–3, 206, 207
  works of, 3, 4, 9, 85, 90, 91, 98–100, 102, 120, 140, 147

life, 1, 3, 8–10, 13, 16, 26, 35, 39, 42, 50, 55, 58, 59, 63, 81, 88, 89, 105, 106, 108–10, 115–18, 120, 124, 127, 166–71, 174, 176–9, 181, 182, 184, 185, 187–93, 195, 197–202, 207, 208

matrix, 15, 16, 20, 21, 23–5, 27, 29, 31–3, 35–8, 40, 41, 43, 45–54, 57, 58, 61–3, 65, 66, 70, 76, 80, 82, 84, 89, 91, 95, 99, 121–4, 136, 137, 145, 146, 179, 193, 194, 201–3, 205–7, 209

pollution, 19–21, 24, 33, 69, 181,
    196
power, 1–5, 9–17, 22, 24, 25, 28, 30,
    37–41, 45, 55, 56, 58, 74, 75, 77, 78, 85,
    86, 88, 91, 104–6, 114, 122–4, 138, 139,
    144, 146, 147, 152, 173–5, 178–81, 183,
    184, 186, 187, 189, 191–3, 195, 197–9,
    201–5, 207–9
purity, 17, 24, 32, 35, 48, 52, 56, 57, 66,
    67, 69, 70, 74, 77, 82, 87, 94, 136, 147,
    205, 206
Qumran, 67, 108, 131, 191, 193, 194, 196,
    197
righteous, 17, 71, 85, 87, 89, 91, 97, 99,
    100, 103–6, 109, 110, 114, 115, 118,
    120–4, 139, 141, 147, 151–4, 161–4,
    166, 168, 169, 173–6, 181, 182, 184,
    191, 194, 197–202, 206–9
righteousness, 3, 5–7, 9, 13, 100, 101,
    115–17, 138–40, 142, 151, 163, 168–70,
    174, 176, 180, 181, 196, 201, 202,
    207
sin,
    Christ, servant of sin, 3, 16, 78, 102–5,
        109, 110, 121, 122, 206
    and the community, 7, 8, 16, 67, 69, 71,
        120, 123, 152, 194, 207
    and death, 3, 168–70, 173, 176, 177,
        181, 183, 197–9, 201, 208
    dominion of, 1, 3, 9, 10, 13, 122, 123,
        165, 168, 169, 174–6, 178, 180–2,
        184, 185, 195, 204, 208
    dying to, 3, 17, 174, 175, 178–80, 183,
        201, 203
    freedom from, 2, 3, 5, 8, 17, 67,
        151, 174, 175, 178–80, 184, 188,
        207
    and the individual, 7–9, 12, 15, 17, 66,
        67, 69–72, 77, 86, 87, 91, 102–4, 118,
        123, 147, 176, 179, 196, 197, 204,
        209
    language, 2, 4, 7, 8, 14, 15, 17, 30, 45,
        63, 91, 121, 173, 204, 205, 209
    and law, 3, 11–13, 17, 75, 76, 104, 109,
        114, 115, 117, 118, 121, 133, 153,
        154, 172–5, 181–4, 187, 188,
        197–200, 202
    law of, 3, 11, 177, 184, 185, 192, 197,
        198
    original, 5, 6, 204
    sin (deed), 1, 2, 7, 12, 62, 64, 66, 68,
        71, 72, 78, 88, 102, 103, 105, 120,
        147, 148, 150–2, 160, 161, 163,
        168, 172, 173, 175, 181, 194, 200,
        206
    sin (power), 1–4, 9–18, 22, 30, 40, 41,
        45, 48, 74, 75, 77, 78, 85, 86, 91, 106,
        114, 122–4, 144, 146, 170, 171,
        173–90, 192, 193, 195, 197–9, 201–5,
        207–9
    sin (verb), 2, 4, 5, 8, 64, 72, 73, 102,
        159, 164, 170–5, 179, 193
    under, 10, 78, 111, 115–18, 139, 147,
        154, 163, 188, 190, 198
    views of, 1, 2, 4, 6–9, 12–16, 18–21, 24,
        30, 32, 33, 41, 45, 56, 57, 61, 66, 72,
        74, 75, 77, 78, 82, 91, 101, 104, 118,
        119, 122–4, 142, 143, 151, 154, 164,
        165, 173, 174, 176, 178–80, 188, 193,
        194, 200, 204–6
sinners, 16, 78, 82, 86, 91, 98, 101, 103–5,
    109, 110, 121, 122, 154, 163, 164, 167,
    168, 173
Spirit, 2, 3, 7, 13, 16, 17, 58, 64, 68, 69,
    71, 72, 75, 80, 86, 88–90, 97, 101,
    110, 112–15, 117–20, 122, 123, 146,
    153, 154, 163, 164, 166, 167, 177, 178,
    183, 184, 188, 189, 193, 197–203,
    206–8
strong, 16, 17, 20, 23, 24, 26, 28, 30, 32,
    37, 38, 46, 49, 53, 54, 62, 64–6, 68, 73,
    74, 77, 80, 82, 84, 91–3, 121, 124, 126,
    128–39, 141–3, 164–6, 171, 175, 203,
    206, 207
Torah, 4, 13, 17, 75, 78, 80, 83, 98, 100,
    101, 104, 112, 117, 121, 122, 124,
    131–4, 141–3, 146, 147, 151, 153, 154,
    174, 178, 180–4, 187, 188, 191, 192,
    195, 197, 199–202, 207, 208
transgression, 1, 11, 19, 20, 21, 24, 82,
    105, 113, 114, 151, 153, 162, 168, 169,
    172–4, 184, 195
transgressor, 16, 78, 105, 106, 109, 110,
    122, 153, 206
weak, 16, 17, 21, 23, 24, 26, 28, 32, 38, 49,
    62, 64, 73, 77, 83, 84, 96, 124, 126,
    128–37, 139, 141–3, 165, 177, 180, 183,
    187, 203, 207

witchcraft, 16, 25, 37, 38, 80–2, 84–6, 90, 91, 99, 100, 104, 110, 114, 121, 206
works, 3, 4, 6, 9, 12, 20, 71, 78, 82, 83, 85, 90, 91, 98–102, 118–20, 140, 143, 147, 150, 207
world, 1, 7–9, 12–14, 19–21, 25, 26, 28–30, 31, 33, 34, 41, 42, 46, 47, 48, 52, 54, 56, 59, 63, 65–7, 70, 72, 74, 76, 77, 80, 82, 83, 86–9, 91, 95, 96, 118, 121–3, 131, 133, 137, 144, 147, 148, 150, 154, 159, 161–3, 166–75, 178, 179, 192, 197, 201, 205, 207, 208

yetzer, 159, 163, 191, 192

INDEX TO ANCIENT REFERENCES

Ancient Greek References
Aeschines

Against Timarchus
139   72
1 195   72

Aristotle

Ethica Nicomachea
7   190

Epictetus

Diss.
1.28.6–8   190
2.26.1–4   190

Euripides

Medea
1077–80   190
1078–80   191

Galen

Hippoc. Et Plat.
4.244.2–9   190
4.274.15–22   190

Oxyrhynchus Papyri

P.Ox.   *3333*   61
P.Ox.   *3798*   61
P.Ox.   *3915*   61

Plato

Protagoras
352b–356c   190

Timaeus
90A–D   70

Plutarch

Moralia
71A   186
446A   190

Ancient Latin References
Juvenal

Satire
1.102–9   60
4:15   60

Ovid

Amores
3.4.17   186
2.19.3   186

Metamorphoses
7.17–21   190
7.21   191

Petronius

Satyricon
38   60
43   60

Suetonius

Claudii Vita
25.4   125

Tacitus

Histories
5:5:1–2   83

Ancient Jewish References

Epistle of Aristeas
139   104
142   104

1 Enoch
19:1   73
99:6–10   73
101:6   106

4 Ezra
8:31   103
8:47   103

Joseph and Aseneth
12:1–13:15   196
21:10–21   196

Jubilees
1:23   153
11:4–6   73
22:16–22   73
23:23   98

4 Maccabees
1:33–34   186
7:19   89

Psalms of Solomon
1:1   98
2:1–2   98
17:22–25   98

Sibylline Oracles
3.701   113

Testament of Levi
2:3   105

Qumran

1QH
1:21–27   193
1:21–23   194
1:21   196
1:31–33   196
3:19–36   189
3:19   196
4:29   196
4:30–38   189
4:33   196
7:17   194
9:16   194
12:24–34   189
13:16   194
18:14   194
18:22–29   189
18:23   194

1QM
4:3   193

1QS
3:14–4:26   189
4:23–25   191
5:4–5   191
5:4   163
9:12   194
11   194
11:9–15   189
11:9–12   193
11:9–10   194
11:9   196
11:11–12   195
11:11   196

4QMMT   99
Josephus

Antiquities
12.22   106
20.38–9   83

Life
14   134

Philo

De Mig. Abr.
89–93   92

De Spec. Leg.
1.52 83
4.178 83

Leg. All.
3.10 106

Rabbinic References

Bab.b
16a 191

Kiddushim
30b 192

Midr. Ps
CXIX.10 191

Sanhedrin
6.2 68

Sifra
93d 186

Sifre Num
112 179

T J Yana vi
4.43d 187

Biblical References
Old Testament

Genesis
2–3 186
6:5 158, 159, 162
6:6 158
15:6 111, 114, 140, 164
18:18 111, 114
21:10 90
47:12 70

Leviticus
4–5 21
11 51
15 51
18:5 117

Deuteronomy
10:16 153
27:26 111–14, 116
30:6 153

Job
33:17 70

1 Chronicles
28:1 70

Esther
14:17 134

Psalms
5:9 154, 156, 160
5:10 156, 158
9:15–17 98
9:27–28 156
9:28 160
10:6–7 157
10:7 154
13:1–3 155
13:1 160
14:1–4 155
14:1–3 154
14:3 154
19:7–13 196
26:10 154
32:1–2 124
35:1 158
36:1 154
36:2–3 158, 162
36:2 162
38 196
40 196
40:6–12 196
51 196
97:1–3 138
97:2–3 138
98:2–3 138
98:2 138
98:3 138
106:20 148
119:169–176 196
139:2–3 156
139:3 160
140:3–4 156
140:3 154
143:2 101, 116, 163
144:8 154
144:11 154

Proverbs
11:17   70

Ecclesiastes
7:21   154

Isaiah
27:9   124
28:16   140
53:11   104, 105
59   158–60
59:7–8   154, 157, 161

Jeremiah
2:11   148
4:4   153
7   21
9:25–26   153
26   21

Daniel
1:8–16   133

Micah
7:3   154

Habakkuk
2:4   116, 117, 139, 207

1 Esdras
3:4   70

Tobit
1:10–12   134
11:15   70
13:7   70
14:5–7   113

Judith
12:2   134
12:19   134

Wisdom of Solomon
11–15   147
11:23   164
12–15   150
14–15   148
14:8   148
14:12   148
14:25–26   148
14:27   148
15:1   150

Sirach
19:2   71
21:2   105
27:10   105
51:2   70

Prayer of Manasseh
9–15   196

1 Maccabees
1:34   98
2:48   98

New Testament

Matthew
5:21–48   151
15:19   159

Mark
7:21   159

Luke
2:35   159
5:22   159
9:47   159
20:37–38   89
24:38   159

Acts
2   21
10   94
11:27–30   92
15   92
15:1–29   79, 92
15:1   92, 96
15:20   94
15:29   94
16:3   93
18:2   125
18:12–17   125
18:22   79, 92
18:23   79
21:25   94

Romans
1–8   128, 146, 202, 207
1–4   17, 125, 164, 207, 208
1–3   147, 150, 184
1–2   163

1:1–15	137	*2:29*	163, 183
1:5–6	135	*3:1–8*	138
1:7	135	*3:4*	102
1:8	125	*3:5*	137
1:13–15	135	*3:6–7*	107
1:16–17	132, 137, 139, 143, 146	*3:6*	102
1:16	139, 165	*3:8*	136, 137, 145, 175
1:17	98, 138, 139	*3:9–20*	163, 208
1:18–4:25	146	*3:9*	98, 124, 146, 154, 163
1:18–3:31	139	*3:10–18*	116, 158, 159, 161, 163
1:18–3:20	139, 163	*3:10–12*	155
1:18–3:9	159, 162	*3:13–15*	160
1:18–2:29	147	*3:13*	155, 156
1:18–32	147, 149, 159–61	*3:14*	156
1:18	147, 149	*3:15–17*	157, 161
1:20	149	*3:18*	157, 161
1:21	159, 160, 162	*3:19*	159, 161, 162
1:21–23	160	*3:20–26*	98
1:22–23	160	*3:20*	2, 124, 163
1:22	147	*3:21–5:1*	132
1:23	147	*3:21–4:25*	12
1:24	148, 160	*3:21–31*	146
1:24–27	160	*3:21–30*	142
1:25–27	148	*3:21–26*	163
1:26	148	*3:23–24*	164
1:28	148, 160	*3:23*	167, 172
1:29–31	148, 160, 161	*3:25*	163, 164
1:30	150, 154	*3:26*	164
1:32	150, 161	*3:27*	167
2	134, 166	*3:31*	102
2:1–3	149, 150	*4*	164, 165, 184
2:1	134, 149, 150, 153	*4:1–25*	140
2:4	150, 164	*4:1*	135, 200
2:5	149, 162	*4:3*	116
2:11–16	5	*4:7–8*	124
2:11	150	*4:8*	2, 124
2:12	172	*4:9–12*	140
2:14	150, 151, 153	*4:15*	105, 115, 172, 173
2:15	163	*4:16–17*	140
2:17–3:8	135	*5*	165, 166, 178
2:17–29	13	*5–8*	1, 12, 13, 17, 124, 125,
2:17–24	151, 153		164–6, 201–3, 207, 208
2:17–23	149, 150	*5–7*	164
2:17–20	151	*5–6*	1
2:17	34, 149, 150, 167	*5:1–8:39*	146
2:21–24	151	*5:1–11*	165, 167, 168, 184, 201
2:23	105, 115	*5:1–2*	167
2:25–26	153	*5:2–4*	167
2:25–27	105	*5:2*	167
2:25–29	152	*5:5–8*	167
2:25	153	*5:9–10*	167
2:26	153	*5:10–11*	174
2:27	153	*5:10*	170
2:28–29	153	*5:11*	167, 170, 189

5:12–8:11   3
5:12–21   1, 2, 5, 17, 165, 166, 168, 169, 173, 176, 182, 184, 201, 207
5:12   3, 5, 147, 169–73
5:13   2, 3, 172, 173
5:14   105, 115, 172
5:15   168
5:15–17   170
5:16–17   168
5:16   172
5:17–21   168
5:17   168
5:18   168, 170
5:19   168, 173
5:20–8:3   13
5:20   2, 3, 10, 12, 13, 168, 174, 178, 184
5:21   168
6–8   12, 165, 176–8, 188
6–7   174
6   13, 165, 166, 179–82
6:1–8:39   11, 165
6:1–23   13, 17, 133, 201, 207
6:1–14   3, 174, 175, 184
6:1–11   188
6:1   2, 145, 174, 175
6:2   102, 188
6:3   176
6:6   176, 208
6:7   68, 79
6:10–11   89
6:11–23   179
6:11–13   178
6:11   175, 180
6:12–23   188
6:12   176, 208
6:14–15   188
6:14   174, 175, 180, 183, 184, 188
6:15–23   3, 175, 184
6:15   102, 145, 172, 174, 180
6:16   181
6:17–23   180
6:17–18   180, 182, 188
6:19–23   180, 181
6:19
6:22   188
6:23   182
7–8   195, 199, 200
7   5, 10, 13, 107, 166, 188–90, 196, 197, 199
7:1–8:17   165, 184
7:1–25   17, 201, 207

7:1–23   175
7:1–6   3, 188
7:1   135, 174, 182
7:2–3   182
7:2   182
7:4   182, 184, 188
7:5–6   200
7:5   124, 177, 183, 198, 199, 208
7:6   153, 183, 184, 188
7:7–25   2, 183–5, 188, 189, 197, 200
7:7–13   1, 10, 72
7:7–12   3, 183–7, 189, 199
7:7   2, 102, 107, 174, 183, 184, 186, 187
7:8–11   185
7:9   184, 197
7:12   183, 189
7:13–25   1, 3, 184, 185, 188, 189, 191, 192, 199
7:13   102, 174, 183, 187, 188
7:14–25   5, 13, 183, 185, 188, 189, 195, 196
7:14   183, 185, 188, 189, 193, 198
7:15–20   189
7:15   185, 192
7:16–17   185, 190
7:16   190
7:17   192
7:17–18   198
7:18–20   185
7:19   192
7:20   192
7:21–25   193
7:21–23   185, 189, 192
7:21   192, 193
7:22–23   193
7:22   5, 189
7:23   177, 192, 198, 208
7:24   11, 177, 178, 185, 193
7:25   178, 185, 189, 195, 198
8   166, 167, 189, 197, 199, 208
8:1–30   183
8:1–11   3, 199
8:1–9   188
8:1–8   11
8:1–4   195
8:1–2   197
8:1   197, 200
8:2–4   183
8:2   184

8:3	12, 197, 198	*12:9–13:10*	141
8:4	198	*13*	130
8:5–9	198	*13:1–7*	14, 136, 144
8:5–8	200	*13:8–10*	183
8:5	198	*13:11–14*	143
8:6–8	198	*13:12*	200
8:6–7	198	*13:14*	200
8:6	198	*14–16*	124
8:9–13	178	*14:1–15:13*	126, 128, 129, 131, 132,
8:9	188, 198		143, 183
8:10–30	188	*14:1–15:6*	132
8:10–13	195	*14:1–12*	130
8:10–11	198	*14:1–2*	132
8:10	177, 199, 208	*14:1*	130–2, 141, 164
8:11	177	*14:2–3*	131
8:12–13	199, 200	*14:2*	131, 133, 141
8:13	208	*14:3*	131, 134, 141
8:14–17	201	*14:4*	130
8:14	201	*14:5–6*	133
8:17–22	135	*14:5*	131, 142
8:18–39	165	*14:6*	141
8:18–30	201	*14:8*	89
8:20	11	*14:10*	130, 141
8:23	177	*14:12*	170
9–11	12, 13, 128, 140, 146,	*14:13–23*	130, 142
	164	*14:13*	130, 131
9	140	*14:14*	51
9:1–11:36	165, 166	*14:16*	130
9:3–5	135, 200	*14:19–20*	109
9:6–18	138	*14:19*	131
9:14	102	*14:20*	130
9:17	116	*14:21*	131, 133
9:22–24	140	*14:22–23*	132
9:24	135	*14:23*	2, 124, 142
9:30–10:21	132	*15:1–6*	132, 143
9:30–10:10	140	*15:1*	130
10:11–12	140	*15:5–6*	131
10:11	116	*15:7–13*	132, 133
10:14–21	140	*15:7–12*	143
11:1–12	138	*15:7*	141
11:1	102, 107	*15:13*	132, 143
11:2	116	*15:14–16:24*	137
11:11	102	*15:14–24*	126
11:13–32	135	*15:14*	143
11:18	134, 141	*15:25–33*	126
11:23	109, 140	*16*	134
11:25–32	138, 140	*16:3–5*	134
11:26–27	124	*16:3*	135
12–16	128	*16:7*	135
12–13	144	*16:10–11*	134
12:1–2	141	*16:11*	135
12:1	177	*16:14–15*	134
12:2	143	*16:17–20*	130
12:3	141	*16:17*	131

1 Corinthians

1–4	58, 64, 77
1:2	65
1:10–13	64
1:11–12	55
1:11	81
1:12	7, 57, 58, 62
1:17–25	64
1:17	55
1:18–3:23	58
1:18–25	50, 55, 65
1:26–29	65
1:26	55, 57
2:1–16	64
2:1–4	55
2:6–16	57
3:3–4	55
3:10–17	64
3:18–23	57, 64
3:18–20	55, 65
4:6–13	64
4:6	57
4:9–13	65
4:10	55
4:12	58
4:14–21	64
4:16	65
4:17	81
4:18	62, 69
5–6	52, 74
5:1–13	70, 77
5:1–8	66, 70
5:3–4	69
5:5	66, 68, 69
5:6–7	67
5:6	67
5:7	67, 68
5:9–10	57, 63
5:11–13	66
5:11	57
5:13	69, 70
6:1–11	50, 55, 65, 67, 70, 77
6:1–2	70
6:1	70
6:5	71
6:7–8	71
6:8	71
6:9–11	67
6:9–10	57
6:9	70, 71
6:11	71, 176
6:12–20	62, 71, 77, 177
6:12–14	71
6:12	52, 57, 71
6:13	57, 177
6:14	177
6:15–17	71
6:15	72, 102, 177
6:16	71
6:18–20	71
6:18	71, 72, 172
6:19	71, 177
6:20	177
7	52, 61
7:1–40	77
7:1–16	52
7:1	61–3, 81
7:2	61
7:10–11	61
7:12–16	62
7:18	78
7:28	62, 172
7:29–31	65
7:34	177
7:36	172
8–11	52
8–10	50, 58, 62, 74, 126
8	129
8:1–11:1	129
8:1–13	73, 77
8:1	62
8:4	73
8:5–6	73
8:7–13	55, 62, 64
8:7	62, 73
8:9–13	64, 73
8:10–13	73
8:12	172
8:13	62
9:1–23	58
9:1–18	57
9:24–26	177
9:27	177
10	129
10:1–11:1	77
10:1–13	73
10:1–4	57
10:16–17	56, 64
10:19–21	73
10:20–22	55
10:22	73
10:23–11:1	64, 73
10:23–33	73
10:23	52, 57, 62
11:17–34	55, 58, 77
11:18	63
11:19	58
11:21	56

11:27–34	64
11:29–32	68
11:30	73
11:33–34	56
12:1–14:33	55
12:1–11	64
12:3	63
12:4–31	64
12:4–11	63
12:12–31	64
12:28	40, 66
13:1–13	64
14:1–19	64
14:26–33	63
14:26	64
14:34–35	48
14:39	62
15:12	55, 57
15:29	57
15:32–34	57
15:34	172
15:42–44	177
15:54–55	75
15:56	3, 4, 45, 75–7
15:57	75
16:1–3	79
16:10	81
16:21–24	131

2 Corinthians

2:6	68
3:1–18	183
3:6	153
4:7–5:5	177
4:16	189
5:2	171
5:3–4	171
5:3	171
5:4	171
5:21	2
7:6	81
7:9–11	68
7:13–14	81
10–13	74, 77, 80, 206
11:7	2

Galatians

1:1	79
1:4	78, 88, 101, 110, 122
1:6–9	78, 79
1:6	79
1:7	82, 84, 86
1:8	82, 84, 108
1:9–2:14	108
1:9	79
1:10–12	84
1:10	81, 108
1:11–12	79
1:13–2:10	79
1:13–21	109
1:13–16	81
1:13	90, 108
1:16–17	84
1:22	90
1:23	108
2	92
2:1–10	79, 81, 92
2:2	82
2:4–5	93
2:4	90, 93
2:10	92
2:11–21	79, 103, 106
2:11–14	95, 103, 104
2:12	79
2:14	96, 97, 108
2:15–21	78, 97, 107, 206
2:15–17	91, 107, 108
2:15–16	97, 99, 101, 104, 110
2:15	97–100, 103, 106, 121, 150
2:16–20	98
2:16–17	90
2:16	81, 90, 98–101, 116, 120
2:17–19	110
2:17	3, 16, 78, 102, 103, 105, 106, 109, 117, 122
2:18–21	108
2:18	16, 105–9, 113
2:19–20	89
2:19	89, 105, 107–10, 115
2:20	102, 109
2:21	101, 108
3–5	81
3:1–5:1	79
3:1–14	112, 207
3:1–2	83
3:1	80, 82–4
3:2–5	88
3:2	120
3:3	82, 120
3:5	120
3:6	110, 111
3:7–5:1	110
3:7–4:7	90
3:7–14	16, 91, 110
3:8	116
3:9	111

3:10–11	90
3:10	90, 112–14, 116, 120
3:11–12	117
3:11	81, 112, 113, 116
3:13–14	108
3:13	110
3:14	90, 113–15
3:19–25	114, 207
3:19–22	91
3:19	11, 13, 83, 105
3:21–22	3, 91, 115, 116
3:21	115, 116
3:22	13, 78, 98, 116, 122
3:22–24	10
3:23–25	117
3:23–24	90
3:24–25	108
3:26–4:7	90
3:26–27	89
3:26	90
3:27	83
3:28	83
3:29	189
4:1–7	90
4:1–3	83
4:1	90
4:3	108
4:8–9	83
4:8	150
4:9	109
4:10–11	82
4:10	83, 92
4:12–20	108
4:13	79
4:15	108
4:17	84, 86
4:24–26	90
4:30	80, 82, 90, 116
5	200
5:1	111
5:2–6:10	80
5:2–6	80
5:2–3	78
5:3	78, 111
5:4	84
5:6	89
5:7	85, 86
5:7–8	84
5:9	82
5:10–12	108
5:11	79, 81, 83, 84, 92
5:13–14	83
5:14	120
5:15	83

5:16–6:8	121
5:16–26	83, 118, 120, 199
5:16–21	78, 91
5:16	119
5:17	119
5:18	120
5:19–21	120
5:19	120
5:22–6:8	207
5:22	98
5:23	120
5:24–25	89
5:24	83
5:25	115
5:26	83
6:1–2	83
6:1	8
6:2	120
6:3	83
6:7–8	120
6:8	78, 115, 120
6:10	83
6:11–18	80, 131
6:12–13	78, 82, 84, 119
6:12	78, 79, 83, 86
6:13	78
6:14	82, 89, 108
6:15	89, 120
6:17	108

Ephesians

3:16	189

Philippians

3:9	98
3:12	171
3:21	177
4:10	171

1 Thessalonians

3:2	81
3:6	81
5:23	177

2 Thessalonians

3:17	131

Patristic Sources

Augustine

Ad Simplicianum

1	*1.10–11*	5

Confessiones
8.10 5
2:6 186

Contra duas epistolas Pelagianorum
1.8.13–11.24 5
4.4.7 170
4.7 5
8.14 185

Contra Julianum
II 3.5 5
II 4.8 5
II 5.13 5
III 26:61 5

De civitate Dei
13.14 5

De gratia Christi
1.39.43 5

De nuptiis et concupiscentia
II 5.15 5
27.30–31.36 5

De peccatorum meritis et remissione
I 10.9 5
I 11.10–39.70 5

De spiritu et littera
9.6 5
49.28 6

Enchiridion
26.27 5

Epistolae ad Romanos inchoata expositio 4
Retractationes
1.22–5 5
2.27 5

Chrysostom

Ep. ad. Romanos hom.
26.3 142

1 Clement
27.4 106

Eujelius Praeparatio Evangelica

4.3 73

Hippolytus

379–774 191

Tertullian

Adv. Marcionem
5.3 93